A Footprint in Time

A Footprint in Time

Brian D. Everett

To order additional copies of this book, contact:
Xlibris
800-056-3182
www.Xlibrispublishing.co.uk
Orders@Xlibrispublishing.co.uk
783933

DEDICATION

To Sheila, the wife who showed me the value of social madness, my family who kept me on that track ever since, and my friends who have been there and supported me throughout the journey

ACKNOWLEDGEMENT

My sincere thanks to my editors and the staff at Xlibris, and in particular Charles Del Mar, who have guided me through the intricacies of producing this recollecting of events, which can loosely be described as an autobiography. To Mavis Rivers-Horton without whose constant pressure I would never have had the presence of mind to write this book - so the blame is entirely hers! But not least, and to me of significant importance, is my gratitude to my children, their families and my friends, without whom these recollections would have been meaningless.

ACKNOWLEDGMENTS

CONTENTS

I may not have gone where I intended to go,
But I think I've ended up where I needed to be.
Douglas Adams

PROLOGUE

While travelling home by train to the north from London one summer's evening and watching the setting sun in all its glory against the blue sky with a backdrop of silver-grey clouds, I thought of the many times I had seen similar settings in other parts of the world, but none of them were ever the same. In so many ways, this reflects events in life: many similar but none quite the same. We all follow different paths which are not always of our own design or desire—some more demanding, some more interesting, and some more rewarding but all in their own way unique and illustrating a tale of progress through time.

This is an encapsulation of one person's travel through time and space, not necessarily meaningful in its portrayal or its outcomes but in its own small way leaving an imprint in the sands of time. It is a personal record of one who has lived through and in some small way participated in a few of the events that have shaped our history. It also encapsulates events which embrace family, friends, and acquaintances. At the same time, it touches on those events and locations that have also had both major and minor impacts on the world stage in an age in which we have witnessed incredible changes in technology across a wide area of human endeavours. Developments which have seen man leave his own environment for the first time to venture into the space that lies beyond—something that our predecessors could never have dreamed possible. Changes that have also brought economic and social improvements and yet have not resolved the issues of human conflict or our responsibilities as custodians of our planet.

Perhaps in some small way, in relating this story, I will have added to the explanation of some of the events that have taken place and given my thoughts on what has taken place or indeed what should have happened, but these are not necessarily views shared by others. As I have passed along my own track in life, I hope I have also left a footprint in time which may in some small way attract those of a somewhat curious or bizarre nature—preferably not fossil hunters!

CHAPTER 1

1066—The Norman Conquest

It was out of all this that we came.

Before launching into my personal background with all my dubious recollections, it would be apposite to look back in time to 1066, when a rather self-indulgent Norman leader and his bunch of social controllers (these days we might possibly refer to them as politicians or lawyers) crossed the Channel and altered the course of English history, much as the Romans had done centuries before and the Vikings in the intervening period. Clearly the Normans, as a form of colonial power, would call it civilisation, much as we have done ever since to justify our own empirical ambitions. The Vikings, on the other hand, suffered no such illusions; it was simply a case of help yourself to what you can.

But why did the Normans want to invade Britain? After all, the Romans had long since decided it was a wasted cause, and the Vikings had turned their attentions to the east. There were a number of disparate and ungovernable tribes fighting amongst themselves to establish dominance—not so vastly different from the Europe of latter years, I hear you say. Call it pride, avarice, lust for power, family dominance, or a blend of them all. The problem can be laid at the door of Edward the Confessor, who died at the end of 1065 and, according to his wife, named his younger son, Harold Godwinson, as his successor. This was swiftly endorsed by the Witans, the ruling advisory body of the day, and Harold was crowned within weeks, much to the consternation of the other claimants to the throne.

Firstly, Tostig, the younger brother of Harold, was the Earl of Northumbria until he was banished from the kingdom for brutality and misrule in October 1065. Tostig persuaded Harald Hardrada of Norway to undertake a joint invasion of England to help him seize back the territories he had lost. Secondly, there was William, Duke of Normandy, who maintained that Harold, whilst in his custody as a prisoner, had sworn allegiance and support of William's claim to the throne, for which reason he felt justified in declaring that he was prepared to invade England and take what he considered rightfully his. Well, he would, wouldn't he?

In anticipation of William's planned invasion, Harold had assembled his troops on the Isle of Wight, but the invasion was delayed for several months due to bad weather. Much to his dismay, Harold felt unable to keep and feed an army indefinitely. He disbanded his merry men and returned to London only to find that Harald Hardrada had landed at the mouth of the Tyne and, joining Tostig, marched south to York. There they defeated the newly established Earl of Northumbria. Having received the news, Harold put together another army and led them almost two hundred miles to York in four days, an incredible feat for those days; it really was a forced march. Nevertheless, despite his men being somewhat exhausted, he caught the invaders by surprise, defeating them at Stamford Bridge and killing both Tostig and Hardrada in the process, but not before he had offered Tostig reinstatement as the Earl of Northumbria if he swore allegiance, which he refused. It is suggested that Harold rode up to them before the battle and made the offer to Tostig, who then enquired what Harold would offer Harald Hardrada. It is alleged that he replied, "Seven feet of English soil" sufficient for Hardrada, as he was a big man. I suppose it could be considered a grave offer!

As if that wasn't enough, two days later Harold received the news that William's invasion fleet had set sail for England, destined to land on the south-east coast at Pevensey. No rest for the wicked. Harold had to turn around and march his army 241 miles south to intercept the invaders. He and his men must have been exhausted. The two armies clashed at the Battle of Senlac Hill, later to be called the Battle of Hastings, on 14 October 1066. The English were outnumbered three to one and lacked mounted cavalry, which the Normans had landed from their six hundred ships in support of the invading army. After nine hours of fighting, Harold and his brothers Gyrth and Leofwine were killed and their army was defeated, thereby marking the arrival of the Normans and the end of the Anglo-Saxon reign, which had existed from the end of Roman Britain in the fifth century. Justified or not, it was to be a turning point in British history.

Amongst the influx of Normans came the supporting contingent of troops, camp followers, and hangers-on, including those from Evraux, an area of Normandy in what we would now refer to as France, a settlement that had been created in the distant past by the migrating Eborhards. As the Germanic name implies, my ancestors were pig hunters from central Europe. Well, nothing has changed, then. Truly, I'm uncertain as to which pigs they were hunting! As a result, it was out of all this that we Everetts came, presumably as vassals of the Normans or latter-day Vikings, and settled in the pleasant green lands of southern England, close to the old Roman fortification of Londinium. You could therefore describe us as the first true migrating Europeans—heaven forbid! Although to be fair, they were steeped in Viking blood or somebody else's.

How do I know this? Well, mainly supposition based on historical research and by embroidering fact with fiction a little, as those early-day chroniclers did in creating the Norman's reputation and many others in history have subsequently done. What a pity Harold had to fight two major battles and in between travel halfway across England. He couldn't turn a blind eye to these events, could he? But for this, things might have been vastly different. However, there is little doubt that the Normans, for whatever reason, brought significant improvements and a sense of order to our country. It was something that had been missing since the departure of the Romans and the arrival of the Dark Ages.

From the invasion, one can track the Everett pedigree through those early warriors from Evraux who, like many in those days, bore the name of the area or town from which they originated—hence the derivations such as Eborhard, Everard, Everett, and (for those who can't spell, like the early census enumerators) Everitt. Following the Norman invasion, many of these families can be traced to locations around the Thames Estuary and, in particular, the county of Essex. Well, it had to have something in its favour because the Romans made Colchester the capital of England, although I would have mixed feelings about my daughters being referred to as Essex girls.

In more recent years, I've discovered that this was a somewhat circuitous route followed by my ancestors because my father's blood line goes back to the Vikings. The irrefutable evidence arises from my DNA that was analysed in 2016 (haplogroup I-L22, I-P109) and shows it to be 85 per cent Scandinavian and 9 per cent British. I'm uncertain as to what the remaining 6 per cent comprised; perhaps there is a little bit of Roman remaining. The Scandinavian element must have been from one of those early Viking incursions into Normandy or maybe elsewhere. You could call the Viking progression a two-pronged strategy: what they might have achieved in direct attacks on the English, they further reinforced by moving through the rest of Europe to become the Normans (Norsemen) and thereby adding to our problems! My maternal line, on the other hand (haplogroup K2b1a), indicates strong Ashkenazi elements, or back to Moses—but let's not go there! They've got enough troubles of their own in the Middle East without delving back into the history of the Everett—or should I say the Bayliss—families.

The rest, as they say, is history. In the words of the author Julian Rathbone, "William the Conqueror, like most successful bastards with guilty consciences, saw to it that history was written the way that he wanted it to be written." So why shouldn't I follow William's example? At least my version is probably closer to the truth.

CHAPTER 2

The Pre-war Years—1935 to 1939

Through tension and conflict.

I was born in Grimsby—or, as I was informed by my mother, delivered by a stork, a bird for which I've a great admiration for its ability to discern in which household it should despatch its consignment. I fear my bird may have misconstrued its instructions because instead of delivering me to No 1 The Mall, London, it deviated considerably in its course and despatched me to a typical early 1930s semidetached house on Yarborough Road in Grimsby (which is in North Lincolnshire for those who are not so well informed) on 17 June 1935 at about four o'clock on a Monday afternoon. A most inconvenient time for those partaking of tea. Nevertheless, I arrived duly destined to become the third of five children. Little was I to know, even if memory stretched back that far, that I was entering a rapidly changing world—one that may well be referred to by future historians as an era of technological and social revolution.

Memory plays funny tricks, but usually the long-term memory is more reliable than the short-term, even for those of us approaching the early years of dementia. Nevertheless, it is difficult to be exact when one attempts to open the rusty doors of childhood. Some people claim that their recollections go back to their first year. What a dreadful thought—all that bawling and shouting and disgusting nappies. Others, like me, have a hazy recollection of minor, isolated events that have no time frame. My memories, fragmented as they are, certainly encompass a time before the arrival in 1939 of my younger sister. For example, I recall having a picnic whilst watching my father play rugby at the Grimsby Town ground at Peakes Lane. Why that should stay in my mind, I have no idea. Similarly, the day we travelled by car—his newly acquired pride and joy—to see an air show at the recently opened RAF base at Manby; by the process of elimination, that had to be 1938. As to the air show itself, there is not a great deal that I can recall, only that we travelled in my father's new car (well, almost new; I think it was a 1937 Morris Oxford). However, I do remember seeing a strange flying machine, which was called an autogiro (apparently the predecessor of the helicopter), and of course I remember the ice cream van. What child could ever forget such an essential element of childhood? There are other snippets relating to the same year, or was it earlier? Alas, we shall never know—fact or fiction?

Declaration of War

In January 1939, I do remember being sent to stay with my father's parents, who were at that time relief managers of the Red Lion Hotel in Skegness, a hotel owned by Hewitt's Breweries. I recall being given a small tin drum, presumably as an incentive to leave home for a short while. On reflection, this must have driven my grandparents to the borders of insanity. They should have done what my father did with my son, Jonathan, years later when my parents had the White Hart Hotel in Hawes, and that was to collect bottle tops, a far more peaceful occupation. The reason for my sojourn in Skegness was clearly to avoid frightening yet another stork that was in the process of delivering my baby sister, or so I was advised at the time. Busy breed of birds!

I don't recall a great deal about the rest of that year until the autumn, when my grandparents had returned to their home in Laceby. We were visiting them one Sunday, which by the process of elimination happened to be 3 September 1939. It was to be a day that left me with an indelible memory, even at the young age of four. It has since made me realise how a young child can so clearly retain those memories. On that morning, we gathered in the front room to listen to the radio, and I was told not to speak whilst the adults listened. I do recall that it was a man speaking in a slow, monotonous, and very sombre manner, informing us that we were at war with Germany. This appeared to me a most disturbing announcement, although the adults played it down. However, I was aware that my grandfather had a very heavy, thick book, which was a history of what they called the Great War. It contained many horrific pictures, with soldiers in trenches being gassed and others being shot, so the impact of war, even to someone not yet five, would not have gone unnoticed. The speech was something to do with Germany invading Poland. All I understood was that we were going to war. It was in fact the announcement made by then Prime Minister Neville Chamberlain.

> I am speaking to you from the Cabinet Office at 10, Downing Street. This morning the British Ambassador in Berlin handed the German Government a final note stating that unless we heard from them by 11 o'clock that they were prepared at once to withdraw their troops from Poland, a state of war would exist between us. I have to tell you now that no such undertaking has been received, and that consequently this country is at war with Germany.

Clearly war had been anticipated for many months because it was during September that everyone was issued gas masks, and by the end of that month, some thirty-eight million had been issued to the general public throughout the country. The terrible experiences of the Great War were still uppermost in people's minds, especially the devastating effect of mustard gas, which politicians feared could be used by Hitler against civilians. This was the most deadly and poisonous of chemicals. It was odourless and took twelve hours to take effect, and only a very small amount would have devastating results on thousands of people if launched by shells or bombs.

My first days at Pelham School in Grimsby as a five-year-old involved walking about a mile to and from school and in the process crossing three main roads, negotiating a substantial road barricade set up by the army, and being completely unescorted after the first week of learning the route. It's hard to image the same thing happening in this day and age, but then the world (despite the war) was a much more secure place for us. I recall that on one occasion that year, I deviated from my usual path home, enticed by some of the older boys to the local cattle market to watch the auctions. Not that I needed much persuasion, because I was fascinated by the cattle, which as a townie I had never seen before. However, when I arrived home some considerable time later, I was faced with a lecture from a local policeman and a distraught mother, the result of which left me in no uncertain doubt as to my irresponsibility—a lesson I was never to forget! Nevertheless, it didn't deter my mother from letting me continue to walk to school unescorted on future occasions. I can't recall my father's reactions, but they must have been in a similar vein. However, I may be wrong because fathers are more likely to consider it part of growing up, an aspect they tend to overlook in their own development.

On a lighter note, what I wasn't aware of at the time—as I had no interests which took me in that direction, until I became involved in 1952–1953 when Bill Shankley was the manager—was that in 1939, Grimsby Town Football Club was in the First Division (the precursor of the Premier League). Their record shows that they finished in the top half of the league, having beaten teams such as Arsenal, Liverpool, Chelsea, Manchester United, Everton, Leeds, Aston Villa, and Bolton. In the same year, they reached the semi-final of the cup but lost to Wolverhampton Wanderers at Old Trafford. The attendance of 76,962 remains the grounds' highest attendance record; now, they are lucky if they get a few thousand. Three years previously, they had lost in the semi-final to Arsenal 1-0; they were therefore a team of some standing, having been one of the first to enter the league in 1892.

The Phoney War

It must have been sometime later that year or early in the following year that we had to have our gas masks fitted by an air raid warden at a local assembly hall in Grimsby. I was told that I must never go out without it. Unlike those issued to adults, which were of black rubber with an attached filter, a child's mask was of red rubber with a flapping nose piece. It went by the name of Mickey Mouse, presumably to reduce the possible fear they generated amongst some youngsters. Nevertheless, the basic principle was the same with all gas masks. The idea was that you breathed in through the filter whilst the process of exhaling was achieved by the air pushing the seal away from the face for a very brief period. My sister, being only seven months old, was placed in something akin to an incubator with a glass panel to let in the light when the lid was closed. Air was pumped in and out through filters. The children's masks were very hot and sticky, creating a feeling of nausea, added to which the glass eye pieces would fog over. Certainly, from my experience, it created a claustrophobic reaction inducing a desire to tear the mask off, which could have been fatal had there been an attack. These gas masks came with a cardboard container in which they were housed, suspended by a cord over your shoulder. For the remainder of the war, we had to carry these wherever we went. People could be fined if caught without one. For us children, there were of course not only parental punishments but also the fear of being caught by a policeman or an air raid warden. Luckily, we never had to put these masks on in a real-life situation. There was a humorous aspect to the Mickey Mouse in that exhaling through the nose-flap made a rude noise, which of course made it attractive to us of simple minds. We were also given a small tin of cream, which we had to rub on our skin if any blisters appeared. This was presumably to counter the effects of blister gas, but again we were totally unaware of what that was or of the consequences.

In retrospect, I suppose this was the period loosely referred to as the phoney war—all talk and no action—which stretched from September 1939 through April 1940. True, there was no British military action, but the government took the opportunity to build up defences. It was a time of intense preparation. Large barricades began to appear, straddling the roads and creating chicanes to slow down vehicles and repel tanks. These were manned by soldiers with guns, and we had to show our identity cards. Similarly, large balloons suspended from steel wires began to appear in the sky. All public buildings had sand bags protecting the entrances and often the lower windows. Anderson air raid shelters were provided to all those who had a garden in which they could be erected. These consisted of six corrugated sheets bolted together at the top with steel plates at either end, providing family accommodation in an area six and a half feet by four and a half feet. The shelters, which cost seven pounds, were rather flimsy but provided some protection because they were half buried in the ground with earth heaped on top to protect against bomb blasts.

CHAPTER 3

The Turmoil of War—1940 to 1945

Most of us have far more courage than we ever dreamed we possessed.
Dale Carnegie

The bombing raids would mainly be at night, and I remember that most nights we went to the shelter the minute the air raid sirens sounded and stayed until the all-clear. Unfortunately, the noise of the bombs would keep us awake because one was never quite sure where they had been dropped and when they would explode. Luckily, we were not in the centre of town and so generally remained unscathed, although there were a few bombs that dropped nearby. The local ARP warden was a friend of my parents, and whenever he could, he checked that we were safe. Tragically, he was killed whilst serving with the army in North Africa in 1943.

Grimsby was the first town in the UK to suffer from the dropping of antipersonnel mines. These were small bomblets termed butterfly bombs that were dropped in their thousands and didn't explode on landing but only when picked up or dislodged from trees or the guttering on houses, or when stepped on. As children, we were told never to touch any metal object but to tell the police or the ARP wardens. On one night alone, the bus station in Grimsby was filled with bodies from such an attack. Looking back in time, this was an indiscriminate attack on civilians with the sole purpose of demoralising the population—something that people should remember when they accuse the British about the bombing of Dresden, which happened much later in the war.

Wartime Education

Many children were evacuated to rural areas and some to other countries during the war, but we weren't. We did pay frequent visits to my mother's parents in Oxford or my father's parents in Laceby. Whilst my younger sister and I travelled around with our parents, my older siblings stayed in one place. My father volunteered for the RAF in 1940 and after commissioning was posted to Grange-over-Sands, in Lancashire, and later to Harper Hill in Buxton, Derbyshire, where we as a family were to join him in 1941. For me, this was the start of a circuit of different homes and different schools in a very short space of time. We lived in six different houses in and around Buxton, and I attended five different schools (one village, one convent, one private, and two state primary schools). This was to become a feature of life as a service child and regretfully continued for my children when I decided to make the RAF my career in later life. Although it gave you a much wider perspective of life, it did little to enhance your academic grounding.

It was here in Buxton that I learnt how to assemble a very basic radio; I think we referred to it as a cat's whisker. Through this fundamental receiver, we caught parts of conversation or music that was being broadcast. An older cousin had arrived to spend his holidays with us, and he had what one would describe as a crazy boffin mind. Other days were spent on the surrounding snow-clad hills with toboggans, although because I was amongst the younger group, I had to make do with a large cardboard sheet, which I recall was nowhere near fast enough, much to my bad-tempered frustration. I must have been the brat, a title with which my siblings taunted me!

During 1942, my father was posted to Connell, an airfield in Scotland close to Oban. My elder brother Graham went to stay with my grandmother in Laceby to continue his education at Wintringham

Grammar School, and my elder sister started at Cheltenham Ladies College, leaving Gillian and me to travel north with my parents. In those days, travelling by steam train to the north of Scotland was an adventure stretching over many hours, and it was an experience long since forgotten. I still look at the remaining steam trains with some degree of fondness, I suppose because they were an established and memorable link with growing up.

It was an interesting phase of the war because the entrance to Loch Etive, where we were living, became a hive of activity. The Americans, having entered the war, started arriving in force during January 1942, with the US Navy recovering the battle-damaged ships from the Atlantic, many of which were then repaired in large floating docks close to where we lived. Connell Airfield became a marshalling area for many Liberator and B-25 bombers flown in from the States. I can recall the smell to this day when I was allowed on one of the aircraft whilst on the base. That familiar factory smell is similar to the smell of a newly made car, yet it's not nearly so inviting.

A squadron of Catalina flying boats was located near Dunbeg, close to the mouth of the loch. The entrance to the loch was naturally protected by the Falls of Lora, over which there was a double-spanned bridge leading to North Connell and the airfield. It was not unusual to see American servicemen during their off-duty times, perhaps the worse for drink or out of sheer bravado climbing to the highest points and standing upright as they walked across the high A-shaped girders of the double-spanned bridge. Had they fallen, they surely would have been killed, but to my knowledge none did. On some evenings, we gathered on the pebbled shoreline as Liberty boats were manned by American sailors, who tried to row across the swirling rapids created by the tidal surge over the Falls of Lora—an equally dangerous practice. In many ways, it expressed the gung-ho attitude of the Americans. But let me not be too critical, for their generosity knew no bounds; we all benefited from their handouts of food, chocolates, and what they called candy but we called sweets. Bearing in mind that all our food at that time was rationed and remained so until well into the 1950s—but more about rationing, its reasons and its impact, later.

My younger sister Gillian and I attended the village school and soon integrated with the local children. Because of our strange English accents, we were regarded as somewhat of a novelty at that time. The headmaster was a stern disciplinarian. Punishment was inflicted using a large leather strap rather than a cane. It was administered unsparing at the least excuse and irrespective of age; even five-year olds were not spared. Somewhat akin to the treatment received in some monastic establishments, I think the school had the well-established belief "spare the rod and spoil the child". I recall on one occasion having received it for a minor indiscretion. I had been playing in the local railway sidings with other boys, which to me seemed harmless. To the station master, we presented a major hazard. The pain lingered throughout the rest of that day. But then, there was that perverse pride in having received and survived such punishment!

Nevertheless, life as an eight-year-old was very exciting. New experiences abounded, such as being taught by one of the locals to fire a twelve-bore gun on the heather-covered hills, although the sight of dead seagulls left me feeling squeamish. On the other hand, climbing up a cliff face to collect eggs was exhilarating. The eggs, which we later ate, tasted very strong and fishy, but at least they were a luxurious replacement for chicken eggs that could only be obtained in very small quantities due to rationing. There were days when we were shown how to cut peat for the fires, and we were allowed to help in the milking of cows and rewarded with a small churn of warm milk to take home. Some days we spent time fishing for mackerel by hand rather than by rod, totally unsupervised alongside the fast-flowing loch with dangerous currents. We often walked for miles across the heather-covered hills with gulls screaming overheard and rabbits leaping out from behind huge rocks. During the school holidays, I travelled for considerable distances down the only road on the north side of the loch in the local postman's van delivering letters and having my first (unofficial) lessons in driving a car at the age of eight. I could hardly reach the brake pedal without standing, let alone see clearly over the steering wheel. It was a good job in those days, and one rarely saw another vehicle on the road, either because there weren't all that many or nobody had petrol coupons. There were other days that I recall clambering over the newly arrived Liberator bombers and being taken out by boat to sit in the Catalina flying boats whilst my father did his inspections.

There was one particular day that caused great excitement when I saw a parachute descending towards the islands. It was early evening, and I ran home to tell my father, knowing that he would let people know. But as is usual with grown-ups, they were highly suspicious that this was a young boy whose imagination got the better of him. I bristled with anger at the manner in which my observation had been treated, and to this day I don't know what happened or who was on the end of the parachute. But I had no doubt at all about what I had seen.

How different life is these days, protected by a whole host of rules and regulations! Some weekends we would go out to Bendaloch as a family, usually without my father, and sit on the beach overlooking Ardenmuchloch Bay, where the masts of a sunken ship protruded through the grey waters. Allegedly the ship had been carrying the Aga Khan's horses when it sank, but where it was coming from or going to, I remain as puzzled now as I was then. In a subsequent and perhaps nostalgic return to Oban and Connell in 2001, accompanied by Sheila and our Labrador Sheba, there was no sign of the wreck and few remnants of the wartime occupation of Connell Airfield. We walked the pebbled beach to exercise the dog, and I thought of those far-off days and the ghosts of yesteryear.

This was an idyllic life for a child: wide open countryside away from the horrors of bombing. But it was not to last because by the end of 1942, my father was posted to North Africa, and we were not to see him again until after the war. The letters my mother received were heavily censored, so we had no idea where he was or what was happening, although later we discovered that like many others in the armed services, after Africa he moved up with the invasion of Sicily and Italy into Europe.

During early 1943, we moved south once more, initially staying with my grandparents in Oxford and then moving back to Grimsby to stay with my father's parents for some months. My mother and her four children all occupied the same bedroom. I attended the local village school as I had done on three previous occasions. I was welcomed back by the headmaster, Mr Rowson, in familiar terms. "So, you have deemed to grace us with your presence again. For how long this time?" He had the innate ability to draw the attention of any wayward child who he considered had not been paying attention by hurling a solid wood blackboard rubber at the offending child; his aim was deadly accurate and the results traumatic. Repeated miscreants had their trousers dropped (I hasten to add only the boys) and their backsides addressed by the cane. Having said that, he would join us playing football with a tennis ball in the playground during our morning and afternoon breaks. To extend the breaks, we would always make sure that the opposing team (his) would be one goal behind; he hated being on the losing side! I think on reflection, this became my first lesson in diplomacy!

Once a week, we were taken to the school playing field, part of which was converted into an allotment, and we were encouraged to "Dig for Victory". To my mind, this was akin to forced labour because we never got the easy job of picking the products or indeed, to my recall, sampling the products! "Just keep on digging, young Everett, and think of the good you are doing." Many years later, his youngest daughter Janet was to be a bridesmaid at our wedding, by which time he had passed to the high school in the sky.

It was about this time that we started receiving aid from America and Canada in the form of tea chests full of drinking chocolate, the contents of which were rationed out to us twice a week. At school, we were encouraged to do our best for the soldiers by collecting books, and as a reward we were given military ranks according to the number collected. It was amazing how many generals appeared on the scene, but I often wonder how many homes had large quantities of missing books. I almost made Field Marshal before they started missing the books that I had purloined. Well, as I explained, it was all for a good cause.

Rationing

We had by this time become conditioned to rationing, which had been introduced earlier in the war as the German U-boats attacked the ships bringing food to the UK. Before the war, Britain imported fifty-five million tonnes of food. A month after the war started, this figure had dropped to twelve million tonnes, which meant that food and clothing were scarce commodities, as were many other things. This brought about two consequences: firstly, the drive for people to grow their own food either in their gardens or on public allotments and parks, and secondly, by the introduction of rationing covering food, clothing, and scarce items. There were three types of ration books, the aim being to ensure that everyone had the right category and amount of food to remain healthy. Buff coloured books for adults, green books for pregnant women and children under five, and blue books for children between five and sixteen. The typical rations per person per week were as follows.

- Meat, 6 ounces (150 g)
- Bacon, 2 ounces (50 g)
- Cheese, 4 ounces (100 g)
- Egg, 1
- Fats (butter, margarine, lard), 4 ounces (100 g)
- Sugar, 8 ounces (200 g)
- Tea, 2 ounces (50 g)
- Sweets, 2 ounces (50 g)

Young children and expectant mothers were allowed extra rations, including concentrated orange juice and cod liver oil. Other food in short supply was rationed by points systems. However, shops often ran out of food because there was never enough to go around, so whenever new supplies arrived, word would get out and large queues would soon form. Many years later, when working in East Berlin I, witnessed similar scenes and recalled the hunger pangs. Although not rationed, white bread was almost unobtainable due to the lack of flour. Similarly, vegetables were hard to find, and many people resolved this problem by digging up lawns and growing their own.

Public parks were converted into vegetable-growing areas called victory gardens, and people were encouraged to cultivate grassed areas wherever possible. The only fruit available, and only in small quantities, were the home-grown items such as plums, apples, pears, and berries. Clothing was limited to basics, and it was often a case of being fitted with hand-me-downs from other siblings (I didn't look very fetching in my sister's skirts) or making repairs where necessary, with shoes mended and torn trousers patched. It was a time of make do and mend. Although life was difficult and one always felt hungry, there were virtually no examples of obesity. What a difference almost eighty years makes; now obesity seems to be the norm.

Village Life

Laceby, being a village on the perimeter of Grimsby, managed to avoid the enemy bombing raids to a large extent. Let's face it: there were much better targets nearby. Although there were two instances of bombs being dropped on the village, both of them were unexploded and therefore had to be defused. However, like so many other villages in the east of England, Laceby sat close to a wide swathe of RAF bases. Of all the UK counties, Lincolnshire had the greatest number of airfields with some forty-six bases, of which thirty-three were populated by bomber squadrons. The noise of heavy bombers, day and night, was a constant reminder of the war being fought. There were inevitably many crashes as damaged planes returned from bombing raids over Germany; others crashed on take-off or were destroyed on the ground by accidents. There was the odd enemy Heinkel He 111 shot down by the Spitfires, but as the war progressed, there were fewer enemy aircraft operating that far north. There were plenty of opportunities for the curious to visit crash sites, which were generally heavily guarded either by the army or the Home Guard. Word of such crashes soon circulated, and we took every opportunity to get to the scene as quickly as possible, always eager to get close to the action. I do recall on one occasion visiting the crash site of an American Lightning fighter, the only one of that day that had a twin fuselage.

The Home Guard

Following the German invasion of Belgium and the Netherlands by parachute brigades in May 1940, which resulted in the British army having to evacuate Europe via Dunkirk, the government took the decision to form a local defence force to protect the five thousand miles of coastline from enemy invasion. On 10 May 1940, the government called for volunteers, and within days half a million had volunteered. This total soon rose to over one million. It was initially called the Local Defence Force but was later changed to the Home Guard. They were formed from those too old or too young to join the services or who were medically unsuitable. However, many in the LDF were drawn from those important occupations necessary to maintain the UK infrastructure, such as farm workers, teachers, transport operators, essential manufactures, and bank staff. As in many other towns and villages, Laceby had its Home Guard contingent, in which my grandfather served. They held meetings in a shed adjacent to the local sandpit, and in addition to their military activities, they constructed trenches at strategic places around the village and trained for a possible invasion. Following the Battle of Britain, which resulted in the Germans postponing their invasion plans, the role of the Home Guard changed to include the defence of essential buildings and key targets such as factories, aerodromes, munitions dumps, and crashed aircraft, as well as sealing off the sites were unexploded bombs still had to be defused.

My mother managed to rent a house on the outskirts of the village towards the end of 1944, which meant that we could move from my grandparents much to the relief of everyone, although we were only a mile away. It was during the late summer of that year that my puppy Bing was run over by a car, driven by airmen from the nearby RAF base at Binbrook, as we were walking down the road. It was a horrible sight and one that took me many months to get over. A German prisoner of war who was working at a nearby farm, presumably as a trustee prisoner, picked up the remains and helped me bury the dog in our garden. It was not unusual to see German and Italian prisoners of war in the brown one-piece overalls with a large yellow circle sown on the back. Many of them could speak very good English and were mainly employed working on the farms around the village, and it was hard for us to always regard them as the enemy.

Following the defeat of Rommel in North Africa, the Allies launched the invasion of Sicily and Italy in September 1943. It was not until the following January that the landings at Anzio took place, and even then the Allies did not enter Rome until 4 June. My father took part in the drive through Italy as part of the RAF support group and was present in Rome shortly after Vesuvius erupted; I believe that was in 1944. Elsewhere in Europe, plans were afoot for the major invasion, and D-Day was launched from the UK on 6 June 1944. In that same month, Germany launched the first of its V-1 rockets on London from their base in Peenemunde, killing 2,500 people. By late July, its infamous successor, the V-2 (predecessor to the Saturn moon rocket) had been launched with devastating effect on London and the surrounding area. Luckily, although we didn't know it at the time, we were well outside the range of the missiles and not part of the target zone.

Life in the village settled into a routine. We spent our holidays and weekends helping on the farms. However, I think to the girls in the Land Army, farm workers, and prisoners of war, we were more of a hindrance. My favourite task was riding on the carts and leading the giant Shire workhorses pulling the loads back to the farm. In the spring, we riddled and then planted potatoes. In the summer, we followed the reapers and stacked sheaves of wheat and oats. In the autumn, we picked fruit and potatoes. In the winter, we cut cabbages and sprouts. Nevertheless, it kept us out of trouble, provided a small amount of pocket money, and taught us much about the fatigue of hard work. It was also a reminder of the old adage "Early to bed, early to rise, makes a man healthy, wealthy and wise", but I'm not quite sure about the wealth and wisdom!

Although the war was going well for the Allies, there were still some setbacks both at home and overseas. It was on 27 November 1944 that one of this country's worse disasters occurred. An explosive storage cavern at RAF Fauld in Staffordshire exploded, close to where I was later to carry out my National service training and where, many years later, my son and family were to make their home. Some 4,000 tonnes of ammunition and bombs created what is one of the world's largest nonnuclear explosions in history, creating a crater some 400 feet deep and three-quarters of a mile across and resulting in the deaths of 75 people and serious injury to a further 370.

CHAPTER 4

The Post War Years—1945 to 1950

Out of the dark and into the light.

The year 1945 was a time of mixed fortunes with the end of the war coming in May of that year following Hitler's suicide on 30 April and the fall of Berlin to the Russians. Three days prior to his demise, the Italian Fascist leader Mussolini had been captured by Italian Partisans and executed, and his body was strung up with his mistress and other collaborators in the centre of Milan. By early May, it was clear that the end of the war in Europe was in sight. On 7 May the Germans unconditionally surrendered to the Western Allies and the following day to the Russians. Field Marshal Bernard Montgomery had already taken the unconditional military surrender in northern Germany at Luneburg Heath on 4 May. Some years later, I was to meet the field marshal in Norfolk. He was a rather diminutive man, but more about that later.

VE and VJ Celebrations

Within three weeks of the conclusion of war in Europe, 7 May was declared Victory in Europe Day, or VE Day for short, and a plethora of street parties erupted throughout the country in every city, town, village and hamlet. Although food at this stage was even scarcer than earlier in the war, everyone contributed to make these parties the focal point of community life. Bakers produced the bread, grocers the vegetables, and mothers the cakes. It was amazing what people had squirreled away and now produced in the way of tinned fruits and sweets. In essence, it demonstrated the community spirit that had been the vital spark that kept the nation going through its darkest hours of the war.

For me, however, it was a bittersweet occasion. My mother had given me the task of transferring plates, cutlery, and some food down to the village hall, less than a mile away, on my cycle. I set off with several bags strapped to the handle bars, and apparently on reaching the village square, I met a haulage lorry travelling in the opposite direction. I had my first unfortunate lesson in flying— head first through the windscreen. Luckily in those days, they didn't have toughened glass, but neither did they have ambulances readily available. Not that I was aware of what transpired, but I was taken home and the doctor was called. Fortunate for me, he was an ex- army consultant surgeon invalided back from Dunkirk and a man who had operated on many serious head and brain traumas. For the next four months, I was confined to bed in a darkened room, bored out of my mind and subjected to repetitive questions on what I could recall about the accident. My accounts of street parties are solely due to the comments of others because I missed out on both VE Day and VJ Day.

VJ Day was a celebration of the ending of the war in the east. The Japanese had fought on with their characteristic fanaticism, no doubt of the view that the emperor would prevail over all obstacles, including the might of the United States. The Americans, fearful of the enormous losses that could arise by an invasion of the Japanese mainland and that had already arisen on Okinawa, decided to drop nuclear bombs on strategic targets in Japan. Earlier in the war, with the help of British and Italian scientists, the Americans had initiated the Manhattan Project, the development, production and testing of an atomic bomb. On 6 August 1945, the first of these bombs was exploded above the city of Hiroshima, creating devastating damage. A second device was dropped on Nagasaki three days later, and as predicted, that led to the immediate surrender of the Japanese. The formal and unconditional surrender was concluded on the morning of 2 September aboard the USS *Missouri* in Tokyo Harbour between Japanese General Urmezu and US General MacArthur.

It was about this time that the first pictures began to emerge of the horrors of the Nazi extermination camps at Bergen-Belsen, and posters appeared on walls and advertising boards throughout villages and towns to point out these atrocities. In the last months of the war, Allied soldiers had discovered several locations used by the Nazis since 1933, where they'd held and eliminated over eleven million people: those who opposed their doctrine, those of ethnic and religious differences (especially Jews), and many of other nationalities for a variety of reasons, justified or not. They were held in what were described as concentration camps (Konzentrationslager), but there was little difference between these camps and extermination camps. Notably amongst the worst were Bergen-Belsen, Buchenwald, Dachau, Ravensbruck, Auschwitz-Birkanau, and Treblinka, but there were many more. The Germans were not alone. It was not long before details of the horrific treatment meted out by the Japanese began to emerge. The years that followed saw many of those responsible brought to justice through such entities as the Nuremburg War Trials held in Nuremburg between 20 November 1945 and 1 October 1946, as well as other courts of retribution.

Further Education

Yet another personal problem arose in 1946, a time when I was confronted by the scholarship examination which was a necessary qualification to transfer to a grammar school—the forerunner to the eleven-plus examination. The frequent changes of schools, which at that point I calculated as twelve different primary schools before the age of eleven, and the consequential disruption created by changes in teaching practices, my accident, and my lack of application meant that I was by no means ready for such a test. I sat the written exam and passed, which I understand from the subsequent discussions with the headmaster was a surprise to both of us. I then had to attend the grammar school for what was termed an oral examination.

This centred on describing events portrayed in a picture of ancient Egyptians digging around in the desert with buildings and camels in the background. Whatever answer they were searching for did not readily spring to mind, and consequently I wasn't considered acceptable.

My mother decided that I was in dire need of private education to enable me to catch up with others, and I would travel the five miles into Grimsby to attend St James's, a private school. There, I had to make the transition to deal with strange languages such as French and Latin, and mathematical equations which included algebra and logarithms, the likes of which I had never experienced; my confidence was at its lowest ebb. There followed months of intensive pressure and resultant pain whilst I came to terms with these strange phenomena with which everyone else seemed to have little difficulty. I do recall sitting an examination in French shortly after having started at the school and achieving the quite remarkable result of 5 per cent which in anyone's view has to be the most glorious of failures. I think I only got that mark through my presentation, certainly not my content. Strange, isn't it? Half a lifetime away, I was able to converse in Arabic, German, and (with some limitations) Russian. But then, not everyone's forte is languages, especially when there are better things on offer, and English was becoming a universal language. Mind you, I did excel at sport. What was it that Kipling said? "If you can meet with Triumph and Disaster and treat those two imposters just the same." Well, I certainly learned that at a very early age!

Nevertheless, despite my lack of academic grounding, within the next year I was able to sit and pass the Common Entrance Examination necessary to obtain a place at public school. Once again it was a surprise to my mother, me, and no doubt the headmaster, because the Common Entrance Exam was far more difficult than the Scholarship, having languages and mathematics at its core. But I digress, for this was not until the following year. My sister Gillian had started school at St Martin's in Grimsby, so we travelled together by bus. I was always reminded by my mother to doff my hat, be polite, and give up my seat to elders, as everyone expected and respected good manners. What happened to those days? I am, however, a recipient of it occasionally on the London Underground these days; usually it's a young girl from overseas, never a male. I of course decline—pride is a strange attitude in those of us who are reaching the downward spiral! But here I go again, straying away from the facts.

Education in primary schools then was very different to that the present day. Teaching, especially in maths and English, was often by rote, delivered to children seated in rows of two-seat and four-seat desks. There were no such things as ballpoint pens. (Now I'm beginning to sound like my grandparents: "Eh, lad, life was hard in them days!") Children, acting as ink monitors, filled up ink wells on the desks in which each child could dip a pen; younger children were given pencils with which to write. The teacher would write information with chalk on a blackboard, rubbing out the details as each part of the lesson was completed. As I pointed out earlier, the large wooden block rubbers (or erasers; I must refer to them as such, otherwise our American cousins will get the wrong idea. Rubbers in school is not a place I want to go.) made the teacher's task of getting the pupil's attention with an accurate throw so much easier; in those days, such disciplines as health and safety had never inculcated society, let alone the classroom, the playground, or indeed the home. Such items as spinning tops, metal hoops (not plastic; that came much later) skipping, or leapfrogging abounded as natural past-times, as well as conkers. These were to be replaced with iPhones, iPads, and the Internet at a much later date—the age of obesity. Looking back on those days, when everything had a place, and everything was in its place, there were icy downhill slides in the school playground. It all proved exhilarating and, no doubt for me, was the forerunner for skiing in my later life.

My father returned home in the middle of 1946 displaying his new suit with which all service officers were issued on demobilisation. He had qualified as a Fellow of the Auctioneers' Institute before the war and decided that he was going to start his own business as an auctioneer and estate agent, but in 1946 business in Grimsby (as in other parts of the country) was at a standstill. Added to which, there were thousands of ex-servicemen returning into civilian life in search of work or resuming careers. Life was extremely difficult whilst he struggled to build up the business and support the family. He took on extra work sorting out the accounts and stocktaking for a variety of public houses, small hotels, and sports clubs in and around Grimsby.

Rationing was still in force, and food was still difficult to obtain. I do recall one Saturday, on my mother's instructions, standing in a long queue in the Grimsby marketplace, clutching my young sister's ration book and waiting for almost two hours. A consignment of bananas had just arrived from the West Indies, and word had spread. As luck would have it, we were in Grimsby at the time. Only those with children's ration books could purchase them, and then only three bananas per child. I had never seen a banana, but it didn't make any difference because they were destined to be shared amongst the family.

This was also the year in which Graham, my older brother, flew the nest. Having been a cadet in the Air Training Corps, he had set his mind on joining the RAF and left to start his training as an aircraft apprentice at RAF Halton. The Brats, as they were known, underwent three years training in the technical engineering aspects of aircraft and their systems. It was whilst he was at Halton that he met his future wife, who lived in Amersham; they married in July 1950. I remember the wedding well but saw nothing of the reception because I had to sit in the car and entertain my younger brother, who was not yet two—a post-war present from my parents. Or was it that dratted stork again?

But these were not times of parochial concerns alone. The war had recently finished, but a new threat was beginning to emerge as the powerful, dominant Soviet Union began to flex its muscles. Winston Churchill, ever the man for the evocative pronouncement, made a speech at Westminster College, Fulton, in the United States in which he drew attention to the threat by saying, "From Stettin in the Baltic to Trieste in the Adriatic, an iron curtain has descended across the continent." This was later regarded as the starting point of the Cold War. At home, shortages continued to affect the public, and on 27 June the government imposed bread rationing,

The post-war Labour government progressed with their aim of nationalising key elements of the nation's infrastructure. In 1947, the

Rail Transport Act was passed in Parliament, and the National Coal Board was created. It wasn't long before whole rafts of enterprises and utilities were state owned, organised, and run. However, they were heavily subsidised and therefore added to the increasing debts we owed as a nation.

The 1947–1948 Winter

Early in the winter of 1946–1947, there were no signs of the weather deteriorating, but by January 1947 things changed significantly. Bear in mind that the technique of long-term weather forecasting had not yet been developed; the only available information was based on forecasts given by the Air Ministry. Whilst these were generally accurate, they did not have sufficient long-term predictability, and nobody anticipated the changes that were to occur. The winter of 1947 was not quite as cold as that of 1962–1963, but it was certainly one of the most dramatic ever experienced in living memory. The first snow fell on 23 January, and the country experienced blizzards which were worse than at any time since 1891. Temperatures fell to -21 Celsius. The government introduced power cuts across the country from 9 a.m. to midday and from 2 to 4 p.m. every day of the week. By February the weather had deteriorated further, and in many areas snow fell every day throughout the month, with temperatures failing to rise above freezing. We were cut off in Laceby by heavy snowdrifts ranging between twelve and fifteen feet in height (or in modern terminology, about five metres). During the first week, my parents were travelling back from seeing my grandparents in Oxford when their train got stuck in a snowdrift near Louth; after several hours, the train had to be abandoned. I don't know who was the more worried, them or us, because in those days there were no such things as mobile phones.

As the month progressed, the freezing conditions turned the snow and ice into solid masses. All schools were closed, and we occupied our days by digging out pathways to our homes and at other times tunnelling under the drifts to form hidden passageways and ice-block igloos. At least the activity was one way of keeping warm. There was very little coal left, and because the houses had no central heating, the water pipes soon froze, creating yet another problem in restricting freshwater. There was no such thing as double glazing, and windows soon iced over. Many houses had outside, unflushed toilets that were not connected to mains sewage. This created a twofold problem: the tasks of cutting a path to the toilet and of removing waste excrement. The weather by itself was severe, but the effects were compounded by the continuing shortages of the post-war era—shortages that included not only food but also the main driving force of the economy, fuel. Britain was already half a million tonnes of coal short of requirements even before the winter started. Eggs, cheese, meat, and bread were on limited ration, and petrol remained rationed and scarce, but then few people had cars at that time, and that included my parents. As a child, I can think of nothing worse than being continually cold and hungry.

In the second week in March, milder air started to push north, but this created a further problem as flooding occurred throughout thirty counties, and we suffered from rivers overflowing and fields flooding for many miles. Inevitably it was a traumatic time, but dealing with these problems became a cause célèbre amongst communities, fostered no doubt by the wartime spirit, neighbours ever ready to help each other battle through the atrocious conditions.

The euphoria of victory in the war soon gave way to the gloom of austerity with the announcement by Prime Minister Clement Attlee of his Dictatorship Bill, placed before Parliament on 8 August. In the bill, he set forward plans for the recovery from the economic crisis arising from the termination of aid from the United States and the need to pay off the huge debts amassed during the war. What the plan envisaged was a pattern of Britain going without more of what were considered "necessities" of life whilst the nation's industrial and material resources were thrown behind growth in exports and reduced imports. The austerity measures included cutting food by twelve million pounds a month (a reduction of 33 per cent), ensuring hotels and restaurants only served two-course meals; cutting imports of luxury goods by five million pounds a month; and reducing petrol for private use by one-third and for commercial users by 10 per cent. Housing was slowed by reducing timber imports by ten million pounds a month. The bill also envisaged longer working hours and the mobilisation of one and a half million workers into essential industry, with the aim of boosting exports. All this from a Labour government!

Minister of Food John Stacey announced the start of a twenty-five-million-pound scheme to grow groundnuts in Tanganyika, with the aim of producing vegetable oil. This turned out to be a gigantic failure and an embarrassment to the government because it was established in the wrong place, in the wrong conditions, and at the wrong time. Moreover, in the two years of its development, most of the expensive equipment had been ruined, and the land turned into a dust bowl. It was abandoned in January 1949 when it became clear that no profits were feasible, and the cost to the taxpayer had risen to over forty-nine million pounds.

In April, two significant events occurred. The school leaving age was raised to fifteen, and the largest nonnuclear explosion in history took place when the Royal Navy exploded 6,800 tonnes of surplus ammunition in an attempt to destroy Heligoland, Germany. Elsewhere, in August of that year, both India and Pakistan gained their independence whilst remaining in the Commonwealth.

It was a time of poverty, queues, rationing, and resilience. Far from the glory of defeating Germany, it was a time of even greater hardship than during the war years. Rationing now covered meat, butter, margarine, lard, sugar, tea, cheese, soap, clothing, sweets, bread, and petrol. A shortage of coal resulted in the closure of power stations, causing massive power cuts. The weekly ration of meat dropped to one shilling (five pence) a week, and potatoes appeared on the restricted list for the first time.

Whilst all these measures impacted on day-to-day living, life in Laceby continued to follow the pattern of any small community. We supplemented food intake by growing our own vegetables and fruit from the hedgerows. Meals were available in state-run canteens in the main towns, and Grimsby had one, predominantly used by workmen but open to families if one could afford it. We continued to assist the family income when the opportunity arose, however small the amount: picking blackberries and selling these to greengrocers; fruit picking for Crosby's, a local jam making company; and working on the farms during holidays (potato setting and picking, chopping beet, stacking corn, helping with threshing, stacking hay, and feeding animals). Farming was highly labour intensive, and cheap labour was always sought after—and let's face it, nothing was cheaper than us!

The economic situation looked gloomy, and the consequences for my father's business were dire. He therefore decided to apply to the Air Ministry to return on a permanent commission, having left as a flight lieutenant, and by the end of the year he was luckily accepted and re-joined the RAF. As a result of the improvement in the family income, it was decided that I would be sent to All Saints College, Bloxham, which was a minor public school near Banbury that my father had attended as a youth and where he met my mother, who with her sister was a boarder at the nearby Banbury Ladies College. Following an interview with the headmaster of the college and having passed the Common Entrance Exam mentioned earlier, I was selected for admission in the spring term of 1948, which was fortunate because by this time my mother was pregnant with her fifth child. It must have been the excitement of post-war Britain, and of course the stork had to make a living. I dread to think where it had been in the meanwhile!

In January, the government continued on its path of nationalisation of failing industries when the railways were placed under central control as part of the newly formed British Rail, which existed until privatisation, which occurred between 1994 and 1997. For me, this took away a lot of the fun in trainspotting, and although some of the individual train engine names remained, the magic of LNER, LMS, and other well-known companies, with their distinctive colours and logos, disappeared. For me, trainspotting was never the same. However, here we are in 2018, and the government has brought back LNER. In a way, it was probably a good thing steam trains were replaced by diesel and electric because I might have become an anorak and joined one of the brigades who, even in this day and age, congregate on the ends of platforms, exchanging their hard-earned knowledge and their flasks of tea. But look on the bright side: all those wives benefitting from this peace and freedom, at least for the best part of the day!

I suppose the big event of the year, from an Everett perspective, was the arrival on 19 April of Charles Ian Robert Everett some eleven years after the birth of my younger sister and nineteen years after Graham, my elder brother—an astonishingly wide gap. As I mentioned earlier, I'm not sure what that stork had been doing in the intervening years, but I suppose the intervention of the war had something to do with it. However, it's fascinating to review the year in which he was born, a continuing period of austerity. The economy was starting on its long, tortuous road to recovery. Nationalisation was the cornerstone of the Labour administration, and it wasn't long before railways, coal, iron and steel, road transport, airlines, gas and electricity, docks, and inland waterways followed the Bank of England and came under the umbrella of state ownership. It is therefore important that the lives of those who lived through these difficult times should be viewed against the backdrop of the general economy of the time.

On the national stage, the most important and far-reaching event was approval in the United States of the Marshall Plan in April of that year. The plan, officially called the European Recovery Plan (ERP), was to fund the rebuilding of Europe over a four-year period by providing $13 billion in economic and technical assistance. The aim was to counter the spread of communism. Access to the fund was also offered to Russia and its allied states, but they refused. Without this massive influx of funds, it is unlikely that Europeans would have been able to kick-start their economies, and even then it would be many years before a full recovery could be achieved. Conversely, without that aid, many countries such as Germany would have fallen under the control of communism.

Rationing was still in force and was to continue well into the 1950s. In 1948, one-quarter of all homes had no electricity, no indoor toilets, and no telephone, and only a limited number had cars. Although television had been introduced before the war, it was still in its infancy and in a crude form, and even this had been shut down for a year due to the fuel crisis. There was only one channel, and it only operated over short periods of time with limited programmes, which bore no relationships to modern systems. Moreover, coverage did not extend much beyond London. The pictures were projected on a somewhat fuzzy and distorted green picture projected on to a nine-inch frame. Ghostly figures followed by their shadows, largely unrecognisable, transited across this very small screen. I recall my grandparents in Oxford having one of these early contraptions; their seven children had contributed to its purchase to celebrate their parents' wedding anniversary. How they got any signal at all mystifies me.

In 1948, houses were heated by coal fires, which added to the commercial uses of coal meant that in adverse weather conditions, some locations suffered from a blanket of choking smog with visibility down to zero—and I mean zero. I recall one day walking back across Grimsby and feeling the walls of shops and houses to get a sense of bearing, with little idea of where the pavement ended and the road began. Luckily, in those circumstances there was little worry about being knocked down by a vehicle. However, one had to rely on an inert sense of location and overcome the fear of claustrophobia. Few houses had central heating in any form. Indeed, few houses had carpets; the floors, being wood, were covered either by carpets, rugs, or linoleum. Household equipment that we take for granted these days either did not exist or was impossible to obtain. It was well into the 1950s before such items as washing machines, tumble driers, and freezers began to appear in numbers alongside other labour-saving devices, which freed up the housewife to seek employment. There were no supermarkets, and shops specialised in their own merchandise. There were butchers, bakers, grocers, clothing and textiles, furniture, chemist, and cycle shops, which meant that shopping was often diverse and time-consuming, even if products were available and not restricted by rationing.

Although this was a time of austerity, it did not stop the nation hosting the Summer Olympics, or as the press referred to them, the Austerity Games of 1948. These were probably the last and only games to be funded on a shoestring. No new buildings were erected, and male competitors were housed in RAF stations around Wembley Stadium; female competitors were located in university and college buildings. Nevertheless, the games were a great success, helped to boost the sagging morale of the nation, and brought to the fore such names as

Fanny Blankers-Kohn, Emil Zatopek, and Arthur Wint. "Who?" I hear you say. Well, it was a long time ago.

Life in Public School

As mentioned earlier, it was at this time that I was ejected from the nest, decked out in my immaculate uniform with a trunk full of clothes (not easy in those days because of rationing and also costs), a tuck box with some fruit and cakes. With a worried mother, I set forth for the south and my induction into life in a public school. The first day after my mother had returned home by train was gut-wrenching. I was released into a maelstrom of pupils, the vast majority of whom had already crossed the River Styx into the unknown and were fully conditioned to the harsh discipline of life in both prep and public school through their previous domiciles. It was unnerving, to say the least.

I was placed in a dormitory along with thirty other boys, and the room was filled with bunk beds. We were supervised by prefects who I'm sure had been indoctrinated by a Germanic philosophy of life, "Arbeit macht frei." Punishments abounded, all administered in the bathroom by a beating with a leather slipper, which I believed they were permitted to do. I later found this not to be the case. Talking after lights out, late out of or into bed (I mean by minutes), running down the stairs or in the corridors, and the cardinal sin of walking on part of the playing field. Life in those first weeks was hell, and beatings came aplenty, but I soon learnt to adapt to the system. In later life, you will learn, I met one of those who had been of that ilk and relished in his memories. It's a good job he wasn't of my vintage, or I might now be serving a sentence for manslaughter. On the other hand, it equipped me for future survival, and on such a basis I considered that I would probably have survived Colditz had I have been of that age!

The days from Monday to Saturday began at 6 a.m. with the ringing of the Evangelist Bell in the school chapel, which was a call to arms for the beginning of the day's routine. Washed, dressed, and ready for breakfast of porridge and toast, we had to be in the queue by 6.45 and sitting down by 7 a.m. By 8 a.m. we had to be in our classroom, all geared up to start the first of our lessons. Lunch was between 12.30 and 1.15. This was followed by an afternoon of organised sport, Army Cadet Force training, or a cross-country run fondly called the Grind for obvious reasons until 4 p.m.; this was a run of some three to four miles depending on one's age. Tea was from 4.30 to 5 p.m., and prep or further lessons were held between 5.30 and 7 p.m. Choir practise would impose itself in the latter hours or by compressing the tea break. Whatever happened, it was into bed by 8.30 p.m. and lights out by 9 p.m. Sunday was a day of rest—believe that if you can! We were up early in the morning to take communion followed by the morning service, and if one was in the choir, as I was, it was practise in between. The afternoon was referred to as a leisurely one comprising of a long walk or a lecture, weeding in the housemaster's garden, or merely writing home to complain about boredom or the intensity of life away from home. I suppose on reflection, it was very similar to what many would maintain was their life as a national serviceman.

On the walls of the internal corridors were plaques relating to former pupils killed during the First World War. What intrigued me was the age of those killed, even to a relative youngster where the gap between ten and twenty is significant. The young age at which they had been killed left an indelible impression. The other factor was the enormity of the numbers killed. I think on reflection that it also created a feeling of humility that so many of them had made the ultimate sacrifice, and that so many families had suffered in the process.

Unknown to me, at that time my grandfather's spinster sisters, Lottie (Charlotte) and Bessie (Elizabeth), lived about eight miles away in a little village called Swerford, a place I visited many years later when I was researching my family history. One day Lottie, who must have been in her sixties but to me appeared very much older, arrived at the school having cycled from her home that morning. I'll swear that the cycle was a penny-farthing but I could have been wrong. I was summoned to the headmaster's study (which put the fear of God into me) to meet her and be told that I had been invited to tea the following Sunday, and that there was a bus which would deliver me there and back. I had the headmaster's permission to go.

After paying my respects and retreating to a safe-haven, I reflected on the difficulties I faced. I had been selected for the second team at cricket on that very day, and the housemaster seemed to think that my prowess as a batsman would make all the difference to the team's result. Needless to say, I did not exactly share his optimism. On the other hand, I wasn't exactly enamoured with the thought of tea with two elder ladies whom I had never met before, and in a place I'd never visited. The result was that I wrote to them giving my apologies. I stopped the local bus and asked the driver if he would deliver the letter to their cottage. Can you imagine how such a request would be dealt with nowadays? "Get lost, lad," springs to mind. Although I went on to make thirty-two runs and take two wickets, and we were victorious, the sense of treason stays with me to this very day, and reluctantly I never did get to meet my grandfather's sisters.

Much of the year that followed was a mixture of elation and grief, the latter reflecting my lowly academic achievements. I struggled with most subjects, I suppose as a result of my frequent change of schools, and consequently my confidence was at a very low point. There was one particular experience that I feel, on reflection, was to lead to a change of direction in my future career, although I was hardly in a position to recognise it at the time. I had been suffering from an ear infection stemming from swimming during the Scholl Sports Day, and I duly reported to the school nurse. Her medication, in an age when antibiotics were unheard of, was to use an enormous syringe to wash out the ear. I remember the excruciating pain that occurred, and I'm sure that it resulted in a ruptured eardrum, but who's to know? Hindsight is a wonderful thing. Needless to say, however ill I felt in the remainder of my days at Bloxham, I never ventured near the medical establishment again.

From Public School to Secondary Modern

News came in my second term, just as I was beginning to adapt to life under the new regime, that my parents could no longer afford the fees. I would therefore be returning home. At this time, my elder sister had been accepted for training at Anstey College, Birmingham, as a teacher in physical education, and I suppose she was in need of the financial support. In those days, it was not possible for anyone to transfer from public school to grammar school, and I was therefore destined for a place in a secondary modern school, Waltham Toll Bar (now another of those so-called academies) in Lincolnshire, a move that was probably to be the making of me. The transition was not too difficult, but I had to not only establish myself in a new environment but also face those with whom I had attended primary school in Laceby from time to time. Initially, I was regarded as a toff with a posh accent and was taunted accordingly, although I'm sure most of them didn't understand what a public school meant. Public lavatories yes, but not public schools. Besides which, they felt (quite rightly) that they were in a public school already. Whilst in primary school at Laceby, I had acquired the nickname Tiger; to this day, I'm not entirely sure why. I did get into fights and have a quick temper, but only when goaded.

There's something about your reputation going before you, justified or not. However, it was accepted that I had established myself as a sportsman, embracing my first love of athletics as well as football, cricket, swimming, and rugby, which always stands me in good stead. Added to which, in my early days at Waltham, I had made good relationships, treading a careful path between the rival school gangs. Not that they were gangs in the modern idiom, but more akin to friends from the same geographical areas. I think my ability to bridge the gap, for what it was worth, was seen by the teachers as a moderating influence. I was soon elevated to the position of head boy without having gone through the initial stage of becoming a prefect, much to my surprise and the annoyance of those already established as prefects.

Fate plays some strange games at times. Two of the teachers at our school were sisters who had lived in Scotland before completing their training, and this was to be their first school. In fact, as teenagers they had been our next-door neighbours in Connell when we lived in Scotland. Although I knew the parents, I was not aware of the girls. Well, who is when you're only eight?

It was whilst I was at Waltham that the Berlin Airlift was in full flow. The blockade of Berlin, which started on 27 June, was one of the first major international crises of the Cold War. The Soviets blocked the Western Allies' railway, road, and canal access to those sectors of Berlin under Allied control. Their aim was to force the Western powers to allow the Soviet zone authorities to start supplying Berlin with food and fuel, thereby giving the Russians total control over the city and extending the influence of communism across central Europe.

The Allies were not prepared to see communism emerge as a dominant force in Europe or a major threat to capitalism in the West. They responded by organising the airlift of supplies into West Berlin. The newly formed United States Air Force and the Royal Air Force flew over 200,000 flights in the first year, supplying some 4,700 tonnes daily. The aircrews included not only USAF and RAF but also Australian, Canadian, New Zealand, and South Africans.

By the early part of 1949, the airlift had carried more than had been previously moved by rail. The success, which had not been foreseen by the Russians, caused them considerable embarrassment, and the blockade was eventually lifted on 12 May 1949. Much later in the 1980s, I was to play a key role in the Allied contingency plans in the event of any recurrence. The three airfields at Tempelhof, Gatow, and Tegal provided the primary gateways to the city for the next fifty years until reunification of the two Germanys, the Federal Republic and the Democratic Republic, in 1990.

In 1949, I emulated my older brother by joining No 195 Squadron of the Air Training Corps. He had been a member prior to going to RAF Halton to become an aircraft apprentice. On one occasion, our science master, who had served in the RAF during the war, took us on a visit to RAF Manby. I was one of six pupils selected to have a flight in a Valetta transport aircraft. The pilot was Squadron Leader Ken Hubbard, originally from Norfolk, a renowned aviator of that era who had set many records for long-distance flights. During the war, he had been awarded the DFC. During my career in the RAF, I was to meet him again on several other occasions, initially when he was a Squadron Leader working for the Air Secretary, subsequently as the officer commanding No 49 Squadron at RAF Wittering, and later when he was a Group Captain commanding RAF Scampton and I was a relatively newly commissioned Pilot Officer serving at RAF Watton in Norfolk. But I digress.

I was given the privilege of occupying the co-pilot's seat whilst Ken Hubbard flew us at low level over the school. This gained a great deal of coverage in the local press and did my acceptance in the school no harm. From the reaction of some of the girls, one would have thought that I had being flying the aircraft myself. That summer, because he had learnt about my desire to join the RAF, I was invited to accompany Ken Hubbard on a training flight to Malta and North Africa. Later, I accompanied him on other flights in the Middle East and North Africa. To me, this was a Biggles type experience which fed my appetite to become a pilot, as well as widening my experience of life abroad. This was the sort of experience that few had in those days, unlike the current situation when most people have frequently travelled to some part of the world.

On the wider stage, this was the year in which NATO was created; that the HMS *Amethyst* escaped the blockade set by the Chinese communists in the Yangtze River; and that the first passenger-carrying jet aircraft, the Comet, took to the air. The first TV station outside London was established at Sutton Coldfield near Birmingham, and on 1 May the gas industry was nationalised. Rationing for sweets and chocolate ended, but within a month it was reintroduced owing to shortages that had occurred. The most significant impact was to come with the 30 per cent devaluation of the pound against the US dollar on 19 September and the resultant increase costs of commodities. It also had a consequential impact on our exports.

CHAPTER 5

Life in the Early Fifties

I'm not afraid of tomorrow for I have seen yesterday and I love today.
Alan White

The 1950s, the sixth decade of the twentieth century, marked the escalation of the Cold War, the conflict between communism and capitalism, which was to dominate the decade; the Korean War; the start of the space race; an increase in the testing of nuclear weapons; and the beginning of decolonisation in Africa and Asia. It was also the year that the mass production of computers began, one in seven families in the UK possessed a car, and the average UK salary was £364. Yes, that's right, £364! On 29 June, the English Football Association had to face the humiliating defeat of their football team by the United States, hardly a country recognised for its football prowess at that time. This was to have far-reaching consequences for the sport in the United Kingdom.

The Air Training Corps

For me and others of my vintage in 1950, these were factors that we read in the newspapers but in general were for others to worry about. That sounds a bit trite, but at the age of fifteen and having passed through a major conflict, this was an inevitable reaction. It was the end of my first year at Waltham and was a full and interesting period of my young life. I was made head boy, as I said, without having gone through the initial stages of becoming a prefect. Perhaps the headmaster, Mr Drury, and the other masters saw something in me that I didn't. Maybe it was the embryonic signs of leadership because it was in that year that I was also promoted to corporal in the Air Training Corps (ATC), within six months to sergeant, and the following year to flight sergeant, the highest rank a cadet could receive at that time.

The ATC became a major part of my life not only in preparation for later service in the Royal Air Force but also in encouraging participation in a wide range of activities, including sport, gliding, being a drummer in the band, and by no means least flying and air navigation. In school, I progressed in both sport and in academic subjects, although the latter could lead to nothing because in those days pupils at secondary modern schools could not sit the recently introduced General Certificate of Education. Nevertheless, I persevered, achieved 100 per cent in science, and was second in class in all subjects. I had similar success in sport representing the school in athletics, football, and cricket. I won the county inter-schools' cross-country championship and later the county half mile. In the autumn, I was selected to play for one of the local Grimsby football teams as well as being recruited into Grimsby Harriers Athletics Club. I had the feeling that I could make a difference in my life.

On weekends I travelled to RAF Kirton-in-Lindsey, which accommodated the Lincolnshire Wing ATC Gliding facilities. We spent many days launching and recovering the gliders, manning the winches or working on the theories of flight, as well as the most important thing, flying the aircraft. The thrill of eventually going solo was countered by the knowledge that unlike powered flight, one didn't have a second chance to land the aircraft, so everything had to be rapidly assessed and quickly actioned—an excellent grounding for powered flight later in my career. When the thermals no longer provided lift, one had to beat a hasty retreat and get back to base to land the glider. Sitting on the edge of the Lincolnshire Wolds almost guaranteed ideal gliding conditions. It proved to be an exciting time for me with plenty of opportunity to be up in the clouds, chasing thermals and having a reluctance to return without just one more challenge. It was so easy to get carried away in more ways than one! Over the next two years, I was to gain my A, B, and C licences, and I never lost that feeling of tranquillity when alone above the clouds. It created a sense of escapism on the one hand and acute awareness on the other—a serenity which I have only captured on the tops of mountains or from the challenges of sailing and listening to the waves breaking against the boat as wind challenges water and both of them challenge you. One has the ever-present awareness that things can change with little warning. It teaches you, above everything else, a healthy respect for the environment around you.

In the summer of 1951, we travelled north to the Royal Naval Air Station at Donnibristle on the Edge of the Firth of Forth for our two-week ATC camp. One of the memorable events was rowing a liberty boat (eight oars) under the massive Forth Bridge. It reminded me of those wartime days at Connell and the US Navy sailors crossing the Falls of Lora. In August I flew with Ken Hubbard once more in a Valetta on a training schedule to RAF Luqa in Malta, via Istres in France. After a two-day stay in Malta, we flew on to Castle Benito in Libya, which as the name implies had been an Italian Air Force base during the early part of the war. Then we went on to Shalufa, Egypt, arriving back at RAF Manby on 19 August.

Later that year, I was selected to play football for Lincolnshire, and it was an occasion when we beat Leicestershire for the Midlands Football Trophy, but not before we escaped in a car crash. One of the ATC officers, the driver of our car, circumnavigated a corner of the country road just a little too fast, and the car rolled over into a rather steep ditch. Trying to extricate yourself from a car that's finished on its roof is somewhat challenging, especially because the doors were held firm against the sides of the ditch. There is nothing that can replace that fear of petrol flowing across a hot engine. As luck would have it, we did manage to squeeze out through one of the widows and into a small gap in the ditch. It happened on an isolated country road not far from Ashby-de-la-Zouch in Leicestershire. Strangely enough, it was only a place I'd heard about through a song which was doing the rounds in the early 1950s: "Ashby-de-la-Zouch, Castle Abbey, a little English town by the sea … it's the only place that I want to be … Ashby-de-la-Zouch Castle Abbey by the sea" (Decca 1946). Actually, it's nowhere near the sea! Suffice to say we eventually got to where we were going after some assistance from a local garage. As to the castle itself, it's had a chequered history since it was built in 1473 by the then Lord Hastings, who was later executed by Richard, Duke of Gloucester. Its other claim to fame was when it featured in Sir Walter Scott's novel *Ivanhoe*.

In June, I reached the age of fifteen, at which stage I was destined to leave school. Surprisingly, the school leaving age had only been raised from fourteen to fifteen in 1947. Although I had set my mind on joining the RAF at the earliest opportunity, the headmaster and my parents decided I should stay for a further year. I was not overly impressed with this idea because I wanted to get out and earn some money, even if it was to be a pittance. There was a compromise, and I stayed for the winter term with little idea of what I would do thereafter. In those days, in secondary education there was a lot of cross-training. Boys took domestic science courses, which involved buying food, cooking meals, baking cakes and bread, and running the school flat for a week, during which time meals had to be prepared each day for a selection of teachers. Girls, on the other hand, had to take carpentry, make furniture, and undertake tasks such as assembling and working on old cars. Windows broken either by accident or during playground football had to be replaced by the offending pupil. This meant measuring and buying the glass and the putty, fitting the window, and disposing of the broken glass. Would it happen in this day and age? I think not.

Festival of Britain

This was a year that was marked with a massive celebration of achievements in the UK. The idea of the government was to provide a tonic for the British public, who had been living through a time of austerity. It was also intended as a celebration of advances in science, technology, and industry. The idea was a nationwide programme of events, to be called the Festival of Britain, the centrepiece of which would be on the south bank of the Thames stretching from Battersea Park to Waterloo. Much of London, as in many other areas, was still in ruins from the bombing, so the development of the sites was badly needed. Buildings such as the Skylon Tower, the Dome of Discovery, and the Royal Festival Hall were the main ones under construction. The cost was substantial for the time, £10.5 million, attracting only £2.5 million in income. The overall loss was £8 million (or about £40 million in today's terms).

Although the early fifties saw the beginning of the post-war economic expansion, with high employment and sustained growth that would continue into the early 1970s, there were many of today's basic household equipment, such as electric fires and washing machines, that were available to only a few. Tumble driers were unheard of, and only 15 per cent of houses had a fridge, with less than 10 per cent having a telephone. However, the era of mass production was on the horizon, and things would soon change. By this time the population of the UK had reached fifty million—not that it had any bearing on what I was up to.

Into Employment

It was also a year in which I swapped the comforts of schooling for full-time employment. Despite my own preferences, my parents decided that because I had shown commercial artistic abilities at school, I should seek employment to train as an architect rather than join the RAF. They recognised that I would have to do that for National service at some stage. During my extended period at school, I had produced, at the behest of the science master, a series of large-scale drawings of jet engines, internal combustion engines, and other electrical and mechanical components; these covered the walls of the science lab. The arts master was not all that impressed with my contributions; in his opinion, such effort should be directed to displaying the rural countryside. Commercial art was, in his view, vulgar and better left to lesser mortals.

My parents decided, as parents are prone to do, that I should approach Hewitt's, a large brewery company with their main office in Grimsby, for a place in their design team. I didn't exactly impress them at the interview when I explained that my interests were flying, sport, and other external activities—and my long-term desire after National service was to serve in the RAF. How naïve can one be? Or was it my way of screwing up the interview? Clearly, I wasn't selected. My next opportunity was working in an iron foundry run by my father's cousin, and again I failed to impress. My next port of call was the Gaumont Cinema in Grimsby; the manager was looking for a trainee projector operator. I lasted but a few months. I don't think the audience appreciated the gaps in the switchover of projectors because I had become so immersed in the film, added to which I didn't like the unsocial hours when I could be better employed in my latest hobby: girls. Cycling home five miles in the rain and snow in the early hours of the morning did nothing for my enthusiasm for the job or my availability to date girls. I therefore took my first steps along the road of procurement, sales, and marketing, but more about that later.

For three evenings a week, I continued with my interest in flying and the other aspects of the ATC, performing in the band as a side drummer. We performed during half-time at Blundell Park, the home of Grimsby Town Football Club, marching up and down the pitch on which I was later to play. That year, despite taking a wrong turning, which even to this day features in my dreams, I won the Lincolnshire ATC cross-country championship in Lincoln, and the following year I retained the title in Brigg. The year after, I completed the hat trick when it was held at Cranwell. Some weekends, time permitting, I competed for Grimsby Harriers in inter-club competitions around the Midlands, mainly in middle distance races.

The borough of Great Grimsby, with its history steeped in fishing and its substantial premier fishing fleet, made awards in the field of navigation at its annual awards night. In 1951 I was nominated and received their first ever award for air navigation.

The year 1952 was yet another eventful period in British history. On 6 September, John Derry, who was the first Briton to break the sound barrier, was tragically killed when his revolutionary new aircraft, the DH.110, broke up mid-air when he was doing a low-level fly past at the Farnborough Air Show. Thirty-one people died as parts of the exploding aircraft cascaded into the crowd. On a less sombre note, the long-running Agatha Christie's play *The Mousetrap* opened at the New Ambassadors Theatre in the West End. But perhaps the most dramatic event occurred at midnight on 2 October when Briton detonated a twenty-five-kiloton plutonium implosion device on Monte Bello Island, off the coast of Australia, becoming the third member of the nuclear club. The United States had refused to share its secrets with the UK even though more than fifty British scientists had contributed to the Manhattan Project, which resulted in the United States becoming the first nuclear nation. This was therefore seen as an act of determined independence by the British government.

Returning to my own little insular world, developments were also taking place in this year. Grimsby was still at that time the world's premier fishing port, served by a massive fleet of deep-sea trawlers. It had the largest fishing fleet in the world, and its dedicated rail services ensured that fresh fish, packed in ice, could be delivered to London's Billingsgate fish market the same day.

I applied for a job in the fishing industry and was taken on by an entrepreneur by the name of Carl Ross. I was a junior fish buyer, a strange title seeing that there was only one senior and one junior buyer. I would leave home at 5 a.m., cycle five miles to the docks, and at 6 a.m. be on the quayside with the senior buyer whilst he purchased the kits of fish at the auction. He was a formidable character, and people would stand aside when he started his bidding. At that time, the Ross Company was small and intimate. I had to pitch in with those who filleted the fish, which then had to be boxed, packed with ice, and prepared to be on the train to London and other destinations that morning. In the late afternoon, I would cycle home, and sometimes I was rewarded with prime fillets of haddock. I reeked of fish. Carl Ross went on to build the Ross Group into a dominant force throughout Europe, firstly as the UK's largest frozen food business and later by acquiring Young's, also a formidable company. At its peak, the Ross Group owned the largest fishing fleet in Europe. In some ways, to my regret I didn't stay to become part of the organisation. Carl's son was later to become a millionaire entrepreneur himself following his involvement with Carphone Warehouse.

On a recent return to Grimsby, I went with friends to have a look at what now remains of Grimsby Docks. How things have changed. During the early 1950s, it had been a pulsating and thriving centre of activity—the largest and busiest fishing port in the world, with more trawlers arriving than could be accommodated alongside the busy quays. Every building was occupied, roads were busy, and trains and lorries were packed with crates of fish. In the background was the ever-present noise of the riveters hammering away on the trawlers chocked up on the slipways whilst being repaired and repainted. The noise was interspersed with the call of seagulls dive-bombing for the remnants of fish. The town thrived on the economic boost provided by the fishing industry.

Now, the docks resemble a ghost town, with shrubs protruding from decaying empty Victorian buildings, the massive Ice House looming like an enormous predator over the derelict fish sheds. Roads are potholed and covered with weeds, and there are disrupted and sunken rail tracks, empty quays, and slipways devoid of ships. No sounds except for faraway gulls screeching at each other in the hunt for food. Why, I asked myself, should such a vital industry have dramatically declined in just a few decades? The answer lies in the political, economic, and commercial uncertainties of the age, which in turn created a number of reasons; overfishing in the North Sea, creating a demand for larger and more powerful trawlers to sail further afield; the Cod War with Iceland, which closed lucrative fishing grounds; quota fishing, the result of Common Market decisions; the introduction and increase in the supply of frozen fish; and the use of factory ships that were capable of reaching other ports, including continental ports, making it more economically viable. The economic impact on the port and the town is all too evident, and unlike other cities and towns, Grimsby has not adapted to the changing times. I did notice that the fields alongside the south bank of the Humber accommodate thousands of cars imported from Europe and elsewhere, added to which there is increasing activity from the newly installed North Sea offshore wind farms.

Flying Training

I could not forecast the decline of the fishing industry, but I needed to find an alternative form of employment that would accommodate my urge to fly. My next move was to Molyneaux, a subsidiary of the Ellerman Wilson shipping line and a company engaged in the repainting of trawlers and other ships. The reason for my move was to enable me to continue with my flying. During 1952, after several selection boards and medicals, I had been granted an Air Ministry flying scholarship which would enable me to be trained up to a level to gain my private pilot's licence, with all costs being met by the Air Ministry. I was allocated to the North Riding Flying Club at Speeton, near Flamborough Head in Yorkshire, initially to do two weeks intensive flying training and followed by several weekends throughout the year. I made this a precondition of my new employment, and strangely enough they accepted. By then, I had been promoted to flight sergeant in the ATC, which was as far as one could go at that time.

I arrived at Speeton, miles from anywhere, on a cold and gloomy November afternoon. I was met by the manager and a somewhat eccentric Scots engineer who was rather partial to his "wee dram" and who was more akin to Doctor Who with his own little Tardis. He was in the act of assembling a Tiger Moth aircraft, the bits and pieces of which were spread around like a Meccano set. I was given to understand that once it had been rebuilt and granted a certificate of airworthiness, I would be flying this aircraft. That filled me with trepidation. Initially I was accommodated at the club, an isolated site close to Flamborough Head and well away from civilisation, although I would hardly describe Bridlington in those terms. My combined bedroom, study, and day room at the club was a storage cupboard/ room containing an array of Calor gas containers and a workbench, underneath which was a camp bed. Not only was it freezing, but the overpowering smell of gas was not conducive to sleep unless one wanted to make it permanent. After a few days of trepidation and remarking about these limitations and the desire not to meet an early demise through gas inhalation, I was moved into Bridlington to stay with a family of Jehovah's Witnesses. (Oh, joy!) I wasn't fully convinced that this was a step in the right direction, converting from gas to religion! With very little money on which to subsist, my evenings were never filled with excitement. I joined the occasional whist drive only because the entry costs were minimal, and it was a way of getting out of the cold and wind. There wasn't even bingo in those dismal days, and certainly nothing to stimulate young blood. I've never been overly excited by days at the seaside since then especially Bridlington.

Although my social life left much to be desired, my days were fully occupied with flying, of which I couldn't get enough—unless the weather was bad, in which case I would either help with the maintenance of aircraft, upkeep the buildings such as repainting signs (at which I had become quite proficient), or immerse myself in air navigation and meteorological manuals. We had some interesting machines on the airfield, including a high wing monoplane called a Compur Swift—a rare breed indeed that belonged to Billy Butlin, who owned the nearby Filey camp. Once qualified, we were given the opportunity to fly it, as we occasionally did in the Auster and Chipmunk aircraft on the airfield.

The chief flying instructor, who went by the name of Larsen, was a difficult man. During my first flight, he asked me if I had ever flown. Having that innate confidence that comes with youth, I told him that I had my gliding licences and had been a passenger in several aircraft, to which there was no response. I didn't know if this was because he couldn't hear me through the Gosport (the speaking tube). I soon found out that it was not the case; the aircraft went into a violent spin as he applied stick and rudder, keeping his feet on the rudder pedals and cutting the engine. He swore at me for not controlling the aircraft. It was his way of saying, "I'm in charge, you arrogant, young sod!" I quickly adapted to his way of thinking and working, and I treated him as God, which I'm sure he believed he was. Later, when I had the temerity to question the lack of parachutes, I was informed that pilots were replaceable, but aircraft weren't! I believe it was to incentivise students to fly with caution. Those were different days.

One day after some five and a half hours of dual flying, during which Larsen had called me all the names under the sun (some of which even I didn't understand), he climbed out of the aircraft and said, "I've had enough. I'm going for a smoke. You can fly the b*****aircraft yourself. Well, don't just sit on your arse—get it up in the air!" With shock horror, I taxied out, took off, and did a circuit followed by a perfect three-point landing before I realised what had happened. I often look back on that situation and think how brave (or foolish) my flying instructor must have been. I had gone solo in less than five and a half hours. But after reflecting on this, I was no different to those wartime fighter pilots who had about the same time before they were involved in dogfights over the south of England. I went solo on 21 December, a day before the Duke of Edinburgh did his solo. Larsen was determined that I should have the first honour, though I'm not sure why; probably to satisfy his vanity. That was also the year in which the prototype V bombers, the Victor, Valiant, and Vulcan, took to the air. I must admit it left me feeling ten feet tall!

Another eventful year saw the coronation of Queen Elizabeth II in June, coinciding with the conquest of Everest by a British team of climbers, though it was a New Zealander, Edmund Hillary, and a Nepalese Sherpa, Tensing Gorki, who reached the summit on 29 May 1953. But because of the lack of adequate communications in the fifties, news did not reach the UK until 2 June, just in time for the coronation celebrations. Being short of oxygen, they remained on the summit for about fifteen minutes before making their descent. Nevertheless, as a nation we bathed in the reflected glory that it was a British-led expedition, and the feel-good factor was immense. As a youngster—well, younger than I was at this stage—I had always been intrigued by the story of George Leigh-Mallory and Andrew Irvine, the two British climbers killed on the 1924 Everest expedition and who were so close to the summit when last seen. Like many others, I often wonder whether they had reached the summit before they were killed. Although Mallory's body was discovered in May 1999, there was no clear evidence, one way or the other; many artefacts were found on his body but no camera. The one aspect that still fuels speculation, and my belief that he got to the top, is that Mallory carried a photograph of his wife, Ruth, which he planned to place on the summit. It was not with all the other personal possessions eventually recovered from the body. Despite a limited search by Hillary and Tensing at the top, there was no evidence to show what might have happed some thirty years previously. I was later to make good my dream and set foot on Everest, but more about that later.

Like his brother and many of those on the three expeditions in the 1920s, Mallory had served in the trenches during World War I. However, what is probably not so readily known is that his younger brother Trafford joined the army as a second lieutenant in 1914. He also saw active service at the front line near Ypres, was wounded, and was eventually sent back to the UK. He volunteered for the fledgling Royal Flying Corps and was awarded a DFC shortly after returning to France in 1914. He was later to become the distinguished Air Chief Marshal Sir Trafford Leigh-Mallory, KCB, DSO, and Bar DFC, famed for his time during the Battle of Britain. He was killed in an aircraft crash in November 1944 whilst on his way to take up his new appointment as Commander in Chief, South-East Asia. But that's another story!

After the Christmas break, I restarted my training at Speeton on 4 January, by which time I was having to travel from Grimsby by train, cross the Humber by ferry, and then catch a bus from Hull to Bridlington, which with connections took over six hours in wet, cold, and often freezing conditions. The Humber ferry was a paddle steamer called *Tattershall Castle*. In the 1970s, when I was working in the Ministry of Defence in London, we would gather on the deck of the *Tattershall Castle* on a Friday lunchtime for a quiet drink or two, where the ship was moored up alongside the Thames embankment as a restaurant and a bar. I often used to look wistfully at the glass-fronted engine room and recall those early days on the Humber—a different time, a different environment.

The rest of my time was uneventful at Speeton—apart from flying through snowstorms without any visual contacts, avoiding low-flying

RAF Meteor aircraft, or avoiding electricity pylons—until the day when I did my final examination cross-country flying test. This consisted of a three-leg circuit from Speeton to Brough on the Humber and then on to Skegness in Lincolnshire, followed by a return leg across the North Sea to Speeton. Having done my pre-flight briefing, I took off for Brough. All was well on the first leg apart from several Chipmunk aircraft taking off across the runway at Brough due to a change in wind direction. I got a rollicking from air traffic control for using the runway and not the grass, indicated by the landing *T*. The senior controller wasn't interested in hearing my plea in mitigation that this is what I had been instructed to do, irrespective of wind direction. Having received a flea in my ear and having picked up some aircraft instruments which were to be delivered back at Speeton, I took off, headed for Skegness, and passed over RAF Binbrook, where heavy air traffic was evident. I wasn't in the game of travelling in the vortex wake of jet aircraft, so I deviated to the east of the Lincolnshire Wolds and flew adjacent to the east coast, thus avoiding RAF flight paths.

I should point out at this stage that the date was 26 February 1953, less than three weeks after the most devastating natural disaster in the history of the UK. On 31 January and 1 of February, a combination of high spring tides and severe wind storms (with winds reaching 119 miles an hour) caused a tidal surge of over 16 feet above mean sea level, creating havoc along 1,200 miles of coastline, damaging large swathes, and breaching sea walls. In Lincolnshire, flooding occurred down the east coast, creating breaches through which the flood waters poured inland for over two miles from Mablethorpe to Skegness. Some 307 people died, over 30,000 had to be evacuated, and 24,000 properties were severely damaged.

Here I was, flying across miles of fields still flooded and heading towards Skegness. I was supposed to land at Butlins' airstrip, which at the best of times comprised of just a grass strip, a fuel pump, and a very small hangar and workshop. I arrived overhead to view a vast area of mud and water and (not surprisingly) no activity. In the distance, swarms of lorries, looking like an army of angry ants, were delivering rubble to build up the sea walls, but at Butlins there were no signs of life. Feeling a minor sense of panic because I hadn't sufficient fuel to complete the return journey, I searched for some solid land, put the aircraft gently down, and climbed down into a field in which there was more water and mud than grass. I could not telephone Speeton or anywhere else because all the lines were down, added to which there was no sign of any telephones. This was the era before mobile telephones, so I couldn't seek advice. However, I was conscious that I had to have some fuel if I was to take to the air again, let alone make it back to Speeton. I looked around, and although there was a fuel pump, there was no power. The building was locked, so there was no chance of a can even if I could get the fuel.

I was now worried that I had been on the ground for a long time, and I had to leave before the light faded altogether. I had no alternative location at which to refuel, and I was left with one option: take off, head for home, and hope that I could make an emergency landing— preferably not in the sea. I decided to head north by the shortest possible route. I found some planks at the back of the building and lodged these under the wheels to act as skis. Then I swung the prop a few times before the engine fired. After getting back into the cockpit and opening the throttle, I offered up a prayer that the acceleration wouldn't tip the aircraft nose down. It was like an exercise in skiing, and it seemed to be an inordinate amount of time before the aircraft, like a demented lover, finally parted company with the ground. At least that was a partial relief. But I couldn't take my eyes off the little glass fuel indicator that sat above my head, taunting me as it bobbed away in the empty zone.

I set a course for Bridlington directly over the mouth of the Humber Estuary, hoping that I wouldn't have to put it down away from land; the North Sea had never held any fascination for me. I anxiously watched the fuel indicator that was already at zero. North of Spurn Head, as the light was failing, I saw tiny spurts of orange shooting in from the North Sea across the path that I was taking, followed shortly after by a pair of RAF Jet Vampire fighters. I could see nothing on the map, indicating that it might be a restricted area. As it turned out, it was the RAF firing range at Skipsea. I eventually landed at base completely out of fuel, the engine having cut out before I'd taxied back to the hangar. I was met by a group of agitated people, including my flying instructor. Because of the problems at Skegness, which the team at Speeton had failed to check, and because I was overdue, the Air Ministry had reported the near miss at Skipsea. I learned later that they were all extremely worried. Whether for me or their aircraft, I shall never know, but I'm sure I was well down the priority list. However, it appeared that I was not being held responsible, although the flying club was admonished for having the incorrect maps. I was congratulated for getting the aircraft back in one piece, which made me think that this was their main concern. I passed my cross-country test and, after a further period of flying, was given my civil aviation licence and wings on 16 March. At that time, I was one of the youngest in the country to have made the grade—but I was too young to take my driving test in a car!

Exchange Tour to North America

In the early part of the year, I had gone through several interview boards and was finally selected as one of twenty UK cadets, out of many hundreds interviewed, to take part in a reciprocal visit to the United States and Canada. Whilst at ATC camp at Middleton St George, near Darlington, an airfield that presently operates under the name of Tees Valley Airport, I underwent a further medical for aircrew selection, which I passed without any problems.

Our visit to the United States was high profile, an occasion during which we got to meet three heads of State: Winston Churchill as prime minister in the UK, Dwight D. Eisenhower as president of the United States at the White House, and Vincent Auriol as president of France at the Élysée Palace. We left from the military side of Heathrow on 25 June aboard a USAF Skymaster to Washington, refuelling in the Azores. Our arrival in Washington was a blur of activity: visits to the White House, the Capitol Building, the Washington Monument, the Smithsonian Institute, and a host of other important locations and functions. We even had appearances on the fledgling TV programmes.

A few days later, we flew to Michigan in a USAF Curtis Commander transport aircraft, and there we enjoyed the amazing hospitality of the Americans—an experience that was to be repeated on so many occasions during our US visit. Technically, as guests of the Civil Air Patrol (CAP) of America, we were hosted by individual families. Everywhere we went, we were looked after and entertained. Nothing was too much of a problem, even to the extent of having the use of the family car (bearing in mind I didn't have a licence). I initially stayed with a family in Birmingham, a suburb of Detroit, and their daughter Carol was a member of the CAP. I was made to feel at home as part of the family and also with their friends and neighbours. Carol and I regularly corresponded following my return to the UK and during my time in Malaya in later years.

It is impossible to cover every aspect of the visit, which took us to many areas of the north-east of the United States, from Pennsylvania to Michigan and across the border to Canada before turning south to New York. I do recall one occasion in Kalamazoo visiting a store—sorry, I should say a shopping mall—in the town and being surrounded by a mass of people wanting to hear what they called my English accent. I admit to feeling somewhat peeved and pointing out that I didn't speak with an accent—they did! In those days, they hadn't seen many English visitors in the States. I did experience difficulties elsewhere on our tour with the little differences or nuances in our two countries' use of the English language.

On one occasion, I was staying in Grand Rapids with the parents of Caroline, another member of the CAP. That night Caroline had arranged to take me to join friends at a local party. Before we left the UK, Squadron Leader Richard Wakefield, who was our tour escort officer, gave us instructions about recording our day-to-day experiences because we would be expected to give talks about the visit on our return to the UK. He therefore advised us to maintain our diaries in pencil to allow changes to be made; otherwise, we could lose track, especially because this would be something of a whirlwind tour. On this occasion, I asked Carol's father for a rubber to correct an error I had made, and he looked horrified. When I explained why, he smiled and said, "You mean an eraser. I think we need to talk, son." As an innocent teenager, I was mortified over the misinterpretation when it was explained to me. What was it that Churchill said? "Two countries separated by a common language."

We appeared in the press and on TV, with colour being a recent innovation. We received a host of invitations wherever we went, participation in quiz shows, meeting many celebrities, and being guided around so many commercial and industrial sites, schools, universities, and institutions. I couldn't help wondering whether our American counterparts received anything near the same treatment in the UK. One particular memory that stands out regarding New York was the night that a cadet from Yorkshire and I walked down Eighth Avenue from our hotel in our uniform, sightseeing. We bumped into the great pre-war boxing legend Joe Dempsey on the pavement near his restaurant. He wanted to know where we were from in the UK and then invited us in for a steak on the house. We talked to some Americans much later, and they said he had a reputation for this sort of hospitality to complete strangers. Nevertheless, he seemed genuinely interested in what we were doing and what was happening in the UK.

After a few days in New York, being accommodated in the Astoria Hotel in Times Square, we flew out from Bolling Air Force Base to Orley Airport in Paris. We did the usual sightseeing, followed by a reception at the Élysée Palace, where we met President Auriol. The following day, we flew back to the UK. On 14 August, I had to travel up to RAF Waddington in Lincolnshire to give a talk on our experiences to a gathering of air cadets—hence the need for the diaries. We had experienced so much in so short a space of time, but it was an inspirational experience.

National Service in the Royal Air Force

My parents left the UK in 1953 shortly after I arrived back in Sutton Coldfield. My father was posted to Seletar, Singapore. The story of my life: I was either flying the nest, or the nest was being moved elsewhere. I got that uneasy feeling that it might be the latter! The postal sorting office in Birmingham provided me with temporary employment, supplemented by some opportunity flying at Elmden

Airport pending my entry into the RAF, which was scheduled for December 1953. After staying with my mother's cousin and family for a couple of weeks, I decided that I needed to find a more permanent base. I found myself ensconced in a one-room flat in Boldmere Road, but it was a solitary, cold, and unusual existence because on the wages I received, there was little remaining other than to pay for the bare necessities and visit the local pub—not so much to drink but to keep warm and play darts.

In December of that year, I embarked on my future career in the Royal Air Force, commencing at RAF Cardington, the last home of the great airships. I progressed on to start my initial training at Hednesford in the West Midlands, one of the many "square bashing" centres in the UK. It had the onerous and, I would have thought, almost impossible task of reshaping teenage youth into fighting men. National service or regular recruits, potential officers or future NCOs, we were all subjected to the same treatment: reduced to the lowest level of humanity and then rebuilt in the image required of a fighting force.

During early 1954, I received a letter from my parents in Singapore, the envelope of which was stamped "Damaged by sea water—recovered from Flight 781". On 10 January, a BOAC Comet jet aircraft, on its return flight from Singapore to the UK, exploded at high altitude over the Mediterranean between the islands of Elba and Monte Cristo; all thirty-five people on board were killed. There were no black boxes in those days, and it took a year of detailed examination and research at the Royal Aircraft Establishment at Farnborough to establish that it had suffered explosive decompression, a result of metal fatigue in the aerial window aperture located in the roof. The design fault was eventually rectified, but not before other Comet aircraft suffered a similar fate.

The days that followed my arrival at Hednesford consisted of large groups of us pounding the parade ground, being subjected to physical torture in the gym, being chased around combat courses, being exposed to gas attacks, or finding our way around Cannock Chase, a vast area of woodland heath in which we were subjected to several combat challenges. Added to which there were frequent spells in the classroom as we were educated in the history, methods, and protocol of service life. On a lighter side, we followed with avid interest the progress of the two West Midland soccer teams who were making their mark in Europe, Wolves under the great Stan Cullis and led by Billy Wright, and West Bromwich Albion under Vic Buckingham with players such as Ronnie Allan and Don Howe (who later became first team coach at Arsenal before returning as manager at West Brom).

Before completing my training, I was called to RAF Hornchurch to the aircrew medical centre and was subjected to a variety of tests, during which the medical staff determined I had sustained on some previous occasion a pinpoint perforation of the eardrum—something I had referred to earlier as possibly having occurred at Bloxham. It had left a tissue scar, but it created a loss of some high-frequency signal responses. Although marginal, they considered I was no longer medically acceptable for modern jet flying. The bottom of my world collapsed, and I returned a very disillusioned individual. Wartime pilots could fly without legs, but in the jet age I couldn't fly with a minor ear defect. After completing my initial training, I was posted to RAF Bircham Newton, in Norfolk, to train with the prospect of graduating as an equipment officer. My heart was not in it, and I didn't make the grade. I was eventually transferred to RAF North Weald as a leading aircraftsman to complete my two years in National service. The officer in charge of the flight in which I was to work, Pilot Officer King, had been an officer cadet on the same course as me at Bircham Newton. I was not a happy bunny! However, looking back it was my fault—my inability to come to terms with failure and thus my immaturity.

North Weald, near Epping in Essex, was steeped in history as one of those airfields from which the Battle of Britain was launched. Built in 1917 to protect London from German bombing raids, it served the same purpose in World War II. After the war, it was the home of the newly formed RAF aerobatic team Number 111 Squadron, the Black Arrows. Initially equipped with Gloster Meteor T7 aircraft, in December 1953 the squadron, under Squadron Leader Roger Topp, was reequipped with the new high-speed Hawker Hunter fighter aircraft, which had earlier established a new world airspeed record.

The Black Arrows were renowned at that period for their twenty-two-aircraft diamond formation. The two other squadrons (both Royal Auxiliary Air Force Squadrons), 601 City of London and 604 County of Middlesex, were flying Gloster Meteor F8 aircraft.

Apart from the lowly wage of a national serviceman, which somewhat restricted my social life, the time at North Weald was very active. As a base with its proximity to London, many of the servicemen were high-level professional footballer players also servicing their two years in the RAF. Consequently, the competition to get selected for the station football team was incredibly fierce, with players from Arsenal, West Ham, Fulham, Tottenham, Chelsea, Milwall, Chelmsford, Brentwood, and many other teams vying for positions. In my lowly position, I therefore had to seek an alternative to fulfil my ambitions. In the winter, I turned to qualifying as a class three referee and later as a class two, and I cut my teeth in the London Athenian League. In the summer, I sought solace in athletics, competing and winning in the middle-distance events and going on to represent Fighter Command in the inter-command championships.

For some of us at North Weald, our social lives consisted of night classes in Epping and Chingford, English literature on base, and local dances where we attempted to increase our prowess by taking dancing lessons as a way of meeting girls—the genuine Essex variety! On reflection, this was also the reason we attended evening classes, because I wouldn't want to leave you with the impression that we were aiming to reach the higher echelons of academia. The one thing about the services was the encouragement to improve one's education, and I embarked on GCE papers in English language, English literature, general studies, geography, and history to make up for my earlier lack of opportunity. I spent two weeks at Nottingham University immersed in Wordsworth, Tennyson, and the war poets, amongst whom were Rupert Brook and Wilfred Owen. Other areas covered Dylan Thomas and *Macbeth*. Books such as *The Lady's Not for Burning* and *Animal Farm* also featured. It was a golden opportunity, and one I grasped readily. I also ventured into writing short stories that were published in the *London Press*, albeit at a very modest level, but it did wonders for my confidence.

Overseas Service

The one thing I did learn during my time at North Weald was that power, as perceived by us lesser mortals, is not always vested at the highest levels. To overcome my poor penury status, I had calculated that if I signed for a further one year's service as a regular airman, I could double my income and even have the outside chance of a posting overseas. I quickly befriended a clerk in the orderly room who managed to manipulate my application form without too much trouble, not so much about the extra service but more to move it to the top of the pile so that I might be selected for an overseas tour—something I could not have achieved by going through my squadron commander. It's a lesson I learned and tucked away for future years: find out where the real power lies!

Having passed to the dizzy heights of a leading aircraftsman, followed some months later by promotion to senior aircraftsman, I set sail for the Far East in September 1954 aboard the troopship *Asturias*, destined for a tour in Malaya—action plus excitement and an increase in pay. The journey took over three weeks passing through the Mediterranean and transiting the Red Sea and the Indian Ocean. Our first port of call was Malta, a place I had already visited, which was a good thing because we were not even allowed on deck, never mind ashore. In fact, we were housed on G deck, one above the bilge, so we rarely got up on deck for a breath of fresh air, let alone across onto dry land. The only air circulating on our deck was that passed down through canvas awnings to our lower compartment, where over one hundred of us were accommodated in narrow metal bunks four tiers high. This resulted in rather smelly and humid conditions, especially passing through the Red Sea with very little breeze.

Once again it was a call to display initiative. I soon found that the families were housed in the cabins on A deck, to us a rather luxurious open deck, and that armed volunteer guards were required to patrol the decks at night, especially when transiting the Suez Canal. Here was a marvellous opportunity to breath fresh air, stretch one's legs and from time to time, but contrary to the rules of engagement, converse with those teenage daughters travelling with their families. I spent many contented hours in this privileged role, always happy to serve my queen and country! On other occasions, we came up on deck for lectures or rifle practice targeting coloured balloons left in the wake of our ship. We also had a lottery system of guessing the nautical miles travelled each day, all of which helped to pass the time and relieve the boredom.

Singapore and Malaya

We arrived in Singapore Harbour in somewhat humid conditions. In these parts of the tropics, the temperature averaged in the high eighties Fahrenheit with 90 per cent humidity, a climate in which "prickly heat" prevailed until one had adapted a suitable rust-resistant tan. My father, who was a flight lieutenant at the time, had obtained permission to collect his lowly offspring, the senior aircraftsman, and keep him for the weekend. What followed was a relationship that was somewhat difficult to get used to because my father, in many respects, had never been around in my formative years, and neither had he readily adapted to the idea of having a second non-commissioned son in the family. We travelled up to RAF Seletar, where they were based and living in married quarters, and after twenty-four hours of being welcomed back into the family, I was then delivered to RAF Changi, on the north-east part of the island, where I was to start my tour in Singapore and Malaya and experience two years of hard work but much enjoyment.

I saw my parents and younger brother and sister from time to time, much of which was spent sailing in the Malacca Straits, the occasional picnic on the beach, or at functions which didn't breach the etiquette of mixing commissioned and non-commissioned status. I'm not implying criticism; these were vastly different times in terms of military discipline. Activities such as the yacht club, open to all ranks, helped to bridge the gap, but it was short-lived. Within four months my family was heading back to life in the UK (yes, the nest had moved yet again), and I was finding my feet in Changi, by which time I had been promoted to corporal and had the additional benefits of overseas allowances and qualification pay; in the minds of the locals, I must have appeared rich. Well, it looked that way whenever I tried to barter with the shopkeepers!

I soon found that my interest in both athletics and football were a bonus both in terms of character building and opportunity. In the eighteen months that were to follow, I established myself in the Singapore national cross-country squad, having finished second in the national championships, and I represented Singapore in the Asian championships. In the summer of 1956, I followed a similar representative route in the middle-distance events. During that year, at the Jalan Basar Stadium, I also established a new 800-metre record for the Swift Club, and I met the Singapore time qualification for the Olympic Games, scheduled for Melbourne in November 1956. However, there were two factors that were to inhibit my further progress. One was that in those days, one could only qualify through your place of birth, unlike today where residential qualifications apply. That meant as a British national, I had to qualify through my home nation, and I certainly wasn't in the running for that, especially when one saw the talent that was emerging at that time: Derek Johnson and Mike Farrell in the 800-metre, Derek Ibbotson and Gordon Pirie in the 5,000-metre, Dave Bedford for 10,000-metre, and Chris Brasher in the 3,000-metre steeplechase. They were out of my league. Second, even if I had been in contention, I would not have been available because I was scheduled to return home to leave the service in November 1956. A friend and colleague in the national squad, Janet Jesudason, did make it to Melbourne and became something of a local star along with another local sprinter, Kesavan Soo. "Regrets, I have a few." Nevertheless, it was a time of great opportunity to compete against those who were passing through or acclimatising in Singapore whilst representing their countries, and to exchange ideas on training methods.

Although sport, for me, was becoming predominantly athletics orientated, there was still time for football at a representative level, and especially sailing, with ideal facilities around the islands and on the mainland of Malaya. However, to bear in mind that there were still many areas in which terrorists were still operating in Malaya—and not too far from the border. So, wherever we went upcountry, we had to be armed.

There is no doubt that the services provided not only the encouragement and the opportunities to participate in sport but also the facilities that enabled every serviceman to reach for the stars. It was also at this time that I was invited to write some local sports reports for the Singapore daily paper, the *Straits Times*, my second lurch into journalism (albeit on the fringes).

In June 1956 I reached that golden pinnacle of twenty-one years of age. It was a Sunday, and we had anticipated spilling over beyond midnight, so the celebration started on Saturday. As we headed for Singapore City, excited at what lay ahead, a sense of gloom and despondency soon settled on our small group, one of whom had received a Dear John letter from the girl he had intended to marry at home. Another had just learned of the death of his parents in a car crash. Shortly after midnight, we arrived back in a less than jovial mood, hardly living up to the expectations as portrayed in Lesley Thomas's book *The Virgin Soldiers*, based on his experiences in Malaya during national service. Consoling myself with the thoughts of at last having reached the recognised age of independence, I opened my single lonely present, a tin containing a cake sent by my mother the previous week. She hadn't allowed for the violent sea movements in transit, so we sat around my bed space spooning crumbs. Alas, they were not crumbs of comfort, but that's for another day.

Singapore was not all about sport and leisure interspersed with military commitments. It was also about coming to terms with the political developments that were occurring in the transition from World War II. The Malayan emergency had been going on for a number of years following the war. It had developed into a guerrilla war fought during pre- and post-independence. Following the Japanese defeat in 1945 and the Allies' relief of Malaya, the Malayan National Liberation Army, with its roots in the communist party, was bent on taking power from what it considered the reestablishment of colonial power. Its drive, under its leader Chin Peng and mainly supported by some half a million Chinese within the country, was to take control of the economy and the country by any means. There was clearly a resistance to such action not only from Britain and its allies but also from the Malays themselves. There followed a protracted campaign during which many of us became involved in one way or another. Our closeness to terrorist activity during the time we were in or transiting through Malaya meant that we had to be fully armed and ready for any eventuality, especially when travelling between Singapore and northern Malaya.

During my sojourn in Singapore and Malaya, both countries were going through transition. One must remember that the failure of Britain to defend Singapore from the Japanese during World War II destroyed our credibility with the populations of the Chinese and Malays. As a result, there was an inherent drive for independence, and although this was held in check during the Malayan emergency, it began to raise its head during the time that David Marshall took over leadership of the Singapore government. Social unrest, especially amongst the younger and more vociferous Chinese at schools with links to communism, began to emerge. In April 1956, David Marshall gave way to Lim Yew Hock as leader of the Singapore government, and he began to crack down on the communist elements within the schools and the unions. By 24 October, rioting had erupted and over the next five days thirteen people were killed, with over one hundred injured and nine hundred arrested across the island. On the night of the twenty-fourth, we were sent into the centre of Singapore to form military antiriot squads, and we stayed there for five days and nights in what was a very volatile and dangerous situation. Initially our vehicle, a four-ton truck, was overturned by rioters near Paya Lebar International Airport, which had opened in August of the previous year, and we were stoned by rioting schoolchildren and agitators. Although we were armed, the rules of engagement did not allow us to fire at the mob. Later, when we had formed boxed riot squads in the city centre, authority had to be given to fire, and even then only after verbal warnings by a political and legal representative—often too little and too late.

Despite these setbacks, our time in Singapore, including detachments up into Malaya, was mainly peaceful, and contacts with the locals were extremely friendly. Whilst things in Singapore settled back into normality, tensions elsewhere in the world were beginning to have an impact on my planned return to the UK.

The Suez Conflict

On 30 July 1956, Nasser, wanting to reduce the power and influence of the old colonial powers of Britain and France and see them out of Africa, had announced the nationalisation of the Suez Canal. The canal provided the only direct means of travel from the Indian Ocean to the Mediterranean and was a vital trade lifeline for European powers. Two-thirds of oil supplies to Western Europe passed through the canal, as did some 15,000 ships carrying essential goods. Oil reserves in the UK were enough for only six weeks. This action brought an instant reaction from both power, who were nervous of the likely impact on the Middle East. The Israelis were also fearful of the growing might of Egypt fuelled by a build-up in Russian arms and influence in the area. Prime Minister Eden saw the only solution was an invasion of Egypt to return to the status quo, and in July he ordered the planning for an invasion. On 29 October, the Israelis started the conflict with an attack across Sinai with a simultaneous invasion of Egypt by the other two nations, France and the UK. Although the invasion was a great success the United States was strongly opposed to any such action. The US support for Nasser was regarded by many as two-faced, with Eisenhower and Dulles having decided that Nasser would need to go in the longer term, but at the same time they were adamant that countries should decide their own future. The United States applied massive economic pressures on the UK to withdraw and added, through the Saudi Arabians, an oil embargo. The British and French had no option but to declare a ceasefire on 6 November.

The result for Britain and France was disastrous because it severely weakened their positions as global powers. Some would argue that this in turn led to the hastening of decolonisation, instability, and civil wars within the region. It certainly soured US relations with France and to some extent Britain for many years, and it led to the eventual resignation of Prime Minister Eden through ill health. The weakening of ties led to De Gaulle withdrawing from NATO in 1966 and to Britain not supporting the United States in Vietnam. I believe it also strengthened the Russian threat and gave them the confidence to exploit situations in other parts of the world. Evidence of this arose in the Hungarian uprising during October and November of that year. On 23 October, a student demonstration in Hungary quickly spread across the country, and the subsequent riots lead to the downfall of the government. The consequences are too often forgotten. The Russians, bolstered by the actions of the United States, which the Russians considered a sign of weakness and disunity in the West, used their forces to brutally crush the revolution in which over 2,300 Hungarians and 700 Soviet troops were killed, and a further 200,000 Hungarians fled the country as refugees.

The possibilities of what might arise from both conflicts impacted my return to the UK. Instead of returning during November as was scheduled, I was now faced with a great deal of uncertainty and a further Christmas in Singapore. Eventually, in January 1957 we were informed that we were to be shipped back on an emigrant liner, the SS *Captain Cook*, returning from Australia. However, due to the many uncertainties pertaining in the weeks that followed Suez, we were also advised that we might be offloaded in South Africa to await further developments, but at least we had a date for departure. How different a journey to the one two years previously. We were now treated like paying guests on a cruise, albeit six to a cabin, but it was vastly different to the 120 per room on the outward journey. Our first port of call was Cape Town, where word had already spread regarding our arrival—the first military contingent since World War II. As we berthed, below us we could see a never-ending line of cars. These were families wanting to take us to their homes and communities and entertain us for the time we were in the Cape Province. This we were allowed to do on the proviso that we were available for immediate recall when required. Two of us were hosted by Afrikaners who were farmers near Pietermaritzburg, and we were made most welcome by all those around, but I must say that although used to the strong Yorkshire Dales and Northumbrian accents, this dialect was something that I found difficult to grasp. Another difficulty we had to come to terms with, even in those days, was apartheid, or segregation. Having lived in multicultural societies such as Singapore and Malaya, segregation to us was something of an anathema. One felt extremely awkward seeing the segregation of people in public places and on public transport.

The remainder of our journey was largely uneventful with further stops at Freetown, Sierra Leone, and the French colony of Dakar (in what is now Senegal), the streets and shops of the town which were looking very Parisian. We crossed the Bay of Biscay in atrocious conditions, during which I felt sure the ship sailed on its side, and during which crossing the deck was a perilous situation in which one had to be secured by safety ropes. It wasn't much easier below decks, especially at mealtimes. We eventually made Liverpool on a dark, overcast, and rainy morning on 14 February 1957, and after being pulled apart by customs officers, we spent the remainder of the day being processed in the usual long-winded and detailed manner reserved for the military. We were served with our discharge papers, a travel warrant for the train journey home, and the residue of our pay; these were the days before bank accounts. Welcome home to civilian life and the inevitability of readjustment!

In many ways, it was a sad parting of the ways. Having served with those who had become close friends and with whom one had shared many experiences, it was almost like saying goodbye to family. The one big difference was that we would be unlikely to meet some of them again. Liverpool in those days was not the most exciting place in which to arrive, and it was almost a relief to be on the train and heading to London.

CHAPTER 6

A New Direction

It is never too late to be what you might have been.
George Eliot

During my time in Singapore, I had been corresponding with Sheila, an ex-friend and ex-girlfriend whose family had moved from Manchester to live in Laceby. Her mother had engineered a meeting during one of my weekends on leave prior to going overseas. Little did she know that she would live to regret it! Sheila at that time was training at Kesteven Training College in Lincolnshire with the aim of becoming a teacher. Although in the past we had gone out together, she now had a boyfriend, so the meeting was somewhat strained. One benefit of life in the Far East was the availability of US nylon stockings, a rarity for people in Europe in the post-war years, and I started sending Sheila a few pairs because she mentioned the difficulty in obtaining them. I was somewhat surprised, as the months went by, how many pairs I had been sending. It was only many years later, when attending one of her college reunions and being referred to as the Nylon Man, that I discovered I'd probably been supplying most of the college female students with nylons. There I was, thinking her letters were declarations of love and friendship. I should have read between the lines. I wouldn't have minded, but as I seem to recall, this was so that the girls could attend dances at the RAF College Cranwell appropriately dressed. Talk about supporting the opposition!

A Return to "Civvy Street"—Order to Chaos

But I digress yet again. Having arrived back in "God's country", I had two things uppermost in my mind. First, how was I going to get up to Grimsby to see Sheila, because at this stage she was teaching in Grimsby and living at home in Laceby? Second, what was I going to do to earn a living? It was one thing to enjoy the benefits of service life, the conditions, the excitement, and the camaraderie, but this was a totally different environment: cold, unwelcoming, friendless, and uncertain. What I needed to do was to bring order to the chaos that I felt I was now experiencing. Here was yet another crossroads in my life, and I had to decide on which route to take. On my way to London by train, I had sufficient time to contemplate my immediate future. Arriving in Paddington with time to spare, I walked along the surrounding roads and stumbled on what I perceived as part of the solution. There in the window of a garage was an immaculate-looking Lambretta scooter, and in one of those rare rash moments when the logic of decision-making is not readily apparent, I walked in, faced a little bargaining (haggling, as they would say in the Far East), and spent my hard-earned savings on the machine, hardly giving a thought as to how I was to get it by train to Norfolk where my parents were living. Added to which I couldn't ride the thing without a licence. Luckily my parents met me at Diss railway station, and my father, aiding and abetting my illegal activity, followed me in his car whilst I negotiated the scooter back by road to Pulham St Mary, where they lived.

As a point of interest, Pulham was at that time a small RAF maintenance unit, and in its early days it had been a Royal Navy airship station, initially operating patrols over the North Sea. By the end of World War I, it had over three thousand servicemen and two thousand civilians based there. It was then rehabilitated as the chief research establishment for airships until that facility moved to Cardington in 1920. Pulham was also instrumental in setting up the first air traffic control sector in the UK using radio beacons. At one time it had been the home of the R33 and the R34 airships; the R34 having made the first two-way crossing of the Atlantic in 1919, from

Edinburgh to New York and returning to Pulham. So why should it not be home to my advanced piece of technology, my Lambretta imported from Italy—a second-hand vehicle, but one that would become my faithful beast in years to come?

During this first week, I coerced my parents into visiting my grandmother in Laceby, thereby giving me an opportunity to contact Sheila. This initial meeting was a somewhat difficult event, I sensed a feeling of uncertainty, and the conversation was somewhat stilted—not quite the reunion I had anticipated. Nevertheless, it was lovely seeing her again, and I was sure the spark was there; it simply took a while to ignite—hardly surprising in the UK climate! In the months that followed, we wrote every day when apart, and I spent every weekend travelling to and from Laceby as our relationship developed. In the meanwhile, I had started work for the Ministry of Labour and National Insurance in Norwich as an executive officer, but my heart wasn't really in the job, so I applied for others. Initially I was a trainee engineer with the Caltex Oil Company in Bahrain. I soon discovered the salary was astonishingly good, but the offer was conditional on me remaining a bachelor for the first eighteen months. It didn't take me long to reject the offer, but not before the second opportunity arose. I had applied for a commission as an officer in the RAF during the same period, and in March following a detailed selection process at Uxbridge, I was notified that I had been accepted, subject to successful training.

In the hope that I was no longer restrained by the lack of a future, I proposed to Sheila when she came down to Pulham for Easter, and she accepted. I was over the moon. However, at the ripe old age of twenty-two, I had to circumnavigate the next few hurdles and seek the blessing of her parents. That was no easy task for a few reasons. I'm not sure they saw me as the ideal husband for their daughter, and I know her mother thought there were others with more suitable prospects. Second, Sheila had just taken up her first teaching appointment. Finally, I had to get my commission and then find a way around the age for marriage, which for an officer in the RAF was twenty-five or over. How days have changed. Furthermore, I had to scrape together sufficient funds to buy an engagement ring, which was extremely difficult on my income because I was now earning less than when I'd been a corporal.

The year 1957 was one of significant change on the international stage. Eden had been replaced as prime minister by Macmillan early in January. The Russians, much to the chagrin of the Americans, established themselves as the first nation into space and triggered the race to the moon. Britain began settling itself in the top league as a nuclear power, and the Treaty of Rome was approved and signed. In January, Eden was forced to resign as prime minister. Initially it was stated as being due to poor health. Although it is true that he had suffered from poor health towards the end of his term in office, he was also subjected to significant pressure by Eisenhower and the US government to resign following the Suez debacle. Isn't it amazing that the United States will brook no interference or indeed accept criticism from any other country, and yet it has no hesitation in inflicting their demands on other nations. However, after retiring from office, Eisenhower came to see the resolution of the Suez Crisis as his biggest foreign policy mistake: forcing Britain and France to withdraw from Suez weakened two crucial cold war allies. It also strengthened Nasser and, through him, Russian influence in the Middle East. I have to view our current situation in the West and ask if this is something that President Trump should also be considering at this point in time.

Later that year in a speech in Bradford, Macmillan coined the phrase "Never have so many had it so good" in his reference to improved living standards in the UK. Eisenhower, having been re-elected in January, forged a sound, working relationship with Macmillan, who in turn went on to lead the move of ex-colonies towards independence. During that year, Russia took a temporary lead in the space race with the launch of Sputnik 1 in October; an aluminium sphere two feet in diameter. This was followed by Sputnik 2, which carried Laika the dog into orbit. It was not until January the following year that the United States launched Explorer 1, their first satellite; that same month, Sputnik 1 re-entered the earth's atmosphere and burnt out.

On 15 May 1957, Wing Commander Kenneth Hubbard OBE, DFC (the man who had given me my first taste of flying at the age of fifteen and with whom I had flown to Malta and North Africa in 1951), was the pilot of the Vickers Valiant bomber XD 818, selected to drop the first British hydrogen bomb off Malden Island in the Southern Pacific. Scientists were somewhat unsure of what the outcome would be. As a consequence, Ken and his crew were all awarded the Air Force Cross following the successful explosion. He was at that point the commanding officer o 49th Squadron based at RAF Wittering, the squadron chosen for its expertise in high level bombing. Our paths were to cross again in 1959 when he invited me to RAF Scampton where he had become the Group Captain Station Commander. At the time, I was a newly married Pilot Officer on my first tour at RAF Watton, in Norfolk. I managed to fly up to Scampton in a Lincoln bomber, a four-engine successor to the Lancaster. Years later I was to be based at Scampton as a precursor to taking up a post at RAF Faldingworth. Ken was a modest and unassuming man who never talked about his exploits. He later left the RAF in 1975 to become a Director of his cousin's company the Hubbard Reader Group. He died in 2004 at the age of 83

A new Career in the Royal Air Force

In June of 1957 my father took early retirement from the RAF and my parents settled in to a new life as proprietors of the White Hart Inn, a hotel in Hawes in Wensleydale, in the Yorkshire Dales. In the same month, I started out on my new career which entailed officer training at RAF Jurby in the Isle of Man, the Officer Commissioning Unit, followed by specific professional training at RAF Bircham Newton in Norfolk. Having recently returned after two years overseas this proved a difficult time for me, especially as it reduced the opportunities I had to see Sheila. The chances of getting back to the mainland from the Isle of Man were virtually non-existent although two of us managed to get away for a week-end by hitching a lift on a training Anson aircraft from Linton-on-Ouse. It wasn't coincidence that we happened to share a syndicate with an NCO pilot from Linton-on-Ouse! No one was more surprised than Sheila when I turned up unannounced. After 3 months of hard graft we eventually graduated as Acting Pilot Officers, a change of uniform and a strange feeling before moving on to Norfolk to start our professional training. My parents travelled across to the Isle of Man for my graduation, no mean feat in those days when they had the worries of running the hotel, something I was to learn many years later. It was during my time in Norfolk that I managed to save enough to buy Sheila's engagement ring, a solitaire diamond that we had seen some months before. (I added to the pot by selling my Leica camera to a colleague).

On the wider stage, Alaska and Hawaii became the 49th and 50th States of the USA, a Britannia aircraft had flown across the Atlantic in a record time of 7hrs and 57mins, the Comet 4 became the first passenger jet aircraft to enter service across the Atlantic, Edmund Hillary had travelled to the South Pole and the EEC (Common Market) had been formed. Later that year Khrushchev became Premier of the USSR and de Gaulle was elected President of France. On a more tragic note it was in February of 1958 that the Manchester United football team "The Busby Babes" were to perish in the Munich aircraft disaster. Their aircraft crashed on take-off during their return to the UK in atrocious weather. Not only was it a loss to Manchester but many were part of the national squad.

Other events of that year involved the Notting Hill race riots and the outbreak of the "Cod War", over fishing rights, between Iceland and the UK; something that I took a very close interest in because of my previous background. The Commonwealth Games took place in Cardiff following which the Queen installed Prince Charles as Prince of Wales. In August, the first US Thor missiles were deployed in the UK and the 'feel good factor' increased when in November Donald Campbell set a new world water speed record of 248.62 mph. It's hard to believe that this was the year that work started on constructing the M1 as UK's first motorway.

Although we were technically some way behind the USA in consumer products, many homes had fridges, radios, cookers but only a few had washing machines. Television was available in Black and White but only on two channels, neither of which broadcast for more than 6 hours a day. On the commercial side things were improving and becoming more competitive. Sir Alex Issigonis revolutionised motoring by designing and developing the Mini, bringing a small affordable family car within the reach of many families

In the February of 1958, a bitterly cold month towards the end of which we experienced heavy snowfalls, I was posted to the Central Signals Establishment at RAF Watton in Norfolk as a fully-fledged Pilot Officer. I recall the snow and ice was still with us in March. In those days, we worked every Saturday until mid-day. On those weekends when I was not Duty Officer I would set off on my Lambretta scooter to Sheila's home in Laceby, returning on Sunday evening. In icy conditions my feet never left the road for most of the journey of 300 miles there and back. It was a sturdy and reliable beast that served me well over the years although things like brake cables, piston rings and brakes needed replacement, hardly surprising with the mileage I was doing.

The primary task of the Central Signals Establishment was Top Secret at that time involving work on Electronic Counter Measures (ECMs) and intelligence gathering. On my arrival, the three Washington bombers B29s of No 192 Squadron departed to be replaced by three Comet 4s (XK 663, XK659 and XK 655 which arrived in March). These aircraft were fitted with ECM and used for ELINT purposes, intelligence gathering along the borders of Russia and its Eastern States. At the same time the Vickers Valiants of 199 Squadron (V Bombers) were fitted with ECM by the Special Radio Installation Flight. During the latter part of 1958 we played host to an American reconnaissance unit operating the Lockheed U2 aircraft, thought by many of the public at the time as a high-altitude meteorological aircraft; nothing was done to convince them otherwise! However, its activities as a spy plane were fully revealed to the public by the shooting down of Gary Powers by the Russians in May 1960, resulting in an intensification of the cold war. Many years later in August 2013, the CIA released details which until that time had been an absolute in terms of Top Secret protected information. In 1955, the US Government under Eisenhower had developed what is now known as "Area 51", a site located close to the nuclear test site in the Nevada Desert for reasons of additional security. The purpose of Area 51 was to enable to development of the U2 aircraft in absolute secrecy. At the time, no one could envisage that manned flight beyond 60,000 ft was possible, hence the reason for the lingering doubt and fascination the public had, based on rumours, that the Area 51 was linked to extra-terrestrials and UFOs. By the way, although this was secret information at the time, and something I never even discussed with Sheila, you've only got to look on Wikipedia these days to confirm the details.

Sheila came down to Watton for the Summer Ball and we decided then that whatever happened we would get married in the autumn. We settled for the first week-end in October. As I was under 25 I had to seek the permission of my commanding officer which was duly given. I then had to search for a place to live which was not easy in a place like Norfolk with a very high population of United States servicemen who could afford prices we couldn't even contemplate, certainly not on my salary. I found several nice properties only to be 'gazumped' at the eleventh hour. I eventually found a flat in the nearby village of Saham Toney. It consisted of 2 rooms in a massive old rectory occupied by Cannon Richmond and his wife, a rather eccentric couple who were very close friends of the Montgomery's (the Field Marshal of El Alamein fame) who visited during our time at Saham Toney. Our flat was situated in the old servants' quarters behind the traditional 'green beige door'.

We were married on the 4th October 1958 in St Margaret's Church, Laceby, where Sheila and I had our formative years in the village and where she became Guide Captain, so her Guides provided the Guard of Honour on our exit from the church. After our Reception at the Wheat Sheaf Hotel in Grimsby we left for a night in London before our honeymoon in Torquay,

As we were to experience in other parts of the country many of the waiters and staff in our hotel were Hungarians who left after the Russian invasion and, as the saying goes – the rest is history.

We moved into our new abode, a flat in one wing of the Rectory, which was a somewhat strange existence. Cannon and Mrs Richmond were very much of the old school and of course it was their home and so, in many ways we were treated as guests of the family. None of the doors had locks and Mrs Richmond would frequently walk in unannounced – and that included the bedroom – somewhat disturbing for a newly married couple who had their mind on other things. Added to which the Richmonds had been Egyptologists and our bedroom was filled with many ancient relics. It's a wonder that Jane, our first born, was conceived – but it happened. I suppose Mrs Richmond considered it to be her home and that we were merely part of the family that she never had and certainly as newly-weds in need of her spiritual guidance!

The fact that we never attended Sunday services was no doubt a great disappointment to the Richmonds who tried hard to convert the 'heathens' but to no avail, we always seemed to have our minds on other things, well certainly I had. Over the weeks that followed our return from 'honeymoon' Sheila decided that we would take up rug making, no doubt with the view to keeping my hands occupied on things which, perhaps in her mind, were of more material value. There were days when Mrs Richmond invited us down for lunch in her kitchen. The table was always set with 5 places which confused me on the first occasion until we were joined by 'Gillie the Fifth', their Scottie Terrier. I must say that the dog wasn't a good conversationalist and I subsequently tried to arrange a cancellation through pressure of work. However, that merely postponed the inevitable. Although it was very generous of them to include us the portions for a growing lad were, to say the least, somewhat unsubstantial and on those occasions, Sheila would always assuage my appetite in the evening – with steamed pudding and custard - I wouldn't want you to jump to the wrong conclusions!

It is strange to look back and recall the significant events of the day. It was the year in which Barclays Bank was the first bank to install computers. It was also the year in which there was a General Election and the Conservatives were returned for a third term. But perhaps one of the most intriguing developments came with the work that Sir Christopher Cockerill was undertaking with the launch of the first Hovercraft on the 11th January 1959. The concept, which he called "the momentum curtain" was based on a system of lift through air pressure rather than on airflow and contained within a curtain below the vehicle. Like so many inventions beforehand and subsequently, the idea of an air cushioned vehicle (ACV) was rejected by the military. The Royal Navy said it was a 'plane' and they were therefore not interested; the RAF insisted that it was a boat and so rejected the idea; and the Army believed it had no military role whatsoever. Based on what I consider my perceptive views on some of our senior military thinkers they can be so blinkered. One only has to look back on the difficulties experienced by Sir Frank Whittle in introducing his invention of the jet engine over the years to see how some people can't understand what is happening around them or appreciate the impact it can have on the future. What was it that Marshal Foch said prior to WW1? "Airplanes are interesting toys but of no military value", a view shared by some of our gallant horse-riding generals in the Great War. I sometimes wonder how we ever came out on the winning team so frequently!

I recall, to my own embarrassment when years later whilst at the RAF Senior Staff College, I was attending a tri-Service lecture at the Army Staff College at Camberley. Following a presentation on the 'Future use of air power', I had the temerity to pose a question to the visiting Air Marshal by asking if he could ever see the day when unmanned aircraft would be used in warfare. I was politely put in my place and told it was inconceivable that pilots would ever be replaced – a point suitably reinforced by my Directing Staff on my return to the RAF Staff College at Bracknell; but then I wasn't a fully-fledged graduate of military doctrine so what did I know; and there was I, with the naïve view that I was supposed to be developing my thoughts and military understanding for the future! How I would dearly love to turn the clock back and point out to the disbelievers of those times what happened in Iraq and Afghanistan with the military sitting at consoles in the US, flying unmanned drones in war-zone some 7,000 miles away, and indeed by the Royal Air Force with similar operations from a base in Lincolnshire!

Faldingworth - The start of many moves

It was during this time that Sheila succumbed to a strange and repetitive sickness, well strange to me because I had never experienced

such things and repetitive because it always hit Sheila at the same time
and in the same place each day. Well how was I to know? I'd never
been privy to the machinations of the Women's' Union and in those
days, it was learn as you go, nobody let you into the inner secrets. Men
were certainly not expected or indeed encouraged to participate in the
ritual of pregnancy. Sheila began to develop strange cravings – fish
and chips accompanied by a bottle of stout which for a non- drinker
at that time was, to say the least, unusual. These ingredients had
to be smuggled passed Mrs Richmond, who had a total aversion to
such plebeian tastes; it was certainly a test of my ingenuity if not my
integrity for no sooner had I entered the portals of her mansion then
she would appear like a well-trained bloodhound sniffing at the air
with knowledgeable nostrils. These bouts of Sheila's strange behaviour
were also regarded with great suspicion by my mother-in-law during
her 'State' visit to our abode. I'm sure she had a calendar against which
she ticked off the intervening months and only dared to breathe a sigh
of relief when the allotted 9 months passed without sign of the stork.
I dare say that had our well-crafted package arrived early, she would
have shot it (the stork I mean!)

Sheila had the customary scan, which in those early days was
somewhat of a novelty in the medical fraternity and a somewhat hit
and miss procedure. The medical staff were of the view that twins
inhabited the inner sanctum but knowing our daughter Jane it was
probably her inability to keep still during such explorations. This
conclusion threw us into panic mode; one newcomer was difficult to
envisage, two was a step too far. However, before the arrival of one
or two more Everett's, the Air Ministry planners got wind of the
explosion in the national birth rate and intervened. They decided that
I would be posted overseas and take up a position in Gan, a remote
atoll staging post in the Indian Ocean, for a one-year unaccompanied
tour. Strange to see that the island is now regarded as a luxurious
Indian Ocean holiday resort. Mind you the facilities are significantly
different.

Human Resources or personal management or human remains as we
would later refer to it with all its faults, was certainly not a science
that had inculcated the Ministry in the 1950's. My Air Commodore,

who was my Station Commander, a man of considerable humanity who was eventually to become an Air Chief Marshal, intervened and pointed out that if the RAF wished to retain bright young officers (his words not mine) then this was not the way to treat them. I was under 25 at the time and not eligible for marriage allowance, which in those days made up half of an officer's salary, and therefore we had to exist on £30 a month of which £20 went on rent. The Ministry eventually relented and decided that I would move north to a base in Cumberland for one year followed by the tour in Gan, such generosity of spirit! Within a month this had been changed to Staffordshire and then to RAF Scampton in Lincolnshire, pending the opening of RAF Faldingworth. It seemed to the men in the Ministry that this was a suitable compromise – blessed are the meek. I felt like a Pawn in a chess game – easily disposed of for the sake of the end game!

In May 1959, we packed our scant possessions and with the help of my parents, who came down by car, and the assistance of my well used Lambretta scooter, we moved north to Lincolnshire. Although having been married for 8 months I was still under the age of 25 and therefore we were still considered by 'the powers that be' to be living in sin and therefore not entitled to married quarters. So, we rented a rather run-down cottage, which my colleagues affectionately termed "The Hovel", in Owmby-by-Spital, about 3 miles from my new base not far from Lincoln. The cottage came with its own house bound livestock, better known as the "carriers of the Plague", who occupied the coal house. Having only one toilet, situated in the coal shed attached to the house meant that I had to escort Sheila frequently, as pregnant ladies will appreciate, armed with a cudgel to ward off the curious rodents. The kitchen was equally questionable, with suspect electrical wiring which certainly required rubber matting when the washing machine (a new gadget I had acquired at great cost, well so it seemed on my income) or the midget oven was switched on. Yes, this was long before the age of the "Health and Safety concerns". I spent the early weeks, in what spare time I had, redecorating and trying to restore the garden to some semblance of order. By coincidence my uncle, who was an accountant in Lincoln, had a farm (as most accountants do – it helps them get rid of the surplus revenue) in the neighbouring village of

Normanby-by-Spital, up until the year before we moved there. He probably heard the news that we were on the way. For the life of me I can't perceive what the 'Spital' means but having looked it up I see that it's a medieval word for contagious hospital. Well that probably fits the bill!

Initially, I was based at RAF Scampton as Faldingworth was still undergoing major reconstruction having been selected the previous year to become the major storage, maintenance and distribution site for all nuclear weapons, including 'Blue Danube', Britain's first nuclear bomb. The intention being that in times of crises, which seemed to be most the time, nuclear weapons would be distributed to all 'V' bomber stations based at airfields in the East of England; these included Scampton, Coningsby, Waddington and Finningley. In the meantime, we were tasked with maintaining and updating the weapons which meant convoys of our vehicles would make frequent trips to and from these airfields and Aldermaston, the nuclear centre for the UK. Little did the public know in those days what was passing their front-door.

Security was extremely tight with vetting at the highest level. The locals thought it to be one of the US sites, at that time located in the East of England, and nothing was done to disillusion them. However, we were under constant observation by visitors including those from Eastern European countries and it became almost a fulltime job collecting car registration numbers, photographing occupants and passing details through to our Intelligence organisations. In those days diplomatic staffs, and particularly those from the Eastern Bloc, were restricted in travel to no further than 10 miles from Central London. I think that on these occasions they were allowed to get away with this limitation so that intelligence could be gathered on who and what they were up to. The operational site at Faldingworth, situated about a mile from the domestic area, was surrounded by an outer and inner high fenced compound, the perimeters of which were overlooked by 22 towers and the whole area floodlit. Access was by two massive electronic gates and the inner compound, which housed several bunkers, the outer compounds were both patrolled by armed RAF Police with dogs. When on duty we spent 24 hours at a time inside the inner compound and on constant alert, whilst at other times we were out on the road with our convoys.

In July I was sent on a 'Nuclear Controllers Course' to RAF Calshot, Southampton. The buildings in which we were located were alongside the slipway on which the two-remaining huge 'Princess' flying boats were cocooned; this aircraft type being in the same league as the earlier Brabazon, built ahead of its time and yet another example of British aircraft design genius - but lacking commercial forethought. It's just a pity that Rolls Royce hadn't built engines with enough power to equip them. The design of aircraft and aircraft engines did not always go hand in hand in those early days and the commerciality of operations was often overlooked. Calshot 'Spit' had also been the location of the famous pre-war air race for seaplanes, more readily known as the "Schneider Trophy" race. This competition was very significant not only in advancing the development of seaplanes but also aeroplane design, particularly in the fields of aerodynamics with streamlined shapes reducing drag and engine design based on liquid coolant systems. In 1931 Britain won the race for the third successive time and therefore retained the trophy in perpetuity. The winning aircraft flown by John Boothman was a Supermarine S6B which later that year went on to be the first aircraft to break the 400mph barrier. The S6B was also designed by R.J. Mitchell who later went on to design the Spitfire which was to become one of the saviours of World War 2.

The reason for my sojourn in Southampton was my newly acquired role as the RADIAC Control Officer at Faldingworth. My responsibilities in an emergency would be to measure, plot and forecast the radioactive fall-out in the event of any explosion – on the assumption that I might still be alive to do it! Little did Sheila know that I wouldn't be around if anything happened – information that never was, nor ever could be, revealed even as pillow talk.

In the August, Sheila went into labour and I took her by car, one that I had hired from Keith Gill the local garage owner who was also our landlord, to Willingham-by-Stow the local nursing home some 15 miles away. Luckily Jane was late as she has had the tendency to be ever since. When she eventually arrived on the 28th August 1959 I was taken to see this child who was housed in what looked like a glass sided fish tank, as were all the other babies. In the week that followed, for in those days you stayed in hospital for at least 10 days following birth, the nurses would joke that whenever you entered that room and switched on the lights the only one with eyes wide open was Jane Everett – a blue-eyed phenomenon; an eerie sign of things to come. If you haven't already done so, I suggest you read 'The Midwhich Cuckoos' by John Windham, you will then understand my concerns. I think aliens from another planet had a hand in Jane's productive process. The rest of that year is something of a blur, one in which I was coming to terms with parenthood and its consequences; feeding, sleepless nights, nappies and sickness, and a fraught wife – oh and I forgot, work. During those frequent occasions when I was out on the road for days at a time I would arrange for Sheila and her accoutrements, including baby Jane, to stay with friends on the Base.

In the September of 1959 I took my 'B' promotion exam at RAF Syerston, the exam being a necessary hurdle to cross before qualifying as a Flight Lieutenant. It consisted of papers in Law, Administration and Organisation and two papers in professional subjects. Although I passed the exam I was informed that it wouldn't count as I shouldn't have been allowed to take it in the first place. It was pointed out to me that I was only a Pilot Officer at the time and needed to be at least a Flying Officer. Despite protestations my efforts were to no avail. What was annoying was that 3 months later I was promoted to Flying Officer. Not that it made much difference to my status; I was still a very junior officer although the extra money helped. Early the following year, I took and passed the exam again – to make it legal!

Following an article regarding two US Marines attempting to break the world record for a March of 100 miles, Flying Officer Brian Anstey, one of my colleagues at Faldingworth, and I decided that we would go for the same record and over the week-end of 14/15 November we set out from Lincoln with a backup team. Unfortunately, we didn't make it, Brian dropped out after 40 miles close to Peterborough and, although I was well ahead of the record time, I only covered 88 miles before back trouble put an end to my endeavours and caused me more than a few headaches in the years that followed. A year later year, together with Sgt Pat Roach, one of our NCOs, I finished second out of 250 servicemen and women participating in the News of the World "March of the Century" from Birmingham to London, along the A5 a road I've never liked since. The winner was Captain Thomas Hiney and a colleague whose name escapes me (as so many do at my time of life); Hiney was later to receive the Military Cross for gallantry in an ambush in the Congo. The publicity gained by this event resulted in many similar challenges and consequently there were many other people who walked further and faster over the years that followed, so you could say it marked a change.

CHAPTER 7

The Winds of Change – A Time of Strife

*"The experience of history teaches that when an aggressor
sees that he is not being opposed he grows more brazen.
Contra wise, when he meets opposition, he calms down. It is
this historic experience that must guide us in our actions"*
(Nikita Khrushchev – 7 August 1961)

The 1960's, the 7th decade of the Century, saw significant changes; an increasing number of countries gaining independence, greater conflict as the 'Cold War' took a hold, major assassinations, added to which it was a period of changing social values and commitments, with the fall, or relaxation, of some social norms embracing sex and drugs and the demand for greater individual freedom. This was an era which was to become known as the 'Swinging Sixties'.

It was a period highlighted by Macmillan's speech on Africa when he postulated that *"a wind of change"* was blowing though Africa and by Martin Luther King exclaiming, *"I have a dream"*; both issues addressing the emerging rights of ethnic groups. It was a decade in which 32 countries gained independence from European rulers and the Algerian War ended (well at least this one did). It was also a period of ideological differences and growing conflicts. In the early years heightened tension arose when the Russians erected the Berlin Wall in 1961 followed by Khrushchev's belligerent stance over the Cuban missile crisis. In retrospect, this can be seen as the most crucial time in world history and almost triggered a nuclear war with what would have inevitably been devastating consequences. China detonated its first atomic bomb in 1964 and followed this with a cultural revolution which straddled the ten years from 1964 to 1974.

In the latter half of the decade, we saw the start of conflict in Northern Ireland, a rise in US involvement in Vietnam, conflict between the Israelis and Arabs culminating in the six-day war, and coups in Greece, Iraq, and Libya. Added to which, there were the assassinations of John F. Kennedy, his brother Robert, and Martin Luther King. It was during this decade that the Israelis captured and executed Adolf Eichmann for war crimes. There is little wonder that people viewed life on a day-by-day basis during this decade, which saw the growth of the flower power people and antinuclear protests.

Spridlington Hall

In 1960, having reached the magical age of twenty-five, I was finally recognised by the military as eligible for marriage allowance. It gave me a feeling which must almost be akin to receiving a peerage or winning the lottery. As a consequence, I became eligible to occupy married quarters on the supposition of course that there was one to occupy—which of course there wasn't. However, I did manage to find a flat in part of Spridlington Hall, close to my base at Faldingworth, which the RAF agreed to take on as a hiring. Although it was somewhat similar to the Rectory at Saham Toney in size, it was vastly superior in layout and condition. Workmen were in the final stages of painting when we moved in, and unbeknown to me, the workmen regaled Sheila with the history of the building in which a gruesome murder had taken place not too many years before; having hacked her two victims to death, the perpetrator had hanged herself from the banisters overlooking the main hallway. They even showed Sheila the marks left by the rope. Hardly a story to tell a pregnant woman who was frequently left alone whilst I toured the countryside with my weapons or sat behind the security fences on duty. Needless to say, the blame for the information, not the murder, lay squarely at my feet, or so I was led to believe from Sheila. Added to which, there was also the occasion when Jane went missing, and I eventually found her under the water, face up in the large goldfish pond fronting the hall, with her eyes wide open and grinning. It was not the first time, nor was it to be the last time, that she had given us both a dickie fit. Maybe aliens have the ability to survive underwater. From that time on, she was well and truly secured within the flat.

The last national serviceman was called up on 31 December 1960, which meant that although the numbers were to decrease, the commitments and the consequential workload didn't. It was a busy time, but I still found the opportunity to take part in sport representing the RAF at athletics and captaining the command teams at cricket and football. I also played for the local village teams some weekends, an aspect of my life which did not gain me much kudos with Sheila. I must say that on reflection, it now appears to me to have been somewhat selfish, but then, we all grow up eventually and find other toys with which to play!

In the summer of 1960, I received news that I was destined to move to Aden as an Air Movements Operations officer based at RAF Khormaksar; it was a better proposition than Gan, which would have been an unaccompanied tour. However, Sheila's mother, when she heard the news, broke down in tears and wanted to know what I had done wrong to be sent to Aden. We were puzzled by her reaction only to fall about laughing when we heard her concerns. It wasn't anything to do with missing Sheila for two years. As she explained, her father had been a sergeant in the Indian army, and in those days, Aden was a punishment posting for those who stepped out of line in India. It was no good pacifying her with the news that we lived in a different world and that this was a step up, not a step down!

It is worth noting here a little of the history of Aden. In 1839, a party of Royal Marines landed in Aden to put an end to pirate activity which was harassing British ships in the area—more or less what is currently happening off the coast of East Africa. With the opening of the Suez Canal in 1869, Aden became the main bunkering station for ships sailing to and from India and the Far East. A sizable British garrison was based in Aden to protect the southern end of the Suez Canal, and certainly for the next ninety years, an Aden posting was a bleak prospect for any serviceman; hence the reason for Sheila's mother's concern. But following the loss of the canal in 1956, Aden became the main base protecting the lifeline of trade and British presence both in the Middle East and Asia. Since our withdrawal from this part of the world, it is more readily known as South Yemen along whose shores the pirates now operate, and Yemen's internal problems keep re-emerging but in slightly differing shapes. What's the saying? "What goes around comes around."

Back on the domestic scene, and before sorting out arrangements for our move, we had a small problem to overcome as we received confirmation that Sheila was expecting our second child in the August. There must be something about those cold winter nights in December!

My mother had offered to look after Jane up in Yorkshire, so it relieved us of one problem. The day before Julie arrived, we had hired a car and, to ease Sheila's boredom, driven to Skegness. There, Sheila decided that she would have her future read to her by the highly reputed Gypsy Rose Lee. I suppose a glass ball is just as good as tea leaves when it comes to predicting the future. For her money—yes, that's always the rub—she was told to expect a bonny healthy boy in about two months' time. Even I could have had a better stab at getting it a little closer. But I'm a man; what do I know? At 1 a.m. the following morning, she woke me with the news we should be moving because her waters had broken, but she wanted to stay and chat for a while. As by now she was highly experienced in these matters, I was hardly in a position to argue anyway, have you tried arguing with a pregnant woman? We sat and chatted for a while. Then the signs began to accelerate, and I decided it was time to move. When I tried to start the car, I found that it was out of petrol. Something Gypsy Rose Lee hadn't predicted! In a somewhat controlled state of panic, I woke Mrs Stephenson, the wife of the owner of the hall. Despite the hour, she said she would drive us to the nursing home some fifteen miles away. It was one of those summer nights when the cold evenings bring in the fog, and it turned out to be a long and nervous journey for an anxious father to be. Julie was delivered shortly after our arrival. I've never been short of petrol since!

A Move to Aden

Later that month, we packed our bags, the removal firm took over what few possessions we had, and we moved out because I had to undergo three months' training in London before starting the new job. The course was down in Kidbrooke, South London, and we had arranged that Sheila and the children would live with my sister and brother-in-law in Welwyn whilst I completed the course and found somewhere to live in Aden. It was a somewhat hectic time, as all the future moves during my service career tended to be.

It was the beginning of November when, after a thirteen-hour flight on a rather cramped Britannia aircraft, I arrived at Khormaksar, our base in Aden, in what I considered to be searing heat after the cold of UK. As I found often to be the case, I arrived totally unexpected by Alan Rackstraw, whose job I was taking over. After much confusion, I settled into the officers' mess, and the following day I started my new job. It consisted of shift work, twelve hours on and twelve hours off, which was to be the pattern of my life for the next twelve months. In the time off, I sacrificed sleep for the opportunity to search for accommodation so that Sheila and the children could join me, but it was extremely difficult. The growth in housing had not kept pace with the massive influx of servicemen, and without guaranteed accommodation, families were not allowed to join their husbands. I was becoming almost paranoid. Having another Christmas away from the family was bad enough, but the thought of this drifting on into the following year was depressing.

The airfield at RAF Khormaksar was heavily overcrowded because at that time it was the busiest in the world. It was at the hub of air routes to the Far East, to Africa, and to the Gulf and therefore an essential element in protecting British trade routes and interests in the area. In addition to the nine operational squadrons, fighter, bomber, and transport aircraft, the base provided essential facilities for the many transiting passenger and freight aircraft, and it was not unusual for over twenty of the transport aircraft to be on the ground at any one time. Some of these were designated quick turnarounds (QTRs), in which the aircraft had to be serviced, replenished, refuelled, and off the ground in less than two hours. The most sensitive of these were those carrying "hot loads", nuclear materials to the atomic testing grounds at Woomera in Australia. During the confrontation between India and China and at the time of the Cuban Missile Crisis, six Vulcans were deployed to Aden at short notice to deliver their nuclear weapons. It was a worrying time, and one in which we began to have serious doubts as to whether we would have a country to which we could return—the so-called doomsday scenario.

As part of my job, I flew on a variety of aircraft ranging from communication aircraft to helicopters, heavy transport, and maritime aircraft, recovering or delivering equipment to diverse areas including Bahrain, the Oman, Kenya, Somalia, Sudan, Ethiopia, Yemen, Kuwait, and other lesser-known areas. One of the most interesting of these was delivering cash convoys to tribesmen in the mountains of Yemen in payment for their support in the fight against terrorists. There is nothing new in this world! These deliveries consisted of ammunition boxes containing Marie Theresa silver dollars, the only currency acceptable to the tribesmen. Although dated 1798, these were regularly minted in the UK—perfidious Albion! The first time I flew up into the mountains, it was in a Belvedere helicopter, the only aircraft capable of accessing the high mountain ranges. I was met at the top by the tribesmen, who had laid out a meal in my honour. It was my first experience of eating out of communal bowls and having to decide which hand to use. I can assure you it was nothing like *Lawrence of Arabia* and certainly lacked modern-day hygiene! I was handed a bowl containing six of what I took to be black olives and invited to eat one. It was so hard that I simply swallowed. It was only on my return to base that I discovered it was an honour to be handed the sheep's eyes. The lump remained in my throat for many days thereafter!

The Swinging Sixties

This was the start of the decade that would become defined as the swinging sixties, a term coined by *Time Magazine*. It was a period of cultural and fashion development in many fields, with its focus on London. It was a catalyst of recovery from the post-war years of austerity that marked the 1950s. The decade was marked by the rise of the Beatles, followed by the Rolling Stones, the Kinks, and the Who, in setting new musical trends. Mary Quant, Jean Shrimpton, and Twiggy were at the forefront of fashion, with Carnaby Street and Kings Road in Chelsea setting trends in fashion as a symbol of "youth culture" with the advent of the miniskirt. The mid-sixties also saw the arrival of the minicar. It was a defining culture that was encapsulated by the American singer Roger Miller in his hit record "England Swings".

On the international front, the situation portrayed a different and worrying development, especially in relationships with Russia, evidenced by the near catastrophic outcome when Kennedy faced up to Khrushchev in the Cuban Missile Crisis. The previous year, George Blake had been sentenced to forty-two years for his role as a double agent, a period during which he had provided the Russians with a great deal of top-secret information, some of it leading to the death of Western intelligence agents. My brother-in-law was working for MI6 in Berlin with Blake when the Russians discovered the tunnel they were working in, and he and others were lucky to escape. The discovery was later attributed to Blake's treachery. The year 1961 was also when the Portland Spy Ring was uncovered, the Berlin Wall was erected by the East Germans to stop the flow of refugees to the Wes and the Russians exploded a fifty-megaton bomb. At home, severe smog caused numerous deaths in London and heralded in the start of a freezing winter during which there were no frost-free nights until 3 March the following year. On the positive side, Britain and France agreed to develop Concord. In the same year, John Glenn became the first American to orbit the earth, and Jamaica, Trinidad and Tobago, and Uganda all became independent.

One of the untold stories (until 2013) was how close the world came to total disaster in 1961 when a four-megaton bomb was one switch away from exploding over the United States. Two Mark 39 hydrogen bombs were on a B-52 bomber that went into an uncontrolled spin over Goldsboro, North Carolina, during which both bombs were released by a control mechanism in the cockpit as the plane broke up. Each bomb was almost 260 times more powerful than those dropped on Hiroshima and Nagasaki during World War II. One fell in safe mode whilst the other, sensing that it had been dropped over enemy territory, went into detonation mode. It had four safety override modes, and the first three failed but the fourth, a single low-voltage switch, prevented disaster and saved what, at the height of the Cold War, undoubtedly would have resulted in Armageddon.

Life in Aden

For me, it was also a positive time. Having spent Christmas away from the family, I was delighted when they finally arrived in mid-February 1962, and we settled into our new flat in Tawahi, Steamer Point. This was close to the central market, a colourful part of Aden. Large cuts of unidentifiable meat, possibly goat, sheep, camel, or some form of beef, adorned the open tables decorated with a myriad of flies, whisked off by the Arab stallholders from time to time, only to return in even greater numbers, having passed the word to other colonies of flies and varied bugs. Fruits and vegetables were brought in daily from the Yemen and laid out in colourful displays, prodded and poked by every would-be purchaser. After our first colourful visit, we left further provisioning to Fatima, our cook/ayah. From time to time, the market would be inaccessible to Europeans, especially when deliveries of Qat arrived and the word spread rapidly, producing almost a riot of clamouring Arabs seeking their share of this basic drug. It resembled cuttings from green privet hedge and produced soporific effects when chewed, causing a resultant high. Needless to say, on those days and for some time after, little work was achieved by the locals.

Bartering throughout the town became a way of life, an enjoyable process for both parties. After prolonged haggling and a coffee or soft drink, a price was agreed depending on the desire to buy or sell. After a few months, by which time we had almost been accepted as locals, we were asked to stay away whenever passenger liners arrived in port on the proviso that we would be given good bargains in the future.

The locals were fascinated by our two girls, one an auburn head and the other a blonde, and both with blue eyes. They would want to touch them for no other reason than enhancing their luck. Fatima would regale anyone who attempted such a rash move with rapid Arabic, Somali, or Yemeni versions of "hands off", ever willing to show her status endowed by Sahib or Memsahib. We would sometimes drive out to the deserted beaches of Little Aden in the late afternoon or on weekends, but within a few minutes of arrival, we would be surrounded by very young Arabs who appeared out of nowhere and liked nothing better than joining in with me and the girls, playing football and leaping around in the shallows of the sea.

By this time, Jane had started nursery school, and Sheila and I would take it in turns to deliver and collect her depending on our work commitments. Sheila had returned to teaching whilst Fatima looked after Julie. To say that Jane was independently minded would be an understatement; certainly, her teacher thought it inappropriate that she remained under her jurisdiction due to her overenthusiastic— or as they were prone to label it, disruptive—behaviour. What an embarrassment to have your four-year-old expelled from her first school, and she was the daughter of a teacher to boot! Could this be the sign of things to come?

Despite this minor setback, Sheila continued teaching, leaving the girls in the capable control of Fatima. Due to the high temperatures, the school day ran from 7.30 a.m. to 1 p.m., which meant that some afternoons when I wasn't working a long shift, we could take the children swimming. This was somewhat restrictive because it could only be done within the safety of the shark nets; killer sharks were an ever-present threat. I recall one day that we had to leave the water in great haste as two fins appeared inside the netted area, and the water bubbled with hundreds of small fish. However, it wasn't sharks but a nineteen-foot-wide giant manta ray driving fish to the surface.

Nevertheless, it was an equally man-threatening fish. On another occasion, we left the beach following a shark attack and clambered over the volcanic rock when Jane, in a fit of pique because we were leaving, threw herself down on a rock, behind which there was a broken bottle. She gashed her thigh with a six-inch-wide, deep wound. Sheila didn't drive at this stage, and because I was holding the thigh muscle together with one hand and the steering wheel with the other, Sheila had to change gear. We managed to get Jane to the military hospital, where the surgeon did an excellent job in stitching her leg, but it was many weeks before we ventured back to the beach again. Jane is still proud of her scars, which have grown with the years, as have her stories!

The following year, we moved into a block of flats in the district of Crater, beneath the towering walls and in the central core of an extinct volcano. The block consisted of three flats, and the building was owned and occupied by the sultan of Lahaj and his family, who also lived there when visiting Aden. We had been attending a function at RAF Khormaksar during the summer when rioting took place in Crater. After hurrying back, we found the entry road sealed off by the military, but after pulling rank and convincing the soldiers that we had young children in the flat, I managed to talk our way round the barrier. On reaching the flat, we couldn't get in. Fatima wouldn't open the door, and all she would say was, "How I know you are Sahib and Memsahib?" After we pushed photos and ID cards under the door, she eventually let us in. She had barricaded the entrance with furniture and had every conceivable knife from the kitchen, including a meat cleaver. No one was going to get past Fatima. She was so much a part of the children's lives that they even conversed with her in Arabic and Somali. What a treasure she proved to be.

On another occasion, we found a massive stalk of bananas, over five feet in height, propped against the front door, and Fatima was laughing. She explained that this was the first offering (proposal) for Sheila by the sultan. Naturally I was furious, but to an Arab this didn't seem unreasonable; it was the first and only time he tried it. His daughter, Ruthkier, had been educated at the Sorbonne in Paris and had a more Western view of life, although she admitted that it would take some years before attitudes changed. I have to say I've seen little evidence of this happening there or elsewhere in the Muslim world.

The riots were of course triggered by growing nationalism instigated by Nassar's drive to rid the Arab world of imperialism. Aden, or South Yemen, became (and still is) a hotbed of revolution, initially with the desire for self-determination but subsequently a breeding ground for Islamic domination in the form of Al-Qaeda and then ISIS. The Straits of Aden are a thriving looting ground for Somalia pirates.

Work hard, play hard. Nothing could be more descriptive of our time in Aden. Whilst we worked around the clock, we still had a very active and enjoyable social life. On reflection, it often puzzles me as to how we found the time, but we did. The parties were too many to recall them all. I do remember one fancy dress party with friends who lived in Maala Strait, a location that became a focal point of terrorism during the British withdrawal from Aden. The dress was "come as a local". Sheila had dressed as Salome. I concentrated on something more current and authentic and dressed as an Arab beggar, complete with beard, rags, and appropriate dirt. It was realistic enough to cause confusion. As it was pointed out to me, not only did I look the part, but I smelt the part. In trying to gain access to the apartment block, the Chowkidar (local watchman) refused me entry and decided to thrash me with his cane. He took exception to what he considered a flea-ridden bum trying to gain entry. Friends came to my aid, trying to convince him that I was a proper Sahib and not a beggar. I suppose I didn't help matters by continuing to play the part, cursing him and others in Arabic and pleading for alms from the "white filthy rich". Well, if you're going to infiltrate, you've got to play the part. The answer, however, is not to be too authentic if you wish to survive!

It was with great sadness that we had to leave Fatima and Aden in November, with tears shed all round. The children couldn't understand why Fatima couldn't come home with us. The trouble was that she had been so much of their earlier years, especially Julie, who could converse in Arabic and Somali better than in English. We did contemplate bringing her back to the UK, but she would never have been able to adapt to our strange way of life in the West or the extreme cold. I mean Fatima, of course, not Julie!

The day before we were due to fly home, we were having a relaxing day around the pool at the officers' club. Jane, in her usual high spirits and deciding that she was a big girl, dived off the lower diving board. I don't know what it would be called in diving terms, but in gymnastics it would be akin to a double twist with tuck and probably with a difficulty of three. She didn't quite achieve the desired level, hitting her head on the concrete surround as she entered the pool. It is amusing to recall but was horrendous at the time. She had to be admitted to hospital with a concussion and was retained for observation. It was a further week before we were cleared to leave. Having moved out of our flat, we had to stay with my squadron leader, Charles Delaney, and his wife for a week, for which we were eternally grateful. Jane made a full recovery without brain damage—well, so I'm led to believe, but I have my doubts!

Return to the UK

Our plan was to fly to El Adam in Libya, North Africa; collect our car, which had gone on ahead; and drive back through Italy and across Europe. However, when we got to El Adam, there was no sign of the car, and nobody knew what had happened to it. Luckily, we were able to remain on the plane and fly back to the UK. I dread to think what would have happened if this had not been possible. Two weeks later, we found our car. The crew of a transport aircraft returning to the UK with an empty aircraft had seen the car with my name on it, and they thought they were doing me a favour by flying it back to the UK!

On arrival back in the UK, we had a few days with Sheila's parents in Laceby, adapting to the cold and the wet (there was no such thing as central heating in those days) before travelling up to Hawes. Each night we would have a quick dram of whisky before leaping into bed, shivering. Shortly after we arrived in Hawes, we saw the news on television that JFK had been assassinated. It was one of those defining moments in life when you remember exactly where you were when the news came through and what you were doing at the time. Over Christmas 1963, we were cut off by high snow drifts in Wensleydale, and it was not until the New Year that we headed south. Sheila and the children returned to Laceby, and I went on to my new appointment as a staff officer at Headquarters Flying Training Command at Shinfield Park, near Reading.

As it turned out, 1963 was another of those years which left indelible memories especially, when in January de Gaulle vetoed Britain's entry into the EEC. Although it generated a lot of anger at the time, that proved to be beneficial in the long term. It was the year that Dr Beeching wielded the axe on the railways, closing two thousand stations and cutting sixty-eight thousand jobs. Minister of Defence John Profumo got himself involved with Christine Keeler, and indirectly the Russian Defence Attaché. Philby was named as the third man in the Cambridge Spy network. MacMillan resigned due to ill health and was replaced by Sir Alec Douglas Hume; little did I think that years later, we were to be next-door neighbours in Scotland.

A New Appointment

No sooner had I arrived in Reading in January 1964, and before taking up my appointment as a newly promoted flight lieutenant, then I was sent down to RAF Lyneham to provide support in moving troops out to Cyprus to cover the emergency. It was some three weeks later that I managed to escape and take up my new post before travelling north to collect the family. We moved into married quarters (yes, one of those rare occasions when one was available) in Whitley Wood on the outskirts of Reading, and Jane began school at the local primary school. I started in my new job, which was looking after the arrangement for all the radar stations in the UK and for administering the contracts for all those RAF stations run by civilian commercial organisations. It was a busy time, especially because I had started a Russian language course at Reading University, but this had to be placed in abeyance when I was selected to attend the Junior Command and Staff College at RAF Ternhill in the summer of 1964.

On my return, in the autumn I became the staff officer responsible for the Command Priority Progression Cell, making sure airfields within Flying Training Command had sufficient operational aircraft daily—a far-from-easy task in the days when aircraft reliability was such an uncertain factor, spares were difficult to obtain, and flying patterns and metal fatigue were not easy to establish. We had one problem at Ternhill where we had several major accidents when the main rotor gearbox on the Whirlwind helicopters started blowing apart, causing crashes and fatalities. It was some time before it was discovered that this was caused by the flying patterns taken by pilots which caused the blades to pitch forward, smashing the cockpit and severing the main rotor gearbox, thus causing the helicopter to break up in mid-air.

Having actively competed in athletics on the international stage, I was naturally interested in the XVIII Summer Olympics being staged in Tokyo. These were the first to be held in Asia, and it was to be the first time that South Africa was barred from participating due to the country's apartheid policy. It was also the last Games to use a cinder track, as a result of which times were to get significantly better, and it was the first Games to allow a carbon fibre pole in the pole vault. Also, 1964 was the year that China became a nuclear nation, having exploded its first atomic bomb. Khrushchev was removed from office and replaced by Kosygin as premier and Brezhnev as first secretary. It became known as the baby boomer year. Race riots broke out in several US cities. At home, Labour took over from the Tories after thirteen years of rule, and Harold Wilson became prime minister whilst concern grew over the "brain drain" of British scientists to the United States.

During the early part of 1965, I sat and passed the C examination, a prerequisite for promotion to squadron leader. It was at this time that Sir Winston Churchill died, and following a state funeral at the end of January, he was laid to rest in Bladon churchyard, close to his birthplace of Blenheim Palace. The following month, we took the children to pay our respects to one of the world's greatest leaders. Having lived through those wartime years, we felt it was the least we could do. I must say that we were just some of the many thousands who followed that path. Work, family, and social life was somewhat hectic over this period, with too much detail to record in a fast-developing year.

In the spring, we received an invitation to attend the Royal Garden Party at Buckingham Palace and enjoyed meeting many people from such a wide spectrum and sharing in such a memorable day. It was a few months later that Sheila discovered she was pregnant again, with all her hopes being pinned on having a boy. I was uncertain as to how the message would be transmitted to our friend the stork, or how the it would know that we were moving to the east of England. In the autumn I had learned that, yet another move was imminent and that in December we were to move to RAF Upwood, in Huntingdonshire. I was to become an instructor on the Equipment Officers' Management and Data Processing courses. However, our girls were delighted with the news that there was to be an addition to the family.

On the world stage, 1965 saw further nuclear tests, with China exploding its second device whilst the United States stepped up its weapons testing throughout the year. Russia notched another first when cosmonaut Alexsei Leonov left the spacecraft Voskhod 2 for a twelve-minute walk in space. France, still smarting over the Suez setback, withdrew from NATO, and the United States increased its involvement in Vietnam.

The following year, the traitor George Blake escaped from prison and defected to the Soviet Union. On several occasions since, I have questioned the viability of his escape both from prison and from the country. It doesn't stack up. Blake had been an MI6 case officer working in Berlin during the mid-1950s at the same time as my brother-in-law, Martin, who was also working for MI6 as a case officer on Operation Gold, a joint American and British project, amongst other missions. Gold involved a tunnel under the Soviet sector of the city, where agents could tap into Russian and East German underground communications lines. Blake remained proud of the fact that his betrayal of this information to the Russians led to the discovery of the tunnel. He also revealed details of over forty spies working for MI6 in both Eastern Europe and the Middle East, many of whom were executed because of his treachery. Blake in turn was betrayed to the British by a Russian double agent. He was arrested and sentenced to forty-two years' imprisonment. What a pity we had done away with the death penalty. It was in the mid-1950s and thereafter that we were still suffering from the impact of other Russian spies, the worst and most damaging of which were the Cambridge Five: Kim Philby, Donald McClean, George Blake, Anthony Blunt, and allegedly John Cairncross. All of them were together at Cambridge University in the 1930s and were part of what were called the Apostles. John le Carre's novel *Tinker, Tailor, Soldier, Spy* was based on his experiences associated with the exposure of the spies in the 1950s and 1960s.

In October 1966, we heard about the Aberfan disaster in which 116 children, 4 teachers, and 24 adults were killed. On the morning of Friday, 21 October 1966, we had the news of a catastrophic collapse of a colliery spoil tip in Wales. After several days of rain, a huge tip of loose rock and mining spoil broke away from the hillside at great speed, demolishing a farm and engulfing the primary school in Aberfan, with mud and spoil twelve metres high. Like every parent and many others, we were shocked and depressed to hear the news.

Officers' Management Training School—RAF Upwood

We arrived at Upwood on what was a dark, wet, cold, and dismal period between Christmas 1966 and New Year's 1967. We had already been advised that the only accommodation was a rather dingy prefab, a remnant of the last war. I was beginning to think that we were destined to become homeless gypsies, forever on the move. I think the service authorities called it career progression, whereas we saw it as acute depression. New Year's Eve was celebrated by candlelight and paraffin heaters as we suffered a three-day power cut. Not for the first time, I wondered what else lay in store.

It was shortly afterwards, on 4 January, that we heard of the death of Donald Campbell. He was on course to break his own world water speed record when, two hundred yards from the end of his second leg on Coniston, his boat hit an object and catapulted fifty feet into the air. At a speed in excess of three hundred miles per hour, Campbell was killed instantly when his boat disintegrated. It was impossible with the technology of that time to recover either the boat or the body; the water was too murky at 140 feet down. However, forty-six years later, on 12 April 2013, both were recovered, and closure for family and friends was possible.

On a more positive note, Sheila was taken into the RAF hospital in Ely on 16 February, and Jonathan, her long-awaited son, duly arrived the following day. There was no sign of the stork; probably it thought it had done its job. Should I ever get to that stage of being inducted into the House of Lords or any other such order (what a laugh), I would no doubt have to consider a coat of arms on which sits a stork! Luckily, by this time we had moved into married quarters, and the neighbours helped with looking after the older children (both of whom were now at school) whilst I visited Sheila.

As the year progressed, I took on additional duties running courses for new officers arriving after their basic training, the ADP courses (computer operations), as well as lecturing on the senior officers' management courses. Sheila was finding life a little difficult with a new baby and two girls who were now at primary school, added to which she didn't drive. We were in a rather isolated location on the edge of the Fens, and this caused a few problems. She also began to suffer from postnatal depression. However, as the year progressed, things began to improve. We joined in the social life both with friends in the locality and on the station. As work became more structured, my thoughts turned once again to resurrecting my Russian language, and with this in mind, I applied for and attended RAF North Luffenham, which was the centre for RAF Russian language training. Yet again I was to be thwarted because out of the blue, at the beginning of November, I was informed that I was being promoted to acting squadron leader and posted to No 1 Advanced Navigational School at RAF Stradishall in Suffolk, as a squadron commander. I was beginning to get the impression that all I had to do to climb the promotion ladder was to apply for the Russian language course. I wish!

Turning the clock forward fifty years, I received an invitation from some of my previous students to join them for a reunion in 2016 to mark the fifty years since they'd graduated from No 275 Officers Course at RAF Upwood. I was the last surviving member of the instructing staff, and some of the students hadn't survived either. I had met a few during later years in my service, and some had actually worked for me in MOD and Malta. It was strange seeing some who had changed very little over the years, whereas others had, well, let's say matured. As well as those living in the UK, others came from Germany, France, and Canada to join in the celebrations, which were held at RAF Brize Norton, allowing us to see the changes that had occurred in the intervening years not only in the RAF but also in ourselves.

Promotion and a move to Suffolk

Although it was nice to get advanced promotion, this was yet another move with the family being uprooted. Once again, the problem of the lack of accommodation and a change of school for the girls confronted us. There was nothing available in the Stradishall area of Suffolk, and we found ourselves at Duxford, on the outskirts of Cambridge, some fifteen miles from Stradishall. In the bad old days, squadron commanders were allocated ex-officio married quarters, but it seemed that by the time I had my own squadron, this process had been set aside. I started a daily commute along country roads taking almost an hour each way, and that was to continue for the remainder of my time at Stradishall. However, looking on the positive side, it meant that being off base, I was not on continual call.

In the summer of 1968, I took on the additional role (what is strangely termed a secondary duty) as president of the mess committee of the officers' mess at Duxford. It was akin to running a large hotel in one's spare time, although the staff management was under the supervision of a full-time mess manager. In that year and the following year, I was also given the additional task of selecting and training a team that would compete in the Nijmegan Marches in Holland. Remember the saying "Give the job to a busy man"? Later that summer, I was in need of a break. We packed our trusty Volvo with tenting equipment borrowed from my sister and headed for Callala de Palafrugel in Spain for two weeks in the sun. It was a tiring but worthwhile journey and an enjoyable break from all that was happening in the UK. On 1 January 1969, I was notified that I had been promoted to substantive squadron leader. Although I had been given acting rank at a very early age, it seemed to me somewhat disappointing to have to wait almost eighteen months for confirmation of substantive rank. But looking on the positive side, at least I had been promoted.

During the months that followed, the officers' mess was revamped, I hasten to add at the expense of the film company, to accommodate the film stars and crew who had arrived in Duxford to film *The Battle of Britain*. RAF Duxford was one of those strategic airfields, together with Biggin Hill, North Weald, Kenley, and Hawkinge, that saw the brunt of the activity during the Battle of Britain. We sectioned off part of the officers' mess to provide actors and support staff with rooms, and in return the film company paid for all the alterations and provided catering facilities, which we used on some of our social occasions, thereby saving the taxpayers and ourselves a considerable amount of money. It was an interesting time during which we met many of the stars, who included Sir Laurence Olivier, Ralph Richardson, Trevor Howard, Patrick Wymark, Susannah York, Christopher Plummer, Kenneth Moore, Edward Fox, Michael Redgrave, Michael Caine, and many lesser-known actors. Whilst we had our own working lives to concentrate on, our families did have the opportunity to see some of the filming from time to time, including the uncut rushes. It's amazing what the film producers could do by using the same piece of action filmed from many directions. A North American B-25 Mitchell bomber was the primary platform for aviation sequences, with cameras located in various positions around its fuselage. One of the surviving World War I Belfast hangars was blown up in a mock raid and later had to be demolished. The film company paid for it, of course! Money seemed to be no object with Spitfires, Hurricanes, and Messerschmitts, together with various German aircraft garnered from around the world by a retired group captain by the name of Hamish Mahaddie. Replica buildings and aircraft made of wood were set up around the airfield to be systematically blown up by attacking aircraft. Perhaps we can all learn lessons from this: if you want anything done in a hurry, call in the film-makers—they can get things done quickly, and they have the funds to pay for it!

There were a few significant events that occurred during 1969. In April, de Gaulle stepped down as president of France, much to the relief of all but the French. The Harrier, the new vertical take-off and landing aircraft, entered service with the RAF. British troops were deployed to Northern Ireland following the Battle of the Bogside, and Gaddafi seized power in Libya. But the most dramatic event was the successful landing of the US Apollo 11 lunar module on the moon—proof that at last the United States had overtaken the Russians in the race to the moon. Neil Armstrong, whom I was to meet on a subsequent visit, made the first step onto the moon and gave that unforgettable announcement: "One small step for man, one giant leap for mankind." I'm sure that it was a prearranged quote. The other two astronauts were Buzz Aldrin and Michael Collins. On the evening of 20 July, we kept the children awake so that they could watch the lunar landing on TV. The picture, in black-and-white, was very much grained, but one must remember that this was not only the infancy of space technology and communication; it was also a time before major advances in computer technology. Nevertheless, the photography was sufficient to distinguish the astronauts walking on the moon's surface and to leave a lasting impression on at least two of the children. Jonathan, in the meanwhile, had collected my medals, accumulated over many years in athletic competitions, and had found a hole in the boxed-in staircase and meticulously posted them one by one through a very small gap. There they repose to this very day, and perhaps one day they will be unearthed by some budding archaeologist or house developer. It was to be thirty years later when Jane called in on the occupants of what is now a private house, one of those trips down memory lane, and related the story, to which everyone collapsed with laughter—that is, all but me!

It was during 1969 that my parents-in-law, who were now in their seventies, decided that they would sell their house in Laceby and depart to live in South Africa. I believe this decision was based on a developing friendship they had made with a younger couple who were returning home to South Africa. They tried to persuade us to do the same, but in view of apartheid and my decision to continue with my career in the RAF, the move was a nonstarter. Besides, I was not inclined to set out on yet another language course, this time in Afrikaners. Added to which, I had just been informed that I was to move to Malta as senior air movements officer and staff officer to the air commander the following November. I was also into my second year of the ISS examinations to qualify for Senior Staff College. These were some of the other reason that dissuaded me from making such a move.

A Time of Transition

The seventies will be remembered by many as a decade of strife and abundant strikes—postal workers, miners, dustmen, and local council workers amongst the many involved in the protests against the government of the day. It started in 1970 and ended with the Winter of Discontent in 1979, when ITV went off the air for five months. The government imposed a three-day working week during February 1972 with the aim of saving electricity. There arose a further problem when the lengthy dry spell in the weather resulted in water supplies reaching a critical level. Add to this the oil crisis caused by the OPEC embargo on oil to Western countries and the emerging economies of the developing world, and it is easy to see why industrial nations experienced economic stagnation. Looking back on the decade, it was a time of both concern and depression. The novelist Tom Wolfe defined it as the "Me Decade", an attitude of counter-culture of the 1960s. However, social progress made during the sixties continued to grow whilst the so-called hippie culture waned and faded completely by the middle of the decade. It was a period in which there was a stagnating economy, uncertain global conditions, and a government that lacked the courage to take truly radical action in pursuit of growth—a familiar and repetitive political failing.

The world saw an upsurge in terrorism and wars throughout the seventies. Terrorism was in the form of the Red Brigade and the

Baader-Meinhof gang, followed by the massacre of Israeli athletes at the Olympic Games in Munich during 1972 by the Black September Group. From the Israeli/Arab Yom Kippur war in 1973 to the Iranian Revolution in 1979, conflicts abounded around the world, especially in Africa and the Middle East. The Cold War continued unabated, as did the internal conflict in Northern Ireland. Elsewhere, coups took place in Syria, Chile, Ethiopia, Argentina, and Uganda, and Russia found itself in a conflict in Afghanistan, which was to continue into the 1980s. Throughout the decade, the world faced an economic downturn and a global energy crisis brought about by the intransigence of OPEC. There was, however, a glimmer of good news with the arrival of the first 747 jumbo jet at Heathrow in 1971, heralding the dawn of cheaper and more readily available air travel. People could now watch television programmes in colour broadcast on three programmes, and during the decade, the first domestic microwave, VHS recorder, and personal stereo became available.

RAF Luqa in Malta

On the domestic front, we duly moved out as a family to RAF Luqa in Malta during November 1969 to find that my predecessor had handed over his married quarters because his wife had returned home to the UK earlier. Brilliant—here we were yet again ensconced on a base without anywhere to live. We were placed in temporary accommodation in the Transit Hotel at Hal Far. Don't be misled by the title—it consisted of one bedroom which served as a living room as well, but then, there are people who have far less. Nevertheless, it was a distraction I could do without when settling into my new job, and I spent most of the first two weeks looking for accommodation. I eventually found a two-bedroom flat in Guadamanga which was of a very dubious standard; the cockroaches were abundant and of a substantial size that took some eliminating, but we had to make the best of a bad situation. Forgive me if this appears as a repetitive theme or moan, but it becomes a factor that not only impacts on married life but also adds a distraction to working life. I certainly made the powers that be aware of my annoyance, which probably didn't do my career a great deal of good, but it was not of my making, and the situation shouldn't have arisen if there had been a little more forethought and planning.

Leaving that behind, we did eventually move into a block of flats at RAF Luqa some four months later in March 1970, which meant further upheaval in the children's education. It was during this year that we became aware that with so many changes of school, Jane was falling well behind her contemporaries. Having gone through this process as a child, I should have realised, but it's a little difficult when you have to concentrate on your job. Added to which, Sheila had always maintained that as a teacher, she would never interfere in the children's schooling, and I supported her in this. How wrong can one be? Jane was, at the age of ten, at least three years behind her peers. We decided enough was enough. I took leave, and we flew back to the UK to seek advice from educational specialists (ACE) in Cambridge. After much heart searching, we settled on a small school, Fyling Hall, in Robin Hoods Bay, near Whitby in North Yorkshire, which combined good academic standards with a friendly and family environment. Suffice to say, it was an excellent choice and one we've never regretted. Not only did it enable Jane to recover the lost years, but it meant that she left school with a confident attitude, a sound grounding, and most important O-level qualifications. In the years that followed, not only did Julie and Jonathan join Jane, but their children have also graduated through the same school and progressed to university thereafter. However, I digress yet again!

We returned to Malta and settled into very busy work and social commitments. Sheila didn't want to return to full-time teaching, and instead she took on the job of running the independent nursery school, which I think was a far more demanding task. My parents came out for a brief visit. Shortly afterwards, Sheila's mother died, and we flew home for a brief period and brought Sheila's father back to Malta to live with us. In between, we had many visits from friends and relatives in the UK who decided that Malta was a convenient holiday spot, and our house was rarely empty thereafter.

Sheila's father's arrival made for some interesting occasions. Once a year, we held a drinks party in our house for the senior officers in

Malta, which included the admiral and the other heads of services. On one such occasion, Sheila's father, who was a veteran of World War I and who had been wounded a few times, regaled them with stories about how bad the officers were in the trenches and how some had been shot by their own soldiers during battle. I tried to dismiss it as embellishment, and of course they fell about laughing when they heard the story. Little did they know that it was probably true. It was not long before he met the mother of a friend of ours and swept her off her feet—or was it the other way around? They both set sail for the UK. What would Sheila's mother have said? I dread to think. By this time, they were both in their seventies, but looking back, I can now understand it. After all, they were mere youngsters!

There were many well-known and important people whom we met during our time in Malta. We looked after Sheila Scott, the famous aviator, on her record-breaking flight around the world; world politicians, actors, and singers, such as the Beverley Sisters, for whom I managed to get Malta football strips for the children; footballers, including Stanley Matthews, who eventually settled in Malta; Wings Day of *The Great Escape* fame; and many, many others—not forgetting our daughter Jane!

Jane flew out during the school holidays on British Airways aircraft via Rome, escorting four younger children from the same school. Clearly they were all under the control of the cabin crew, but Jane was full of her important role at the age of ten as the nominated school escort. We duly awaited her arrival at the civil air terminal, and when all the passengers had disembarked and passed through customs, there was no sign of Jane, which made us very agitated. She eventually arrived, and when we asked her why she had taken so long, she said she had been talking to the nice customs man. He asked her what she had in her suitcase, and she said some beef, sausages, bacon, and fruit (all banned imports in Malta). He laughed at what he thought was a joke, and after chatting for a while—because Jane can chatter—she was cleared through. When I asked her why she had said what she had, she replied, "Well, Grandma sent you a big piece of beef, lots of sausages because you can't get them here, and lots of apples, and you've always told me to tell the truth." I almost had a fit as we whisked our little criminal out of the terminal!

Strategic Importance of Malta

Luqa airfield was a hive of activity, both military and civil, and was central to British and NATO military presence in the Mediterranean. Malta's Grand Harbour was similarly congested by Royal Navy, US Navy ships of the Sixth Fleet, and ships of the Italian navy. Visitors included the carriers *John F. Kennedy* and HMS *Ark Royal* accompanied by a plethora of guided missile destroyers, frigates, commando carriers, fleet auxiliaries, and submarines of both nations. The growing attention given to the Mediterranean by the Soviets in the 1960s had become alarming to NATO. The eastern seaboard was becoming a Soviet lair for their submarines and provided them with warm water access to the Atlantic. The situation was becoming of even greater concern to the Western allies as more Arab states, shaking off the influence of colonial powers such as Britain and France, espoused the Soviet cause and accepted their weapons in exchange for the use of ports and harbours in the Mediterranean. Malta became the hub of combined air and sea operations, with the harbour and airfield providing the essential replenishment resources.

Resident-based RAF squadrons, including the Shackleton Mk 3s of 201 Squadron and the Nimrods of 203 Squadron, continuously swept the Mediterranean, tracking Soviet submarines and surface shipping, whilst Canberras of Nos 13 and 39 Squadrons carried out photographic reconnaissance and electronic countermeasures. Numerous other aircraft occupied the limited space at Luqa, including V bombers, Phantoms, Javelins, Harriers, Buccaneers, and Lightnings. Replenishment support was provided by VC10s, Argosy, Hercules, and a variety of helicopters buzzing to and from the ships offshore like angry bees. Not forgetting, of course, the flag-waving Red Arrows Gnat aerobatic team.

Amongst the many visitors who used our facilities for training were the Special Boat Services (SBS), the Navy equivalent of the SAS, who carried out parachute drops in some of the quieter harbours. I had the opportunity of joining them in low-level parachute jumps, what were termed water drops, from the Argosy aircraft. These were the first jumps I had carried out over water, and they were completely different from land drops. At low level, you quickly had to release yourself and your equipment from the harness before hitting the water to avoid drowning under the parachute or becoming entangled with your reserve chute and equipment. Since then, parachutes have evolved to such an extent that they are virtually flyable through controlled steering.

As time progressed, so did the workload. I was responsible for all air transport operations out of RAF Luqa and, together with an army colleague, for the Joint Services Port Unit in Grand Harbour. In June 1970, we had many visitors from NATO participating in exercises: Dawn Patrol during June, and Lime Jug in the November. Because of the nature of military operations in the Middle East, and because of the political situation, RAF Luqa seemed to attract an inordinate number of VIPs both day and night. This included leading politicians such as the foreign secretary, at that time Lord Carrington; senior NATO, US, and UK military officers; senior civil servants; and others from all walks of life. Whilst they were on the base, it was my job to look after them.

During my early days in Malta, I had been writing a series of articles on life in Malta called "Through the Eye of an Eagle". Much to my chagrin, I was also given the secondary duty of public relations officer for the RAF, a position that would normally have been carried out by a full-time civilian journalist. It was the old adage that I mentioned earlier: "If you want a job done, give it to a busy man"! This activity got me involved with helping Lady Dorman, the wife of the governor general, in supporting her charity works, but that's another story.

In my first few months, I met up with Vernon Pragnell quite by accident whilst working down in Grand Harbour. He was the son-in-law of the lady my father-in-law eventually eloped with the following year. Life does get complicated! Vernon was working with GCHQ/

MI6 monitoring Russian activity in the Mediterranean, and we became firm friends and colleagues over the years that followed.

The Beginning of the End

In July 1971, Sir Maurice Dorman was replaced as governor general by Anthony Malmo, the first Maltese to hold that important office. On his departure from Malta, Sir Maurice gave his public farewell speech to the people of Malta just before flying out from RAF Luqa. He asked me if I could discreetly have his notes typed so that he could release them to the press; he did not want some of the alterations revealed. I therefore agreed to type it myself. In the haste, I didn't return the original but made sure later that it was secure. Some twenty years later, after I had left the RAF and we had purchased Purves Hall, a country house hotel in the Scottish Borders, the Dormans came to stay with us. One evening we were reminiscing about life in Malta. I told him that I still had the original draft of his speech, which I was delighted to hand back to him. He was extremely pleased because he said he was contemplating writing a book about his life in the colonial service, but I'm not sure that it ever materialised, and he died in October 1996.

Shortly after Sir Maurice's departure from Malta, the Labour Party under Dom Mintoff, the prime minister, started to agitate for the removal of British military presence from Malta. How much of this was an endeavour to seek added finance, or whether it was to eliminate what was conceived as colonial influence, is hard to ascribe. Suffice to say that by the autumn of 1971, Mintoff was demanding $46.8 million, an almost fourfold increase in the lease of $13.65 million paid by Britain. With the refusal of the British government to accommodate this increase, Mintoff set a deadline of 15 January 1972 for the complete withdrawal of all British and NATO military from the island. This gave us an immense problem because there were about 7,000 dependants and 3,500 services personnel based on the island. This didn't include the multiplicity of equipment, some highly sensitive. Despite ongoing negotiations, plans were put in place for the start of an immediate evacuation of families and equipment. It was a massive task, calling for significant military and civil shipping and airlift from the UK. On 14 January, one day before the deadline, I said farewell to my family as they left on what was to be the last of the family flights. During this time, Mintoff continued with his brinkmanship. Not only was he having intense negotiations with Lord Carrington (the defence secretary) and Joseph Luns (the secretary general of NATO), but he was also flirting with the new ruler of Libya, Colonel Gaddafi, and with the Chinese and Russians. He threatened that if the West didn't meet his price, the Russians or the Libyans would. He had already turned down an offer of $26 million in December and invited the Libyans in to operate the civilian air traffic control system alongside the RAF.

Whilst Mintoff continued his demands and frequently switched the deadline, the withdrawal continued at a pace. Clearly many of the buildings and equipment were purpose built and of high security, and we therefore had to follow a scorched earth policy to avoid highly sensitive equipment falling into the wrong hands. The work continued around the clock with airlift and shipping in full support. After Christmas, as the deadline approached, negotiations continued,

NATO offered to bridge the gap by providing $10 million towards Malta's failing economy. Before the deadline arrived, we had evacuated just about everything and everybody. The carrier was about to sail from Valetta, and a handful of us, the remnants of all three services, were left to await the last aircraft. With a matter of days to go, I had been put into a temporary hospital at Luqa with a compacted vertebra, wondering if I would be left behind.

It was at this time that I had a visit from Dr Paul Farrugia who told me that Mintoff was now worried about the conclusion and what might happen if agreement was not reached. I should explain that due to the Maltese system of taxation at that time being only based on the primary job, many Maltese had two or more forms of employment and applied the tax system to the lowest paid. It's not too difficult to see where this is leading. The British employed many Maltese nationals in basic clerical and lower management positions and on a very low salary, which meant that many clerical jobs were occupied by people who held high-ranking positions in the community. I had a few working for me. My chief clerk, Dr Paul Farrugia, was also the personal physician to Arch Bishop Gonzi, a powerful and influential man. At that time, Paul was also the director of the Malta Blood Bank, a knight of Malta, and one of the island's most influential men. After the British withdrawal from Malta, he became the ambassador to the Vatican and later Malta's ambassador to the United Nations. Having discharged myself from the medics, I relayed this information to the air commander and was then taken to see the British high commissioner to explain what had taken place and the role that Paul had played. Paul was in a state of panic and concerned at what might be regarded as treason, and he feared that he might be eliminated. He was reassured that nothing would be revealed. On 15 January, six hours before the deadline, Mintoff defused the crisis by calling off the "pay or get out" demand to Britain.

As one of a small group representing the three services, I was invited for a farewell dinner as a thank-you by the senior officer on the island, Rear Admiral Templeton-Cottill. It was a very pleasant and convivial evening, but the following evening, the eve of our departure from Malta, the island was hit by an earthquake, the epicentre of which was just off the coast of North Africa. It didn't cause a great amount of damage, but it did crack the runway, and for some hours we wondered if our aircraft would be able to take off. However, with great relief we departed for home having successfully completed our job.

Little did I anticipate that I would be heading back to Malta in less than two weeks to set up arrangements for the return of the military to island. After a few brief days in Wensleydale with the family, I was recalled by the Ministry of Defence and headed out to Malta. Upon arriving back at the civil airport, I was greeted by many of my staff in a jubilant mood, glad to see us return. I was less than happy, having to leave my family behind and uncertain as to when we would be reunited. Added to which, there was no enthusiasm in the ministry to deal with the return in the same swift fashion as the evacuation, and it was many weeks before a semblance of order could be achieved. After a great deal of hassle and signals to and from the UK, we started to receive the assistance we sought. I made several flights to Cyprus and other locations, arranging for the recovery of vital equipment to restart operations in Malta.

I was eventually replaced in March but still faced the uncertainty of what or where my next post would be—and how and where I would accommodate my family, who were still living with my parents in the north of England. My thoughts went back to Rudyard Kipling and his poem "Tommy", written in 1892.

> O it's Tommy this an' Tommy that, an' Tommy go away.
> But it's thank you Mr Atkins when the band begins to play.

Concerned over the way my career was drifting, I asked for a career interview in MOD. As usual, it was a summation of my progress to date and was full of platitudes, but there was no clear indication of the direction it was going. It was the usual explanation of the consequences likely to arise because of defence cuts and how this impacted on future predictions, but if I continued, et cetera, et cetera. The one thing I did discover was that I was to take up a position at the RAF Computer Centre at Hendon as duty controller. At this time, the SCC computer system was the second largest and most modern of its kind in Europe. At least this was a challenging proposition.

The RAF Computer Centre—Hendon

I moved Sheila and the family down to Hendon, and we stayed in a hotel whilst we searched for accommodation—the ever-present problem with service life, but in London it was almost impossible to achieve. There were some surplus married quarters at RAF Henlow in Bedfordshire, about an hour's drive from Hendon, so we moved in during June 1972. Julie and Jonathan started yet another school whilst I commuted to and from work. We decided that the continual change of schools was also beginning to disrupt Julie's education, so we arranged for her to join Jane at Fyling Hall. In the months that followed, I searched around for housing which was closer to Hendon and therefore would allow Sheila to return to teaching now that two of the children were established in their education; besides which, we had increasing expenses to meet. We eventually found a very nice semidetached house in North Harrow owned by a couple who were in the diplomatic service and moving out to Nigeria. This enabled Sheila to get a job teaching at North Harrow Primary, a school which Jonathan would attend and one which was very convenient all-round—not a view shared by Jonathan, who suddenly found that having a parent as a mother and teacher was a lose-lose situation!

Despite the shift working brought about by the need to provide coverage around the clock my work at Hendon was very interesting. The IT system, or Automatic Data Processing (ADP) as it was known in those days, was the second largest of its kind in Western Europe, comprising four mainframe AEI 1010 computers and ancillary equipment, providing around-the-clock service to the RAF worldwide. The whole operation occupied over five thousand square feet of accommodation. I marvel to this day that all the processing capacity can now be dealt with by a PC or desktop computer at a fraction of the size. How far technology has travelled in such a short space of time. It makes me aware of that we've been living through an age of technical revolution.

RAF winter balls are usually occasions where at midnight, the station commander or his deputy announces promotions and awards, if there are any, before details are released to the press. Usually the recipients are gathered together and told the news during the day so that they can tell their families and share in the celebration before details are released to the public. On 31 December, we had invited friends for the evening, and following the end of the festivities, during which we had an enjoyable evening and heard details of a couple of promotions, we returned home a little after midnight because I was on an early shift the following day (although having to work the next day was not an ideal way of welcoming the new year). After having briefed the staff on the day's activities, I returned to face the usual stack of mail and found, much to my surprise, a letter from Rear Admiral Templeton-Cottill congratulating me on the award of the MBE for operational services in the Middle East. Initially I thought it was an error, but on opening the Daily telegraph, I found that it was correct. What a way to find out! Civilians are normally told months in advance that they are to be offered the award. Not so in the military, whose loyalty and acceptance are rightly assumed. Apparently, the CO had gone on leave and forgotten to tell his deputy that confirmation was in his safe. I had mixed feelings: elation at having been made an MBE, and annoyance that the CO had screwed up what could have been an ideal opportunity to celebrate. After all, it is not every day one gets the privilege.

The year 1973 was when the UK joined the European Community. VAT was introduced in the March budget at 10 per cent. Oil prices increased by 70 per cent. The National Union of Mineworkers introduced an overtime ban, which resulted in a state of emergency being introduced with the announcement of a three-day week due to shortages of power; the NUM were holding the country ransom. The miners went on strike the following February and stayed out for a month. To me, the nation appeared to be tottering on the verge of anarchy, but worse was to come.

Later that year, we duly received an invitation to attend Buckingham Palace for the investiture. We were limited to two guests and decided to take Jonathan rather than bring the girls back from school; we certainly couldn't take one without the other. Jonathan was more impressed with the Ghurkhas, who lined the palace staircase, than with the ceremony or seeing the queen. On learning that I had been in Malta, the queen said she had very fond memories of the island, having lived there with her husband, Prince Philip, while he was still a serving officer. My parents came down for the day and waited to have photographs taken with us. I felt sorry for them because it was a bitterly cold day standing outside the palace. On his return to school, Jonathan was asked by his teacher to tell the class of his experiences, but all he could talk about was the "Gherkins" that stood on the staircase!

Senior Staff College—Bracknell

Towards the end of the year, I received notification that I had been selected for Senior Staff College at Bracknell in 1974. This was to be a year-long course, so we were all allocated married quarters. Whilst this was a very welcome arrangement, the houses, early 1950s in design, lacked any form of heating apart from an electric fire in the living room, which was adequate in the summer but useless in the winter. At least it was one less problem to worry about.

During this year, and in the middle of the miners' strike, the government called a general election, resulting in no party having overall majority. In August, US President Nixon resigned over the Watergate scandal. That autumn was also marked by IRA atrocities in Guildford and another general election, in which Labour won but with a majority of only three. In November, following a reshuffle of the Shadow Cabinet, Margaret Thatcher challenged Ted Heath's leadership of the Conservative Party, resulting in her assuming leadership of the party in February 1975.

The year at Bracknell passed very quickly and was packed with activity: intense study periods interspersed with visits to operational units both at home and overseas, as well as briefings from many leading commercial companies and institutions, government departments, and industry and union leaders. We had a mix of students from all services and different nationalities on the course. One of the American students, a US Navy commander, had been the executive officer on the aircraft carrier the USS *John F. Kennedy*, whom I had worked with in Malta. Also, on my syndicate were an Indian and a Pakistani who the previous year had been at war with each other. Another student, John Assan from Nigeria, eventually became head of the Nigerian Defence Force but was subsequently executed on the beach in Nigeria following a coup. There were many others with interesting backgrounds. At the end of the course, I was one of the more fortunate students, being promoted to acting wing commander and appointed head of movements operations in the Ministry of Defence, a post I had cast envious eyes over and one that would put me at the centre of UK defence activities.

CHAPTER 8

A Whitehall Warrior

Challenges are what make life interesting. Overcoming
them is what makes life meaningful.
Joshua Marine

In December 1974, we moved into married quarters at Bushey Heath
near Watford, and I had my first taste of daily commuting between
Stanmore and London. The following January, Sheila started teaching
in Bushey, and Jonathan began school at Bushey Heath. As head of
movements operations in the Ministry of Defence, I had responsibility
for planning and overseeing the worldwide UK military air transport
operations, major exercises, special and clandestine operations, and
VIP arrangements)including those for heads of state, the prime
minister, and various ministers). It was to be one of the most intense
periods of pressure, spanning 1975 through early 1978. In the latter
half, I had the added responsibility of being appointed as the ministry's
escort officer to the prime minister, James Callaghan, and the foreign
secretary, David Owen, on their overseas visits, which meant working
closely with the staffs at Number 10 and the Foreign Office.

Within the MOD, I worked with a brilliant and dedicated team
who tackled the many and varied problems in areas that spanned the
globe, getting urgent spares out to submarines; moving special forces
out to or recovering them from hot spots in Africa, Asia, or South
America; and supporting troops in areas of operations or on military

exercises. Each alternate year, we had the task of airlifting members of the Victoria Cross and George Cross Association for their meeting in London, and I would get one of my squadron leaders, usually Chris Ranasinghe, to act as their escort. I felt very honoured to be invited by Admiral Godfrey Place VC, the president of the association, to both their tenth and eleventh reunions at the Café Royal in April 1976 and again in May 1978. The guest of honour on each occasion was a senior member of the royal family. Despite his reputation for not suffering fools gladly, I got on well with Godfrey. He was very modest about his wartime exploits, having won the VC and the DSC and the Polish Cross of Valour. It was in September 1943, as a twenty-two-year-old lieutenant in the Royal Navy, that Place was one of two midget submarine commanders who, in a most daring raid, successfully attacked the German battleship *Tirpitz,* resulting in it being out of action for eight months. At each of these occasions, I felt overawed in the presence of such collective bravery and honoured to sit at the same table as such modest men. Unfortunately, Godfrey Place died in 1994 at the relatively young age of seventy-three.

It was at this point in time that I had another aberration, possibly a hangover from my academic year at Bracknell. I launched into an Open University BA course in the hope of completing it in two years—always a dreamer! Over the next two years, I found myself burning the midnight oil, frequently up against impossible deadlines and occasionally working through the night. The evenings were never a problem, arriving back from London at 8 p.m., snatching a quick meal, and working on. Had it not been for the fact that Sheila, back into full-time teaching, had work of her own to do, it might have posed a problem. Anyway, Jane, having left Fyling Hall and attending the local college, seemed to fill the house with teenagers of dubious character, and there was therefore never enough room for me to occupy a seat in the living room despite the many hints that fell on stony ground. Nevertheless, we made sure that my additional work didn't impose too much on our social life; all work and no play is a recipe for disaster. When the pressures come from all directions, it certainly focuses the mind.

There were many interesting elements to my time in MOD, too many to relate, but from an historical viewpoint some were to be later part of our heritage. One of these was the day I received a telephone call from Magdi Yagoub, who subsequently became one of the world's leading heart surgeons. He sought assistance in flying a heart from France to Harefield at the early stage of heart transplants in the UK. Many of the other aspects were and remain highly sensitive or subject to security limitations.

During 1976, together with colleague Jim Cooper, I flew out to Washington. Our remit was to carry out an in-depth study of the transport facilities across the United States and Canada. Jim looked at the elements south of the border whilst I concentrated on Canada. It is only when you travel from coast to coast that you realise what a vast country—or should I say continent—it is, and what a wide range of cultures Canada possesses, from its Scottish roots in Nova Scotia to the French influence in Quebec, American influence in Alberta, and British influence in British Colombia. Much of the British Army's tank training was being carried out on the prairies around Medicine Hat near Calgary whilst the RAF used the facilities at Cold Lake in Alberta. I had arrived in Calgary in early February, when temperatures, exacerbated by the wind chill factor, plummet to around -27 Celsius. Only a problem if you don't have the appropriate clothing. I arrived in Calgary minus my cold weather clothing, which courtesy of North American Airlines, was on its way to Florida. It was not the first time my baggage had gone astray in my travels across the North American continent, and it wouldn't be the last. It was an anomaly that I was to experience after leaving the RAF. I was met at Calgary and travelled to Medicine Hat in an army two-seat Beaver aircraft. By the time I clambered out of the cockpit, I had turned a darker shade of blue, and after thawing out, the army kitted me out with cold weather clothing and applied me with the appropriate doses of alcohol to help my blood supply recirculate. At the end of our investigations, we had two days in Washington where we completed our report before flying back to London.

I arrived back to the news that my father, who had been suffering from leukaemia, had died that morning. After a quick debriefing within the MOD, I collected Sheila, and we headed off to Skipton to help my mother sort out her future, see my father for the last time, and attend the funeral.

Escort Officer to the Prime Minister

It was whilst I was in the Ministry of Defence that Harold Wilson used the Main Hall to announce on 16 March 1976 that he intended to resign. There was much speculation as to what had brought about that decision, and without a reason being given, it led to speculation by the media. But some years later after having left the RAF I was in the British Rail Booking office in Victoria, and in front of me were Mary and Harold Wilson. He looked a shadow of his former self, and it was very evident that the ravages imposed by Alzheimer's had taken its toll. I was somewhat surprised that someone who had led the country as prime minister should be reduced to having to queue for his ticket, but I suppose that is a democracy.

In January 1978, I accompanied then Prime Minister James Callaghan, in my new role as MOD escort officer, on his tour of Bangladesh, India, and Pakistan. Our first port of call was Dhaka in Bangladesh, where we duly arrived on the night of 4 January 1978. After dispersal of the VIPs, the crew and I ensconced ourselves in the hotel in which we were staying to catch up on the day's events and enable the crew to be fully rested. I met and discussed events with Superintendent K. A. Bhuiyan, head of the special branch, before going up to unpack.

Bangladesh

I should point out at this stage that on 2 October 1977, Bangladesh suffered one of its many coups. Premier Zia Rahman was to suffer twenty-one coups during his five years in power, but he eventually succumbed to assassination by six of his officers in 1981. The coup in October 1977 was initiated by airmen of the Bangladeshi Air Force (BAF), six of whom had died in the abortive coup, and because of this failed attempt, the whole of the air force had been confined to their base at BAF Bashar. This situation pertained up until our arrival, and a state of martial law was still in place with a nightly curfew imposed at midnight until 0700 hours. Nervous young army conscripts, armed with loaded rifles, patrolled the streets to maintain order. That evening, a letter was slid under my bedroom door in which there was a formal invitation for myself and the crew to attend a reception at the air force base. It was in this context that I was somewhat concerned and sought guidance from the prime minister's principal private secretary. There was a great flurry of activity in the dovecote, and after discussions with the PM (and no doubt with the premier of Bangladesh), it was decided that I should go ahead and attend with the crew. Apparently, there had been no contact with the BAF since the coup, and it was thought helpful if we could feed back details of morale on the base. To say that I was apprehensive was an understatement. I had no wish to be part of an international incident no matter how high or on what grounds it had been sanctioned, and I didn't wish to find myself a victim in some foreign land. However, "mine is not to reason why, but just to do and die", and I assembled the crew. We found ourselves transported through the streets of Dhaka to the BAF Base at Bashar.

We were greeted on arrival by a remarkable reception, initially by staff in immaculate white uniforms and blue turbans. We were guided in to meet the base commander and his officers. It was a greeting that was on a par with anything we could have wished for. What I found even more astonishing was the wide variety of alcohol on offer. In a dry state such as Bangladesh, this was unheard of, but it was openly proffered, and the company was most convivial, although they stuck to cordials! Strangely enough, the conversation never touched on the current or past political issues; it was all about flying and general aviation matters.

At about 2300 hours, I was becoming a little apprehensive of the approaching hour of curfew, and I passed the word around the crew that we would shortly be departing. I used the pretext that the crew were needed the following day to work out future routes and timings. The base commander would have none of it and insisted we stay until midnight. I think he was trying to prove a point to the army, but I had no intention of being meat in the sandwich. We duly set off with twenty minutes to go before curfew, accompanied by a heavily armed escort. On my return, I duly reported what had happened. Everyone was delighted at the outcome, and it was shortly afterwards that relations with the BAF returned to normal. I like to think we had a hand in that happy event. The following evening, I was invited, with the PM and others, to a reception given by British High Commissioner Barry Smallman and his wife, and we met some very interesting people working behind the scenes, especially those involved in covert intelligence activities. It was a most informative evening.

India

On Friday 6 January, having said our farewells, we departed for India. There were many aspects to this visit to the Indian subcontinent, but there are a few that have remained in my memory, even though I have been back to India since that time. For example, the size of the country, the sheer density of its population, the historical beauty of its buildings, and the legacy of its colonial and precolonial past. One has to witness the seething mass of people in the cities; it is awesome. Amongst the hustle and bustle of the country are some truly remarkable sites, too many to cover them all. However, one such building that stands out is a timeless place of worship, the Golden Temple of Amritsar in the state of Punjab. It is a significant place of worship for those of the Sikh faith, and it is said that Buddha spent some time there. "I have seen many places, but none like Thee" (Sri Guru Arjan Dev). Yet another building, often described as one of the seven wonders of the world, is the Taj Mahal, situated on the south bank of the Yamuna River. To visit it at night and to see its white marble structure reflected by the moonlight on the river makes it a truly magical experience, especially when one knows its history, which can only be described as a labour of love—maybe not for the mass of builders who constructed it, but certainly for the man who instigated the idea and funded its building. The construction of the Taj Mahal began in 1632 in Agra, Uttar Pradesh, under the instructions of Mughal Emperor Shah Jahan following the death of his third wife, Mumtaz Mahal, during the birth of their fourteenth child. The grief-stricken Shah decided to build a white marble mausoleum of magnificent and stunning proportions for Mumtaz. Unfortunately for him, he was later deposed and imprisoned by his son Aurangzeb in Agra Fort, also on the bank of the Yamuna River. The fort can more accurately be described as a walled city. In 1526, the Mughals captured the fort and a vast treasure, which included a diamond that later became known as the Koh-i-Noor. Shah Jahan's prison was in the Ausamman Burj, a tower with a beautiful marble balcony, and it was the place where he eventually died; it looked out directly onto the Taj Mahal, giving him a daily reminder of the death of Mumtaz.

Finally, to see the legacy of the British raj reflected in its administrative buildings, together with its civil service that impacts on everyday life, takes one back to Victorian days and the remnants of colonial rule. I begin to wonder whether we gifted the civil service to India, or whether it was the other way around.

In the centre of Delhi, there is a cycle rack, similar in many ways to the Boris cycles of London but more in keeping with the butcher's bicycles of the last century. What intrigued me was the large metallic plate strung from the crossbars with the advert "Everett Transport Company". To this day, I wonder which of my many ancestors created this company!

For those unaware of the circumstances surrounding India Air Force One, the president's personal aircraft, it was a Russian Tupolev 124 bomber converted into a VIP aircraft. In November of the previous year, the president was on board another such aircraft with the same designation when it crashed while coming in to land at Jorhat in Assam. The pilot overshot the runway in poor visibility, and the aircraft crashed into a paddy field. It was over two hours before rescue services could reach it. President Dasai was one of the few survivors of the crash. During our visit, as we were covering vast distances in such a short period of time, most of our travel was by air. On one such occasion, we were flying within India aboard the VC10 whilst being accompanied by President Desai in India Air Force One. Before take-off from Delhi, the president asked me if he could fly on the VC10; in return, our prime minister could fly on Air Force One. I broached the subject with the prime minister, and I then realised why people found him so astute. He said, "I think it would be better if you flew in Air Force One and your counterpart fly in the VC10."

I responded, "Does that mean I'm expendable, sir?" He laughed at that—always the gentleman.

My place in the Tupolov, whether intentional or not, was in the bomb aimer's position in the nose of the aircraft, a somewhat confined space, and access to it is through a gap between the pilot and co-pilot's rudder pedals. Being aware of what had happened on the earlier occasion, I had an unpleasant and claustrophobic journey in more ways than one, especially as we came in to land with the vision of the runway hurtling up to meet us. I think it's what one might describe as a bird's-eye view of impending disaster! However, I'm sure the PM would not have had to endure this confined area but would have had a far more comfortable seat in the VIP section of the aircraft.

Pakistan

To the third leg of the visit, our journey to Pakistan. We were late taking off from Delhi on 11 January, the result of last-minute political discussions. On state visits such as these, representatives of the national press (lobby correspondents) accompany the official party from the UK. Naturally, favourable deadlines are what it is all about; late news is no news. Shortly after take-off, I was faced with a barrage of questions as to how our late departure would delay our arrival; they were all concerned about filing their reports to ensure they would be released in the press the following morning, bearing in mind that papers are put to bed well before midnight of the preceding day.

On hearing the noise, the PM asked me what the problem was. I told him and said that I'd assured them that on such a visit, we would arrive on time despite the delay. He turned to the press and said, "If that is what the wing commander has said, then that is what will happen. The RAF has a well-earned reputation on its planning to the minute." He then returned to his part of the aircraft. Unlike him, I was far from sanguine. I knew that in normal circumstances, it couldn't be done. But it had to happen—where was Merlin the wizard at times like this? The aircraft captain, who remains in charge whilst the aircraft is in the air, was worried about exceeding the airframe speed limit imposed on the VC10. I reassured him that I would accept responsibility for what might happen, returned to my seat, and prayed like hell.

We duly touched down to the minute, and before leaving the aircraft, the PM turned to the reporters and said, "Gentlemen, put your trust in the RAF. They know what they're doing." I was so relieved and grateful for the pilot's common sense. The reception was both colourful and impressive with the president, General Zia, the British ambassador, and many other dignitaries lined up alongside the red carpet with a backdrop of mounted cavalry and a band playing a military tune at triple speed. Once the ceremonies were over and the VIPs and main party had departed, we left for our hotel for a quiet night's relaxation.

On Thursday, 12 January, I and others in the party were invited by the British high commissioner and Mrs Bushell to a reception in honour of our prime minister and Mrs Callaghan at the Hotel Intercontinental in Rawalpindi. Years later, whilst staying with friends outside Rothbury in Northumberland, we had dinner with their immediate neighbours, Sir Lawrence and Lady Pumphrey. He had been Bushell's predecessor as high commissioner in Pakistan. It's a small world, especially because Caistron is a small hamlet of just five houses some distance from Rothbury! As a word of explanation for those who are not aware of relationships within the Commonwealth, the high commissioner of a commonwealth nation is the same as an ambassador.

Another coincidence had occurred whilst at the high commission in Islamabad. I met the parents of a girl who was just back from school in England. When I asked where her school was, she said a school in Yorkshire. It turned out that she was a very close friend of my daughter Jane; they shared the same room in the same school! We had another very interesting and informative day being entertained by the staff at the high commission, about which much could be said.

On the morning of our departure from Pakistan, General Zia invited PM Callaghan to attend the final one-day cricket Test match between Pakistan and England in Lahore. We had the opportunity to meet both teams during the lunch break and sit with some of them in their dressing room whilst the match was in play. England managed to lose the match, although they took the series 2-1. It was interesting to see what took place with the hand messages passing between batsman and the coordinator in the dressing room. I was presented with the signed autographs of the England team, which I later gave to Jonathan as a keepsake.

Middle East Peace Talks

During the final months of 1977, Callaghan had two meetings with Menachem Begin, the Israeli prime minister, at Chequers, in which they discussed the possible withdrawal of the Israeli troops from occupied Sinai. During our brief visit to Pakistan, a message was received from Anwar Sadat, the president of Egypt, asking PM Callaghan if he would stop over in Egypt on his return to the UK. As a result, I was asked if arrangements could be made to divert our VC10 aircraft into Aswan so that talks could take place. To the uninitiated, this would seem a simple problem to resolve. However, it raised a host of issues. Because of fatigue and therefore safety issues, no crew could operate more than twelve hours in any twenty-four-hour period without a break. The crew of the VC10, carrying the PM, had to be categorised to a very high standard with security cleared. Diplomatic clearance had to be obtained from any third country over which the aircraft would fly, irrespective of who was on board. Finally, the airfield into which we were flying had to be capable of handling the aircraft.

Using the same crew would necessitate an overnight stay in Aswan, the airfield chosen by the Egyptians, which would cause major disruption to the PM's heavy Parliamentary schedule. The airfield, built by the Russians, had never been used by us; we therefore had no real feel for factors such as runway length, its load-bearing strength, the navigational equipment, or support facilities available. Simple little things like the right grade of aviation fuel, access steps, and power support became major issues. The only backup crew in the UK available at short notice was headed by an American major on an exchange tour. Could you image the United States presidential aircraft being flown by a Brit? How the press would portray this beggars belief. Last but by no means least, how could we obtain diplomatic clearance to overfly either Somalia or the Yemen, and Saudi Arabia or Sudan? Diplomatic clearance takes up to thirty days, and no dispensation is normally given to VIP flights, irrespective of who was involved. But this was a problem I left to the Foreign Office to resolve. Number 38 Group, the RAF operations group, managed to recall a crew from leave and fly them out through Saudi Arabia with authority to exceed their crew duty time, if necessary, to enable the aircraft to return to the UK. All of which left a lot of people, including me, in a somewhat stressed state of mind. However, the meeting did take place in Aswan, not Cairo as reported in some elements of the press, during which the partition of the West Bank was discussed, and Sadat's views were passed on to President Carter. The result was that in September 1978, the Camp David Agreement was signed between Egypt and Israel. Under the terms of the agreement, Egypt regained Sinai and in return recognised the state of Israel. History can record that Callaghan played an important role in the solution.

Prime Minister's Visit to the United States

In August 1977, David Owen, then foreign secretary, had appointed Peter Jay as ambassador to the United States. Jay at this time was the son-in-law of the prime minister and a friend of David Owen. The appointment was regarded by some elements of the press as nepotism, and they questioned Callaghan's judgement in this respect, but perhaps that was nothing unusual in politics. One only had to look back at the honours list compiled by Harold Wilson following the announcement of his retirement in 1976.

In March, we had to arrange a visit to the United States where Callaghan was to meet the newly installed President Jimmy Carter and address the United Nations. The two were to form a very close working relationship. It was a brief visit; we arrived to be met by the Jays and accompanied by the usual greeting party. I was not required to be on hand the following day, so I had a relaxing time visiting the Smithsonian Institute and the FBI offices in Washington. Then I watched a game of softball out at Arlington whilst the PM and president had talks at the White House. A day later, we flew out from Bolling Air Force Base. There was one incident of interest as the PM and party were about to board the VC10. The Americans decided to do a last-minute security sweep of the baggage with Alsatian sniffer dogs. One became very agitated and kept returning to a green parcel, eventually cocked its leg, and urinated. Mrs Mulley, the wife of Secretary of Defence Fred Mulley, rushed across to explain that the box contained a ham, a gift she had been given to take back to the UK. The ham was coated with almonds, which give off a signature similar to explosives, so there was no wonder the dog was trying to draw attention to the contents. There were a few red faces all-round but a contented grin on the face of the dog!

As an aside, or rather a point of interest, whilst in America Margaret Jay met Carl Bernstein, who helped to expose Watergate. They subsequently had a much-publicised extramarital affair. Later in life, she became Baroness Jay, and despite never having been elected to public office, she became leader of the House of Lords.

We arrived back at Heathrow in the early morning of Saturday. Sheila was there to meet me with her car parked alongside the VIP chauffeurs—one way of getting free parking. She said she had an interesting hour being chatted up by the other drivers, who thought she was one of them. There were a few red faces when they discovered she wasn't! We then had to get to Alexandra Palace by midday because it was my graduation day, having taken my degree finals the previous December. I recall I slept through most of the ceremony, having had a hectic three days followed by jet lag. Just as well as these ceremonies become a production line of graduates awaiting their turn to be presented to the academic hierarchy. I was grateful that these VIP trips didn't occur too often. Later, I did a few flights with the PM and other ministers out of Northolt to Bonn and other locations in Europe, but thankfully these were usually out and back on the same day.

MOD Engineering and Supply Policy (ESP)

People who say it cannot be done should not
interrupt those who are doing it.

George Bernard Shaw

In the middle of 1978, having completed almost four years in a very demanding job—for work in the office still went on despite the overseas visits, and the days in MOD often stretched well into the evening—I moved across to the Old War Office and took up my new appointment as head of one of the policy branches (ESP 31) dealing with engineering and supply officers' careers. I thought that as head of ESP, I was destined for a world beyond ours. Nevertheless, it was a task that almost demanded extrasensory perception! However, a much more sedate pace of life ensued, although it was still very important. It's amazing how popular one becomes, especially when one is recommending others for key appointments.

On a more serious note, it was an opportunity to gain recognition for those who were to be the stars of the future. It was a testing time, marshalling arguments with the academics as to why they could and should recognise the training and experience gained by middle-ranking officers when selecting people for master's degrees and doctorates. I spent weeks travelling to and from meetings with members of the university senate explaining and illustrating the depth and intensity of much of the training that officers had to undergo at the postgraduate level. I felt that there was often a complete lack of understanding because many academics had an outdated opinion of officers—and at times almost an extreme left-wing view that anyone who had military connections or connotations did not fully understand the concept of management. Nothing could be further from the truth. Many of the new management techniques which have emerged since the war originated through a new generation of military philosophy and management concepts. It was no longer "do as I say" but "do as I do". Indeed, as far back as the early 1950s the armed services had led the field in management techniques. It was the illustration of management through leadership as well as knowledge and experience. When I moved into commercial life in the 1980s, I quickly discovered how few managers had the ability to extract the best out of their systems, managers, or workforce in general. I felt a great sense of achievement and satisfaction in the work I did over this time, the results of which were only to emerge many years later. In my years at London Transport as a director, I was asked to design the training of those with potential to become future directors, and many of my arguments and justification were based on my MOD experience and generated similar positive results. Indeed, I engaged the assistance of York University Management Department, the professor of whom had been one of my fellow officers in the RAF.

In 1979, we decided it would be nice to get away for the summer and have a family holiday in Rhodes. Julie was in France, staying with a French family to improve her language, and Jane was on holiday with her boyfriend Kevin. That meant we had only Jonathan with us. Although the holiday was relaxing, I think Sheila missed the female company; she was ensconced with two males who she described as not the world's greatest communicators. During the second week, Jonathan, who had never ridden a motorbike before and was not yet fourteen, hired a motorcycle to ride across the island. We followed at a discreet distance by car. He disappeared, and for the next two hours I had to deal with a frantic Sheila, who was convinced he had been involved in an accident, kidnapped, or ridden over a cliff. We called in at a small village to establish the way back, and there was Jonathan sitting at the bar having a soft drink. Well, that's what he said it was. Did he get stick from his mother—and so did I, which was nothing unusual!

Football Tour to Sri Lanka

Throughout the 1970s, I had participated in sport and returned to football, but this time in management rather than as a player, though I still played from time to time. I had taken on the role of chairman of RAF Football, and towards the end of April 1980, I took the RAF football team on a two-week tour to Sri Lanka. One of my squadron leaders, Chris Ranasinghe, whom I first met when he was one of my students at Upwood, and who later worked for me in Movements Operations in MOD, had asked if he could accompany the team because he knew many people in Sri Lanka—a fact that was to be displayed during the tour. Before joining the RAF, Chris had been a major in the Ceylon Army but had fallen foul of the regime in Sri Lanka (Ceylon) in the early days of Bandaranaike. Although in India attending Staff College, he was nevertheless associated with those who had been involved in the coup at that time; guilt by association, I believe. In later life, Chris remarried and shortly thereafter developed Alzheimer's to the extent that he no longer recognised his wife, Doreen. He died in 2013.

It is worth pointing out that Solomon Bandaranaike came to power in 1956 and profoundly changed Ceylon's politics. He downgraded English, regarding it as a colonial language; made Sinhala the official language; and promoted socialism. He removed the British military bases in Basar, China Bay, and Trincomalee. He was assassinated in September 1959, and his wife, Sirimavo, eventually took power, becoming the world's first woman prime minister and mother of the fourth president. She continued her husband's policies, moving her country closer to Russia and China and against the United States and Britain. She crushed an attempted military coup in 1960 before losing power in 1964, which she soon regained in 1970. There was another abortive coup on 27 January 1972, the Colonels' Coup, with the key leaders being arrested before the coup could be carried out. It was during 1970 that the name of the country was changed from its old colonial name of Ceylon to Sri Lanka. Sirimamo eventually lost power in 1977, convicted of abuse of power and rejected by the people who had previously worshipped her. Chandrika, her ambitious daughter, continued the dynasty when she was elected president in 1994, although others had presided in between.

At the time of our visit, Junius Richard Jayewardene, a friend of Chris's, was in power after being elected prime minister in 1977 and president on 4 February 1978. He remained as such until 1989, aligning himself with the West.

Our first game, which I was invited to referee, was against a Sri Lankan XI in Colombo. We won comfortably, but I had a poor game; it's often the case when a game is so one-sided, and the losing side commits a steady progression of fouls, something I later noticed in the FIFA World Cup of 2018. Inevitably, you can't arbitrate on every single offence without major disruption to the game. I was also conscious of the mood of the spectators. The following day, we were invited to lunch at the British high commissioner's residence, during which High Commissioner David Aires outlined the political situation in the north of the island. Problems had arisen in the north where the minority group, the Tamils, were set on a course of self-determination. He intimated that it would be advantageous if we could travel to Jaffna to play their football team. He also added that it would be an act of diplomacy if we could perhaps lose! Whilst I advised the team manager and the players that we would be heading north, there was no way that I was going to suggest they should contrive to lose the game. I would have been strung up had I even contemplated such an outcome. Besides which, I have very strong views that sport must never become embroiled in politics. We travelled north and were well received by the locals, and the match was a hard-fought contest. I have learnt that wherever one goes and whatever the level, everyone gets great satisfaction out of beating the Brits. Perhaps it has something to do with our empirical history. We lost 2-1 to a better side and returned somewhat disappointed to Colombo, where we were feted for our diplomatic skills. Little did they know we deserved to lose, and it wasn't arranged, but they wouldn't listen to our protestations.

The Sri Lankans were also lauding us for other reasons and on this occasion basking in the glory of being associated with the Brits. News of the successful attack on terrorists at the Iranian embassy in London had just come through. At 11.30 on Wednesday, 30 April 1980, a group of six men stormed the Iranian embassy in Kensington and took twenty-six people hostage. Over the next six days, negotiations lead to the release of five of the hostages in exchange for minor concessions. Concerned by the length of time taken, the number of hostages involved, and the fact that it was in the forefront of world news, Prime Minister Margaret Thatcher called in the SAS. On the sixth day, the terrorists, frustrated by the lack of progress, shot and killed a hostage and threw his body out of the embassy. The SAS, having been given the go-ahead, abseiled down from the roof and stormed the embassy, rescuing all but one of the hostages and killing five of the six terrorists. The total operation took just seventeen minutes. By the delighted celebrations in Colombo, one would have been forgiven for thinking they had carried out the operation themselves.

Not that it has any bearing on our visit, but there is another subsequent quirk of fate that I must add. In June 2007 I was invited to the wedding of Roger, the son of very close friends of mine, Michael and Sheila Walker. Mike and I had served together on many occasions, and Sheila had been a teacher at the same school as my wife. The subsequent wedding reception was at Fawsley Hall, Daventry, where I met Mrs Chandrika Bandaranaike Koumaralanga, the former president of Sri Lanka. Her daughter Ysodhara was marrying Roger, who was a consultant surgeon. Ysodhara was also a doctor, and they had met during training.

The Winter of Discontent

In January 1979, with the Winter of Discontent at its peak, the lorry drivers went on strike, and one million local authority workers added to the misery with a Day of Action. The IRA and the INLA continued their murderous vendetta with the assassination of the Tory MP Airey Neave in March and the Earl of Mountbatten in August—a sure challenge to Margaret Thatcher, who became Britain's first British female prime minister It was in December that the USSR invaded Afghanistan, and the repercussions stretched into the middle of 1980, with several nations (including the United States) boycotting the XXII Olympiad in Moscow in protest. Four years later, the Soviets retaliated by boycotting the games in Los Angeles.

Later in 1980, we decided to join my brother and his wife holidaying in Monastir, Tunisia. Unfortunately, we had overlooked it being Ramadan, the Arab religious holiday which involves fasting throughout the day, which impacted the quality of service provided.

The hotel complex in which we were accommodated was very crowded but nevertheless enjoyable. However, we had two disturbing incidences, the first involving Jonathan and the second involving me. Three days into the holiday, Jonathan limped out from the sea complaining of intense pain in his leg. I noticed two marks on the underside of his sole, so I quickly carried him in to see the hotel doctor, by which time Jonathan was going into muscular spasms. The Tunisian doctor didn't seem to know what to do, and each enquiry was met with a shrug. We put Jonathan into a taxi. I told the driver I would pay any speeding fines as we raced into Monastir to the hospital. The driver made the most of my offer and drove to the limits of his ability with great gusto! Luckily, we were met at the entrance by a French female doctor who recognised immediately what the problem was and administered an antivenom serum for snakebite. It was an excellent reaction and one for which we are eternally grateful.

The second incident was not so dramatic, but it could have been. I had been up to my room to collect some things for Sheila, and on the way down I took the lift by myself. The lift was limited to five people. The next floor down, six Germans crowded in, two of them smoking. As I discovered after a few minutes, none spoke English. The lift stopped in the foyer, the lights went out, the fan stopped working, and the door remained locked. The foyer was crowded and noisy. Despite our banging, no one noticed because all the other lifts were working. There was no escape hatch in the enclosed metal cage and no response to the emergency button (after all, it was Ramadan—no engineers). We managed to force a minute gap between the doors at the base in the hope of getting some air and attracting attention. However, it was a further twenty minutes before we were heard and subsequently released, by which time we were soaking wet with perspiration and more than a little short of oxygen. It convinced me that I would have to brush up on my German if I was to survive in the future. However, it took me a few months before I would get back in a lift, which probably improved my overall health because I negotiated many steps. The long-term effects of claustrophobia lingered on during my later years in London, especially during the rush hours on the Underground. A similar event occurred in City Hall, Westminster, some years later when we got stuck between floors. I knew that we would be extracted eventually, but it was still a fairly traumatic time!

January 1981 saw Ronald Reagan succeed Jimmy Carter as US president, and in March the first London Marathon attracted 7,500 runners. There were contrasting events in early summer. The Israeli Air Force destroyed Iraq's Osirak nuclear reactor in June, and at home the following month, we had riots in Toxteth, Liverpool, Moss Side in Manchester, and Chapeltown in Leeds. This was in stark contrast to the jubilation surrounding the royal wedding of Prince Charles and Diana in London, which was watched by a TV audience estimated at over 780 million. But for me, one of the saddest items of news was to learn in October of the assassination of Anwar Sadat, who had steered Egypt through many difficult years in the Middle East since taking over from Nassar and attempted to stabilise relations with Israel. He was of course replaced that month by Hosni Mubarak, who ruled Egypt until his overthrow in the Spring Revolution of 2011–2012.

CHAPTER 9

Keepers of the Peace

We may be likened to two Scorpions in a bottle, each capable
of killing the other, but only at the risk of his own life.
US Foreign Affairs Journal

In May 1981 I attended the Joint Services Movements Staff Course,
in the Empress State Building in London, prior to taking up my
appointment as the command movements officer at the Joint
Headquarters of British Forces in Germany. The motto of the RAF in
Germany was aptly titled "Keepers of the Peace" and was a continuous
reminder to us all of the reason why we were in this part of Europe
and the role that we were all committed to maintain: the prevention of
the spread of communism and the dominant threat of the Warsaw Pact
countries to peace in the West.

Joint Headquarters Rheindahlen—Germany

I arrived at JHQ Rheindahlen, near Dusseldorf, in July to start
my German language training. In my new appointment, I had
responsibility for all land, sea, and air movements in conjunction with
my army counterpart. Having to work closely with other nations, and
in particular with our German hosts, I first had to undertake language
training. For the next three months, I underwent intensive training
in colloquial German on a full-time basis. (I could have done with

this before I went to Tunisia!) There were eight of us on the course, including two civilians destined to be linguists, and throughout the day we had to immerse ourselves in German. The two German frau linguists would not entertain us speaking in English at any stage, so it was quite a struggle but was inevitably the best way to adapt to learning a language in a short period of time. In the initial stages, we each had to tell a well-known story in German. I chose Red Riding Hood. I could have chosen Hansel and Gretel, but I wasn't sure that would have been appropriate. The fraus had never heard the story and were convinced I was making it up; after all, who had ever heard of a wolf in bed?

I found the technical aspects of the language, and in particular the military aspects, difficult to absorb. It almost seemed that joining words together into a lengthy single word was the predominant way of describing technical aspects in German. For example, Gebrauchsanweisung meaning operating manual, and Hochfrequenzlantsprecher meaning Tweeter. However, I survived the course to gain my diploma in colloquial German. Had I failed, I would have had to return to the UK and another job, added to which it would hardly have done my career or my pride much good.

As I neared the end of the course, Sheila joined me in Germany, and we moved into a house in the village of Waldniel. I wasn't long in the job before UK Director of Movements Alf Beil decided to visit Germany, and I had the task of escorting him around the "Parish", including a trip into Berlin by the military train and a visit to East Berlin. Since the end of World War II, except for the period of the Berlin Airlift, this train had travelled every day (including Christmas Day) between Hannover and Berlin and was a crucial means of maintaining our rights to travel to and from Berlin, which the East Germans, through the Russians, had always challenged. The rail link, operated by the Royal Corp of Transport, ran from Hannover through Helmstedt on the West German Border, to Magdeburg in East Germany, where the engines were changed before the train arrived in Berlin. Like most visitors, Alf found the visit to Berlin both interesting and informative, and he could see for himself what life was like the other side of the Berlin Wall. The Russians and the East Germans, both civilian and military, were always close at hand; it was the usual cat-and-mouse game.

At this stage, Jane and Julie were working in the UK. Jane had started nursing in London, and Julie had a job in the accounts department of Fenwick's in Brent Cross. Jonathan was still at Fyling Hall School. Julie came out to Germany for a brief visit at the time we moved into Waldniel, saying that she had decided to take up nursing at St Mary's Hospital in London. She started during 1982, shortly before the birth of Prince William. However, in the intervening period, she stayed with us enjoying the social life and playing hockey for the Rheindahlen team.

The Falklands War

This was the year the Falklands war took place, initially when on 19 March 1982 a contingent of Argentinian military invaded and occupied South Georgia. By the beginning of the following month, a much larger force overwhelmed the small contingent of marines and took over the Falkland Islands. Whilst not involved in the overall detail of contingency planning, I found myself travelling back to MOD, the planners having decided that some of the Harrier aircraft in Germany would replace the RN Harrier aircraft departing for the Falklands as part of the RN task force, which had departed from Southampton. The overall concept of sending a task force across the world to fight the Argentinians was astounding, but by the end of April, Britain had declared a two-hundred-mile exclusion zone around the Falklands, and Royal Marines had recaptured South Georgia. The nuclear submarine HMS *Conqueror* sank the Argentine Cruiser *General Belgrano* in May, and the rest, as they say, is history.

By 14 June, after seventy-four days, Britain had defeated a much larger army against all odds and retaken the islands. However, in all the glory, I do recall one very depressing day. I was in the MOD in Whitehall for a briefing when we received news that the *Atlantic Conveyor*, a requisitioned hybrid container ship crewed by the merchant navy, had been destroyed through enemy action. The ship was hit by Exocet missiles fired from Argentinian Super Etendard jet fighters in the close vicinity of the Falkland Islands. (French missiles fired from French-built aircraft). Although by the time of the attack the eight Sea Harriers and our six RAF GR3s had been transferred to the aircraft carriers, four of the five RAF Chinook heavy-lift helicopters, six RN Wessex, plus essential radar, reserve aviation fuel, and a large quantity of ammunition had been destroyed. The loss of the Chinooks had a massive impact and gave rise to the historic yomp of British forces across the Falklands to seize Port Stanley and end the war; it is recognised and respected even to this day as an historic military feat. As a matter of interest, and a fact not widely appreciated, Prince Andrew played a significant role in the war. He was the pilot of the Wessex that rescued crew members from the stricken ship and later flew his aircraft in a decoy role against incoming Exocet missiles.

At home, the IRA kept up their attacks on mainline Britain with bombs in Hyde Park. Despite these distractions and the heavy commitment in the Falklands, the focus of attention remained on the Central Front and the threat posed by the Soviets. It was therefore important that the contingency plans associated with this area were continually updated. Planning for Exercise Lionheart, the major exercise scheduled for later in 1982, was well underway at the Joint Headquarters at Rheindahlen. As the guardians of the lines of communication, vital for the resupply of the front-line forces in a time of conflict, it was important that we examine all the possible options working both with armed services of the other nations involved and the host nations. Our first task was to visit and check on all the ports bordering the North Sea, large and small, from Belgium through the Netherlands and to the Danish German border. It was interesting to note that even in the smallest fishing port, there always seemed to be a Russian or Polish trawler—often bristling with aerials! As we moved up the coast and across the Zuider Zee towards Bremen, more were in evidence.

The next task was to look at the road and rail infrastructure. Although that was primarily the responsibility of the host nation, we still had to satisfy ourselves that they met every eventuality—for example, roads having the capability of providing emergency aircraft landing strips without disrupting resupply. There was still much to do in the coming months not only on our part but in the many organisations at every level to ensure that Lionheart, both in the UK and on the continent, was a success.

QBAL Planning

In the months that followed, as well as monitoring the work of the movement's activity across the command in Europe, I was heavily involved in the Quadripartite Berlin Airlift (QBAL) contingency planning, especially in looking at the role the French would be playing with their 747 aircraft in the future and fitting them into the overall flight paths. QBAL was comprised of the air forces of the UK, France, and the United States, with the ground support organisation being provided by the West Germans. The aim was to resupply Berlin should the Soviets ever again close the road and rail links to Berlin through East Germany. With a mixture in the various aircraft of the three nations, a new factor was emerging: the flight separation times between the aircraft using the corridors into and out of Berlin. The jet vortex and the air turbulence produced by heavier modern jet transport aircraft created handling problems for following aircraft. This meant we had to look at the impact of either greater separation between aircraft flying at the same altitude or look at ways to adjust altitude. Second, the much greater capacity of these aircraft meant that different ground handling techniques and equipment had to be considered and provided to meet any possible contingency. I had been tasked by the USAF air commander, Major General Overacker, in leading a small team to work out the solution to this problem. It was not an easy task, and it took us well into 1983 before we came up with the solution.

Each year we had a QBAL planning meeting spread over a week and hosted by each nation in turn. In 1982 it was in Paris; in 1983 it was in Charleston, South Carolina; and in 1984 it was in London. The last one in 1985, my swan song, was in Frankfurt, where to the horror of the Germans and the amusement of the Americans, I gave my farewell speech in German. I had never revealed the fact that I understood what the Germans were discussing over the years, which helped in our negotiations and our diplomacy—at least up until that point!

Jane's Wedding and the Aftermath

In our absence, our eldest daughter, Jane, had planned her wedding to Kevin to be held in Brize Norton Village in Oxfordshire, this being the home of Kevin's parents and the major RAF air transport base. But there was still the reception for about one hundred guests to be organised, which we arranged to be held in the hotel at RAF Brize Norton. By courtesy of HM customs, I purchased the champagne in Berlin, and we brought it back by road, a rather cluttered car loaded to the gunnels. Sheila had a girl in her class whose father, a warrant officer in the catering branch, had made the cake for the wedding of one of the royals. With a little pressure and financial reward, a wonderful wedding cake was produced and travelled from Germany in Sheila's car. Our decision to use the facilities at Brize Norton was because the hotel had plenty of accommodation at affordable rates and excellent catering facilities. It also offered secure surroundings— particularly important with the IRA targeting military personnel and organisations. It had an added advantage which made the reception unique. The evening following the reception, we gathered in the bar to meet and greet the first of the troops flying back from the Falklands in the early hours of the morning. After the wedding, Sheila, Julie, Jonathan, and I headed off for a week's recovery in the Lake District, walking, visiting every lake in the district, and chilling out.

We had planned for Sheila's father to fly out to join us for Christmas from Luton. A taxi was arranged to pick him up from Grimsby, and a seat was booked on a charter flight three days before Christmas from Luton to RAF Wildenwrath in Germany, where we were due to collect him. I will always remember waiting in the terminal and seeing everyone off the aircraft, but there was no Jack Holland—he wasn't even on the passenger manifest. Sheila was somewhat distressed, to say the least. I telephoned the police in Lincolnshire, and after some searching they confirmed that in the early hours of the morning they had received a report of a car buried in a snowdrift south of Lincoln;

the only reason they found it was because the lights were still on. They also said that it was Sheila's father, and they had recovered his car by transporter and taken him home to Waltham in Lincolnshire, where he lived. He was OK apart from hyperthermia and confusion. Confusion, all right—he shouldn't have been in his car, but in the taxi we had arranged and paid for! I immediately set off from Germany by car and motored up to Waltham. I wrapped him in blankets and journeyed back via Dover and Ostend. This was Christmas Eve and a round journey of some twenty-two hours. Jane was also due to travel out by bus, and I called her and arranged for her to meet me in Dover.

Once New Year's was over, Sheila and I talked about the difficulty we faced, especially because it was apparent that either old age or dementia had taken its toll of her father. Jack wouldn't contemplate living in Germany, his experiences of the First World War having completely coloured his views of Germany and the Germans; nothing was going to change that. We agreed that we would have to resolve this problem and quickly, so we travelled back to the UK, found a lovely retirement home for him in Louth where he soon settled, and then returned to our commitments in Germany.

By this time, we had moved into married quarters at Rheindahlen. Sheila had returned to teaching. Jonathon, who had completed his O levels in the UK, was now at the Sixth Form College at Rheindahlen working on his A levels. We started working on a fitness programme, and Sheila joined me on early morning runs before the working day started. It wasn't long before she was setting her own routes and timings, although I couldn't convince her to join me over a longer distance. I turned my attention to Jonathan, who by this time had joined me on the Hash House Harrier (H3) runs every week, and on weekends we would frequently compete in long-distance runs in the Ardennes. I was extremely proud when we finished equal first in one of the half marathons, not so much from my perspective but knowing that Jonathan was turning into a good runner. Besides which, you always take greater satisfaction from the achievements of your children and those who follow than your own.

Later in 1983, Sheila and I went to Paris for a short break with Tom, Sheila's headmaster, and Beryl, his wife. It was just what the doctor ordered, a most relaxing break from the hustle and bustle of military life, working around the clock, and teaching in Germany. We also managed to fit in short breaks with Frank and Margaret Stainer, who, after their sojourn in the Falklands, had moved to Darmstadt near Frankfort in Germany, where Frank was working with the European Space Agency. It gave me the opportunity to sit in the operations room and watch the monitoring of satellites, which is quite relaxing when you are not associated with the project! During our time in Germany, we had many cruises down the Rhine and experienced Oktoberfest in Munich, which was similar to that in the north of Germany, but I would guesstimate that it involved drinking a far more substantial amount of beer. In October 1983, we decided to throw a party in the officers' mess at Rheindahlen to celebrate our silver wedding, to which we invited over 150 of our friends and relatives, many of whom flew out from the UK.

My penultimate year in Germany, 1984, saw me involved with others in planning the next major QBAL exercise, Starting Gate VIII, held in Hannover and Berlin during May and aimed at testing the support of Berlin by air. Throughout 1984, we were also heavily involved in what was destined to be the largest military exercise since the end of World War II. Code-named Lionheart, it was one of a series designed to test the military lines of communication across Europe in support of NATO on the Central Front. Lionheart, which ran from 3 September to 5 October, cost the UK over £30 million and involved 131,000 troops. It saw the deployment of 40,000 territorial army, 17,000 regular troops, and 13,000 airmen from the United Kingdom. During our preliminary planning phase, we toured across the top of Europe from France in the west to Germany and Denmark in the east to examine potential port facilities. Even in the smallest of fishing ports, it was not unusual to see trawlers or similar small cargo vessels flying Eastern European or Soviet flags, bristling with aerials. It wasn't difficult to see what they were there for, and it certainly wasn't fishing.

Berlin, London, and Other Major Marathons

As I mentioned earlier, I had been participating in several 25K and 40K runs in Holland, Germany, and Belgium. Frequently I went with Jonathan, but it was always a conflict on a Sunday morning when clearly his priority was to remain in bed! One success I did have—and it was nothing to do with running—was to accumulate six strikes in a row in ten-pin bowling competitions. For the uninitiated, this is the equivalent of a bowler taking two successive hat-tricks in cricket. Well, that's my rather biased view! I still have the badge to this day. Isn't it sad when you become an anorak? Talking of anoraks, I had by this time taken over the Hash House Harriers as chairman, secretary, and organiser of this multinational group of individuals, and before we left Germany, I had recorded my one hundredth run and Jonathan his fiftieth. Having also been involved in football over many years, including having been chairman of the disciplinary committee and a representative on the FA Council, I was also invited to take over the role of chairman of RAF Germany football when I first arrived in Germany. Clearly there was little time outside work and sport. It was a good thing, in many ways, that Sheila was fully involved in the demands of teaching.

One thing I always wanted to do was to compete in a major marathon. I had finished equal first in the Ramsey, Isle of Man, Marathon in 1959, my first and only previous attempt, but I'd never participated in a major race in Europe. I had my first opportunity in Berlin on Sunday, 25 September 1983. It was a hard run, with officials on hand to pull you out of the race if you fell behind your estimated running time. I was extremely glad that I hadn't stated a time I was not capable of achieving, but their ominous presence pushed me to my limits. Encouraged by the ever-present crowd and overlooked by the East German guards in their goon towers, I had every incentive to keep going. I completed the course in a time of 2:51:34, which I've rarely managed to better. Maybe the answer is that I should always perform under threat!

The day-to-day responsibilities of running our movements' responsibilities across Europe continued despite these heavy additional tasks. However, I still found time to return to the UK and run in the London Marathon for the first time. Isn't it amazing that everyone who has run a marathon says that it is fantastic and uplifting and leaves you with a feeling of great achievement? Looking back on my first marathon in the Isle of Man, and then in Berlin, there is no way I would describe it as that—but I would stress that's looking back! But isn't it strange that nobody seems to recall the pain, the burning blisters, and the utter exhaustion of running 26.2 miles as the reserves of carbohydrates run out and you hit the preverbal wall, leaving the remaining 5 to 6 miles to be completed in a zombielike stupor? Also, isn't it odd that until the 1948 Olympics, where changes were made to accommodate the distance from Windsor to Wembley, it used to be 25 miles? What's the problem? It's only another 1.2 miles. Well, try telling that to anyone who has reached the 25-mile points and is almost walking backwards! Whatever the mileage, the body is not adapted to this form of torture, a mileage more suitable to a car driver than a runner. Nevertheless, over the years I've found myself being what one might describe as a masochist, having completed no less than twenty-five full marathons in my dotage. I always recall the great Czech Olympian Emil Zatopek, who said, "We are different, in essence, from other men. If you want to win something, run 100 meters. If you want to experience something, run a marathon."

Whilst on the subject of records, and for no particular reason apart from national pride, this was the year that Richard Noble of the UK set up a new world land speed record of 633.4 miles per hour in his car Thrust 2 in Nevada. It was in 1997 that another Briton, Andy Green, a serving RAF officer, was the first to go through the sound barrier at ground level, driving Thrust SSC and setting a new world record of 763 miles per hour. Turning the clock forward to 2018, after years of preparation, Andy Green and team are set to take the new car, Bloodhound SSC, which has been several years in the making, to a specially prepared part of the South African desert at Hakskeen Pan to attempt to raise the world record to 1,000 miles per hour.

This new vehicle, the most complicated car ever built, is powered by a Rolls Royce EJ 200 engine developing 135,000 brake horsepower and assisted by a rocket engine, with the potential of getting the car to reach 1,000 miles per hour, or a mile in 3.6 seconds (Mach 1.4). What are the limits to man's abilities?

The Enemy Within—The Government's Fight with the Unions

At home, the focus of attention was on the power struggle being launched by the unions against the Thatcher government and the miners' strike. It should be remembered that Margaret Thatcher and the Tory party had won the national election in 1983 with a majority of 144 seats—a significant degree of national support. In 1984, the National Union of Miners was one of the strongest unions in the country, having brought down the Heath government in 1974 and hell-bent, under their communist union leader Arthur Scargill, in flexing their muscles to an unacceptable degree. The mining industry had been nationalised by Atlee in 1947, but by the 1980s most of the mines were unprofitable, and the government wanted to stop this haemorrhage and close these pits. In 1982, the NUM had succeeded in winning a 20 per cent increase in wages; by 1984 they were demanding a further 30 per cent increase, a fact often overlooked by the public of today. Confrontation between the new chairman of the Coal Board and Arthur Scargill, the leader of the miners, came to a head when, on 12 March, Scargill announced a national strike without first having carried out a ballot. This caused a split with some miners forming their own union, the Democratic Union of Miners (UDM).

The government had no hesitation in taking on Scargill. It was a defining moment in British industrial relations, and although the strike dragged on, the union soon ran out of money and the miners had no income. Inevitably, despite the serious incidents arising through the strike, many workers drifted back to work. Never again would the government be held ransom at the hands of a few. The impact of the strike led to stockpiling of coal at power stations, a switch from coal to electricity and gas, trains being converted to electricity and diesel, and homes being converted to electricity and gas. Of the 176 pits, only six were left by the end of 2009. Despite the inevitable bitterness at the poverty created, Scargill lost a lot of support when he turned to the Soviets and the Libyans for financial support, the latter being particularly unacceptable after the death of PC Yvonne Fletcher outside the Libyan embassy in London in April.

Berlin and East Germany

By November 1984, a new director of movements, Bryan Hughes, had been appointed in MOD, and I found myself once more heading around the circuit to give him an overview of our commitments in Europe and how we were meeting these. Inevitably, this involved yet another journey to Berlin through East Germany, something that I had done many times already in my short time in Germany. But on some occasions, such as this with military police escort, I was inevitably followed by the gentlemen in suits and no doubt others taking photographs from a number of grubby windows. I don't know why they bothered because I'm sure that they were obtaining all they wanted through the leaks in our Foreign Office security. As we passed the many long food queues in East Berlin, I promised myself that I would bring Sheila across to East Berlin before we finished our tour in Germany to give her the opportunity to see the contrast between East and West. But strangely enough, when I suggested to the children that they might like the experience of travelling to Berlin, none of them seemed interested in taking up the offer. In retrospect, I think they regretted not doing so.

On 4 February 1985, knowing that I would soon be leaving Germany, I arranged to travel up to Berlin to take Sheila on a tour of the city and meet up with British, American, and French colleagues. This time I was keen to make the journey by road, travelling up through the corridor from Checkpoint Alpha. At Helmstedt we received our briefing on timings and were reminded of the need to avoid contact or any incident with the East German locals or the Russians whilst en route. Transit times had to be adhered to, so there was no stopping unless in an emergency. Towns and villages that we passed in Eastern

Germany often seemed devoid of people or shops, and there was little sign of mechanical transport apart from heavy trucks, tractors, and buses; rare was sighting a car, and those we saw were the traditional East German Trabant, a car that was a virtual antique at the time it was designed. The Trabant was the East German answer to the VW Beetle. However, it wasn't in the same class. It had a body made from fibreglass, like Duroplast, a recycled and reenforced material with fibres like cotton mixed with wood. Its air-cooled, two-stroke engine was most inefficient, and thought it could reach a top speed of seventy miles per hour, it had a mediocre performance and smoked like an Iraqi oil fire. It had no brake lights or indicators and was indeed a joke of a car. Incidentally, its name in German means satellite or companion, inspired by the Russian Sputnik. It should have been launched into space and left there!

Apart from the distinct lack of humanity, the remainder of the journey was uneventful until we reached the Russian checkpoint, where I had to present my documents. I first had to exchange salutes with the guard, a matter of international courtesy. He was a very nervous conscript soldier who I'm sure had not seen many relatively senior officers; as we understood, the guards were not allowed to remain in any post for too long for obvious reasons. Within the building, there were no signs of human habitation, just a few chairs and a hole in the wall, behind which there was no doubt some activity on the fax machines! The walls were adorned with the large photographs of Lenin and Leonid Brezhnev, but none of Stalin (understandably) and none of them leader Konstantin Chernenko. I wondered if that was indicative of the changes that were about to take place with Mikhail Gorbachev's rise to power two months later. A hand appeared through the small slit in the wall indicating that I should hand over my documents, and after a wait of about twenty minutes, during which I'm sure the details were transmitted to other parts of the organisation ahead of my arrival, I rejoined the car, in which sat a very worried Sheila. I must say that during my wait I didn't feel particularly sanguine and wondered if this would be commented on when I duly arrive at checkpoint Bravo at Dreilinden. However, we arrived without further ado and spent the night in the United States officers' mess at Tempelhof.

The following day, I took Sheila with me to the Berlin Air Safety Centre, where she met her first real Russian, the major who was on duty with his KGB minder (or was it watcher?). The day after that, we went through checkpoint Charlie on the junction of Friedrichstrasse and Zimmersrasse, the single crossing point into East Berlin, with our military police escort. We soon picked up our usual followers, who stayed a discreet distance behind, but their photographers didn't have the same inhibitions or perhaps the same masters. That's what was fascinating about Berlin and the Cold War: it was all a game of cat and mouse. I took Sheila to visit the remains of Hitler's bunker, the Reichstag, the opera house, and the Russian war memorial, amongst other sites. Many years later, when I was doing a cruise in the Baltic, I returned to Berlin, my first visit since the wall had come down; but more about that later. Sheila couldn't believe her eyes. The bomb-damaged buildings, augmented by many high-rise, featureless blocks of flats clearly developed in the post-war era, presented a very dismal setting. It was made even more depressing by sight of the long early morning queues for bread, meat, and vegetables—a stark contrast to the affluence of the Kurfurstendam (the Oxford Street of West Berlin), with its colourful shops and pavement cafes.

The RAF Band Tragedy

We were coming towards the end of our tour in Germany when, in February, we were invited to join friends at the RAF Winter Survival School in the Bavarian village of Bad Kohlgrub for a few days of skiing. The RAF band was due to travel down to play at the ceremony marking the thirtieth year of the school's existence. We had been skiing on the slopes above the village when word came through that the RAF band from Rheindahlen had been involved in a crash on the autobahn at a place called Langenbruck, near Stuttgart. When we got back, we were met with the dreadful news that eighteen of the band, one RAF policeman, and the driver had died in a sea of flames, and the remaining nineteen had been injured. The double-decker bus carrying the forty passengers had crashed into a fuel tanker carrying nine thousand gallons of aviation fuel. It appeared that the bus skidded on fuel leaking from the tanker and immediately burst into flames.

Not only was it tragic, but it was also very distressing because we knew many of the bandsmen from RAF Rheindahlen, including their director of music, Squadron Leader Robin Tomsett. In the days that followed, celebrations were cancelled and replaced with a memorial service arranged in the local village church, following which we all returned to Rheindahlen in a very gloomy state.

CHAPTER 10

Farewell to Arms

Don't cry because it's over, smile because it happened
Dr Seuss

The year 1985 arrived with a feeling of disappointment. Promotions are normally announced on 1 January, and yet again there was nothing to indicate any advancement for me. It was eleven years to the day since I had been promoted to wing commander, and here I was at the age of forty-nine with nothing but promises. It was not that I'd set my expectations too high, because I had been the recipient of six "Special Recommendations" and eight "Highly Recommended" assessments for promotion—extracts of which I've kept to this day, having obtained the details in 2009 through the Access to Information Act. It seemed that because of cutbacks in the RAF, and because of the age bracket, I was now in the wrong place and at the wrong time in a highly competitive environment over which I had no control. If, as some very senior officers had said, I had potential for high office, then I felt I needed to move into a commercial environment where I could prove it in open competition, rather than remain in the RAF until the age of fifty-five, become disillusioned with life, and reflect on what might have been.

I had thoroughly enjoyed my service career, and I was indebted for the experience I had gained over the years, but I had no wish to let my career limitations affect this view. On returning to the UK in February

1985, I decided to apply for premature voluntary release (PRV). Even this was not as easy as it might appear because quotas were applied to the release of officers with specialist experience, added to which there was a waiting list. However, I eventually managed to persuade the Ministry of Defence to release me on 1 August. This meant that if I waived my entitlement to terminal leave and the training for civilian life that was part of the agreement, I would be able to start work on 1 June. In the meanwhile, I took on the appointment of head of aero engine management for the three services: RAF, RN, and Army. We were based at the Ministry of Defence procurement establishment in the windy town of Harrogate, North Yorkshire.

On my final day in the office in Harrogate, I had farewell drinks with my staff in a local hostelry at lunch time and returned to the office. I couldn't help feeling that this was not a very satisfactory conclusion to a long and active career, in which I believed I had made many contributions in commitments to the service as opposed to the family. But on the bright side, I was off on the start of another career. While packing my papers and metaphorically clearing my desk, I heard noises outside, and on looking out of the window, I saw a Rolls Royce limo parked with the number plate KGB 1. A beautiful Cossack girl was in the rear seat supping champagne, and the music blared, "I did it my way!" My brother-in-law, having been told by the senior commanders at Harrogate that no farewell arrangements were normally acceptable, decided I was not leaving without due recognition. He was of the view that it was disgraceful that after thirty years in the RAF, my departure was not to be marked—his comments, not mine. Inevitably, there are those within one's career, whatever that might be, who are better defined as job worthies rather than risk takers. Unfortunately, I found that there were a few at Harrogate who fell into this former category. Dave had therefore made his own arrangements. I suppose as an ex-RAF man, he was doing what he does best: putting two fingers up to authority. In addition to this spectacular send-off, Dave had arranged a farewell party for family and friends in Harrogate, which turned a sad day into one I shall always remember with gratitude.

Before the date of my departure from the RAF, I had been offered a job with British Caledonian Airways at Gatwick. Although tempted, I didn't regard this as the right career move; it was simply switching one uniform for another. Other job applications and some interviews came and went, and I began to realise that making the transition was not going to be an easy task. Added to which, many potential employers had an outdated concept of what life in the services was all about; in some instances, it was almost the Colonel Blimp concept. I didn't even get to the interview stage for secretary of a small local golf club in Yorkshire; they considered I wouldn't have sufficient commercial experience. Boy, did they do me a favour!

City of Westminster

It was at this time that Sheila and I spent the weekend with my brother and his wife, Sue, in Leeds. On Sunday afternoon after a splendid lunch and a few drinks (probably too many), we sat down and trawled through the newspapers for job adverts and even sent off an application for the post of director of planning and transportation in London, which appeared as a centre-page advertisement in that morning's copy of the *Times*. It was a rather flippant gesture and one to which I did not expect to receive a response. But life is full of funny quirks, and the truth is you never know what results from one's actions. Two weeks later, I was invited down to London for an interview with the chief executive of the city of Westminster. It seemed to go well, but I had no great expectations. I was told that they were looking for a chief of staff who could pull together the five rather diverse divisions within the organisation: planning and development, transportation, works and highways, the management of car parking operations in London, and information technology.

Within three weeks, I was summoned down to London again, this time to be interviewed by the politicians. The journey down from Harrogate was a bit of a disaster: the train was almost an hour late, further delays occurred on the Underground, and the day of my arrival coincided with a Royal Garden Party in Buckingham Palace. I caught a taxi in the hopes that I would reach City Hall in Victoria before everyone had gone home. The driver unfortunately was one of those nonstop moaners, complaining about everyone and everything—congestion, the state of the economy in London, unsightly new buildings, bus lanes, estate agent's boards, conditions of the roads and pavements, lack of control in car parking, no consultation with the public. You name it; he covered it. We would normally have travelled to Victoria via the Mall but that was closed due to the Garden Party at Buckingham Palace, and of course he added that to his list of complaints. By the time we arrived at City Hall, I was almost two hours late for the interview and suffering from a severe bout of tinnitus, defined as "the perception of sound within the human ear in the absence of corresponding external sound", caused by the taxi driver's diatribe. The only difference was that I knew I had been on the receiving end of an ear bashing.

On arrival, I was whisked into the interview, apologising for my late attendance. The panel was headed by the leader of the council, Shirley Porter, daughter of the Tesco family and later to become Lady Porter, as well as six local government politicians and the chief executive. Shirley led off with the first question by asking how I would set about reshaping the centre of London. It was the obvious question which I should have anticipated and hadn't! Well, there are two possible solutions in such a position: call it a day and walk out or talk your way out of an embarrassing situation. One thing that had been inculcated into me throughout my service life was to stay calm in a crisis. Thinking of my recent experience from my taxi ride, I related and embellished on its details. I concluded by saying, "In essence, you shouldn't be interviewing me for the job. You should be employing the taxi driver. He knows all the problems, and he's got all the answers!" After the laughter died down, I was asked a few routine questions, and the brief interview was over. *Another interview blown,* I thought.

Having arrived back in Harrogate at about 11 p.m. that night, Sheila told me that the chief executive at Westminster had telephoned, and I was to call back. I was surprised that there was anyone there at that time of night. Little did I know that this was to become the norm. The chief executive informed me that they had agreed to my appointment and that the decision was unanimous. I had serious doubts about my ability to carry out the job, but Sheila proffered what later turned out to be excellent advice. She said that they must have seen qualities in me that they wanted and, if in the months ahead I felt out of my depth, I could always leave and find another job. Thus, started a new career, a new beginning, and a return to work in London.

I arrived at Westminster on 1 June, one month before I had officially left the RAF. Shortly after my start, Shirley Porter told me that she thought my analogy of the taxi driver aptly described many things that needed to be done in London. I told her it was genuine and that I hadn't invented the story, but she didn't believe me. Over the months that followed, I found her to be extremely forthright and at times somewhat of a bully if one allowed her to be so. Like all bullies, whilst wanting to dominate, she would at times respect those who stood their ground to some extent. I certainly don't accept bullies, so for the rest of my time at Westminster, however uncomfortable confrontation became, I stood my ground, particularly on matters of importance—which was not always favourably received, especially by politicians of that ilk.

After having stayed in Bolney, a small village in Sussex, with friends from our days in the RAF, we set about looking for a house not too far from London, preferably in the Hayward's Heath region of Sussex. We eventually settled on a property in Gander Green, a pleasant location on the outskirts of the town, within walking distance of the railway station. It was a 1950s detached three-bedroom house and needed some updating, but it had a massive and well-cultivated garden. We set to work on the improvements, and except for the extension, we did all the work ourselves in whatever spare time we had—building new fireplaces, replacing doors and building archways, plumbing, tiling, painting, decorating, and replanting, restocking, and maintaining a massive garden. All of this increased the value of the house by almost 50 per cent at the height of the property boom, although this wasn't our aim; we simply wanted a house we would enjoy when we finally retired. Certainly, it was one of the best investments we made, but the work left us shattered, especially after the long days in London.

It was during this time that Sheila suffered the trauma of a slipped disc whilst getting out of her car, which left her with a distinct lack of mobility for many weeks, following which she had to undergo an operation in Haywards Heath Hospital. Julie was living at home and was working in one of the local hospitals near Haywards Heath, and Jonathan had started at North Staffordshire University in September 1984. In his time down from university, he worked in Haywards Heath in a perfume factory (much to the satisfaction of his sisters) and in a local restaurant (more to the satisfaction of his parents, although I didn't experience much in the way of discounts).

My working life at Westminster began during the summer of 1985. As a new boy on the block, the first thing I did was to call in the union reps for a breakfast meeting. We ironed out a few minor problems, and I told them that my door was always open. They were highly suspicious, not having had that sort of contact in the past, but after two such meetings I never had a problem in relationships with the unions thereafter, not even when we moved to privatisation at a later stage. This was another essential lesson from service life: leadership and good communications are essential but all too often lacking in the commercial and services sector. There were, however, several changes that I had to manage within my disparate divisions and a few manning problems that I had resolve. The remainder of the year was spent adjusting the organisation whilst improving the service.

The event that was to have a direct impact on my future came with the passing of the Local Government Act of 1986, which gave rise to the abolition of the GLC under Ken Livingstone. In the years prior to my joining Westminster, a clash of ideologies had arisen because of the antics of the leader of the Greater London Council, Ken Livingstone (or Red Ken as he would become known), and the Conservative government of Margaret Thatcher. It was the "cut and save" philosophy of Thatcherism versus the "high tax and high spend" of Marxist socialism as defined by Livingstone—free enterprise and privatisation against high taxes and union involvement. Livingstone went out of his way to deliberately antagonise Thatcher in his anti-government propaganda, using government subsidies to reduce bus and underground fares and meeting with IRA and Libyan terrorist leaders. In an effort to contain Ken's extravagance, the government reduced and then abolished the GLC's grant as a punishment. In retaliation, Ken decided to reduce the fares on the Underground and bus network, and to raise a local tax of £117.3 million to cover the shortfall, 20 per cent of which would come from the city of Westminster. Consequently, the government argued for the abolition of the GLC, which had now become a thorn in its side, and on 31 March 1986 the Local Government Act was passed abolishing the GLC. Its powers were devolved to the boroughs.

As a politician, Shirley Porter wanted to emulate Margaret Thatcher. There were comparisons between the two women. Both had centres of power in Westminster, both were daughters of grocers, both married successful businessmen, and both were bossy and at times strident. Yet they were as different as chalk and cheese. Whereas Margaret Thatcher was always on top of her subject and led by example, Shirley Porter was renowned as having a butterfly mind and an excessively dominant attitude. What they did share was contempt for bureaucracy. Shirley was hell-bent on two things: in following her father's doctrine in introducing one-stop services for the benefit of customers and residents, and in maximising efficiencies to the extent of moving some services into the private sector. Each week, every director and senior staff had to spend at least one day on the shop floor, an area which combined the activities of all the city's departments, dealing with customers. In pursuing these and other doctrines, she was absolutely ruthless. But I have to say that putting the customer first was one of her major successes.

Bearing in mind Shirley Porter's determination to cut costs, she had accepted the transfer of these responsibilities without an increase in central funding. From my perspective, this meant that our department had to assume the devolved responsibilities for bridges, highways, and underpasses; building control; street naming and numbering, and road safety, along with the inherent overheads such as IT and administration. With over 220 miles of additional roads; 390 miles of footway, bridges, piers, and tunnels; and the relevant signage, this was a massive commitment. These tasks were absorbed without additional resources or additional funds in an almost impossible time scale. It wasn't long before other hidden costs became apparent with the discovery of blue asbestos in the lining of the Strand Underpass. Of such things, political dreams are made—or nightmares revealed!

During the latter part of 1986, the newly appointed managing director arrived to work under the chief executive. This was regarded as a political appointment to circumvent the opposition to some of the projects being proposed by Shirley. The most notable of these was the Home for Votes scandal, which duly led to the downfall of Shirley Porter and her being surcharged £36 million for what Lord Bingham was to describe as "a deliberate, blatant and dishonest misuse of public power for electoral advantage and it was corrupt" (Bingham 2001).

Privatisation—A Developing Concept

In March 1987, the MD gave me the task of devising and implementing privatisation reviews and setting each of the identified areas on a fully commercial basis. I completed the study recommending that two elements should be considered for privatisation, the first being cleansing and refuse and the second being parking operations. The incumbent directors of cleansing, headed by Paul Pinder, subsequently the chief executive of Capita, set up an in-house bid, and so launched the first successful privatisation in local government on 7 May 1987.

Seeing the way that the political situation was developing in Westminster and bearing in mind that decision made by officers as well as politicians could result in surcharging, I was not too sanguine with my position at Westminster. Added to which, I found myself servicing six different committees and having to attend public meetings, most of which were held after 6 p.m. at night. I often slept in the office, and this was becoming an intolerable burden on family life. I discussed it with Sheila, and we decided that we would buy a country house hotel in a decent location, run it for perhaps ten years, and then retire. Eventually, after much searching by Sheila (assisted by Julie), we settled on Purves Hall, a fourteen-bedroom hotel set on twelve acres of grounds in the Scottish Borders. A lovely location with clientele drawn in the main from corporate hospitality, shooting, hunting and fishing, and other field sports, as well as those who enjoyed the tranquillity of country life. However, the business was not sustainable without further growth or capital injection, and in the words of Shakespeare, "thereby hangs a tale".

In the meanwhile, following the review I had carried out into privatisation, I was caught between two stools. I was asked to stay on to see through the first privatisation in local government, but I also needed to be up at Purves Hall. I talked it over with Sheila, who thought it would be a good thing in the short term if I remained in London because it would provide us with the extra cash. She was prepared to soldier on by herself for a while, with the aid of Lesley Brown as her support manager (the daughter-in-law of the previous owners). Because of the successful privatisation, I was appointed as director of parking operations (the largest of its kind in the UK) with the aim of creating a fully commercial operation suitable for a second privatisation. Within the year, we had reduced operating costs by 50 per cent and increased net profits from £7 million to £17 million. We improved the image, quality, safety, and operation of the seventeen city-owned off-street garages without any increase in costs, and we renegotiated leases, further increasing income. Similar improvements in the on-street parking activity generated a further £3 million. On the downside, I was still commuting to and from Purves Hall each weekend, and Sheila was having to bear the brunt of running the hotel. She was not only the proprietor; she was also the chef (a proven and brilliant cook), manager, and general factotum—not my words but those of the guides and hotel inspectors. Amongst the accolades she gained was that of the prestigious Michelin Guide.

World Events, 1985–1987

> No matter how much we want things to stay the same, life
> is all about change.
> *Anon*

The year 1985 was one in which Ronald Regan became US president for a second term, being sworn in on 20 January. It was also the year that Gorbachev became general secretary of the Communist Party and thereby the new leader of the Soviet Union—a change that was to have a profound effect towards the end of the decade. At home, the miners' strike came to an end after a year. However, it was also a year in which social unrest and racial tension led to riots in Handsworth, Birmingham, and Broadwater Farm in London. Soccer faced one of its worst years with the Heysel Stadium disaster, a European football match in Belgium between Liverpool and Juventus, in which 39 spectators died and 600 were injured, and the Valley Parade ground, the home of Bradford City, where a flash fire killed 54 spectators.

The year 1986 was not a good one on the international scene or indeed on the British political scene. In the early part of January, both Defence Minister Michael Heseltine and Trade and Industry Secretary Leon Brittan resigned over the arguments surrounding the Westland Helicopter Company. In the same month, Space Shuttle *Challenger* disintegrated after launch, killing all seven of the crew on board. In Europe, the Single European Act was signed setting the EC objective of establishing a single market by the end of 1992. In the UK, 1986 was dominated by three or four key events: the marriage of Prince Andrew and Sarah Ferguson, the Wapping dispute, the Channel Tunnel plans, and the abolition of the Greater London Council.

The announcement was made in March that Prince Andrew and Sarah were to marry, and the wedding took place on 23 July 1986 in Westminster Abbey, watched by an estimated TV audience of over 500 million with thousands of people lining the route. The queen conferred the title of Duke of York on Prince Andrew just ninety minutes before the wedding—a title that is normally conferred on the second son of the monarch.

Confrontation between the union print workers and Robert Murdoch's News International, generating violence in Wapping, was yet another example of unions unable to drag themselves into the twenty-first century. The Wapping dispute following on similar lines to the miners' strike of 1984–1985 was a significant turning point in the history of UK unions. It started on 24 January when six thousand went on strike over changes within the printing and newspaper industry. It centred on the abolition of outdated practices and the introduction of new technology. The strike shared similarities with the miners' strike in that it lasted a year before collapsing in February 1987 for the same reasons, a year without wages. By 1988, all the national press had been removed from Fleet Street and relocated in Docklands.

In early 1986, Margaret Thatcher and Francois Mitterrand announced that contracts had been finalised for the construction of the Channel Tunnel linking Britain and France. Work on the tunnel was to start on 15 December 1987. The idea of such a tunnel was first explored by the French mining engineer Albert Mathieu, who formulated early designs for Napoleon in 1802. The first attempt to build the tunnel was made in 1880 but abandoned when the British military became concerned over national security. How do I know this? Well, when I did my officer training in the Isle of Man in 1957, I had to give a presentation on a provocative subject of interest, and I decided to talk about the feasibility of a tunnel under the channel and its impact on military thinking.

But perhaps the most significant and worrying event of all in 1986 was the Chernobyl disaster in Ukraine, the worst nuclear power plant accident in history, which was to have a pronounced effect on the future development and use of nuclear power as a source of energy. Also, politics and sport became entwined once more: thirty-two nations boycotted the Commonwealth Games held in Edinburgh because of the political situation in South Africa. In the soccer World Cup, Argentina beat England by a goal, which Diego Maradona clearly pushed in with his hand—an offence he gleefully admitted later as "the hand of God". And they say cheats don't prosper. Maybe we should have played the match in the Falklands!

The arrival of 1987 brought with it heavy snowfalls across the UK, leaving houses, roads, railways, and towns isolated and motor vehicles stranded. This was followed in October by a hurricane which hit the south-east, killing twenty-three and causing massive damage. Throughout the year, there were two disasters that shook the nation. On 6 March, the *Herald of Free Enterprise*, a roll-on, roll-off vehicle and passenger ferry belonging to Townsend Thorenson, capsized and sank half a mile off the Belgian coast. It had only just left the port of Zeebrugge on its return to Dover. The cause of the accident, which resulted in the deaths of 193 people trapped inside the stricken vessel, was later ascribed to two factors: the ship having sailed with the bow doors still open, and the poor design of the ship, which did not have damage control compartments. The second disaster was in November when a fire broke out on London Underground at a major interchange terminal at Kings Cross, resulting in the death of thirty-one people and injuries to sixty others.

In March the Provisional IRA, continuing their bombing activities, set off a bomb in Germany at the British headquarters in Rheindahlen, but the most significant atrocity occurred on 8 November during a Remembrance Day ceremony in Enniskillen, County Fermanagh, when eleven civilians were killed and sixty-three were injured. The remaining months of the decade saw increasing IRA activities, including the use of proxy bombing.

On the political front, Margaret Thatcher called an election on 11 May which the Conservatives won, and she was elected PM for the third time in June. That makes me wonder how the unions could honestly believe that the country was behind them and not the government of the day. In November, the government announced the controversial Poll Tax.

CHAPTER 11

Two Businesses—One Aim

If you're going through hell, keep going.
Winston Churchill

From a personal perspective, it was all beginning to happen in 1987. In April, Julie joined the Queen Alexander's Royal Army Nursing Corps as an officer cadet, graduating from Aldershot in June of that year. In May, Laura, our first grandchild, arrived on the day we had to motor up to take over Purvis Hall. In the June, Jonathan graduated from university just in time to help us with the hotel.

Purves Hall was the original home of Sir William Purves, the solicitor general of Scotland, and the old buildings date back to 1665. However, the new hall was built in the early nineteenth century. Situated in the Scottish Borders between Duns and Kelso, it is set in ten acres of wooded parkland and surrounded by secluded lawns and gardens. Facing south with panoramic views of the Cheviot Hills and reaching out into open countryside, it rests in what can only be described as idyllic rural countryside. Within the grounds are a walled garden, two paddocks and stabling for twelve horses, a swimming pool, and a hard court for tennis. It was only converted into a country house hotel in the mid-1970s.

We had arranged to take over the hotel on 16 May 1987, but unfortunately that was to be the very day that our first grandchild decided to enter the world. I was certainly not flavour of the month with Sheila or Jane, but we did get to see them for a few hours before we headed north. Our arrival was, for us, a frenetic introduction to the hotel and hospitality industry because two days after our arrival, a wedding reception had been arranged with a large marquee, seating some 150 guests, being erected on the lawns. Thankfully, Jonathan having graduated from university, was on hand, and together with friends and some locals, we helped quell the thirst of the many guests. Nevertheless, it was certainly a baptism under fire.

Within the first few months, it soon became apparent that our business plan for the hotel had been somewhat ambitious, and although it was sustainable over the longer period, it did not allow us to employ a full-time cook or assistant manager. Added to which, like many in business, we had not predicted the impending economic downturn. We decided that I would retain my job in London until a clearer picture emerged. To put it bluntly, in the changing economic uncertainty, we needed the extra money to keep the business solvent. I therefore began to commute each weekend whilst living weekdays in Watford with Jane and Kevin and now the new baby, Laura. I was relieved to know that Jonathan would be on hand to provide Sheila with some support, at least until the following year when he would leave to start at the military academy in Sandhurst. Vincent, a son of one of our friends, had also arrived to start training in hotel management under Sheila's watchful eye, as well as under our assistant manager, Lesley Brown.

Throughout our married life, Sheila had not only worked as a teacher, supported me in my many endeavours, and raised three wonderful children, but she had always found time to entertain friends and the many visitors that I would frequently impose on her, often at very short notice. Over the years, she had developed into an excellent and sociable cook, unlike those who bask in the limelight of television, and it wasn't long before her talents were recognised at the highest levels—Michelin, Johansen, Ashley Courtney, The Good Hotel Guide, and many other leading critiques. The following assessment given in 1990 summed up their assessments: "But the real reason for visiting Purves Hall is the food. Sheila Everett is a very talented cook. We ate superb dinners three nights running, the food was inventive, interesting and well-presented but not outlandish, the quality and freshness remarkable." Such inspections were totally unannounced and often unknown even after the event, but I'm delighted to see professional independent inspectors calling cooks by their proper name and not using the overrated title of chef. However, it wasn't just the food that attracted people but also the friendly, comfortable, and family atmosphere that Sheila had created.

During 1988, Jonathan had decided to follow his sister into the army. It must have been something I'd said in proffering advice when I'd suggested that he not follow his father into the RAF, as he had indicated that he was going to do, but he found himself a job first. So, what did he do? He joined the Royal Artillery. Well, I suppose it was the logical outcome because I had paid for his training in his early days—all that money fed into those Space Invader games in the Scarborough Arcade during weekend visits, where I'm sure he developed his missile attack schemes. We travelled south to join Jonathan as he graduated as a lieutenant from the Royal Academy at Sandhurst in August of 1988. It was a day of immense pride for me, with two of my brood having gained commissions from the Queen and the third well established in the nursing profession.

December 1988 ended on a tragic note with the blowing up of Pan Am Flight 103 over Lockerbie with the loss of 270 passengers, crew, and people on the ground. The impact of this reverberated for many years after the event and was certainly resurrected during the uprising in Libya during 2011–2012. Whether we will ever know the true extent of what happened or Gaddafi's role in the planning as revenge for the bombing of Libya by the United States is difficult to see.

After a short stint in the UK and Germany, Jonathan arrived in Cyprus as part of the UN peacekeeping force. In the meanwhile, Julie had been posted to Munster in Germany in 1988 as a captain in the QARNCs, where she was to meet Nigel. I must admit to a feeling of great pride in having seen all three children having started out on careers of their own choosing and achieved so much in such a short space of time. Of course, they would all go on to achieve much greater success and produce talented and thoughtful grandchildren. It must be something that has emanated from their mother's genes!

During 1989, Julie returned to the UK for the theatre training course at Aldershot, during which time she started planning the UK element of her wedding to Nigel. They were married in Aldershot on 7 April 1990. Julie, the second of our daughters, was now an army captain in the Queen Alexander's Royal Army Nursing Service (QARANC), and Nigel was a surgeon in the RMC; they'd served together in Germany. It was whilst in Munster that Julie met Nigel in the operating theatre during a clash of wills (which despite their protestations continue to this day), when she told him he might be a surgeon, but in her operating theatre he would have to abide by her rules. What makes me think that she's so much like her mother? Obviously, Nigel, as a major at that time, was so intrigued by being reprimanded by his junior that he thought he ought to invite her out—and thereby hangs a tale, four children later!

Because Sheila was running the hotel and I was working on in London, Julie had to arrange much of her wedding details herself, which included the reception, accommodation, and church details. I met up with Sheila, and we travelled down to join the family in the hotel near Aldershot. It was then that Jonathan and Katie decided to call off their engagement. I don't know the reasons, and I never I asked why. It was clear that Katie, who was from Wales, did not agree with Jonathan remaining in the army; at that time, he was serving with the United Nations in Cyprus, and she wanted him to get a job near her family in Wales, so I guess this had a bearing. Nevertheless, apart from that, it was a fabulous day. Nigel and Julie left for their honeymoon in Phuket whilst we returned to the pressures of business—me to London and Sheila to Scotland.

The Capital Parking Group

With the emergence of privatisation, especially within London, and the likely benefits that could be gained by local government pursuing the concept of outsourcing, it was quite clear to me and my assistant directors that car parking in Westminster was a sustainable business which could be developed in the private sector and across Europe. We therefore declared an interest and on the same day parted company with the organisation in City Hall and set up an embryonic business, Capital Parking. We prepared a business plan to acquire the work from the city of Westminster. However, one of my assistant directors, who headed the parking operation, decided against progressing with the concept after having a divergence of opinion with one of his colleagues, and he returned to his native Yorkshire to follow other opportunities. We were therefore left with a problem of finding the right balance of commercial experience that would enable us to convince the banks that we were a viable organisation capable of taking on the market. I had an added problem. How was I to run two businesses at opposite ends of the country and yet retain one aim: the long-term profitability of both?

In January 1989, upon having left Westminster, we established our first venture into a truly commercial world and faced up to the reality of competition. For me, this was not a first, following close on the heels of Purves Hall. Our aim, in addition to securing a contract with Westminster, was to establish a company with the objective of designing, implementing, and operating city centre parking both on-street and off-street schemes. A secondary objective was to provide a traffic management and parking consultancy service throughout Europe. It sounds impressive, but initially that was all it was. As new kids on the block, we had a lot to learn. First, we had no track record as a newly formed commercial company apart from our record at Westminster, and we had no customer base. Second, we had no substantial financial backing. Third, we had no established base from which to operate. Finally, we had to address those areas in which we needed existing expertise, a commercial director and a finance director, to augment our operational background. All rather naive, but one must grasp an opportunity when it arises and make the most of what is available.

We set ourselves up in rented accommodation in Victoria and used our contacts within Capita to assist our setup, the costs being deferred on the understanding that we would offer 5 per cent of the shares in our new company to Capita. Having done this, we set about compiling and submitting our bid to secure the contract with Westminster. Lesson one, quickly learnt, was that without a proven track record, such contracts are unlikely to be secured; even Westminster was reluctant to make that move. Our solution was to negotiate and secure the acquisition of a company, Sureway Parking Services, who already had such a record with Westminster and other local authorities. This inevitably led to further erosion of our shareholding and a new director, who was the managing director of Sureway. However, it gave us the launch platform from which we could secure new business. I remained as chairman and managing director of Capital Parking and a director of Sureway.

Our first bid for work at Westminster proved somewhat of a disaster in that we only secured part of the work, the management of the Resident's Parking Scheme. The bulk of the work for which we had bid was given to APCOA, with Westminster having changed their selection criteria in the latter stages of the competition—a familiar but questionable behaviour, and a government tactic adopted by local government. This motivated us to secure work elsewhere, and over the next few months we managed to win contracts with a range of local authorities including, Oxford, Bracknell, Waltham Forest, Redbridge, and Milton Keynes. It was at this time that I was taken into hospital for an operation to remove a growth in my throat—something that my surgeon son-in-law Nigel had noticed. Although clearly I was aware of the problem, with the importance of the work we were undertaking, I was reluctant to take time out to have it sorted. Luckily, it turned out to be non-malignant, and I was back at work within days. Nevertheless, it was a worry that I could have done without.

With a new finance director and a new marketing director, it was inevitable that the balance within the company would change, especially because their views were in many ways contrary to mine and would in my view inhibit growth at the rate we had predicted—always a critical factor in a new start-up company.

I had established other contacts through the British Parking Association, of which I was treasurer, and from the Westminster days, as well as in other countries such as the United States and Hong Kong, which proved helpful to us in formulating potential markets. However, although it did not impact on our operations, my colleagues were unhappy that I was still involved with developing Purves Hall, and although I had considered selling the business, I thought it too early because the market was in recession, added to which it did not, in my view, pose a conflict of interest with my role as chairman, having already handed over the role of chief executive to the finance director. I therefore continued to travel north late on Friday nights, returning on Sunday evenings. On those occasions when we had meetings overseas or in the city, I had to leave Sheila to cope alone.

Over the months that followed, we focused on finding work for the Capital Group in several new areas. I concentrated on the National Health Service whilst the others sought contracts with local authorities. I had been negotiating with hospital trusts at Withenshaw in Manchester and Addenbrookes in Cambridge because I saw this as a very strong potential market. Once the health services grasped the impact paid parking could have on their revenue, they became anxious to create the space for parking. Some unfortunately became avaricious and wanted to extend charging across the board and retain the income themselves, to provide equipment that should have been funded by the NHS. They saw it as a cash cow which they could milk, largely at the expense of patients and visitors. Nevertheless, this was potentially a very large market. I was also keen to get into Europe, and I had contacts working in that area. Paul Prestwood-Smith, whom I had known when he worked in the GLC, was prepared to arrange a meeting with the mayor of Madrid, who was keen to use our services. But again, there are lessons to be learnt, this time associated with cash flow in a newly formed business. We found that in some instances, payments from the Spanish authorities were often six months or more in arrears, and the bureaucracy and communications difficulties added to the problems.

In the meanwhile, there appeared to be a growing divergence of opinion within the board of Capital Parking on the way the business should be developed. Once again, I learned a very salutary lesson in business: keep your friends close and you enemies even closer. Having been the main motivating force in setting up the company and having invited the others to join me, I now found myself in a minority, and herein I learnt another lesson: never own less than 51 per cent of your own company. All of this was to no avail. The knives were out, and it was evident that my ideas and opinions no longer prevailed. In my view, it had no bearing on what we had done or what we were considering; it was all about individual power on the board. Although I remained a shareholder and a consultant, I parted company from my colleagues and Capital Parking and retired to the north to sort out the hotel business.

The following year, Capital Parking was acquired by a leading French company involved in the parking industry, to whom I sold on my shares. Although I didn't lose from a financial viewpoint, it was nevertheless a bitter experience to lose the company that I had sacrificed so much to create and to see long-term development suffer in the interest of short-term gains. But steel is forged in the heat of fire, and by such experiences one becomes more focused, hardened, and determined that future successes will be achieved, whatever the field.

Nepal and India

> I don't regret the things I've done, only the things I didn't when I had the chance.
>
> Abhisehek

In October 1989, Sheila and I took time out from work to recharge the batteries. We decided to look for an adventure holiday and eventually settled on a trek in the Annapurna range of the Himalayas. As is inevitable on these occasions, we met up and became very close friends with five Americans, two Australians, and a Yorkshire farmer who had shared our arduous climbs. It was a long and extremely hard trek, starting with the bus ride from Kathmandu to Pokhara across dusty, narrow mountain tracks (one could hardly call them roads). On one occasion, we had to leave the bus and help remove the debris of a landslide which had blocked the road. Back on board, we then had the nerve-wracking process of the driver negotiating around the rockfall with his wheels precariously gripping the edge of the track down which there was a 1,500-foot sheer drop to the valley below. Upon arriving in Pokhara, we were ensconced in tents surrounding the lake with what seemed like hundreds of other trekkers. This was our first, but not our last, experience of "holes in the ground" latrines. It was not the best of introductions to the Himalayas, but we survived.

We set out the following day on our way to the Annapurna range, passing through many small Nepalese villages and progressing up through the wooded jungle area as we headed north. As the days progressed, Sheila became the pied piper of Nepal with an ever-increasing number of youngsters eagerly following in her footsteps as she handed out sweets and biros. I must say they were eager and happy disciples, but then, she had that effect on children, which made her such a natural and talented teacher. She was also gifted in redistribution from the rich, or should I say not-so-rich, to the poor. In other words, many of what I regarded as essential items (pens, pencils, paper, scissors, sewing kit, etc.) found their way into Nepalese hands without me even noticing!

Apart from the hard going as we progressed higher, the ever-changing landscape with the terraced fields cut out of the mountainside surrounding the villages presented a fascinating backdrop to the now visible, snow-capped peaks of Annapurna and its sister mountains. Pressing on across ravines with suspended rope and wood bridges which had seen better days, we moved through dense and colourful rhododendron bushes towards the oak forests below the snow line. It was here that we had our first major problem to confront. The previous day, a tiger had attacked animals in a nearby village, and it was considered too dangerous for us to camp close to this wooded area. The alternative was to cover two days in one by trekking for twelve hours to reach the hill above the Ghurkha village of Siklas before bedding down for the night. Unfortunately, one of the assistant cooks, a female Sherpa, got left behind and spent the night high up in a tree. She caught up with us the following day, and her husband, also one of our porters, hadn't even missed her! A further day on, while traversing a narrow mountain pass, we turned the corner to see the path washed away and water cascading down the hill into the valley far below. There was no room to turn around and retrace our steps, and so the only way was forward. The next few minutes, which seemed like hours, were some of the longest and gut-wrenching that I have ever experienced as we individually picked our way carefully over the water and slippery rocks. Needless to say, this was not the way we returned! Since that time, I have frequently had cliffhanging nightmares from which I am thankful to awake.

On the way down from Annapurna, we wallowed in the pleasure of washing ourselves in the ice-cold river. When I stumbled back to Sheila, shivering in the early morning temperature, I discovered that my sweater, track suit bottoms, and thick socks had disappeared. Sheila had decided that the Nepalese were more in need of my clothes than I was. You can imagine we had a distinct variance of opinion. To be fair, she had given her own clothes away, though, I hasten to add, not all of them! This was something I was later to refer to in the eulogy I gave at her funeral.

There is much that can be said about the trek, the people we met, the friends we made and still contact, the awesome views of the Annapurna peaks and the surrounding mountains, and the panorama that surrounded us, particularly the early morning sunrise that gave life to the mountains. All of this made it a memorable experience. It created in me the urge to go higher and fulfil the long-term desire to climb Everest.

We eventually arrived back in Pokhara, and after a tearful departure from the others, Sheila and I, with Jack Bamberger, one of the Americans, set off to fly over Everest. It was an incredible sight to look down on that massive structure surrounded by equally dramatic mountains. It reinforced the desire to climb the ultimate mountain at some future time. The remainder of the team went on to join in the journey down the white-water rapids. We had a hair-raising journey back to Kathmandu, with many of the mountain roads having been destroyed by landslides yet again. Our next part of the journey was a flight to India where we were to spend a few days, primarily in and around Delhi, the Golden Triangle, before heading back to the UK. Jack had his first experience of life in the raw, Asian style. Whilst in

Agra, we had decided to go for a swim before lunch at the Hilton. Jack was just completing his swim when a young, well-dressed Indian boy unzipped his trousers and urinated in the pool. Jack must have established an Asian all-comers record for the fifty metres, and I'm sure to this day, he finds it impossible to get his head around how such a thing could possibly happen, especially in the Hilton of all places. But then, he's got a lot to learn about superficial standards and life outside America.

Purves Hall

During our time at Purves Hall, we entertained many well-known celebrities and others who were equally important, or perhaps more so, in our estimation. Some wanted to be out of the limelight, others were passing through, and some had specific security arrangements that needed to be addressed. In October 1990, we vacated our bedroom, which was on one end of the building, so that Ian and Kathy Botham could use it. Ian was on his walk from John O'Groats to Land's End, raising funds for charity, and he needed to be away from the rest of the supporting group. Sheila lived on the story for evermore recording the night that Ian occupied her bed! Kathy and Ian are a lovely couple, so different from the views sometimes portrayed in elements of the press. He invited me to join the walk on the next section, but I declined because there was too much to do at Purves Hall and too little time when I was there.

On another occasion, I was approached by Special Branch, who were anxious that one of our guests, a prominent judge in Northern Ireland, and his wife (who were targets of the IRA) were afforded maximum protection. The reason for selecting Purves Hall was the fact that it was isolated, and I had a background in the services. The judge and his wife had to be seated away from windows and possible lines of fire in the lounge, the bar, and the dining room. Their bedroom had to be regularly checked and the staff screened, although they could not be told why. On returning to the hotel one evening after visiting friends, we were confronted by men emerging from the woods in our grounds. They wanted to know who we were and what we were doing. Instead of being angry, I was grateful that they were plainclothes policemen and not IRA! Other guests such as Sir Maurice and Lady Dorman, the former governor general of Malta, didn't want any fuss, just the peace and tranquillity of Purves Hall.

After having already let some of our stables out to the owners of the local National Hunt Stud Farm, we were approached by a couple who had moved into Greenlaw and were importing and breeding miniature horses, both South American Falabellas and Scottish Shetlands. They wanted to use our facilities, but I wasn't too keen and suggested that instead Sheila might want to go into partnership providing that the others did the work. The Falabellas were between twenty-six and thirty inches in height, and the foals were twelve to twenty-two inches at birth—smaller than our dogs. Although it was not a successful financial venture, they added some colour and interest for our guests, as did the peacock (McTavish) and peahen (Henrietta) we had inherited, although they could be somewhat noisy in the early morning, which was not always conducive to the restful environment sought by some residents. I now understand why peacocks have a reputation for being brainless after watching McTavish displaying himself in all his finery to our large green motor mower whilst Henrietta looked on somewhat puzzled. Despite this misdirection of affection, they did manage to produce an offspring, Hamish. I noticed that our cheese bills in the meanwhile had increased to an astonishing level, due to Sheila feeding them from the kitchen door each evening.

The outdoor pool, rarely used by the guests, caused me some headaches. It had an inner lining that was prone to splitting, especially when the dogs managed to find their way through the gate, particularly Sheba the Labrador, who loved water. I couldn't obtain the chemicals locally and had to bring these up from London, but maintaining the pool kept our insurance premiums down because we were some distance from the local fire services. I notice from a recent aerial shot taken by Nigel when he flew over the property that the present owners have filled in the space previously occupied by the pool.

Hunting, shooting, and fishing were major attractions for guests, as was golf. We were in the centre of these activities. Fishing on the

Tweed was available on the stretch owned by the Hirsal, the adjoining estate, the home of Sir Alex Douglas-Home. He was of course the prime minister who, on renouncing his title as the fourteenth Earl of Home in 1963, succeeded Harold McMillian following his resignation. One of the interesting facts in the connection between the Purveses and the Homes was that the two families were linked by marriage. Indeed, the new Purves Hall, built in the nineteenth century on the site of the old hall, was the home of the daughter who married into the Homes of Hirsal.

The Baronetcy of Purves

In Scotland, some titles are associated with the land and the family estates. It is also customary for the deeds of any property to be held by the individual owner. In our particular property, the deeds, dating back to the 1600s, were secured in an old metal ammunition box housed in the attic. Deeds dating back beyond the mid-1700s were in Latin, the official legal language of the time, whereas those after 1750 were in English.

One evening in 1990, I was busy showing some American guests the velum parchments and hoping to impress them by blowing the dust off the scrolls before unrolling them. As a relatively young country, anything dating back beyond two hundred years usually has Americans awestruck. As I was placing them back in the box, one of the other guests asked if he could see them. Sometime later, when I went to lock them away, he asked me if I knew what I was sitting on. I said, "Yes, a large pile of debts." His name was Fred Hogarth. Strangely enough, he was someone who had served with me in the RAF in Aden. He told me that he now worked for Burke's Peerage, and his task was to visit country houses such as ours, tracking down dormant titles. Having examined the deeds, he thought that there was a barony associated with the property and that as far as he could establish, it was still extant. Burke's always had clients interested in purchasing such titles. However, it would first have to be proved by Lord Lion of Scotland, who was responsible for heraldic titles.

Over the course of the next two years, it was established that there was indeed a title "in the Baronetage of Nova Scotia". It was created in 1665 for Sir William Purves, who became solicitor general for Scotland during the reign of Charles II. The title became dormant on the death of the eighth baronet in 1960. Burkes found a faulty disposition in that the Deeds did not include the words *"all and whole the lands and barony of Purves"*, proving that the old barony of Purves was still extant and therefore in our ownership. Although proved in November 1991, negotiations were not concluded until early in 1993, so for a short period of time, we had the distinction of being the baron and baroness!

The First Gulf War

During 1990, further tension had been building in the Middle East. Saddam Hussein had amassed huge debts with the West as a result of the Iraq and Iran War and was desperate to find some way to repay the debt. There were three reasons for him to cast his eyes over Kuwait. First, his intense dislike of the Kuwaitis, who were mainly Shi'ites. Second, Kuwait had, along with the UAE, exceeded their OPEC quota of oil production, thus driving down the price of oil. Third, Saddam needed some justification to invade to gain control of the oil wealth, using the excuse that the Kuwaiti oil was being drawn from wells underneath Iraq. In July, he threatened action against Kuwait. On 2 August, the Iraq army crossed the border and invaded Kuwait. Bearing in mind that the Iraq army was the fourth largest in the world, it took it only twelve hours to take control and achieve the surrender of the Kuwaiti rulers. This brought immediate condemnation from the UN, followed by the imposition of economic sanctions on 6 August. Saddam annexed Kuwait and announced that it was now the nineteenth province of Iraq, at the same time US forces arrived in Saudi Arabia at the request of King Faud.

During the summer, Julie as part of Number 33 Field Hospital and being on emergency standby, was deployed to Dhahran in Saudi Arabia on 20 August, the day before her birthday and less than four months after her marriage. Throughout the months that followed, Nigel argued his case with the Ministry of Defence that he should also be sent to the Gulf, in the hope that he would be with Julie. However, he was told that as a senior surgeon, he would not be sent because they had sufficient medical cover. Breakfast TV caught on to the story, which they called "The Wife Who Went to War". As I recall it, the interviewer was Lorraine Kelly. The interviews of Nigel and Julie were shown on a split screen; Nigel at home and Julie in the Gulf, which left Nigel even more upset over the separation. He did eventually get his way and was sent out to Saudi Arabia at the beginning of January 1991 when the war started. The deadline for the UN ultimatum to Saddam Hussein to withdraw his troops from Kuwait was exceeded, and the coalition launched an aerial bombardment on 17 January 1991 followed by a full ground assault on 23 February, resulting in the liberation of Kuwait and the invasion of Iraq. On 25 February, the Iraqis attacked the airbase at Dhahran, where Julie was based, with Scud missiles, killing twenty-eight US soldiers. They also launched similar attacks on Israel in the hope of dragging Israel into the conflict and thereby alienating the Allied forces from the Arab countries, but this wasn't achieved. The Scud was a tactical ballistic missile developed by the Soviet Union. On 27 February, Saddam ordered the retreat from Kuwait, but not before adopting a scorched earth policy by setting fire to 737 oil wells and looting as much as they could of Kuwaiti wealth. These fires were not finally extinguished until well into November, and much of the loot was destroyed during the Iraqi retreat. The Iraqis had also released millions of gallons of oil into the Gulf to prevent an attack by sea. The resultant pollution and its impact on marine life took many years to recover from.

This war marked the beginning of live news from a war zone, with CNN recording the launch of missiles as they occurred. This brought instantaneous news coverage of the conflict to audiences around the world, and our American friends, who were on holiday in Hawaii, telephoned us to ask for news and shared our worries over Julie and Nigel. While watching the late news in Purves Hall, we were horrified on two counts. Julie was based at Dhahran airbase, and we were led to believe that Saddam might be using chemical and biological weapons. One night the TV news was cut short, and the screen coverage from Dhahran went blank. The news reporter said they had lost contact with Dhahran, which was under attack by Scud missiles. In the early hours of that morning, we spent a gut-wrenching time walking in the garden and waiting for news. Eventually the news channel recovered. The loss of signal had only been a technical fault! Troops in the gulf were allowed two telephone calls a week to the UK, a totally new departure from previous conflicts where security was paramount. On one such occasion, Julie had to cut short her call to us, saying that she had to put on her gasmask because they were under attack from Scuds.

On 28 February, the president of the United States, George Bush, ordered a ceasefire and a halt of the coalition forces that were close to Bagdad at the time. Perhaps if they had been allowed to finish the job and there had been an exit policy thought through by the politicians, there would not have been a second Gulf War, and many lives would have been spared, but that's a subject for historians to ponder over.

The Final Days at Purves Hall—The End of an Era

There are several other stories to relate concerning our time in Purves Hall, but many of these are covered elsewhere. Suffice to say that as well as being a business, it was a beautiful home, and it had been our intention to eventually live there when we finally retired. Our friends from our time in Nepal came from the United States and Australia to join with our Yorkshire friends in a reunion at Purves Hall. We took time out to show them the Borders and the many historical sites up and down the coast, which was just as well because our time at Purves Hall would soon be at an end. Two things where to impact on our long-term plans: one was the economic recession of the early 1990s, and the other was Sheila's car crash the following year.

The collapse of the stock markets across Europe and the Western world that occurred on Black Monday in October 1987, a few months after our arrival at Purves Hall, saw the value of shares fall by over 22 per cent, larger than the crash of 1929. The economic downturn marked the end of the boom years which had created the high interest rates. This led to falling house prices, negative equity, and lower spending. The result was a significant slow-down in the economy, which in turn created unemployment, social unrest, and some rioting at the height of the recession in 1991–1992. The Gulf War added to the problems by creating a spike in oil prices. Economic growth was not re-established until 1993. All of this had a major impact on our business. Many of our clientele, as I mentioned earlier, were drawn from corporate hospitality or those involved in outdoor pursuits such as golf, fishing, shooting, and hunting. In a time when people are having to economise, these were the very things that were set aside. Consequently, we were struggling to survive as a business.

Alexandra, Julie and Nigel's first child, was born in Queens Hospital, Nottingham, on 2 June 1992. We travelled down for the christening. Little did we know that less than five months later, our world would be turned on its head. In December, Sheila was anxious to get the Christmas presents to the grandchildren on time, and she was driving to Berwick when the car skidded on black ice and hit a tree. The Audi 200 she was driving burst into flames. Although badly injured, she managed to get herself and Sheba, her favourite Labrador, out before the car was totally destroyed. In the process, she had broken her back, her ribs, and her sternum. By the time I got the news, Nigel was already on his way from the south to the hospital in Galashiel's, where Sheila had been taken. I drove up from London and arrived shortly afterwards. Jane came up the following day, and for three weeks she managed to cover Sheila's role as cook and manager. Much to our amazement, she provided a wide range of meals on time and to a high standard. Like mother, like daughter!

To add to the stress, Jonathan had been posted for a tour of operations in Belfast. On one of those rare occasions when we were watching the news on television, we had the worrying experience of seeing him leading his soldiers on patrol in the Falls Road, one of the notorious trouble spots in Northern Ireland.

It was evident that without Sheila's skill and expertise, we could not continue indefinitely to function to the high level we had achieved, which led me to the decision to close the hotel and put the property on the market. Easier said than done. By the end of July 1993, having failed to sell the hotel, I instructed the estate agents to put it on the market as a private house for the same asking price, and within a month it was sold. Yet another lesson learnt: pick the right market! Our life in Scotland came to a sad ending. We had made many friends and had loved the house, the locality, and the countryside. The downside was that we were so far away from our family and the many friends we had in the south. But perhaps the saddest part of all was that Sheila had lost her dream palace – a place that would always be a second home for her children and grandchildren in later years, and one in which she could entertain our many friends. Truly it was a "Heartbreak Hotel".

Not only was this the conclusion to our time in Scotland, but it was also the end to an era that had seen dramatic changes. The 1980s had seen another decade of significant social and economic change. Daily advances in technology are almost accepted as a natural progression in life, yet it was only in 1981 that IBM released the first personal computer, and it was towards the end of the decade that Tim Berners Lee invented the World Wide Web. It was also a decade of major changes in and between nations—a period in which the European landscape changed dramatically with the disintegration of the Soviet Union and communism. Major violence and civil unrest occurred around the globe with the Iran and Iraq war, which resulted in the deaths of one million people; the Lebanese war; the bombing of Libya; the first Intifada in Gaza and the West Bank; and of course, the uprising in China, such as at Tiananmen Square. But the greatest impact had to be in the events unravelling in Eastern Europe, staring with the uprising in Poland, the velvet revolution in Czechoslovakia and Hungary, the overthrow of Ceausescu in Romania, and culminating with the fall of the Berlin Wall and the disintegration of the Soviet Union and the Warsaw Pact, which led to the end of the Cold War. It was a period in which Western government readopted laissez-faire (let us be) policies of economic liberalisation—a removal of centralised controls to encourage economic development. Towards the latter half of the decade, greater attention was being paid to the likely impact of global warming.

CHAPTER 12

London and a New Beginning

> What we call the beginning is often the end. And to make an
> end is to make a beginning. The end is where we start from.
> T. S. Eliot

In the meanwhile, after having put our furniture and possessions into storage, moved down to Church Crookham in Surrey, and parted from Capital Parking, and finding myself back on the market again, I set about finding employment. That's not an easy task in the twilight of one's working life. I was interviewed and shortlisted for the job of secretary of the New Samaritan Fund, and I was duly offered the job. However, I was in two minds and eventually proffered my apologies in turning down the offer because I was really looking for something more challenging and dynamic. I was also offered a job with British Caledonian Airways, but as I said before, to me this was akin to re-joining the RAF at an even later stage of life, so I declined the offer. Talk about being overly optimistic! At that point in time, we were staying with friends in Bolney in Sussex. John suggested that London Buses had a vacancy and was looking for someone from outside the bus industry to take on the role of senior contracts manager, preferably someone who had experience of privatisation. He said that I should apply for the position, which I duly did.

I was interviewed by the finance director of London Buses in the offices in Victoria. It was a strange interview, which I thought was more a statement about his capabilities than an enquiry about mine! I must have been a good listener because I got the job, which was located in what used to be the old MI5 Headquarters in Old Broadway Buildings. It was somewhat ironic because my office in the new location was just a short walk from Devon House, 12 Dartmouth Street, the office I'd occupied as chairman of Capital Parking. What comes around goes around! Within months I found myself on the move once more—only in terms of location, I hasten to add, this time to offices in Putney. At this stage, I was still commuting on weekends to Purves Hall, but only for a short while, so I continued to live in Watford with Jane and family during the week. Sheila came down for the birth and christening of our granddaughter Alexandra at the beginning of June.

My responsibilities as senior contracts manager involved the purchase of buses for the eleven London bus companies. This involved something in the region of five hundred buses a year, and it was a very interesting activity. In addition, I had the job of planning and arranging the refurbishment of five hundred of the remaining ubiquitous Routemaster buses. The reason for retaining them was that they were the only open-platform bus still allowed to operate under EC regulations. As hop-on, hop-off double deckers, it was imperative that they continued to operate in central London to avoid the heavy congestion which would arise with door-operated buses. We were keen to stimulate competition in the marketplace by splitting the order for buses between several of the key manufacturers mainly in the UK and Northern Ireland. We were also anxious to introduce new concepts into our vehicles, such as low floor chassis and platform entries. It was an opportunity to introduce ultra-low sulphur fuel to improve the environment, and it became known as city diesel. This fuel was not available within the UK, and we had to have it shipped in from Rotterdam. Strange, isn't it, that we now accept it as a regular fuel in all the garages throughout the country—but we were the first!

The years 1993 and 1994 were a period of transition for the family. After leaving Purves Hall and searching for a new home, we moved into Julie and Nigel's vacant property in Church Crookham on 16 May 1994, a temporary arrangement because they in turn had moved into married quarters. So, began a return to commuting into London, which also enabled Sheila to spend more time with our growing family. Throughout the early nineties, Nigel, being special forces trained and attached to the SAS, found himself at very short notice disappearing to all parts of the world. In 1993, Nigel was also sent to the Falklands on detachment for four months—one of the vagaries of life in the armed forces. This was followed the next year with a similar move to Rwanda as part of the UN force between April and June, during the country's civil war and genocide when almost one million people (20 per cent of the population) were massacred in fighting between the Tutsi and Hutu people following the assassination of the country's leader, Juvenal Habyarimana.

It was during March 1994 that Julie gave birth to her second child, Samantha, so we were on hand to help out and be there for her christening.

> Two Nations Divided by a Common Language
> Winston Churchill

In the early part of 1994, Sheila and I had been invited by our American friends to stay with them again in Santa Barbara during June, and I set about making the arrangements. What I had failed to realise was that this happened to be the year in which the United States was hosting the Football World Cup. What a Wally! Try as I may, I couldn't get any seats on any aircraft during June, and both our friends and we had other commitments, so we couldn't change the dates to later in the year. I explained this in somewhat plaintiff terms to one of the travel agents, who said, "Why not book one of our bus tours around the States?" We could leave at any given point and rejoin—for example, in Santa Barbara. She explained that the tour would be spread over three weeks, visit four states, include all accommodation in first-class hotels, allow us to spend a week with our friends in Santa Barbara, and cost no more than a business flight across the Atlantic. I couldn't see how that would be possible, and I had visions of joining a group of elderly geriatrics travelling the roads of North America and sleeping in run-down motels—a group of latter-day hippies. After discussing it with Sheila, we concluded this would be the only chance of meeting our friends in the foreseeable future. With much apprehension, we accepted the offer.

We set off for Los Angeles, from where the tour was due to start, on 8 June, whilst the rest of the tour group went on their merry way. Arriving at the airport in LA was, in my view, a more daunting experience than aliens transiting Heathrow, with long queues at passport control and a subjection to a convoluted interrogation as to our reasons for being in the country. One should remember that this was before the events now known as 9/11. We were eventually released into the care of our friends and enjoyed a very pleasant week in Santa Barbara, where they have a ranch on a smaller scale than the one next door owned by the Reagans. However, the ranches both shared the same problems in that they sat atop of the San Andreas fault line, which has experienced a few not insignificant earthquakes and landslides. During our stay, we attended the graduation of their granddaughter, who gave the address to the parents on behalf of the school. One thing about the Americans: they don't lack confidence at an early age and on these occasions! Throughout the week, we rarely had any time to ourselves because the hospitality shown by everyone was truly remarkable. Invitations included dinners not only but lunches, teas, family parties, and even breakfasts. The difficulty, as always, was trying to say no or to be in two places at the same time!

At the end of the week, we caught our coach and rejoined the tour, which was passing through Santa Barbara on its way south to San Diego and Mexico. The next three weeks were amazing and exhausting, travelling through five states from New Mexico in the south to California in the north through Arizona, Utah, and Nevada. Countryside ranged from the deserts to the forest, from the hills to the plains. It included cities such as Phoenix, Las Vegas, Reno, Sacramento, San Francisco, San Diego, and Los Angeles, to name a few. Sights ranged from the Colorado River to the Pacific Ocean, from Grand Canyon to Yosemite National Park, and travelling through the intense heat of Death Valley. The hotels surpassed all that I had experienced on a holiday tour. At one stage, I wondered who was going to meet the bill when we had the penthouse suite in the Hilton in Las

Vegas, but that was not unusual on this tour; most of the hotels fell into this exceptional category. On our return from San Francisco, we left the coach and had a final night with our friends, trying to repay some of the hospitality.

There was one remarkable incident during our tour. After having booked into our room in the Marriott Hotel in Los Angeles, we turned on the television and watched the remarkable escapade of O. J. Simpson following the murder of his wife and the chase along the highway (Route One). Our hotel sat at the intersection of Highway 1 and Route 405, so not only did we follow the events on TV, but we saw it in real life from our hotel window. How does it go? "Been there, seen that, got the tick in the box!"

Later that year, Julie and Nigel's third child, Victoria, arrived, followed by Richard a year later. We were delighted of course but wondered how Julie was going to cope with four born so very close in time. She did so, and as they say, the proof is in the pudding, or some such thing. They have developed into four very intelligent, capable, and rounded individuals—as have, I hasten to add, all my grandchildren. As a grandfather, I'm immensely proud and delighted.

Appointment to the Board of London Transport

> Never mistake knowledge for wisdom; one helps you make
> a living, the other helps you make a life.
> > Eleanor Roosevelt

Back home, life continued at a pace. We moved our LT offices from Chiswick to the headquarters in Victoria, and 1994 became for me a time of intense activity. With the move to replace the aging fleet of buses in London, of which there were close ten thousand, and the need to maintain a high level of competition in the bus-building industry prior to privatisation, I spent most of the year visiting manufacturers across the country and, in some instances, in European countries. Negotiations took place with chassis and engine manufacturers (Volvo, Scania, and Dennis), with body builders ranging from Leyland in

Cumbria, Wrights in Northern Ireland, Plaxtons and Optare in Yorkshire, East Lancs and Alexanders in the north, and Dennis in the south. I now know what the life of a travelling salesman must be like. The only difference was that I was buying, not selling. This is a huge difference in the game of negotiating, especially when you hold many of the aces!

London Buses Limited was set up in 1985 under the London Regional Transport Act of 1984. Three years later, it was separated into different business units, in preparation for selling off. Each company was established on geographical lines. Every weekday, more than 7,000 scheduled buses carry over 6 million passengers (2.18 billion in any one year) on 700 routes, some of which run for 24 hours a day, 7 days a week. I'm sure it now carries considerably more. The routes, fares, and service levels were specified by us, with the right to run the services contracted to private companies through a tendering process. During the early part of the 1990s, each of the twelve in-house bus operating companies were put on a fully commercial base, tasked with becoming profitable within their own area of operations so that eventually they could compete with those companies already operating elsewhere in the UK. The privatisation of London bus services was a progressive process of the transfer of the services from public organisation to private companies.

The secretary of state announced the intended sale of the companies in December 1992, to be completed by the end of 1994 Therefore I was moved from my role as head of contracts to become part of the LBL team that would negotiate with the bus companies involved in the competition for routes. These negotiations involved not only the individual companies but also their legal, management, and accountancy advisors. Amongst the many objectives we were set was the examination of the entire bus operation in London, including bus routes, the system of contracting that would apply both before and after privatisation, the division of zones between potential contractors, and the identification of assets to be sold off. We had strict guide lines set out by government ministers limiting such factors as the size of the market, avoiding contiguous segments, becoming owned by one operator, profitability, improved operations, and many other aspects.

For example, we were also tasked with providing an opportunity for the management and staff to take a stake in the new companies.

The months that followed were an intense period of activity, and we literally working around the clock. There were site visits and inspections, as well as detailed discussions with government ministers, developers, company directors, management advisers, accountants, and lawyers, to name a few. Often meetings and discussions would go on into the early hours of the morning, especially as negotiations neared a conclusion. I had a quick shower, a change of clothes, and a cup of coffee before back to the negotiating table—sleep wasn't even on the menu, only catnaps during breaks for coffee. By 1 January 1995, all the 10 remaining bus companies had been sold off generating gross proceeds of £233 million at a cost of £9.7 million. The National Audit Office (NAO), in their subsequent revue to Parliament, concluded that we had achieved the aims set by government on target, having generated gross proceeds substantially higher than anticipated, whilst also adopting best practice and managing the sale in an effective manner—high praise indeed from the NAO!

Following the sales, I was appointed as the procurement and infrastructure director with responsibility for running the day-to-day management of the bus operations in the London area, a role I continued to fulfil until my retirement in June 2000. The same year I was appointed as a director on the board of London River Services Limited, a company formed after we had taken over responsibility for the river services and piers from the Port of London Authority. The years that followed saw significant changes in the operation as we sought to maintain the improvement in the services. We didn't have the monopoly on new ideas, although I could see many opportunities for enhancing the bus service whilst improving the bottom line. During 1995, I spent several weeks, together with the Clive Hodson, the managing director, visiting many of the countries on the continent and in Scandinavia looking at their operations. We discovered some ways we could improve it was gratifying to see that, in many ways, but we were well ahead of them, particularly in cost-effectiveness and customer service. Towards the end of 1995, after intense negotiations with the bus operating companies and the substantial work of my management team, I got my colleagues on the board to approve the introduction of quality incentive contracts, introducing direct financial incentives for operators linked to the quality of service they provided. These came into force shortly before my retirement in 2000.

It was also a time where the services we provided to the public were under intense examination, and during that year I found myself, along with Clive, under interrogation by the infamous Glynis Dunwoody and her House of Commons Transport Select Committee, as well as arguing our case before the Monopolies and Mergers Commission. But in the main, we were largely successful, and a better service began to emerge.

Molesworth

With retirement only six years away, in January 1994 we began to look for our final home. After many months of searching, we settled on Molesworth, a small village in Huntingdon. With almost an acre of land, it was the type of property that we had looked for, set in a rural farming community. It also had the added advantage (disadvantage) of having my younger brother and family living next door—not that it had an impact on our decision, but better the devil you know! On 6 May 1994, we completed the purchase and duly moved in. I started my daily commute to London, but not before we had gone down to Greenwich for the birth and christening of our fourth grandchild, Samantha. The years 1994–1995 were filled with drama and change on the domestic front. In September 1994, Sheila was admitted to the Hampshire Clinic for an operation on her back. Jonathan was selected for Junior Staff College in November and posted off to Plymouth in January 1995, where he joined twenty-nine Royal Marine commandos, to remain until December 1997. We now had two roughie toughies in the family.

Molesworth was a lovely village just off the A14, and for many years it had been the home of the nearby RAF airfield dating back to 1917. In World War II it became part of the US Air Force bomber force in Europe. Flying Fortress bombers operating from Molesworth were the first American bombers to operate over Europe. In July 1943, the comedian and entertainer Bob Hope entertained the troops on the base. Although Bob Hope has always been thought of by many as an American, he was English American, his real name being Sir Leslie Townes Hope, KBE. Another interesting fact about Molesworth is that US airmen from the base married more English women than the compatriots from other American bases in the UK, for whatever that's worth! In the early 1950s US operations from Molesworth were carried out by the Air Resupply Group, a deliberately misleading title, because they operated B-29s on clandestine operations over Soviet-occupied territories.

During the 1980s, the Ministry of Defence rebuilt Molesworth with storage bunkers to accommodate nuclear missiles, ground-launched cruise missiles (GLCMs), a Gryphon-type missile developed from the Tomahawk Sea launched version, similar to those stored at RAF Greenham Common. As a result, both bases were focal points for protests by a variety of protest groups, and RAF Molesworth was the scene of frequent protests for much of the 1980s by groups ranging from New Age Travellers, Quakers, and Anarchists to CND, who between them set up a "Rainbow Village" outside the perimeter of the base. In February 1985, a decision was taken to increase protection and remove the protestors. About 1,500 military servicemen and police secured the Base. A seven-mile perimeter fence and an inner fenced compound were constructed, and floodlights were erected every one hundred yards. Between the inner and outer perimeters, armed guards patrolled twenty-four hours a day. Clearly, the events left an impact on the villagers, influenced by their political views in one direction or another. Between 1990 and its eventual closure in 2015, the base was home to the Joint Analysis Centre, the US European Command's intelligence gathering and analysis centre.

After arriving in Molesworth, we were soon involved in the very active social activities, which were many and varied and made the village such a pleasant place in which to settle. Knowing that the village church was awaiting the appointment of a vicar to replace the incumbent who had died in office, and that the services had to be maintained and the grounds and building looked after, Sheila decided that she would offer up my services as church warden—something I found out about only when the Church Council accepted and thanked me for the offer! Little did I anticipate that this would involve us in much more. Someone had to cut the grass in the churchyard (no mean feat), clean the church (made filthy by bats, a protected species), read the lessons, maintain the accounts, run the PCT, support and maintain the structure of the church, and do a myriad of other duties. In addition, I seemed to have acquired the responsibility as assistant treasurer for the three churches also in the vicinity, in addition to being the Deanery and Ely Dioceses representative. Remind me of that saying once again: if you want a job done, give it to a busy man!

However, things were to change in a dramatic way. Less than a year after moving to Molesworth, in May 1995 Sheila discovered a lump in her breast. She kept the discovery to herself and, unbeknownst to me, had undergone a mobile screening in the locality. It was only following a series of tests that she revealed any of the details to me or the children. Once the results of the tests had been disclosed by the GP, we arranged to go with Sheila to the Marie Curie Centre in Cambridge, where the consultants confirmed the diagnosis as metastatic cancer of the right breast and some of the lymph nodes. He informed us that it was an aggressive form of cancer and the prognosis was that she only had a limited life span, probably less than five years. The pronouncement was horrific not only to Sheila but also to the rest of us, coming right out of the blue as it did. Nevertheless, we decided to be positive in dealing with the problem and discussed the way ahead.

Sheila had a mastectomy of the right breast in August of 1995, and ten lymph nodes were removed. A traumatic event in any circumstance, but for a woman to have to lose a breast is obviously difficult to accept. During this time, our fifth grandchild, Victoria, was born in Greenwich Hospital on our thirty-seventh wedding anniversary. Sheila was far from well over this period. During November 1995, attempts were made to reconstruct Sheila's breast, and for a while all was well, but underlying infections resulted in a further attempt proving unsuccessful, which led to further infection. It was then decided to go no further, and Sheila started on a course of chemotherapy in 1996, following which she entered a period of remission. We both started using the sports facilities at the Buckden Marina, and we tried to lead a normal life in between her treatments. Sheila had decided, following conversations she had with friends in the village, that she would arrange the flowers for all the church services—a hobby which she was keen to pursue. I was relieved in a way because it would help to keep her thoughts away from the inevitable.

The following year of 1996 saw a spate of bombings on mainland Britain by the IRA, two in London Docklands, one in Central London, and another massive bomb in the centre of Manchester. In between, we had the tragic massacre of sixteen schoolchildren and one of the teachers by a psychopathic gunman in Dunblane in Scotland. Finally, we had the royal divorces of the Prince of Wales in February followed by that of the Duke of York in April. The following year was highlighted by two distinct but very different events. First, the tragic death followed by the funeral of Diana, Princess of Wales. Second, the astonishing world land speed record set up by Squadron Leader Andy Green (RAF) when he became the first man to break the sound barrier on land, reaching a speed of 763 miles per hour.

In June 1998, Jonathan left for a tour in Cyprus with the United Nations on the "green line" dividing the Turkish-held North from the Greek-held South of the island. It was during this time that he met Anna. Meanwhile, back in the UK, Sheila and I were set to embark on the celebrations surrounding our ruby wedding anniversary. Jane, Julie, and Jonathan had very generously arranged and paid for a reception at the Old Bridge Hotel, Godmanchester, Huntingdon, on 3 October 1998, attended by so many of our friends accumulated over the years. Unfortunately, Jonathan couldn't get leave to be with us.

Despite the earlier failures, Sheila insisted on having another attempt at the reconstruction of her right breast in November 1998, but it again proved somewhat of a disaster. This time she accepted the result was not to be as she desired. It was indeed a difficult time for her but was cushioned to some extent by the news that Jonathan and Anna were to marry in April 1999. She was able and determined to focus on this major event in a woman's life. The wedding took place in the church of St Leonards in the little village of Shipham in Somerset, where Anna's parents lived. The couple departed on honeymoon and then started their married life in Cyprus, where James was born, on 30 September in the Queen Mary's RAF Hospital in the UK Sovereign Base Area of Cyprus.

CHAPTER13

First Decade of the Millennium

The future came and went in the mildly
discouraging way that futures do.
Neil Gaison

Counting from the year AD 1, technically the third millennium should start on 31 December 2000, an argument put forward by Arthur C. Clarke in his book *3001: The Final Odyssey*. Nevertheless, the populist argument was that the new millennium should begin on the first of January 2000, as with all other years. Whatever the reason, the populist hypothesis was applied, and the changeover occurred on 31 December 1999. Does it really matter? It will largely depend on which time zone that one occupies.

During the early part of 1999, the anticipated worldwide computer chaos, aptly described as the Millennium bug or the Y2K bug, was being predicted to inflict something of Armageddon proportions. It had been identified by Computer World in 1993 as a problem brought about by the limitation of clocks within computers which, broadly speaking, had the ability to recognise "98" as 1998 but would be unable to relate to "00" except as 1900, leading to computer confusion. Due to the advanced awareness and the actions taken, the Millennium bug failed to result in disaster, but there were some consequences: some flight information for small aircraft failed; in Italy, bills were sent for 1900; and in the UK, some credit cards were rejected. It certainly wasn't the Armageddon predicted. There is a saying, and I can't remember where I read it: "Being a prophet of doom is a low-risk occupation. If things go right, you have warned people ahead of the event, and if things go wrong, then you are a prophet."

This was to be a decade of significant events, the most dramatic and horrendous of which was the al-Qaeda attack on the United States, which has since borne the title of 9/11, the date of the attack carried out by terrorists who hijacked four aircraft on routine internal flights. Two aircraft were deliberately crashed into the twin towers of the Trade Centre in New York, and one into the Pentagon in Arlington. On a fourth, which was destined to hit the Capitol building, the terrorists were thwarted by passengers who had learnt via mobile phones of the previous attacks. The hijackers then crashed the aircraft into a field in Pennsylvania. There were no survivors from any of the flights, and all told there were some three thousand people killed and a further six thousand injured in the attacks. The total cost to the United States was estimated at $10 billion. This also had a significant impact on the global economy. It was established that the idea for the attack was formulated by the mastermind behind the attack, Khalid Sheik Mohammed, in 1996 and subsequently approved by Osama bin Laden, the founder of al-Qaeda, in 1999. Although Khalid's earlier plan had been to select nuclear power stations, this was considered too dangerous. Following these atrocities, the United States, supported by a coalition of its allies, declared a global war on terrorism and took the offensive against al-Qaeda and Islamic extremists, primarily in Iraq in the war to remove dictator Saddam Hussein and in Afghanistan with war against the Taliban.

The hunt for Osama bin Laden and the other conspirators was relentless, and in 2001 he was identified as hiding out in the Tora Bora caves in mountains close to the Khyber Pass in Afghanistan. The subsequent attack by US and UK special forces failed to capture bin Laden, and he escaped over the mountains into Pakistan where, years later, he was eventually killed by US Special Forces (Navy SEALs). Throughout the next few years, there were several other attacks and bombings in Bali, Istanbul, London, and Madrid. There were many other conflicts and wars going on around the world in areas such as

Africa (Somalia, Liberia, Algeria, Nigeria, Chad, and the Central African Republic), the Middle East (Yemen, Iraq, Syria, and Palestine), and the Far East (Sri Lanka, India, Nepal, Thailand, and of course Afghanistan).

However, the decade embraced more than the fight against terrorism. There were other historic events taking place, some of which we tend to overlook, such as the introduction of the Euro as a standard currency across most of Europe and a counterbalance to the dollar. There was the Indonesian earthquake measuring 9.1 on the Richter scale, the third deadliest in history, and the resultant tsunami, which created waves of over one hundred feet impacting fourteen countries and resulting in the death of 230,000 people. And, of course, the global recession, which commenced in 2007, a reaction to the economic boom of previous years and high artificial prices that could not be sustained; by 2009, it was firmly entrenched. Economic experts have called this the worst financial crisis since the Great Depression of the 1930s.

Domestic Issues

But let's return to more domestic issues. It was on 17 September 2000, the day of Sheila's birthday, that we were called to see the oncologist at Hinchinbrook Hospital. Julie, having made the journey specially to spend the day with Sheila and sensing that something was not quite right, decided to accompany us to the hospital. We were confronted with the stark news delivered by the consultant that Sheila's cancer had spread and that she had secondaries in the bones, liver, and lungs. She had only months, if that, to live. It was at this stage that I realised that some people in the medical profession lack interpersonal skills and can be too blunt in delivering such news. Julie telephoned Nigel, whose immediate reaction was, "Get your mother up here, and my colleagues will evaluate what can be done." That day, Sheila travelled with Julie back to Darlington whilst I returned to work in London because there were many things that had to be resolved. We had to establish what treatment was necessary—where, when, and how. If ongoing treatment was to take place in the north, we had to find somewhere to live. Not the least of my problems, I had to sell Molesworth and hand over my job at London Transport. Sheila remained very ill throughout the remainder of the year and had further operations during November to seal the lung, where there was a significant build-up of fluids.

Fortunately, we found a house less than two miles from Julie and Nigel in Darlington, and we completed the purchase on 14 December with the aid of a bridging loan from the bank. Sheila stayed with Julie and Nigel whilst I sorted out the rest of the move to the north, and we spent Christmas together. My only problem now was to sell Molesworth, move the furniture, and sort out my departure from London. The treatment that Sheila received from oncologist John Hardman and his team in Darlington was second to none, and it is something for which I will remain eternally grateful. As I was to discover later by searching the Internet, John was not only held in high regard throughout Europe, but he was considered by the Americans to be a leader in his field. We were indeed most fortunate.

The treatment Sheila received and the subsequent monitoring showed remarkable and rapid improvements, so much so that in the March 2000 I could take her with me to Malta, where I had meetings with the minister of transport and his team of officials. It also gave her a week in the sun to catch up with her Maltese friends. This had proved beneficial, and John Hardman agreed that she could travel (accompanied and closely monitored by Julie) to Cyprus to see our new grandson, James. With these developments, it was decided that I would continue working in London until June, when a successor would be appointed. In the meanwhile, by a stroke of luck, I had managed to sell our house in Molesworth in February and move the furniture and our possessions up to Darlington in March. This meant that for three months, I lived with my sister Shirley and her husband, Martin, in Welwyn during the week and commuted up to Darlington on weekends.

Retirement and the Aftermath

> The trouble with retirement is that you never get a day off.
> Abe Lemons

With my successor having been appointed, I retired from London Transport in June. I brought Sheila and the girls down for the farewell luncheon arranged by the colleagues and friends in LT, largely driven by my excellent secretary, Carol Reeves, and we all stayed in the RAF Club. It was probably a step too far for Sheila; although she wanted to come, I'm sure she was exhausted by the effort. As is often the case with the treatment of cancer, there are good days and bad days.

Sheila, having been involved with the church in Molesworth, wanted to attend church in Cockerton, close to where we lived. Once again I found myself in the position of church warden for another five-year period. Sheila's parents had been devoted Christian Scientists, and she had been brought up in that religion. However, since our marriage she had turned more towards the more traditional church. As Jane had decided that our grandson Jack was going to have a belated christening, and the vicar in her village had declined to perform the ceremony on the basis that they were not regular churchgoers, she asked me if it could be done in Cockerton, to which our vicar agreed. Sheila then decided it would be nice if she could also be baptised in the same ceremony, and the vicar, who by this time had become a good friend, agreed. Well, he wasn't going to refuse such an offer— two for the price of one! The ceremony was conducted by the bishop of Durham, Michael Turnbull, the predecessor to Justin Welby, who went on to be the archbishop of Canterbury. As indicated, the vicar turned out to be a very caring and understanding friend, and it was not until after Sheila's death that he told me that he had also been suffering from cancer. He died shortly afterwards.

During the year, Jonathan had been notified that he had been selected for Staff College in Kula Lumpur, Malaysia, which meant that he would have to complete a Malay language course in London between September and December. Sheila and I decided that we would go out to join Anna for a week in the October, which would give Sheila a break from chemotherapy; by this time, she had lost her hair and was resorting to a wearing a wig. In November, we went down to London for the LTOCA dinner and met up with Jonathan prior to his return to Cyprus.

World Events and the Doomsday Clock

On the world stage, it was yet another year of natural disasters, with the usual round of earthquakes and tragedies interspersed with the Olympics and a change in the Russian leadership. During January and February, over 1,200 people were killed in earthquakes in El Salvador. Vladimir Putin rose to power in Russia, and the Russian nuclear submarine *Kursk*, an Oscar II–class nuclear powered cruise missile submarine, exploded and sank in the Barents Sea. The possible cause of failure was the explosion of one of the hydrogen-peroxide-fuelled torpedoes resulting from corrosion. Once again, it caused a stand-off between the Russians and the West. At home protests over the costs of petrol and diesel escalated. Blockades of oil facilities by lorry drivers and farmers caused widespread disruption. Since 1993, fuel prices in the UK had risen from the cheapest in Europe to the most expensive because of the ever-increasing fuel tax.

As one considers the various natural and man-made tragedies, it is probably apposite to look at how close in history we have come to the destruction of humanity as we know it. The concept of a doomsday clock is one that symbolically marks humankind's closeness to global catastrophe. It is intended to reflect basic changes in the levels of continuous danger to humankind. It was a concept devised by a group of Chicago scientists in 1947 who had been part of the Manhattan Project. Initially, it was set to represent the closeness to nuclear war, but it has been adapted over the years to reflect other aspects, including climate change, bioterrorism, artificial intelligence, and predicted asteroid impacts, any or all of which could create world disaster. It is meant to envisage a clock face with the minute hand moving close to midnight and therefore disaster for humankind. It is, metaphorically speaking, adjusted each year to reflect the changing political, social, and environmental issues that confront humankind.

Family Developments

Sheila continued her treatment in 2001 and was the second person in the UK to be started on Herceptin, considered at that time the new wonder drug for aggressive forms of breast cancer. There were some side effects, but in general this marked a significant improvement in holding the cancer at bay. During the year, I had been made a Freeman of the city of London and a member of the Guild of Company of Carmen. I'm not sure to this day if there is a limit to the number of sheep that I can drive across London Bridge! During this time, I had also been invited to join the board of Thorpe's, a bus company operating out of cramped and inaccessible buildings at the rear of the old Wembley Stadium in London. They had been one of our smaller operators when I had been with London Transport. There was much to be done; technically they were short of the right facilities, lacking in specialist engineering, and short on financial and management accounting skills. Clearly there was a great deal of work that had to be done to turn the company around, not least to get premises that would allow them to grow by competing for new contracted routes. I found myself regularly involved in journeys to and from London and in meetings with London Transport, CPT, and other bus-operating bodies.

In the early part of the year, Sheila was having problems because the nurses couldn't find a good vein through which to administer the drugs, which led to her having a Hickman Line fitted into the chest close to the heart. We had planned a trip down the Nile and were a little apprehensive as to how we would cope, or at least I was. It was agreed that I would undertake a course at Darlington Memorial Hospital so that I could administer the drugs and change the line and dressings. Absolute hygiene was to be the primary care to avoid any contamination in a sensitive area. Although I felt capable, the worry was always there: what if things went wrong? All went well, but it was a nightmare. Sheila got to see all the sites she wanted to and more: The Valley of the Kings, the tomb of Pharaoh Tutankhamun, the pyramids, a trip down the Nile, Thebes, Abu Simbel, Edfu, the inside of the Great Pyramid, and many other ancient sites—including me on a daily basis!

On 24 August, we had a telephone call from Jonathan to say that Charlie, the youngest grandson, had been born at Gleneagles Hospital in Kuala Lumpar. We now had two aliens in the family, one born in

Cyprus and one in Malaya. It would be another two years before we were to see him.

During this time, we had started using Banantynes Gym to give us a base level of fitness, with Sheila spending most of her time in the pool. Not for the first time, I can vividly recall where I was when a major catastrophe occurred. We were there on that dreadful day, 11 September, when TV reports came through showing the attacks on the New York Trade Centre.

In January 2002, Jonathan and family left Malaysia destined for Canberra in Australia, where for almost the next two years, he was to work as part of the Australian Military Intelligence organisation analysing data and briefing at the government level in Australia, the United States, and the UK. I had planned to take Sheila on a worldwide tour during the summer of 2002, flying out to stay with friends in the United States and then move on to Hawaii, New Zealand, and Australia before flying back via Singapore. It was what one might describe as blowing the kids' inheritance. I'd arranged first class to provide a bed for Sheila and cars to meet us. How I got the insurance, I do not know, but it was all above board. Ten days before we were due to leave, the local nurse had been to administer drugs. Shortly after she left, Sheila went into septicaemic shock. I called an ambulance, and she was rushed into hospital, where she remained for a few days, putting an end to our ambitious plans. Though it was a disappointment, I was greatly relieved that this had not occurred during our planned trip or indeed during our trip to Egypt.

Sheila had an operation on 17 January, and in the following month she attended the Lymphedema Clinic under John Hardman, the oncologist at James Cook Hospital, where she had bloods taken and two bone infusions. In March, she was back in hospital for an MRI scan, followed by radiotherapy and a new range of drugs. In April we travelled south for a week, staying with Jenny and Paul Wessendorf in Yeovil, Sheila and Mike Walker in Swanage, and Frank and Margaret Stainer in Blandford—friends we had known over many years. All of this was helpful to Sheila through some very difficult days.

Every day is a new beginning. Treat it that way. Stay away
from what might have been and look for what can be.

                                                    Marsha Petrie Sue

In May, we had the trauma of having Sheba, our black Labrador, put
to sleep on the advice of the vet. She had developed cancer of the
stomach. It was not an easy decision at the best of times but bearing in
mind the closeness that Sheila had with Sheba, it had a major impact
on Sheila, especially in her condition. She felt devastated by the loss
and made me promise that I would bury Sheba's ashes with her when
her time came, which I did. It's a good job that we had a holiday
shortly afterwards. I think the cruise helped her to come to terms with
the loss.

In June, we had a two-week cruise in the Mediterranean, with sister
Gill and her husband, Dave, as well as John and Barbara, friends
from Sussex. We travelled from Spain through to Greece before flying
back from Venice. The mix of the two couples was a little like oil
and water. However, in retrospect they proved enjoyable company once
we had come to terms with the booze and food available in copious
quantities. It was a massive ship, over 109,000 tonnes, 950 feet long,
and over 211 feet high, carrying 3,500 passengers and over 1,000 crew.
We flew out to Barcelona and then sailed the Med, calling at Monte
Carlo, Livorno, Florence, Pisa, Civitavecchia, Rome, Naples, Malta,
and Athens before we moved up the Adriatic to Venice. The on-board
facilities and food were excellent, although I still rate the Norwegian
Line as better. Sheila had a couple of bad days, the second of which
saw her in the ship's medical centre after having taken on a skin
infection, high temperature, and massive swelling of the legs. There
was some doubt as to whether the doctor would let her fly on the last
day, but Sheila insisted. After some debate and antibiotics, she won the
day, but not without considerable worry on my part.

Worried as I might have been, I would do nothing to curtail Sheila's
desire to pack as much as she could into her limited time; every
day was a golden experience and one she could not be denied. We
disembarked after two days in Venice to fly back from Marco Polo
Airport, only to be caught up in the French air traffic control strikes,

which caused major disruption. The result was some four hours' wait surrounded by piles of luggage with almost two thousand other anxious passengers in stifling temperatures. I was particularly concerned about Sheila's condition but got neither help nor sympathy from the airport staff. As usual in these circumstances, especially in Italy, confusion reigns supreme, and at that stage the Italians hadn't joined the strike generated by French air traffic controllers. Eventually we progressed as far as the final departure lounge—great cheers from the Brits—and boarded the aircraft. As we taxied out, the pilot was telling us about his successful negotiations with the Italian air traffic controllers and how he had convinced them that he should take off. Wrong! Two minutes later, as we sat on the end of the runway waiting our turn for take-off, they went on strike. So, for almost two hours, we sat and stewed in the aircraft with only the APU providing limited air cooling, with temperatures into the upper 90s Fahrenheit. We eventually made it home, but I was seriously concerned about the impact it had on Shelia's health. It also made me realise what an unhelpful and uncaring group of people exist within some of our airline transport systems.

Despite a few setbacks, Sheila was still determined to make the most of life, so in July we attended her college reunion. Then in August we travelled to Prague for a week's relaxing holiday—well, trying to relax. In between, we stayed with friends Jacqui and Trevor in Cambridge during November, as well as David and Pat in Northumberland. In December we joined other members of the Everett clan at Nidd Hall, near Harrogate, for a weekend. Talk about living life to the full! Sheila was certainly insistent on that, and I wasn't going to deny her anything.

Since arriving up in Darlington in 1999, I had become involved with the Darlington Gymnastics Club. At that time, Julie was secretary of the club; it was short of money and lacked suitable accommodation. It had a small committee of parents, none of whom had a business background or an understanding of how to grow the business. There were only twenty gymnasts of varying skills trained by three coaches and using facilities in a poorly maintained gym shared with other sports at Eastbourne School. They asked if I could help, and I agreed provided that what I recommended would be acted upon. As a result, I produced five-year and ten-year plans to grow the business and stabilise the finances, following which I was asked to become vice president with specific responsibility for club development. Although I continued to work in London until 2000, I subsequently became a BG-qualified coach and judge, and throughout the years the club grew both in numbers and stature to its current level of over four hundred members and ten coaches. We were not short on enthusiasm, only on money. As a voluntary sports club, we had no means of revenue other than membership fees, and this income barely covered our overheads. Much of the equipment was tired and outdated—and, in some cases, unsafe to use. From time to time, we raised money by bag packing at local supermarkets; the few hundred pounds raised over the year helped to sustain us but was not enough to buy replacement equipment. Julie, as secretary of the club, put together a case for lottery funding to introduce a new element of rhythmic gymnastics into the club. I started out on what was to become an annual pilgrimage of raising money through a series of challenges. Initially this was to raise money for the club, but over the years it broadened out to other charitable causes and has now reached well over £180,000.

Hadrian's Wall

The first challenge was a hundred-mile walk along Hadrian's Wall from Wallsend on the east coast to the Solway Firth in the west. Nigel decided to join me on this the first of many such walks we shared. Twenty miles a day was all right in my mind if you are doing it in a car, dreaming about it, or perhaps even running it, but walking across rugged terrain is not for the faint-hearted. I sound like a wimp. Well, I was, and I am. I had an old pair of boots that were not conducive to the prevention of blisters, and I'm sure that they weren't designed to have nails that protruded into the soles of one's feet.

On the third day of wimping and after having surmounted many stiles and climbed over several walls, we stopped for the night at a pub. I had a brainwave—well, it was either Nigel's or mine, because it doesn't happen to me too often—I stuffed a beer mat into my boot. That overcame the problem of the nail but did nothing for comfort. That night, after Nigel retired to his bed (a place he seems to enjoy), I stayed down and took part in the pub quiz. As the odd one out, I joined a Norwegian couple who were also walking the route. Somewhat to the astonishment of the locals—because the quiz, as one would expect if you are a publican and want to retain customers, was heavily flavoured with local knowledge—we won! I didn't check to see if the Norwegians lived in the Dales!

The next morning, we set out nice and early. We were initially accompanied by the Norwegians, who climbed every one of the 118 stiles. I, being of simple mind, decided that the shortest distance between two points was a straight line, and I took to the road. Well, isn't that why the Romans built them that way? Nigel, like an obedient son-in-law, didn't demure. As we dropped down the hill and followed the road alongside the Solway Firth, I pointed out the signs to Nigel. These indicated that on some occasions, at high tide, the water would be above our heads. Not knowing when this might occur during the next twenty-four hours had a significant impact on the speed with which we covered the few remaining miles! It was a relief to have finished what we set out to achieve. Although we had planned to stay the night in a B&B, Sheila and Julie travelled across to collect us. It was also a relief to get back home because Sheila wasn't feeling too well at this stage, although she still had good days and bad days. With the money I had raised from donations, which amounted to about ten thousand pounds, we were able to purchase new floor mats, a vault, and other much-needed equipment for the gym club.

Forest Park

During the early part of the year, we had quite a bit of work done on the house, revamping the bathroom, rebuilding the study/office (which I used as the base for my consultancy work), and redecorating and replacing carpets. Sheila spent an increasing amount of time at our static caravan down at Forest Park in Cromer. I joined her whenever I could, travelling between Cromer, London, Darlington, and other locations to meet my various work and gymnastics commitments.

Sheila loved Cromer and the peace and tranquillity of the surrounding area. I think in many ways, it helped her to come to terms with her illness, and I think she had accepted the inevitable outcome. Between March and October, apart from holidays we had elsewhere, we spent the best part of the year at Forest Park, only returning to meet Sheila's medical appointments and treatments. We had several trips back to the north for appointments with the various specialists, and in between we spent as much time as possible on holidays with friends. For the best part of this year, my voluntary commitments such as the U3A, church, and gymnastics coaching had to be put on hold, although there were occasional times when it was possible to cope with the many demands. In March I took Sheila back up to Scotland to join in the celebrations for our friend Sheena's eightieth birthday.

On 1 April, I received notification from our medical insurance company, PPP, telling me that they were withdrawing funding for the Herceptin treatment that Sheila was undertaking on the grounds of increasing costs. Despite letters of protestation, I found that from the legal advice I was given, they were entitled to take this action even though it was morally wrong. I discussed the matter with Sheila's medical consultants involved in her treatment, and they put the case to the Regional Health Authority, who eventually agreed to continue the treatment under the National Health Service. It was this decision that led me later to become a nonexecutive director of the Primary Care Trust and continue with voluntary work in support of the NHS. It was my way of repaying the magnificent support they had provided for Sheila. I'm afraid the decision taken by PPP did nothing to alleviate my cynicism regarding insurance companies in general or PPP in particular. Although the treatment was prolonging Sheila's life and, more important, improving her quality of life, we both knew that there was no magical cure and that this was very unlikely for many years to come. We had to face up to the reality that the future was at best uncertain and at worst limited to a few more months. In these circumstances, I was determined that we should make the most of what little time we had left.

Scandinavia and the Baltic

In June we travelled down to Sussex to meet up with friends before we all joined the *Oceania* in Southampton, setting out on a cruise to Scandinavia and the Baltic. I was hopeful that this would provide Sheila with an ideal compromise, enabling her to relax but also to have the opportunity for some sightseeing if she felt up to it. At least it took the stress out of travelling once established on board. To eat or not to eat—that was the only question. Our first port of call was Stavanger, the fourth largest city in Norway. Situated on the Stavanger peninsular in south-west Norway and facing the North Sea, it is often referred to as the oil capital of Norway. There are many old wooden seventeenth- and eighteenth-century houses huddled together along narrow streets in the old part of the city. Its modern claim to fame, apart from oil, is that it houses NATO's Joint Warfare Centre.

The following day, we moved on through the small scattered islands that surround the coast to Bergen, Norway's second largest city, occupying most of the peninsular on which it sits. Its claim to fame as a North Sea fishing port is its large export of dried cod. Sheltered from the North Sea by the islands of Askoy, Holsney, and Sotra, it is surrounded by what are claimed to be seven mountain, but I'm not sure that I counted that many. I must say that the only downside to sitting close to a mountainous backdrop is the abundant rainfall to which these hills give rise. The other worrying factor that the local inhabitants must live with is the rising sea level, leaving the city exposed to the constant threat of flooding. I suppose they will not be alone if global warming becomes the issue that many expect. I'm just glad that I no longer live in the Fens!

The on-board entertainment was good, but most nights we retired early because Sheila needed to recover from the daily treks around town. We did curtail our walks and intersperse them by sitting in or out of cafes, dependent on the weather. Sheila enjoyed the days at sea reading and relaxing. I notice the Scandinavians are very competitive people, especially when it comes to historical claims, and Kristiansand was no different in this respect, stating that it was the fifth largest city in the country and the home of many festivals throughout the year. It had a busy harbour close to the charming old town of Posebyen. The town consisted of low-rise, wall-to-wall, white wooden houses huddled together on cobbled streets. It was a similarity shared by many of the towns on this rocky coastline, synonymous I suppose with much of southwest Norway.

A day later, we found ourselves in Oslo, and after a hearty and relaxing breakfast, we ventured out to explore the city. It is of course the economic and governing centre of the country, so it is somewhat of a bustling city—not quite as hectic as London, Paris, or Berlin but nevertheless busy in its own way. It is set against a backdrop of green forest hills rising above the city and creating the form of an amphitheatre. According to Norse legend, the settlement was founded by King Harald Hardrada in 1049, the one who featured in the battle prior to the Norman invasion, but over the years fires have destroyed major parts of the city many times, and in the course of each rebuild, its character has changed.

We moved down into the straits between Denmark and Sweden and arrived at Elsinore, a medieval town with a long and exciting history dating back to the Viking era. Again, the similarity in Scandinavia is striking. Once more we saw cosy timbered houses, some ochre in colour, sitting alongside narrow cobbled streets, the oldest of which was 1577. Farther on alongside the busy harbour were the white, well-preserved brick houses of the merchants. The castle of Kronberg, dominating the skyline, is built on the top of the old fortress made famous by William Shakespeare in Hamlet: "There's a divinity that shapes our ends, rough hew how we will."

Copenhagen needs no introduction. It is the capital and the largest city, sitting astride Zealand Island and Anager Island in East Denmark. We were fortunate in our visit to Amalienborg Palace; not only did we get to see the royal family in the presence of Queen Margrethe and her husband Prince Henrick, but we also arrived in time for the changing of the palace guards in their resplendent uniforms of red and blue surmounted by black busbies and carrying ceremonial swords. In our tour of the city, we visited Rosenburg

Castle, Kobmagergade Street in the Latin Quarter, and Kings Garden. We were determined to see the "Little Mermaid" perched on a granite boulder close to the edge of the harbour. It was much smaller than I had envisaged, and though it was a well-sculptured bronze statue, I was left with the impression that it was in an inappropriate place, too close to the pavement that you could almost miss it. Finally, we saw the Gefion Fountain, named after the powerful goddess of Nordic mythology.

Our last port of call in Denmark was Aarhus, the second largest city, the principal port on the east side of the Jutland Peninsular, and roughly the geographic centre of Denmark, with its historical Viking origins dating back to AD 960. We probably walked too far that day because Sheila was thoroughly exhausted without knowing it and consequently suffered when we got back to the ship. As always, she was determined to pack everything into the day. However, I cursed myself for getting carried away with her enthusiasm and not seeing the telltale signs. Upon leaving Denmark behind us the following morning, we headed for Belgium and Zeebrugge, for no other reason than to have the opportunity to visit the ancient city of Bruges. After catching the train from the port, the four of us arrived in Bruges mid-morning in time for a barge ride down the canal before lunch.

Madeira

I was somewhat involved in gymnastics during October with the English National Championships, but within a month we were on our travels once again, this time to Madeira for ten days. Yes, another jet-setting holiday, but primarily relaxation in the sun. It was the first time that I had been away from London in November, which meant missing the Remembrance Day March in Whitehall and our annual dinner, and I felt a bit guilty. On the other hand, it was important to Sheila to lift her spirits because the clock was ticking, and her well-being was the most important consideration at this stage. Although we travelled around the island, I made sure things were done at a leisurely pace. It was a fantastic and relaxing break made memorable by the cable car ride to the top overlooking Funchal Harbour, with the panoramic views from the Monte Palace Tropical and colourful gardens. But perhaps the most exciting aspect was taking the toboggan ride down into Funchal, a journey of some seven to eight minutes in a wicker basket hurtling down at breath-taking speed. The only means of control is the driver zigzagging to avoid hitting the walls. Why I allowed her to talk me into taking the ride, I can't recall; put it down to a moment of mental aberration! There is no doubt about it: she had every intention of maximising the days left to her, and as she said, "What the hell. I'm going out on a bang, not a whimper."

In between trips, we visited friends in Scotland and England, making the most of the time that remained. We spent Christmas in Darlington with all the family around us, including Jonathan, Anna and the boys, and Jane and Richard. Christmas Day was at Julie's, and on Boxing Day we took the family plus in-laws out for a celebratory meal to Brewster's. On 30 December, after they had all left to return home, Sheila and I set off for Lincolnshire to see in the new year and have a nice, relaxing few days on Pat and Bill's farm in Laceby; they were friends from our school days when we both lived in the village.

On the world stage, 2004 closed on yet another major tragedy when an undersea megathrust earthquake, estimated between 9.0 and 9.3 with its epicentre off the coast of Sumatra, occurred on Boxing Day, killing over 260,000 in several countries around the Indian Ocean rim. It created waves thirty metres high (ninety-eight feet), destroying everything in its path. Although it had no direct impact on us as a family, it did have a bearing in 2005 in its aftermath. Jonathan, having left the army, was sent out to Indonesia by the Foreign Office as part of a team to assess the damage to the infrastructure and to encourage the internal military dissidents/rebels to enter discussions with the local government. He acted as a go-between with rebels and the Indonesian military and was part of the eventual successful peace agreement. He has the remains of the rebel flag hanging encased on his study wall.

Sheila's Demise

I'm glad that we could pack so much into the years after Sheila's prognosis because 2004 proved to be a traumatic year with a more rapid decline in Sheila's health, which led me to resign as a director with Thorpe's and as chairman of the Society of Engineers in London. I also stopped my gymnastics coaching and other local activities because there was no way that I could continue. It was during the early months, and the following further visits to Forest Park, that I discovered that Sheila had stopped taking Tamoxovan in the self-belief that she was cured. Well, that was what she said at the time, but I very much doubt that was the reason. She had been having side effects from the drug, added to which I think she recognised the inevitability of having survived over four years rather than a matter of months—and, I have to say, four years of reasonable quality life. From here on, it was a downhill progression with increasing sickness and fatigue. Despite the advice of the doctors and nurses, she was adamant that she wasn't going to go into the local hospice, and I was in complete agreement with her. Home was where she needed to be, with her "brood" around her. In the autumn, she became confined to her bed, so we moved her bed downstairs. I managed to get her a tall bamboo screen, which gave her a modicum of privacy without her being separated from us.

In October, on the advice of her doctors, I sent for the children to be with her for the last few days before she passed away, which she did on 29 October with all of us there. Although it was a devastating event, it was also a relief that her suffering was at an end. Two months after her funeral, we took her ashes down to Lincolnshire and scattered them beneath her favourite tree in the woods of Aircrops in Laceby. She would have loved this, surrounded by family and friends sharing in her childhood memories. It's a strange and unwelcome feeling, and one that never leaves you, when you lose your other half, your friend, your lover, and your lifetime soulmate. There isn't a day that goes by when you don't recall a memory or miss the intimate conversation, even on trivial issues. I suppose it's hardly surprising when you've spent forty-nine years of married life together. For me, whatever may occur in the future, life will never be the same again.

Christmas was very much a family affair, with everyone spread between my house and Julie's. In a way, it was probably a good thing because we were all there to help each other through a difficult period. As a family we had always (whenever we could) made the most of Christmas together, and like many mothers, Sheila would go overboard in making certain that everyone had a memorable time.

CHAPTER 14

A Challenging Future

You must do the things you think you cannot do.
Eleanor Roosevelt

Thankfully, there was a great deal to keep me occupied during the early part of 2005. I spent New Year's with Bill and Pat in Laceby. It was strange, being there without Sheila, but it was something that I would have to get used to. I took myself off to the woods where we had scattered Sheila's ashes, sat on a tree stump, contemplated life, and had a mental reflection on the many memorable occasions we had spent together. I thought it was no good talking to Sheila; nevertheless, I did so, conscious of the fact that if she was there, then she would know everything that was happening. If not, there were always the memories of the time we had in this village and during our life together.

The following day, I returned home to sort out the fitting of a new kitchen. What I failed to say was that on the evening of Sheila's death, we had a fire in the kitchen—not surprising with everything else going on, and thereby hangs a story, but you would have to ask Jane about that! Nevertheless, it was in serious need of a makeover, so I had carpenters, fitters, plasters, and painters in to make a complete revamp. Sheila would have loved it, and I bet she would have said, "What took you so long, and why didn't you claim on insurance?" She always maintained that if you pay for a service, you should get it.

In the circumstances, it was the last thing on my mind—no pain, no gain!

Despite the massive gap in my life, I was reluctant to dwell on our loss too much, and it wasn't long before I found myself fully active once again. I had several English Gymnastics meetings to attend, having been appointed to the English Board during 2004. After a weekend with Pat and David up in Rothbury, I found myself heading south to Plymouth. In February, I learnt that Jonathan was being sent on detachment to Belize, in Central America, and because it coincided with his birthday on the seventeenth, he suggested that I travel down to Plymouth to stay with them until he left for Belize on 21 February. He was heading out on what was to be a four-month detachment. By this time, he was showing the signs which I had probably displayed some years before: disillusionment regarding his future in the army. I think it is often the case that when you have experienced the involvement in high-level responsibility, finding yourself in a less interesting or demanding job dampens your enthusiasm. On his return from Belize, he decided to call it a day as far as his military career was involved.

The remainder of the early part of the year, I was heavily involved in gymnastics, U3A, and church development work; the days, weeks, and months seemed to run into each other. It wasn't long before Anna and the boys were heading north to Darlington during the first week in April, and I was able to enjoy those grandfather moments, driving digger cranes and earth movers with the boys and of course the other grandchildren. I think the girls handled the cranes and diggers better than we boys.

In the year that followed Sheila's death, I wanted to show some appreciation for those within the health services who had been tackling the dreadful disease which had afflicted Sheila, and I also wanted to support the gym in Darlington. I decided to do two more challenges during the year. The first, in continuing the support of the gym club in Darlington, was to raise sufficient money to enable the purchase of an air track for training (costing £5,000). The second was to provide some financial support for one of the cancer charities, Cancer Research UK.

Throughout 2004 and 2005, I worked with the church authorities on a case to justify the building of a new gymnasium and community centre in Cockerton on the community site owned by the church. Despite our joint efforts and the agreement of the planning officers, in the autumn our case was rejected by the politicians. It was a significant setback costing us a great deal in both time and funds, and it was a lost opportunity. Not only was it a major disappointment, but it also left us with a high degree of disillusionment with local politics, or should I say politicians. It was evident that there was a distinct lack of interest in the community towards the healthy development of children in the locality. The tackling of fitness and overcoming obesity appeared as buzzwords, but support never got beyond the printed word. Putting aside our despondency, we agreed to make the most of our limited facilities but improve and replace outdated equipment.

West Highland Way

The aim of my 2005 challenge was to raise £10,000, to be divided equally between the two charities, by completing the West Highland Way Trek in April, and then by completing a 300-mile East Coast cycle ride in seven days during June 2006. The West Highland Way runs from Milgavie (pronounced Mull-guy), a suburb of North Glasgow, to Fort William in the Highlands some 100 miles away, which we aimed to finish in five days. I say *we* because Nigel was keen to participate in the planning and the walk itself, but he left me to raise the money for the charities!

We arrived in Glasgow on the evening before the walk. We met up with Nigel's sister and her husband, who lived on the outskirts of Glasgow, for a meal that evening before checking into our first night stop at Milgavie. On 12 April 2005, we set off for Glasgow and the start of the walk. Following a leisurely breakfast, the next morning we set out for Drymen, about twelve miles. The route runs in and over mountain countryside on the west side of Scotland, so almost by definition it is subject to very changeable weather at any time of the year. It is particularly prone to windy and wet conditions, especially the farther north and the higher one must travel. The walk was not too arduous apart from the first half mile, which was uphill—hardly conducive to exercise after a full breakfast. Nevertheless, it was a relatively simple start, climbing up through Allander Park, rough moorland of birch and gorse, before moving on over footpaths, tracks, country lanes, and disused railway tracks. There were steady climbs but nothing too strenuous. I always find the first day of such treks tiring until the body adjusts to the punishment. We pressed on through mainly farming countryside and soon passed the Dumgoyne distillery in the Strath Blane, formally known as Glenguin and noted for its production of unpeated malt whisky. Thank goodness it was morning otherwise, we might have fallen to the "temptation of the Devil", as our good puritan Scots would have us believe.

After an overnight stay in Drymen, we set out the next day somewhat refreshed, heading towards the head of Loch Lomond on our way to Rowardennan, about fourteen miles away. Loch Lomond is the largest body of inland water in Britain, covering over 27 square miles; it is also one of the longest at 23 miles and the deepest at 623 feet. The whole of this area is steeped in romantic history, much of it fictional, having attained its stature through the writings of notable novelists and poets such as Sir Walter Scott, William Wordsworth and his sister Dorothy, and others like Samuel Taylor Coleridge. There is no doubt, however, that its beauty lends itself to this extravagance of romantic settings. The lochside route, which follows the eastern shore for many miles, is twisty and surprisingly undulating—the scenery constantly changing as the path winds up and down hills, into gravelled bays and around promontories, through open woodlands and into densely cultivated plantations of conifers—before eventually emerging into bracken clad moorland. Here one has a stunning view of Conic Hill (358 metres), which dominates nearby Balmah.

From Rowardennen to the head of Loch Lomond, the track hugs the eastern shore and is, in my view, one of the hardest sections of the trek, particularly north of Inversnaid where the track at times seems to double back on itself. One minute it crosses the pebbles on the shoreline, and the next you're stumbling over boulders rising high above the loch; it's all up and down from there on. Beyond Ptarmigan Lodge sits Rob Roy's Cave, not so much a cave as a rocky indentation well concealed amongst the boulders. Rob Roy McGregor was an eighteenth-century Scottish folk hero or cattle rustler, depending on which version of history you believe. It is alleged that here, in 1711, Rob Roy kept his prisoners and kidnap victims, as immortalised (or rather romanticised) by Sir Walter Scott. I won't repeat Nigel's views of the terrain for fear of offending those who are not normally subjected to this language; suffice to say, he was not amused. Beyond the cave, the sense of wilderness soon returns as the path meanders up and down many, many, times from the gravel shore of the loch through the boggy marshes and high bracken, as well as up through densely wooded land covered by many fallen trees. We eventually emerged at the end of the loch into Glen Falloch, passed the Falls of Falloch, and headed our weary way towards the settlements of Crianlarich and Tyndrum.

The next leg of the journey was to lead us through the Bridge of Orchy to Kingshouse. This is perhaps one of the most scenic and enjoyable sections of the walk. It has the magnificent backdrop of the Blackmount Mountains as you cross Rannock Moor, a wilderness of scrub and bog, beyond Ba Bridge and alongside Loch Ba. Dramatic it may be, exposed it certainly is—not a place to find yourself lost in during inclement weather because it offers no protection whatsoever. Eventually we arrived at the Kingshouse Hotel, reputedly Scotland's oldest inn. It stands in stark isolation at the intersection of Glencoe and Glen Etive, beneath the twin summits of Creise and Buachaille Etive More. We had a more leisurely start the next day, having a shorter leg to complete across the Devil's Staircase, one of only three ascents along the way worthy of being called an ascent. The gradient flattens out as the col is approached, and then begins a long gradual descent to Kinlochleven. Here we were at last at the start of our last day and our final stage on our way to Ben Nevis to collect T-shirts to mark our achievement. So ended yet another challenge!

In May, hoping to raise more money for charity, I arranged for the players of Newcastle Football Club to sign one of their shirts, which

I then had framed and sold it for three hundred pounds at one of our awards nights. Every little income helps, but one would be surprised how difficult it is to sell Newcastle memorabilia in the land of Sunderland and Middlesboro!

Cricket Tour

A rush of blood in July found me accepting an invitation to tour with the Northwood Cricket team during July, this time to the Channel Islands, travelling overland with Richard, Jane, and family through France. I wouldn't say it was a conspiracy, but during the first match I found that wherever I was placed in the field, the ball seemed destined to pass in my direction—a shattering experience at my stage of life, trying to recreate the athletic ability of a greyhound and the physical ability of a teenager with the accuracy of a spear-throwing Zulu. I have to say that by the end of the day, I didn't argue against those wishing to pass the amber liquid down my throat, which seemed to be the ritual that I have come to associate with Northwood Cricket Club. On our return through France, Richard had arranged for us to stay at the Chateau de la Doree, near Tours, a one-time home of Lucien Bonaparte. I was accommodated in the luxurious suite "La Chamber Mata Hari". You may recall that Mata Hari was an exotic dancer of Dutch origins who was executed by the French in October 1917 as a double agent working for the Germans. It is alleged that her activities resulted in the deaths of over fifty thousand soldiers. After having lain awake most of the night, I had to express disappointment that I didn't experience a visitation. Yet another lesson: you can't win them all!

International Events

The year 2005 was a mixed one on the international scene, with significant space achievements coupled with major natural disasters. Scientific discoveries included the dwarf planet Eris with the greatest density in the solar system. In January, the Huygens spacecraft landed on Titan, the largest moon of Saturn. This was followed by the launch of Deep Impact from Cape Canaveral with the purpose of studying the comet Tempel 1. Later in the year, the Mars Reconnaissance Orbiter was launched from the same location to explore Mars.

It was also the year in which two major earthquakes occurred. The first, of 8.6 magnitude, was in Sumatra during April, killing 1,314 people. A second, of 7.6 magnitude, caused far greater damage in Pakistan during October, killing 86,000 people and displacing thousands more. In August, Hurricane Katrina caused havoc on the Gulf Coast of America, killing over 1,000 people and causing over $108 billion in damage. I'm uncertain as to whether these events are occurring on a more regular basis or if it's just that better communication means news travels faster.

Two other notable events occurred with the death of Pope Paul II and the election of his successor, Pope Benedict XVI, in early April, followed shortly after by the wedding of Prince Charles to Camilla Parker-Bowles, an event that could not have occurred sixty years earlier but that reflects the changing times in which we live.

Family Matters

In August I found myself travelling down to Plymouth once again. Jonathan, having left the army and because of his background, was asked by the Foreign Office to fly out to ACHE in Indonesia as part of a UN team to see what could be done to help in the tsunami recovery. Primarily, the aim was intelligence gathering and to assist in negotiations between the Indonesian authorities and the ACHE rebels. Jonathan flew out on 12 August, and I stayed on in Plymouth, helping Anna in the purchase of their new house before returning to Darlington on 21 August.

On 8 September, I had a telephone call to tell me that Sheila's younger brother, Bernard, had been found dead in his flat in Bolton. He had had no contact with his immediate family in recent years, so I took it upon myself to make the necessary funeral arrangements after talking to his daughter Sally, who lived in Kent. But first I had to contact the coroner to get dispensation for the burial because there was some doubt over the cause of death. I arranged for the funeral on Monday the nineteenth and travelled across to Bolton with Julie. It was rather a sad occasion because apart from Sally and her husband; Jane; Richard and Jack; and Sheila's cousin Joyce and her husband, Mike, there was no one else.

Jane and Kevin's marriage had been on the rocks since 1999 when she'd discovered he'd been having an affair. Ever since then, the divorce had dragged on, and here we were six years later with still nothing resolved. A court hearing was set up in Leicester for Tuesday, 27 September, and Jane telephoned and asked me to support her at the hearing. Although things are quite amicable now that the divorce has been completed, at the time I couldn't forgive Kevin for the grief he created not only for Jane but for Sheila and the children. It was a very difficult time all round. Inevitably, that is the role of a father: to protect and support his offspring. The only people who gained from this significant delay in the divorce proceedings were of course the lawyers, that merry band of predators.

I returned to Plymouth on 26 October to help to move Anna and the boys out of married quarters and into their own home. "Marching in and out, as it is fondly referred to in military parlance, is a system that ensures that everything is spotless before the next family move into the married quarter. That took me back a few years because nothing changes. Having seen them established in their new house in Raleigh Woods, Plymstock, I headed home to Darlington ready to hand over as chairman of the South Durham U3A on 8 November. A quick turnaround, and it was down to London for the LTOCA events associated with the Remembrance Day. Jonathan returned home for Christmas, and I was invited to join them in the first Christmas in their new home, following which a few days later, I headed off to Laceby for yet another New Year's with Bill, Pat, and family in North Lincolnshire and New Years' Day with Tish, John, and friends in South Lincolnshire. I was beginning to have that distinctive feeling of a jaded globetrotter, having finished off another year on the move.

On 3 January 2006, Jane had a further court hearing in Leicester, which she asked me to attend. Here we went into another year of lawyer's fees—and this time a judge to intervene, which accounted for very little apart from an increase in costs. Maybe in the next life, I will become a lawyer and pick over a few bones.

Abu Dhabi and Bernard's Inquest

On 15 February, I flew out to Abu Dhabi and joined Jonathan, Anna, and the boys in the Hilton Corniche for a week whilst they sorted out the arrangements for their future life in the UAE; it was the first of many such visits I would undertake. Abu Dhabi was indeed a modern thriving metropolis somewhat on a par with Rio de Janeiro, if somewhat smaller. Its population had grown from a few hundred in the 1960s to about seven million—a phenomenal growth arising from the discovery of oil in the 1970s. I tried telling Jonathan that when I flew over Abu Dhabi from Aden in the early 1960s, it was a small collection of mud huts, no more than twenty in total. His response was, "Yes, Dad, I know. And you still got change out of a farthing!" I proved young smart arse wrong when we visited the sports club in which there was a framed aerial picture of Abu Dhabi in 1962. I had great satisfaction pointing out that there were in fact nineteen houses! Having returned home, the following month I travelled south to help Anna pack and move out of their house in Plymouth, which was then going to be let to tenants for the duration of their time in Abu Dhabi. Jonathan came back to collect them on 1 April, and I saw them safely on their way from Heathrow the following day.

On 26 April, I decided to attend the inquest into Bernard's death, held at Bolton Coroner's Court. I was somewhat surprised to be called as a witness, answering questions as to his mental state, especially because I hadn't intended to be there. Up until that time, I hadn't realised he had taken his own life through an overdose. Whether it had resulted from Sheila's death or his own depression, no one will ever know. His earlier life had been hard enough without the break-up of his marriage and a subsequent broken relationship. The female doctor present at the inquest said that he had previously made attempts to take his own life and had been undergoing treatment for severe depression.

On 1 May, having done very little training in preparation for Morocco, I travelled to the Lake District with Nigel and climbed "The Old Man of Coniston"; less than three weeks later, we would be out on the Atlas Mountains. In between the two events, I managed to squeeze in a short flight. The previous Christmas, the kids had bought me a one-hour flight in a Tiger Moth, and Jane's daughter Laura had received a similar family present. On 14 May we gathered at Sywell in Leicestershire (an old RAF airfield which I had previously visited in my RAF days). It's not often you get the opportunity to join your grandchildren in their first experience of flying. This was also the first time that I had been back in the cockpit of a Tiger Moth since those heady days of 1952, but it all seemed very familiar. The only difference was in radio communications, which didn't exist in my day; there was no internal communication except by a Gosport tube, let alone communications with airfield control towers. All we had in the fifties was visual contact, and then only if the weather was favourable! Laura turned out to be a natural, but the costs of flying these days is quite prohibitive, so I think it unlikely that she will progress further. What a pity.

It was 2006, and we were into another year, one filled with the usual variation of problems. It was in that year that the H5N1 strain of highly pathogenic avian influenza was fast mutating with HPA1, being found in many bird species and creating the worry that it had crossed the boundaries into humans. It was also a year of more human tragedies when in February, a massive mudslide in the Philippines killed over 1,000, followed by an earthquake in Java during May which killed over 6,000. Other events on the international scene included North Korea announcing that it had tested its first nuclear weapon, which clearly left the United Nations unhappy; Fidel Castro handing power in Cuba to his brother Raul, leading to speculation about Fidel's health; and Saddam Hussein found guilty of crimes against humanity and sentenced to death.

CHAPTER 15

Morocco—Across the Atlas Mountains

In Morocco, it's possible to see the Atlantic and
the Mediterranean at the same time.
Yahar Ben Jelloun

In May 2006, Nigel and I flew out from Heathrow to Morocco with
the aim of crossing the Atlas Mountains and pressing on down to the
Sahara Desert—me as part of the year's charity challenge, which was
for the Royal Masonic Benevolent Fund, and Nigel for the shear hell
of it; he had been given a pink chit by Julie! Having lived and worked
in Arab countries, I thought it might be nice to combine fundraising
with a different form of challenge. Nigel decided to keep me company,
having been given approval from Julie because she no doubt thought
somebody should look after her nutcase of a father, and who better
than a doctor?

Why the Atlas Mountains? Well, you could say that I have a morbid
fascination and fear of climbing. As I mentioned earlier in this story,
in my early childhood I lived in awe of Mallory and Irvine and their
exploits on Everest. I would have liked to follow in their footsteps, but
to tell the truth, I hadn't the courage. Well, maybe I would give it a
try. Despite having flown aircraft and jumped out of them, albeit by
parachute, I still suffered from vertigo, and I suppose this was my way
of trying to overcome the fear, although I had coped on Annapurna.

Situated on the north-east corner of Africa, Morocco faces both the Mediterranean and the Atlantic. It covers almost half a million square miles and has a population of 33 million. It lies on a geographical fault running from Agadir through the Atlas Mountains and has been the subject of many earthquakes; the town of Agadir was destroyed in the fifties, and in recent times over 600 were killed in Al Hoceima. Our visit was in May, and though the temperatures in Casablanca and Marrakech were high, there was a marked contrast as we approached the northern slopes of the Atlas Mountains. Morocco is a fascinating country with an environment strikingly different to our own: arid deserts and rugged mountains interspersed with green valleys. Our trek set us on a course that approached the mountains through the Ourika Valley, a beautiful area of steep-sided gorges and green terraced fields along the winding Oued Ourika. After passing through the foothills of the Atlas, we eventually reached Oukaimedan, which in Moroccan means "the meeting place of the four winds", and it sits at an altitude of 7,500 feet. We left the valley via a steep climb to a ridge that runs between Jebel Toubkal, Morocco's highest mountain at 12,000 feet, and Jebel Oukaimedan at almost 11,000 feet, eventually crossing the Kik Plateau and descending through the high, narrow passes to the southern side of the High Atlas Mountains. This part of the High Atlas revealed a dry, rocky, but colourful land, where the verdant oasis stood out in stark contrast to sand and rock. This is an area fabled by the French Foreign Legion at the turn of the century. I recall the days of my early youth fascinated by stories I read of the days of adventure and the classic story written by P. C. Wren in 1924 of the heroic but tragic *Beau Geste*, the lone survivor in the North African Fort of Zinderneuf, surrounded by and succumbing to the attacking Tauregs. It's an authentic encapsulation of life in the French Foreign Legion prior to World War I.

Continuing down towards the Sahara, we passed through the "Valley of the 1,000 Kasbahs" only to be confronted with a major problem. On reaching Ait Oudinar, we discovered that torrential rains had washed away roads and bridges, creating a problem in crossing the rivers, which by now were in heavy flood. This was a test of our ingenuity. Nigel managed to coerce, with a financial stimulus, a local donkey owner to proffer up his steed to make the river crossing. I, in a similar fashion to a tightrope walker, edged myself warily across the river via two narrow trees which the locals had lashed together. After traversing this moonscape countryside, we eventually came to the town of Ouarzazate, situated close to the Jabel Sahro mountain range and on the edge of the Sahara Desert. It was once an isolated French Foreign Legion military outpost centrally positioned on a crossroads that connects Marrakesh, Agadir, Zagora, and El Rachdia. Nearby is the spectacular and exquisite Kasbah of Ait Ben Haddou, made popular through the filming of *Lawrence of Arabia*, *Jewel of the Nile*, and *Jesus of Nazareth*. Moving on to Boumaine du Dades, we had a break and experienced a Moroccan Hammam, which evokes all that is sensual about Moroccan culture: a series of leisurely hot and cold steam baths, followed by scrubbing to deep clean the skin, and then a massage to fully relax the body. The skin is then rinsed with rose and orange water, organic olive oil soap and essential oils, argon (which is unique to Morocco and has huge antioxidant properties), laurel, citrus, cedar wood, and finally sandalwood. All of these are used in the massage to induce deep relaxation, which in our case was sorely needed. We returned via the Dades and Todra gorges, headed back north over the mountains, crossed the Tizi n'Tichka pass, a route built by the Foreign Legion in the 1930s, to the end of our journey in Marrakech. It left us with just a day to wander through the world's largest Souk, a daunting, claustrophobic labyrinth of dark and narrow alleyways in which one can barter for just about every conceivable item of need—"And if they haven't got it, they will make it!"

As the afternoon drew to a close, we emerged from the depths of the Souk and made our way to Djemma el Fna Square, the heart of Marrakech, a heart beating at a different tempo as night follows day. After making our way to the Café Aragana at the north end of the square, we climbed the steps to the balcony, and took a seat, and looked through its ornate metal railings at the activity in the square below. Here we spent an interesting passage of time relaxing and drinking one of the more distinctively flavoured coffees. As the sun drifted towards the horizon, marking the passing of the day, the atmosphere in the square took on a subtle change. More and more people congregated around the stalls. At the far end of the square stood the Halakas, dressed in their djellabas of blue or grey, traditional head-to-toe garments, their heads surmounted by calico skull caps. These Halakas are the storytellers, spinning their tales of dervishes and djinns, stories passed down through generations of Berber families and no doubt embellished over time in their telling. As we watched, the Halaka paused only when the story was on a knife's edge, thus allowing him sufficient time to pass round his dish in which to collect coins from the enthralled listeners before continuing with the saga. By now the many food stalls were becoming active, their yellow butane lights haloed in the rising smoke; the distinctive aromas of the food complimented by the soothing music of the Gnaoua, musicians from the Sahara. Throughout the square, a variety of entertainers began assembling, each surrounded by their own small audiences: bare-chested fire-eaters pausing only to take in more oxygen; snake charmers with their cobras seemingly in a hypnotic trance, swaying gently to the playing of the pipes; dancers, acrobats, and magicians; and of course the many traders plying their wares. A truly remarkable transition from day to night, as hundreds of people started to gather in the square, adding to the growing cacophony of sound.

Our travel through Morocco had been a journey of two hundred miles in ten days over difficult terrain. It was a challenging, demanding, yet rewarding experience—but you don't have to do it the hard way, just make it a holiday!

Spain

During the latter half of June, I travelled down to Forest Park, Cromer, to carry out some maintenance work on the caravan and to get it ready for Nigel, Julie, and the family, who were going to spend two weeks down in Norfolk whilst I was away in Spain. On 15 July, I flew out to Seville to join Shirley and Martin on a river cruise, during which we were destined to visit Alcazar, Cadiz, Gibraltar, Alcoutin, Barracuda, Arcos de la Frontera, Santa Maria, and Cordoba. I met a very nice woman, a lawyer who lived in Sussex and was travelling with her mother. Well, I suppose there have to be *some* nice lawyers!

We enjoyed each other's company on the cruise, but as Shirley and Martin were prone to do, they worked in a not very subtle way trying to matchmake. I didn't need their help! Shirley and Martin were also reluctant to do too much sightseeing because they decided that the heat of the day was a more appropriate time to sit, nursing gin and tonics whilst surveying the locals from the comforts of a chair. This of course was the time when Europe was basking under temperatures which were more appropriate to Africa. Even in the UK, the heat wave brought temperatures of over 100 Fahrenheit in some places. On buses and the Underground, temperatures reached 126, like those normally experienced in Death Valley.

The East Coast Challenge

I arrived back near the end of July in time to make the annual college reunion at Kesteven Hall, returning via Laceby to spend the weekend with Pat and Bill, where they were experiencing an early harvest. I spent a couple of days helping, which made me realise that I wasn't in the highest category of physical health, especially when it came hefting bales of hay. Although this might seem like a series of holidays interspersed with visits, I still had my NHS work, U3A commitments, and of course the ever-present gymnastics to attend to. Jonathan, Anna, and the family came home during the summer school holiday period and came up to Darlington. Jane also visited with Laura and Jack for Julie's birthday, so we had an enlarged family celebration. I took Jonathon and Anna and the boys down to Gatwick for their return flight to Abu Dhabi on 26 August and spent the weekend with John and Barbara at Bolney. On Monday, I travelled up to Whissendine for a birthday BBQ at Jane's before returning home.

All roads are flat, it's just that some come with an incline.

In between, I had been desperately trying to fit in a few cycle rides in preparation for the next challenge, but I think I resigned myself to a lower (if possible) level of fitness. I should mention at this point that I hadn't been on a bike since the age of seventeen, apart from once round the block on a "sit up and beg" cycle—certainly not one that had a multitude of gears and such narrow tyres. Having been carried away with enthusiasm earlier in the year, I had purchased a Dawes Audex road racing bike. Ever since my early childhood, I'd dreamt of the day when I could afford such luxury. In those days, a Dawes was the ultimate in cycling experience and well beyond my level of investment, costing a mammoth twenty-five pounds, or over a month's salary!

Let me cut to the chase. September saw me astride a saddle, in earnest, for the first time since the age of seventeen (and yes, before you mention it, they did have bikes in those days). On Monday, 11 September, David and I set out to conquer the East Coast, joining up with the third in our party, Roger, a consultant surgeon. Well, such creatures have to be of some use! He was also an avid socialist, so I had two "Guardian Readers" who soon introduced me, through a series of lectures, to the etiquette of cycling. There I was, thinking all I had to do was keep my head down and pedal! Following the old, disused railway track between Robin Hoods Bay and Scarborough, I soon found that I had to overcome a few technicalities—for example, how to unlock one's feet from the pedals before crashing sideways into a bed of nettles, the etiquette of not riding too close to the man in front (as Rodger was quick to explain), slipstreaming is unacceptable behaviour, avoid riding two abreast, and as a back marker, call a warning of cars approaching. These are the problems you must live with when you ride with dedicated cyclists. As a rookie I had much to learn, but in my mind the priority was survival!

Our journey took us along the picturesque routes overlooking the cliffs, through Scarborough, where I recalled the many lost weekends when the children were at Fyling Hall School and we were investing money in training Jonathan as an artillery officer. (We encouraged him to play Space Invaders in the local amusement arcade on wet, miserable Sundays in winter whilst we read the papers in the warmth of the car. Oh, feckless parents.) Then it was on to Bridlington, which brought back memories of the cold and icy days during my flying training. Just beyond lay the massive World War II airfield of Carnaby, where I used to practise my emergency landings across the runway rather than up and down it, and just beyond it our destination for the night. Again, it reminded me of the time I was almost shot down on my cross-country flight. This was proving to be a trip down memory lane for all the wrong reasons! After a good night's sleep apart from David's snoring, we set off after breakfast for Hull—or should I say, Kingston-upon-Hull—in readiness to cross the Humber Bridge. It was a pleasant if flat part of the route with well-defined cycle tracks, which Roger kept pointing out, for my enlightenment, was only because of the sound investment of a Labour Government. And there I was, thinking that it was all down to investment grants from the EC!

By now we were noticing the effects of the easterly winds blowing in off the Humber, and whichever way we turned, it seemed to be head-on. Bearing in mind we had double panniers that carried another 25 kilogrammes of clothing and more, the wind made a significant difference to our progress. We eventually made it to the south bank, and I began to feel more at home in Lincolnshire, my old stamping ground, for a night stop at Bartnetby-le-Wold. I'm never quite sure with these boundary changes when Lincolnshire changed to South Humberside, and then which part of it changed back to Lincolnshire. To me, it will always be the home of the Yellow Bellies, and that's another topic. Bartnetby was never going to be the most thrilling of stops, but at least it was a break; unfortunately, we were too late for dinner. Yes, my Norman/Viking ancestors did make it this far north, but unfortunately they hadn't at that time cultivated their culinary skills—or if they had, they never passed the art down. Our accommodation was almost as bad as the meal, and the subject of my origins in Lincolnshire were thankfully never raised during the remainder of the evening.

The next morning, we set off to cross the Wolds, and anyone who says that Lincolnshire is flat should think again or try cycling across this part of the country, as the Wolds stretch down for two-thirds of the county. I had a couple of technical problems on the way, one in which was self-induced when I managed to dislodge my chain, and the second in which the local council road surfaces played their part, leaving me with a rear tyre puncture. We stopped for lunch in Market Rasen, close to my old base at Faldingworth, and eventually came down from the hills just north of Woodhall Spa, the one-time home of the No 617 Squadron (The Dambusters) after they left their original home at RAF Scampton, where we were to spend our second night. After a shower, we walked into town for a pub meal and a few beers. Fortunately, Roger had the pleasure of sharing a bedroom with David that night, which left me with undisturbed sleep.

As we headed south from Horncastle, the effect of the easterly wind became more evident, the roads were straighter, the rivers (or should I say dykes) more plentiful, and the countryside flatter. We had arrived in the Fens, where we began to contemplate what might happen if we had a Tsunami in the North Sea. My word, it makes you pedal faster. After a brief stop in Boston—you remember, the port from which we shipped all those migrants to our major colony across the Atlantic, and in return it is now suffering from a reverse situation, a massive influx of East Europeans—we pressed on towards Kings Lynn. Roger left us at Long Sutton as he headed off to Wisbech, and we took the road to Lynn and our final night stop before Cromer. We had the added luxury of separate bedrooms that night. Sharing with a beautiful girl is one thing; sharing with David is quite another. While on the subject of David's idiosyncrasies, he was the technical route selector and decided that the shortest route between two points is the longest. We therefore travelled along the coast of the Wash via Hunstanton, then along the north coast via Sheringham, before arriving in Cromer. As a simple aviator—and some would say very simple—I had thought that the direct route via Fakenham seemed more appropriate. But I knew how much David likes his cycling, bless him! It proved a very interesting and sandswept path somewhat congested with "Grockles" (sorry, I mean tourists), but it wasn't too long before I discovered David's secret. It had nothing to do with mathematical probabilities; it was something far more predictable. The pubs, at short intervals apart, had a wide selection of Real Ale. Clearly he had done his homework. How he keeps on the bike, I do not know!

We finally made it to Forest Park and the caravan to find Pat waiting with a lovely meal. How she calculated our arrival time, I do not know, but then, she's been married to David for a long time and must work around his distractions. Pat had travelled down by car, thankfully with a cycle rack that could accommodate two bikes. We spent the following week recovering, sightseeing, and travelling along the Norfolk countryside and reaping the benefit of David's earlier research; it helped that Pat was doing the driving. I think I saw more of Norfolk in those few days than in the preceding years.

Fifty miles a day, with headwinds all the way, seemed more than enough for me on my first real test on a bike. But it's amazing how the memory fades and one soon discards such problems as punctures, headwinds, rain, discomfort, and sleepless nights and starts with that idiotic phrase: "What are we going to do next year?"

CHAPTER 16

Projects and Other Commitments

I don't like to commit myself about heaven and
hell—you see I have friends in both places.
Mark Twain

Much of my spare time, if I ever had any, was taken up with three
projects. The first was the continuation of coaching at Eastbourne
coupled with our efforts to find a new gymnasium. The second
was the work that, as church warden, I was heavily involved in.
The third was the running the South Durham U3A. Towards
the end of the year, having paid for architects and a project officer
and having secured the support of the local planning officers, I felt
convinced that we were almost there. The plans were for a joint use
community centre in Cockerton, fully equipped on the upper floors
as a sole use gymnasium. We had secured an agreement with the
church authorities, who owned the land, that we would partly fund the
project, and they would receive a substantial revenue income. Despite
the support of council officials, the plan was rejected by councillors
on very questionable grounds. We didn't have the funds or the time to
take to appeal or have "called in" by the secretary of state. Suffice to
say, I remain jaundiced in my views on the interests of local politicians
being swayed by the vociferous and ill-informed minorities. Ten years
later, having grown the club from thirty members to five hundred,
all of whom in the age range from five to fifteen, we are still fighting
for local support to establish a permanent, self-supporting home. It's

unbelievable. What happened about improving health, looking after children, and keeping crime off the street? Fortunately, five years later we at long last received planning permission for a factory building on an industrial site, which would provide more than enough space to build for the future.

Like many aging churches, St Mary's at Cockerton did not meet the demands of modern-day legislation: access for the disabled, health and safety issues, toilet and kitchen facilities, and emergency exits. As church warden and thereby the guardian of the church property, it was down to me, assisted by the parish council, to ensure the work was carried out. The alternative was to close yet another church. The problem as always was the lack of funds. Over the five years of my tenure that followed, we managed to garner the funds, supported to some extent by a couple of generous benefactors and from the strenuous support of the incumbent, Father Richard Wallace, who regrettably died from cancer in January 2012 but not before having seen the culmination of all the efforts. Nevertheless, it proved a major headache at the time.

The third aspect was my time as chairman of the U3A. Shortly after arriving in Darlington, and once Sheila's cancer had stabilised, we joined the South Durham Branch of the U3A. Like so many of these organisations, it's not long before you are co-opted onto the committee. In my case, within the year I was landed with the job of chairman because there had been a schism in the committee, as often seems to be the case. There was a clash of personalities between the chairman and secretary on the one hand and the treasurer and colleagues on the other hand. The secretary and the chairman walked out of the meeting having lost the argument. One thing I've learnt in civilian life is that those in power talk but don't practice democracy, especially in local committees! In trying to calm things down and avoid the committee disintegrating, I found myself being reluctantly persuaded to run the branch until the next AGM. However, once in it's very hard to get out, and I stayed for the next five years until I eventually found a willing successor (well, there was a little persuasion!). Despite her illness, over this time Sheila played a very active role in helping to pull together the disparate groups, and she almost single-handedly provided the celebration luncheon for 150 members. Her reputation as a chef (sorry, I forgot my principles— cook) preceded her!

The year, as is often the case, proved to be something of a mixed bag. I heard from Maureen Bennett that John had died of cancer. Maureen and John had been good friends of ours since our time together in Germany. I went down for the funeral during the first week in November. As with all such illnesses, it hadn't been sudden, and Maureen had had some time to adapt, but it was still a shock. Having gone through this experience with Sheila, I think it helped Maureen to talk about the good times. Two days later, I was in Watford staying with Richard and Jane because we had golf on the Saturday and the Northwood Cricket Club dinner the same evening. Two weeks later, following the Remembrance Parade weekend in London, I was on my way again to Abu Dhabi for an enjoyable twelve days in the sun on my pre-Christmas visit. Each time I go, I'm staggered by the rate of development; it's amazing what oil wealth can achieve. Isn't it a pity that we don't have other methods of developing our economy at the same rate of growth? I returned for the usual round of Christmas lunches, LTOCA in London, followed by the RAF Club Christmas lunch with Bob Carr and rounded off with Christmas at Julie's. Jane, Laura, and Jack came up on Saturday for three days, and I disappeared off to Pat and Bill's for the customary New Year's celebration. Was this becoming habitual?

The year 2007 has been defined by some as the year of earthquakes, although from what I recall the world has seen worse years, and not too long ago. There were, however, two or three quakes of sizable force which were to have significance results. In January, there was an earthquake of 8.1 magnitude off the Kuril Islands, which followed an earlier one in November 2006 of 8.3 magnitude. The Kuril Islands form part of the ring of tectonic instability encircling the Pacific Ocean referred to as the Ring of Fire, an area of substantial earthquake and volcanic activity over the years. There were further earthquakes, one in particular of 8.1 magnitude at the boundary between the Nazca and South American tectonic plates, causing havoc in Peru, where 85 per cent of the city of Pisco was destroyed on 15 August, killing 547 and injuring a further 1,300. There were others on both side of the Pacific Ocean, some creating tsunamis. I'm still amazed that we can almost predict in which geographical area these earthquakes, tsunamis, and volcanic eruptions will occur but can do nothing to counter the enormity and ferocity of their actions.

Other Events

Perhaps not of the same magnitude but worth mentioning, other events included Tony Blair giving way to Gordon Brown as prime minister in the UK; some might see that as an earthquake. Yet another pair of Scotsmen running our country. Whatever happened to devolution for England? Finally, there was Bulgaria and Romania joining the European Union as the twenty-sixth and twenty-seventh states; at this rate, we shall soon become the United States of Europe! Perhaps the events of 2007 should not pass without mention of the watershed in the global economy because it was this year that saw the start of what many economists have considered to be the worst financial crisis since the Great Depression of the 1930s, leading to a downturn in the economy and the global recession which spanned the years 2008–2012. There is a great deal of speculation as to the cause of this crisis: a complex interplay of government policies in the United States and Europe, the easy access to subprime borrowers (mortgages on home loans), the lack of capital holdings in banks and financial institutions, and speculation in the Futures Markets are but some of the reasons. The results were inevitable: an increase in sovereign debt and an inability to access credit. The responses of governments varied, firstly with unprecedented fiscal stimulus through quantitative easing, the printing of more money. QE is based on the theory that in a severe recession, the economy needs Keynesian stimulus to revive it (greater spending). However, this may ease the crisis but only adds to the long-term debt. The alternative was to cut the deficit through austerity measures and reduce government spending rather than increasing taxation. Either route is fraught with dangers, but more about this later when I recall events in the remainder of the decade.

Upon returning home from my New Year's break in Lincolnshire, I took up my new part-time role as a nonexecutive director with the Durham and Darlington Primary Care Trusts. I hasten to add that the concept of part-time doesn't exist in the National Health only where money is involved. It wasn't for the money (as the remuneration was a pittance), but I wanted to do something that would recognise the help the NHS had given Sheila over the years. I soon learned that although it was supposed to be for two to three days a month, with all the organisational changes it turned out to be three days a week and, as time evolved, five days a week. I began to find the work interesting and worthwhile, and before long I had been asked to take over as chair of the Provider Committee, the role of which was to arrange the provision of services within the community. At the same time, I took on the role of chair of the Exceptional Cases Committee for both PCTs, the task of which was to examine and fund (if approved) those cases for which treatment was not already approved and funded within the NHS Tariff. Ironically, this was the very committee that had approved the payment for Sheila's treatment of Herceptin back in 2001 when PPP had withdrawn their funding. It was therefore a task that I attacked with vigour, although I knew that we were not dealing with a bottomless pit of money. Balancing the pressing needs of so many with limited resources became a significant factor in my time with the NHS.

In March I took ten days out to join Shirley and Martin on a holiday in Portugal. Travelling south, mainly by train, our journey took us to Oporto, on to Coimbra, and then down to Lisbon and the surrounding countryside. When I had been at the RAF Navigational School at Stradishall in Suffolk, we had flown down through Oporto to Gibraltar, accompanying the students on their major navigational test. This latest venture was not work but a nice, relaxing holiday, Martin and Shirley were quite content to find the nearest bar where they could have their early morning gin and tonic. I, taking on the role of family photographer, did the sightseeing element, clambering up to old castles, taking in scenic views, or soaking up the local history. Upon returning home, I had a few days catching up on work before a spell in hospital—nothing major, just straightening out my nose, which had been kicked out of place whilst I was coaching gymnastics. Not the gentile sport that it would appear to an outsider. Some girls can play rough!

The Cheshire Canal

During May, I joined Jane and Richard and their families, including Richard's mother, Sheila, on a canal boat holiday in Cheshire. Well, I loosely call it a holiday because it was the blind leading the blind; only Richard and his mother had handled a narrow barge before. What's the saying? "In the land of the blind, the one-eyed man is God." Ninety-two locks in ninety-two miles was not something that I had anticipated and was a trial of one's patience as well as strength. I must say that the teenagers were not impressed; it was totally alien to their usual daily routine because it involved getting out of bed before midday and working. They mutinied on day three and left for home! We took the three dogs, and they spent most of their time in "dog overboard" situations in the water. Richard's mother stood in the cockpit (sorry, I forget, it's nautical terms—the Bridge) with her hand on the tiller directing operations. I therefore nicknamed her the tank commander. I know it's not the correct title, but she looked as though she was directing military tank manoeuvres. Mind you, coward that I am, I never used that term in her presence. Having set out the downside, there were the more interesting days. I could even refer to them as pastoral if they hadn't been interspersed with occasions such as the day we spent in dry dock as the result of having a discarded tyre wrapped around the propeller which had to be cut loose. Total mayhem, but a holiday with a difference.

CHAPTER 17

John O'Groats and Back

To the sober person adventurous conduct often seems insanity.
Georg Simmel

Towards the end of 2006, I spent the weekend with Pat and David in Rothbury, a relaxing break. Inevitably our conversation turned to cycling. With David, there are only two things in life, cycling and politics. I try to avoid the latter because we come from opposite ends of the spectrum. I had been explaining my thoughts of a cycle ride from Land's End to John O'Groats, and though he was keen to participate, he thought it would be more convenient to start from the north so that a return journey could be done without having to resort to rail. It would be a little longer, in the region of 1,100 miles, which he thought could be achieved in about fourteen days. I wasn't quite as sanguine, having realised that we would have to average over seventy-eight miles a day—the equivalent of eight hours a day in the saddle. However, David was limited in the time he could be away from his work, so I foolishly agreed.

For the next few months, I attempted to improve my cycling stamina but didn't get beyond thirty miles on those days that I managed to train. Somewhat ill prepared, as has been the case in each of my other challenges, I set off with David for the nether regions of the United Kingdom. On 22 June, I joined David up in Caistron, near Rothbury in Northumberland, and we set out on our ride from there to John

O'Groats and back. "Why not from Land's End?" you might ask. Well, it was all about the economics and the distance. We wanted to do somewhere in the region of 1,000 miles, we had a window of 14 to 16 days, and we wanted to avoid the problems of moving bikes by rail, so we compromised. From my point of view, this was another charity ride from which there was no turning back, the beneficiaries on this occasion being Cancer Research (UK) and the Royal Masonic Benevolent Institution.

The weather on the first five days of the ride can be better described as atrocious, with severe thunderstorms, lightning, and torrential rain coupled with an unexpected north-westerly headwind. Usually the prevailing winds at this time of the year are from the south-west. Many of the roads in the Scottish Borders had sections washed away and resembled rivers rather than roads. Although farther north the rain wasn't quite as heavy, it was persistent and energy sapping. I now know what a salmon feels like, fighting upstream against the current to lay its eggs and then die! Was this a voice from the heavens, or Sheila telling me I wasn't up to the challenge?

We travelled through Northumberland, passing Kielder Reservoir, the largest artificial lake in the UK surrounded by the largest man-made forest in Europe, on our way to Edinburgh for an overnight stay before moving on to Stirling via Falkirk. Stirling, once the capital of Scotland and today the gateway to the Highlands, is dominated by the Wallace Monument commemorating a famous Scots victory. Well, they have to have something they can celebrate! In early September 1297, King Edward's army arrived in Stirling to cut down Scotland's resistance. The Scots, under William Wallace, retreated, thereby allowing half the English force to advance over the narrow bridge. Although the English had the greater number, once over the bridge, they were trapped in the loop of the river in marshy ground and subsequently slaughtered. I knew how they felt as I crossed the bridge in the never-ending torrential rain and climbed the hill out towards the Bridge of Allan along roads that cascaded water and gave no indication of depth. Was I to become the latest English lamb to the slaughter?

The road to Aberfeldy, via Crieff and Glen Eagles, offered little relief because although the rains had eased, the winds had swung round to the north, thus ensuring that we would once again be faced with a headwind. Coming down the hill into Aberfeldy, we were met by Ross Menzies, a friend from my days in Malta with whom we were staying the night. As always, Ross and Nanette made us feel part of the family. Refreshed, we set off the following morning for Kingussie via Dalwhinnie—a whisky that brings back memories. I needed one—a whisky, not a memory! We soon faced the long climb over the Dromochter Pass at a height of 1,516 feet, the watershed where the River Truim flows north and the River Gary flows south. This took us along Glen Truim to Aviemore.

Later that day, having passed the north-eastern end of Loch Ness and climbed up over Slochd, we reached the undulating Meall Mor and headed for the Moray Firth and our night stop in Inverness. After a poor night's sleep, we saw ourselves back in the saddle for a further day of battling the headwinds on our way to Lairg, but not before negotiating Dingwall, Alness, and Bonar Bridge. I can't remember how many times I proffered up prayers for a change in the wind, a flattening of the hills, and some sunshine, to no avail. At this stage, I was beginning to lose the will to live, watching David's ever-rotating, short, hairy legs as he burnt up the miles. I do recall raising questions over his parental ancestry as well as his thirst for punishment; he called it cycling for pleasure, the poor, disillusioned individual. I think he should take up flagellation as a sport. As for me, I let my mind wander, as it is prone to do, thinking of the many more pleasurable activities I could have been engaged upon. Despite these conditions, the considerable challenge of the hills, several punctures caused by the poor quality of the roads, and frequent stops to consult the maps (which never seemed to show the routes or the villages that we believed featured in the locations in which we stopped), we managed to keep up an average of ten miles per hour each day. It may not seem a lot, but when you take out time for meals, calls of nature, sorting out mechanical problems, and the reluctance of the body to get back in the saddle, the speed must increase proportionately.

The famed Scottish midges who reside in this area and are notable at this time of the year were not out in force to attack the English intruders. Maybe it was the name of McKechnie that fooled them, or perhaps like us, they were sick and tired of the perpetual rain. Nevertheless, their places were adequately filled by less familiar insects, and they gorged themselves on any part of our exposed bodies, resulting in a few sleepless nights.

Our accommodation varied from a room in a Youth Hostel in Aberdeen, occupied by eight others whose snoring could have been mistaken for the London Philharmonic had it not been for the lack of unison, to a luxury stately home, Carbisdale Hall, donated by the Salveson family to the Scottish Youth Hostel Association (SYHA). In between there were a series of B & Bs which ranged from comfortable to homely. In my youth, which was light years away, I had on occasions visited youth hostels which were of questionable standards, one step removed from living in the open. How standards have changed. However, I must continue with my version of the saga. Leaving Lairg and Loch Shin behind us, we soon entered upon a road(?) loosely referred to in the appropriate road atlas as a minor road with passing places—on a moonscape occupied by sheep and little else. It was here that my prayers were answered. At the very time that we were met with a snow blizzard and I was about to hurl my bike into the nearby stream, we stumbled on the Cask Inn—what an appropriate name—which had appeared out of nowhere. To this day I'm inclined to believe it was a mirage; however, the road atlas does confirm its existence. Inside were six people occupying seats, all but one being English, including the owners! It was noticeable that the farther north we progressed, the more evident it became that the Scots no longer inhabited the country but had made their homes elsewhere: The United States, Australia, Europe, or dare I say England. By the time we reached John O'Groats, it was hard to find a Scot; there were some English, a lot of Australians, some Dutch, and even a few Germans amongst the assorted other tribes, but few Scots! As for the French, I think they went home in 1746 having lost out in the Jacobite Rebellion. So why are the Scots pushing so hard for independence? Power for the few, no doubt!

Let me not digress but return to my mirage. In an effort to revive our flagging bodies, we had a coffee followed by a rum, and then rum with a coffee, and then rum with rum. Well, too much coffee is bad for you! By late afternoon, with darkness descending and no lights, and with little hope of mounting the bike without falling, let alone riding in a straight line, we sallied forth for Tongue some thirty miles to the north where awaiting us was (we hoped) a comfortable bed. It is about this time that I fear my memory recall is not as clear as it should have been. We eventually reached our destination without mishap, and I do recollect that the following day, we set out on our final leg along the top of world—sorry, Scotland. Other than that, there is little remaining in the memory bank.

I do remember that on approaching Thurso from the west, we passed the Dounreay nuclear power station, which was in the course of being decommissioned. From my previous existence, I had always been somewhat cautious when coming into close proximity with radiation. Knowing it to be safe is one thing, but courting a close embrace is another! Perhaps we pedalled just a little faster in our desire to reach Thurso, our last watering hole before our final destination.

John O'Groats is supposedly named after Jan de Groate, a Dutchman who obtained a grant from James IV of Scotland in 1496 to operate the ferry between his home and the Orkneys. It appeared that he might have been the last resident because as we arrived at John O'Groats around 5 p.m., we found the place deserted. Added to which, the tourist office had taken down the famous directional signpost in the belief that it might be taken by some souvenir hunting cyclist. You've got to hand it to them: I would never have thought of uprooting and carrying a six-foot pole upon which are mounted several finger points giving the mileage to various locations around the globe, let alone lashing it to my bike. After all, it was going to take me some time to get back on the bike without acting as an agent for Pickford's removal service. We eventually moved five miles south to our residence in the local youth hostel, run strangely enough by a couple from Darlington. Well, I did say that they'd run out of Scots. Because there was no food or cooking facilities, it was suggested that we cycle north again to find a restaurant that might be open. We did, and luckily there was, but it was another ten-mile round trip that I could have done without.

The following morning, we made our third sortie into the ghost town of John O'Groats to take a few pictures against the harbour wall and the derelict hotel long since closed. After consulting our maps, as David is wont to do, we plotted our route home. I said to David there were only two roads, but there was always the option of catching the train from Wick. It was a defeatist attitude which he would not entertain, but it was worth a try. Having repacked our kit for the hundredth time, we set out on our return to civilisation. The mythical God of weather—I know not his name, but it sounds not unlike the Anglo-Saxon for bar steward—decided that he had enough of blowing the winds to the south, and it was time to reverse them to the north for our sole amusement. Headwinds up, headwinds down! It was a bit like spinning a double-headed coin.

By cutting across country, we eventually reached the main A9, which follows the coast down to Inverness. We had planned on reaching Nigg and catching the ferry to Cromarty on the Black Isle, and then a further ferry from Fortrose to Nairn on the south of the Moray Firth. However, the Fates transpired against us because on reaching Nigg in the late afternoon, we discovered that the ferry company had gone out of business and stopped operating the previous month. You could describe my response as a sense of humour failure. We retired to the local hostelry to have a recuperative beer served by the landlord whilst what I assume was the landlady reclined on a sofa with her hand on her head, moaning, "I can't go on with this pressure." I looked around and noted that we were the only customers! There was nothing we could do but to backtrack to the A9, by which time it was raining heavily. The heavy goods vehicles appearing out of the failing light seemed to grow in threatening enormity, but not to worry—we only had another sixty miles to go! What followed is history and forgettable, although on many occasions that day, I did feel as though I might be destined to join those Viking laddies who had made it to Valhalla.

A point of interest: why the Black Isle? Firstly, it is not an island because it is surrounded on only three sides by water, so it is technically a promontory. Secondly, it is not black. Its name is derived from the fact that snow doesn't settle there, but it does in the surrounding area, and therefore its dark colouring against the snow looks black—hence the name.

Talking about history, we decided to travel to Culloden, which is but a few miles from Inverness, to look at the battlefield, the site of the last pitched battle fought on British soil; the final confrontation which was to end the Jacobite Rebellion when, on 16 April 1746, some two thousand Jacobites were killed and the Scots routed and driven from the field within one hour, with only the loss of fifty government troops. "Bonny" Prince Charlie was to flee to France and never to return to Scotland. At the time that we made the visit, there was little to show that this had been one of the most decisive battles in British history, but then, neither is Flodden, for the Scots suffer from amnesia when it comes to defeats. I notice it even today on the rugby and football fields!

But I digress yet again. I did warn you that I'm prone to do so, and quite frequently. We continued our travels through the Highlands across to Elgin before turning south through Rothes, Dufftown, and Huntley. Upon reaching Stonehaven on the coast, we moved on down the A9 to Arbroath before travelling alongside the Carnoustie Golf course. I only mention this because it was the year that the town was to host the 136th Open Golf Championship. It was also close to that point that I had a senior moment, forgetting to turn a corner at reduced speed, whereupon the bike took to the air and delivered me into the hedgerow and fencing which was secured with barbed wire. I looked up into the face of an equally puzzled cow who clearly had never witnessed humans flying despite the location close to RAF Leuchars. This strange encounter with barbed wire left me with a scar on my upper arm, and yet the sleeve of the jacket was not torn or punctured, unlike the wheel of my bike!

Our next leg was to take us from Dundee to Newport-on-Tay via the road bridge, one of the longest in Europe when it was opened in 1966.

It is 1.4 miles long (2,250 metres) with a 3-metre walkway/cycle track in the centre, a somewhat nerve-racking prospect for a cyclist and equally so for the poor pedestrian, but it does save time. We travelled down alongside the Fife Regional Park to Glenrothes and then on to Inverkeithing, where later we crossed the Forth Road Bridge, which was opened in 1964 and links the two sides at South Queensferry, only a short distance from the centre of Edinburgh and our overnight accommodation. I almost had the feeling that we were reaching the end of our venture. However, we were still north of the border and a long way from Darlington. The following day, our route took us through the pedestrian and cycle underpass below Arthur's Seat and out to join the A7, which would lead us back through Selkirk and Hawick to cross the border at Carter Bar. After a brief rest, we pressed on, passing Keilder to arrive as light was failing, close to the village of Otterburn.

We were only about twenty-five miles from David's home, I suggested we stop at the local shop in Otterburn so that I could buy a bottle of champagne to celebrate our return south of the border and what we at least considered a tremendous achievement by two elderly gentlemen. I entered the shop and selected what I considered to be one of the better champagnes and proffered my money to the man behind the counter. I was then staggered to hear him say, "You can put that back—we don't sell alcohol to cyclists." He was totally impervious to the protestations of a long-distance cyclist of pensionable age, even one who was polite beyond reason. Isn't it amazing that we have such "Job Worthies" running a business? As I said to him when I was leaving empty-handed, "I hope the local sheep don't shop here—or perhaps they do." Thirsty and anxious to record our achievement of having covered over one thousand miles, we headed for Caistron, and this time I was not worried by the speed with which David attacked his pedals. David's wife, Pat, had already had the forethought to have a chilled bottle awaiting our arrival, bless her. We celebrated our modest achievement in style. I do recall saying never again—but in the words of James Bond, never say never!

The return to Darlington was uneventful, especially in light of what we had subjected our bodies to over the days during which we set out to conquer the north. Upon arriving home, I returned to the daily routine, if you can ever describe it as such, dealing with the ever-increasing problems generated by the NHS and the many other commitments that I had managed to accumulate. At the same time, I thought next year I would have a nice, relaxing holiday and forget the traumas of fundraising and the challenges that they give rise to. How euphoric, or rather how foolish, of me!

> Life is like the river, sometimes it sweeps you gently along
> and sometimes the rapids come out of nowhere.

Time to Recuperate

To repay a sponsor's generosity, I was invited to participate in a couple of days playing cricket for Northwood Cricket Club in Middlesex. I must say that my abilities with the bat, and to a lesser extent the ball, left much to be desired, and some of the other players must have speculated on the alternative option: that I should perhaps have just extended my cycle ride and bypassed Northwood. Not that this was a year packed with holidays, you will understand, but it was simply my way of dealing with the problems of the NHS. After all, I didn't want to burden them with another patient suffering from stress! In order to ease their workload during August, I took myself for a cruise down the Danube. Well, it wasn't really my idea; Shirley and Martin had booked to go and thought I should join them on the journey upstream from Budapest to Germany. Once again, I found myself doing the castles and countryside whilst they did—yes, you've guessed right, the gin and tonics. I believe their philosophy was to never drink water because of the disgusting things fish can do in it. Nevertheless, this beautiful and historic countryside never fails to impress me, and it was a relaxing holiday. Little did I think that it would be just a matter of time before I would be talked into cycling one thousand miles down the Danube to the same location.

Anna and the boys came back to the UK in August for a final week at Cromer with her mother before flying back to Abu Dhabi. They had been out in Slovakia, where they had bought a house in a small village in the foothills of the Tatras Mountains, the idea being to escape there from the Middle East during the heat of the summer.

In late September and early October, I took time out to visit Norfolk and carry out some maintenance work on the holiday home and garden at Cromer. Actually, it was just my excuse to chill out, looking at the seals and the birds (feathered variety, unfortunately). November was a bit of a golfing month, another game I play badly, with games in Northwood, Lytham St Annes, and Durham played over weekends. At the end of the month, I flew out to the Emirates to stay with Jonathan, Anna, and family for three weeks and watch the World Rugby sevens in Dubai. Jonathan played for the Emirates in the first round and achieved two cracked ribs for his efforts, so hilarity had to be avoided at all costs—no chance, having seen his performance! We returned to Abu Dhabi and a more sedate lifestyle and watched the world powerboat championships. We also spent a couple of days at Liwa Oasis on the edge of the Empty Quarter and enjoyed some time in Oman. In between times, I spent several weekends being entertained or entertaining friends who lived in scattered parts of the UK, as well as rummaging through our collective memories of how life was in the olden days. The remaining time was split between NHS activities; work involving the local church, of which somehow I had become church warden; the University of the Third Age, of which I was chairman; gymnastics at club, regional, and national level; family history; and organising Remembrance Day Parades in Whitehall. Added to which, there were two weddings and a funeral, not forgetting dog walking, although I'm not quite sure who took whom!

Late November and early December saw me back in Abu Dhabi once more, a sort of pre-Christmas visit, added to which the boys were playing in the Abu Dhabi rugby sevens competition at the end of November, something I didn't want to miss. During my stay, I was invited to the Dascam Christmas party, the consultants for whom Jonathan worked. It was unusual for a variety of reasons: because it was early, because it was a beach party held on Liwa Island, and because drinks were freely available—most unusual in a prohibited area. Now I could understand why it was held on a secluded island! However, it was all with the permission of the Emirate authorities. On reflection, my sojourns in Abu Dhabi reminded me of earlier days in other parts of the Gulf, but they were far more relaxing.

In mid-December, I found myself back at Pat and David's for the weekend. Christmas was at Julie and Nigel's, followed by New Year's 2008 at Laceby with Pat and Bill. One could almost say the there were signs of repetition in my behaviour. But that's the sign of advancing years, when habit becomes paramount.

CHAPTER 18

South-East Asia and Beyond

Asia is not going to be civilized after the methods of the
West. There is too much Asia and she is too old.
Rudyard Kipling

It was 2008, a leap year, and the eighth year of the third millennium.
It was the year that saw the forty-fourth US presidential election, won
by Democrat Barak Obama, the first African American. It was also
the year that Dmitri Medvedev, former aide to Vladimir Putin, was
elected president of Russia. Strange how some people cling to power
come what may. Putin, having manoeuvred his aide into power, then
stayed on as prime minister, the power behind the throne until such
time as he could legally get himself reelected as president. February
saw Kosovo, a part of the former Yugoslavia, declare independence
from Serbia.

Generally, it was a depressing start to the year, with January seeing
the worst financial crisis since the Great Depression of 1929. Stock
markets around the world plunged with a major domino effect
occurring as global banks, having stalled in the United States causing
a knock-on effect in Europe. Added to which, crude oil prices hit one
hundred dollars a barrel for the first time, and food prices increased
significantly.

On 12 May an earthquake of 8.5 magnitude hit the province of Sichuan in China. The quake was on the border of the Indo-Australian plate and the Eurasian plate, and its impact spread many hundreds of miles from the epicentre with devastating consequences, resulting in 69,197 deaths, 18,392 missing, and 374,176 injured. Cyclone Nagis killed more than 138,000 people as it moved through Myanmar. It wasn't only earthquakes that were causing concern. In March, 160 square miles of the Antarctic Willet Shelf disintegrated, raising further concerns about global warming.

In August, eleven international climbers were killed on the world's second highest mountain, K2. The tragedy was believed to have been caused by an ice avalanche 400 metres from the summit at a point known as the Bottleneck, a narrow couloir which is overhung by seracs. Although an easier route to the top, it is situated at 8,200 metres, well within the death zone, and is therefore a most dangerous route.

There were further successes in space: NASA's Phoenix mission landed on Mars, the Fermi Gamma-ray Space Telescope launched, and India entered into events with the launch of its first lunar spacecraft.

This was to be yet another hectic and eventful year for me, with two visits to Abu Dhabi, a tour of China and Japan, a visit to Slovakia, and the usual visits to Cromer (isn't life a bum). Added to which, we formally opened our new gym in Darlington, of which I was now president, with the usual collection of dignitaries. I had taken on the role of chairman of North of England Gymnastics as well as being treasurer of the Durham County Association. In between times, I was heavily engrossed in the machinations of the Health Services as chairman of the PCC Provider Service, planning for the eventual hiving-off of the services to the private sector; church matters, as the church warden; LTOCA meetings in London; chairing the South Durham U3A Committee; and carrying out the many Masonic commitments. However, I managed to fit in a weekend with friends in Dorset and a weekend in Lytham St Anne's for a fiftieth wedding anniversary, as well as slotting in weekly training for the attempt on Kilimanjaro, scheduled for the New Year. If this is retirement, I wonder how I ever got the time to go to work!

Having settled into our new gym location, a revamped building in Weir Street that was formerly an old factory unit, and having the official opening by the mayor in January, the remainder of my spare time was absorbed in coaching the growing number of members and, with others, organising fundraising to sustain our activities. By this time, we had grown from a club of some twenty gymnasts to one of over three hundred. As chairman of North of England Gymnastics, this was also a busy year for me, with meetings and competitions across the region in addition to those arranged by English Gymnastics, on whose board I represented NEGA.

A Return to Malaysia and Abu Dhabi

In early February, I spent the weekend with Mike and Sheila Walker, old RAF friends, down in Dorset before flying out to Kula Lumpur, Malaysia, where Jonathan's boys were participating in a schools' international rugby tournament. Anna couldn't be there, so we had a boys' time sightseeing, eating, and drinking, as one is prone to do at such events! My arrival coincided with Jonathan's birthday—yet another excuse to celebrate. It was also a time for reminiscences; for Jonathan having spent a year at the Malaysian Staff College; for Charlie, if indeed he could recall anything at all, having been born in Kula Lumpur; and for me having spent many eventful times representing Malaya in athletics at the international level during the 1950s, a time when the "Emergency" was at its height.

I quite vividly recall a senior moment. Jonathon and the boys were leaving our hotel to catch their flight back to Abu Dhabi, and as I waved them goodbye, I was struck by a sudden thought. Wasn't that what I was supposed to be doing earlier that morning—leaving, not waving goodbye? In a state of panic, my internal clock had missed out by twenty-four hours, and I called the airport with some fabricated excuse and managed to rebook for that evening. Luckily, I was also able to rebook my room at the hotel. However, it was all an expensive and embarrassing oversight, and one that I haven't been allowed to forget by my children. That apart, it was a most enjoyable time in Kula Lumpur and a chance to be with the boys.

During the last two weeks in March and the first two weeks in April, I found myself once again in Abu Dhabi. Anna had been admitted to hospital for a major operation, and because Jonathan had pressing work commitments in his new job, there was nobody to look after the boys, so I flew out to fill the gap for three weeks. On my return to the UK, there followed an intense period of work involving both my NHS and gymnastics commitments before I left once again for the Far East on 28 April, a visit which I had planned many months before.

China and Japan

In my earlier days, I'd always had a fascination for those countries which were far outside the boundaries of what I perceived then to be the limits of my future travel. Isn't it incredible how the world has shrunk? That, or my expectations have expanded. China and Japan were places to which one's imagination could travel, but little else. Certainly, in my service career they were places one read about, observed from a distance, and worried over. To me, they were enigmatic both in historical and modern terms. China is an enigma and has been so over many centuries. Many years ago, Churchill said that Russia was "a riddle, wrapped in a mystery, inside an enigma". In my view, this applies more so to China, where both the old and the new are shrouded in mysteries. The only difference is that the doll within the doll is a Russian concept, not Chinese.

China is a massive country covering over 3.7 million square miles, and up until the time of Genghis Khan, it comprised of several warring kingdoms. It has a population of 1.3 billion, and with a GDP (gross domestic product) more than $9 trillion, it is fast becoming the major economy in the world. This year was of particular importance both to the Chinese and the rest of the world because Beijing was set to host the Summer Olympics. Although I didn't get the opportunity to see the Games I did see the Olympic Park in all its glory before the Games opened. I thought the "Bird's Nest" Stadium was particularly impressive and an appropriate building for the venue. The Games, held 6–24 August, proved a great success, with forty-three world records being established

Our entry into China was through the city of Shanghai, and nowhere is the contrast between old and new more aptly portrayed than in arriving at Pudong Airport and travelling into Shanghai. At the airport, you board the Mag-lev, the world's fastest train at 430 kph (268 mph), which takes just seven minutes twenty seconds to reach Shanghai, compared to an hour by road.

Shanghai

Originally a fishing village, it flourished under the 1842 Treaty of Nanking, which opened China to foreign trade following the Opium Wars. It is the largest city by population in China and the largest city proper in the world, with a population of over 23 million. It sits on the delta astride the mighty Yangtze River, which divides the old city from the new. On the west bank lies the Bund, the old colonial commercial centre and once the financial centre of the Far East; on the eastern side, the skyscrapers (such as the Oriental Pearl Tower) define Pudong, the new financial heart of the city. The Shanghai Stock Exchange is the world's fastest-growing financial centre, which at the time of the visit had shown a massive 130 per cent growth in just one year. Overarching the city is the ever-present fog, the pollution resulting from the industries that surround the city—a reminder of the penalties of progress. As well as the many and varied industries, the river plies a constant flow of shipping and feeds the busiest container port in the world, handling over 450 million tonnes of cargo.

It is never possible to do justice to a city of immense size, but there are two aspects worth a special mention. One is the Jade Buddha Temple, and the other is the Humble Administrator's Garden. The temple contains two Buddha statues in Jade, one weighing three tonnes and a smaller reclining one representing Buddha's death. There is an old

Chinese saying: "Gold is valuable; jade is invaluable." The toughness of jade is remarkable. It has strength greater than steel and was put to work by many early civilisations for axes, knives, and other weapons. It was later that jade became a symbolic stone used in ornaments and religious artefacts. Today it's valued for its beauty. The emerald green jade, known as imperial jade, is highly valued and is coloured by chromium. Other colours are influenced by iron (green and brown) and manganese (violet), whilst Nephrite is usually only green and creamy white. As Confucius said, "When I think of a wise man, his merits appear to be liked to jade."

There are several truly remarkable gardens in China, one of which is the five-hundred-year-old Garden of the Humble Administrator. A traditional Chinese Ming-style private garden, it was originally built in 1559 by Pan Indian, a wealthy figure who had been in public service. He had it constructed for his father, who'd died shortly before it was completed. The site occupies twelve acres and has many Chinese pavilions and never-ending paths. Close by is the famous eighteenth-century Huxing Ting Teahouse with its bridge of nine turns, reflecting the ancient belief that evil spirits are unable to turn corners to cross water (a bit like the old Skoda car!). Its name, however, is more prosaic than it would seem: it simply means "mid-lake pavilion".

Suzhou

Suzhou is appropriately called the Venice of the East because it is a city of canals, arched bridges, whitewashed houses, and ornamental gardens. It has a history stretching back some 2,500 years, being the traditional centre of the Chinese silk industry, but it did not prosper until the construction of the Grand Canal during the Sui Dynasty (AD 581–618). The city has long been known as a centre for artists, scholars, merchants, financiers, and government officials, who built fine gardens around their villas. The villas were designed as small replicas of the natural world, with ponds and hills representing lakes and mountains, and pavilions and towers are surrounded by secluded walls. One of the most famous is the Master of the Nets Garden, covering some 5,400 square metres; the pond in the middle covers

400 square metres. It is impressive to see many examples of where light and dark are used as contrasts both within the villa and in the external settings.

Hangzhou

Situated at the southern end of the Grand Canal is one of China's seven ancient national capitals, the old imperial city of Hangzhou, renowned for its beauty. There is an old popular saying: "Above, there is heaven. Below, there is Souzhou and Hangzhou." Marco Polo, who visited the city in the thirteenth century, called it the most beautiful and prosperous city in the world. But then, he probably hadn't travelled very far at that time! Many artists have flocked here over the centuries, turning it into a cultural centre. Two of China's most famous poets, Bai Juyi and Su Dongpo, served as mayors. (Don't worry—I hadn't heard of them either.) The city continued to prosper during the Ming and Qing eras due to the thriving silk industry and its location in the fertile rice-growing region. By far the most attractive part of this location is West Lake, which occupies over 1,400 acres of water. It was once a shallow sea inlet, but in the eighth century it was dammed and dredged, and the lake was created. It's encircled on three sides by misty green hills, where Longjing tea and mulberry trees are cultivated in abundance. The adjoining gardens were first landscaped during the Southern Song Dynasty between AD 1127–1279.

Xitang

We travelled on to Xitang, a strategic town in the south of the Yangtze River delta, famous for its waterways, ancient houses, and long covered walkways. The town and the surrounding areas are also known as a centre for the manufacture of buttons resulting from palace life that demanded gold, silver, agate, pearl, and coral buttons, whereas the lesser mortals made do with seashells or wood. In this day and age of mass production and plastic facsimile, there seemed to me little possibility of this becoming a major growth industry. At midday, we sat alongside the canal and watched whilst fishermen caught the fish which lurked beneath the mud and oily waters. Not a rod and line for them—no, they used cormorant birds with a tight noose around their necks, enabling them to regurgitate our lunch. Suffice to say that between the muddy waters of the canal (into which the day's outpourings of the town found their way) and the digestive systems of the cormorants, I had little desire to increase my intake of Omega-3 but settled back with what I recall was a loss of appetite and a wish to move on to pastures new.

Xian

An internal flight took us on to Xian in pursuit of the Terracotta Army, which has turned Xian into a tourist centre. However, until our farmer friend fell through a hole in the ground whilst drilling for water and discovered the source of his future income, it wasn't always a modern-day theme park. The old city of Xian dates back to the Tang dynasty (AD 618), and its walls form one of the largest ancient defensive military systems in the world that still stands to this day. The manner in which it was constructed meant that soldiers could both outlook and outshoot any attackers. The walls are forty feet tall and between forty and sixty feet thick, covering 8.5 miles. It's well crenelated. The four gates constructed within the walls have drawbridge facilities and inner gates, all of which are protected by watchtowers. The Grand Mosque within the city reflects the diverse nature of religion in China in the ancient times, and even now it shows that although Buddhism dominates, there is still recognition of other religions.

Returning to the Terracotta Army, as one must inevitably do, perhaps I should explain a little of the background to the army and its discovery on 29 March 1974. Local farmers were digging a series of wells in search of water when they discovered pottery fragments and ancient bronze weapons. The rest is history, but one local farmer still makes his living by autographing books of their discovery. In 1998, Bill Clinton paid a visit and met the farmer. Because the farmer was not educated, the Chinese authorities told him that if he had difficulties, he should simply respond with "me too". He was able to ask Clinton how he was and then responded, "Me too." Clinton said he was amazed at the discovery, to which the farmer responded, "Me too." Bill said he liked talking to Hillary in bed about such things at the end of the day, to which he responded, "Me too." Ever since, he has been known as Mr Me Too. Well, it's a story worthy of comment, even if you don't believe it!

To date, three pits containing eight thousand life-sized terracotta warriors lined up in battle formation to protect the entrance of the emperor's tomb have been fully revealed. Qin Shi Huadgdi (259– 210 BC), the first emperor of China, ascended the throne at the age of thirteen, when construction of his tomb began. Well, at least he had the foresight to plan for the future. On completion of his many conquests, he ordered 720,000 conscript labourers to hurry up on the building of his royal tomb. It was finished just in time! According to historical records, all the workmen along with his concubines were then entombed with the emperor in order to keep the location secret. There is another old Chinese proverb: "Dictators ride to and fro on tigers which they dare not dismount—and the tigers become hungry." The royal tomb, which is situated about one mile behind the terracotta army, is larger than the pyramids and occupies two million square metres, its base being 515 by 485 metres and its height reaching 100 metres. Unopened as yet, it is said to consist of an inner and outer city. There is mention that it could be booby-trapped with poisoned arrows and other lethal traps to ward off grave robbers. Only time will tell!

That evening, we attended the Tang Era Musical, a traditional and colourful entertainment, before retiring to dream of the warriors and their pursuits. The following morning, having digested the cultural delights of old Xian we left by air for Beijing.

Beijing

2008 was the year of the Beijing Olympics, and like most cities that engage in this form of self-flagellation, Beijing was bustling with activity to ensure that the building programme was completed so that the Games would start on time. Needless to say, the city was a hive of activity, whilst at the same time the authorities were trying to reduce pollution by keeping nonessential Chinese in the countryside and out of the city. The days were grey, the fog seemed endless, and the frenetic work went on. The many tourists, of whom we were a few, continued with their sightseeing pilgrimage, which inevitably included the Bird's Nest Stadium and the surrounding Olympic Park. The four days spent in Beijing seemed to spiral into one as the guides vied with each other to pack in the maximum amount of sightseeing with an endless encyclopaedia of history.

The view of ancient China was that the country sits in the centre of the world; it is a view which still strongly influences their culture— China speaks, and the world listens! Nevertheless, there is (or rather was) a lot to see and even more to learn. What follows is a brief resume of the locations in the order in which we visited them, though not in the order of importance.

The Temple of Heaven is where the emperor came every winter solstice to worship heaven and pray for a good harvest. Because his rule was legitimised by a mandate from heaven, a bad harvest could be interpreted as his fall from grace and threaten the stability of his reign. The design of the temple complex, true to its sacred purpose, reflects the mystical, cosmological laws believed to be central to the workings of the universe. For example, the number nine is considered the most powerful digit, and the slabs forming the circular altar are laid in multiples of nine. Within the Hall of Good Harvest, the interior twenty-eight columns are divided into four central pillars to represent the four seasons, twelve inner columns to represent the months, and twelve outer columns to represent the two-hour tranches that make up the day. There are many other examples.

Situated on the outskirts of Beijing is Yiheyuan, or as it is better known, the Summer Palace. It was here every summer that the imperial court would take up residence to get away from the heat of Beijing. It has a 700-metre-long covered walkway, ornately decorated and running along the shoreline. Emperor Guangxu and Empress Dowager Cixi received ministers in the Hall of Benevolent Longevity. Having heard of the exploits of Cixi, one has to say the name was most inappropriate. It was her powerful domination that coined the phrase "the power behind the throne". She sat at the back of her son's throne behind a curtain and whispered directions on what judgements he should make. True to form, she placed her son under house arrest before he reached adulthood and the full trappings of power, and there he remained until his death in 1908, allegedly poisoned by Cixi. She died twenty-four hours later! At the west end of the lake is the testament to her avarice: the famous full-size marble boat she had built with money intended to create a modern Chinese navy.

After travelling back to the city, we arrived at Tiananmen Square, one of the largest squares in the world covering some 247 acres and situated at the front entrance to the Forbidden City. Although a public gathering place since the Ming dynasty, it became the focus of world attention on 4 January 1989 with the massacre of a gathering of students following seven weeks of protest. To the south side of the square is the Memorial Hall housing the body of Chairman Mao Zedong. The Forbidden City was part of the imperial city during the dynasty of Mongol Yuan. However, the first Ming emperor moved the capital from Beijing to Nanjing and ordered all Mongol palaces to be razed to the ground. When his son Yongol became emperor, he moved the capital back to Beijing and started constructing the Forbidden City. It took one million workers over fifteen years to complete and is the world's largest palace complex, covering over seventy-two hectares. It is surrounded by a 7.9-metre wall and a 6-metre-deep and 52-metre-wide moat. The main halls of the inner and outer courts are all arranged in groups of three—the shape of the Qian triagram representing heaven. The residences of the inner court are arranged in sixes—the shape of the Kun triagram representing earth. The sloping ridges of the roofs are decorated with lines of statuettes, which represent the status of the building; a minor building has three whereas the Hall of Supreme Harmony has ten. It's the only building in imperial times that was allowed Hangshi (ranked tenth). To the north lies Jingshan Park, also known as Mei Shan (Coal Hill), an artificial hill built from the waste removed to build the moat and the nearby lakes. It is the highest point in Beijing and served as an imperial garden from AD 1179 onwards. On 17 March 1644, the last

Ming emperor, Chongchen, hanged himself from a pagoda tree in the grounds when the forces of Li Zi Cheng captured the inner city.

Some thirty-one miles north of Beijing are the Ming Tombs, where thirteen of the sixteen Ming emperors are buried along with their wives. The most important is that of Yongle, the third Ming emperor. It is said that sixteen concubines were buried alive with the emperor, a practice that was abandoned later in the Ming dynasty. We stopped off for a brief visit on the way to see the last great Chinese enigma, the Great Wall, known to the locals as the 10,000 Li Wall (a li being half of a kilometre). Stretching from the east coast to the Gobi Desert it was at one time an important link to the Silk Road, and it can be seen from space. The original wall was begun two thousand years ago when China was unified under Emperor Qin Shihuang, and it incorporated many of the other walls. The construction work required hundreds of thousands of workers and incorporated 180 million cubic metres of earth and the bodies of deceased workers, of which there would have been many! It was manned by over one million soldiers, but the wall never performed its function as a defence line. However, it did work as a kind of highway for movement across the difficult mountain terrain.

We assembled for a last night, partaking in a meal which included Peking duck. Peking may have changed its name back to Beijing, but the duck hasn't—yet another enigma!

Japan

The flight from Beijing to Tokyo via Korea, which a few of us undertook as an extension to our tour, proved entertaining. I was allotted a seat next to a beautiful Japanese girl who had a marvellous chat-up line (how I wished that I was many years younger than even I felt I was) before I discovered that she belonged to some religious sect; she was obviously seeking another conversion. Well, you can always dream—a clear sentiment for both of us! Like so many of my generation, brought up on the horrors and atrocities of the war, I had preconceived ideas of what Japan and the Japanese held in store for my visit: rigid discipline, a handful of rice, and (if luck was on my side) a glass of sake. I was to find that this was another land in which ancient went hand in hand with modern—yet another intriguing enigma.

Tokyo

We duly arrived at Tokyo's Narita Airport and transferred to our hotel in the Shinjuki area of the city famed for its hotels, restaurants, skyscrapers, shops, and nightlife. The next two days were spent amongst the hustle and bustle of Tokyo. It's not so much a city as a constellation of cities grown together over time. In five hundred years, it has grown from the modest fishing village of Edo and now forms the largest metropolitan area in the world, with a population in excess of 35 million. It has been described as one of the three command centres for world economy, the others being New York and London. Within the metropolis the Chiyoda District is the seat of the capital's power, both political and economic; the location of the Imperial Palace; as well as housing the Parliament, various government ministries, and the headquarters of many of the leading companies. As with other cities in Japan, the many gardens are a sight to behold and are both decorative in colour and layout.

The Imperial Palace (Kyuden) is situated on the site of the old Edo Castle, home of the shoguns Tokugawa, who ruled from 1613 until their overthrow in 1867. It has been completely rebuilt since its destruction during World War II and is now occupied by Emperor Akihito and his family. Needless to say, they were not on hand to greet us, only appearing on high days and holidays. Clearly our visit didn't carry an A rating. We did get to view the inner palace ground from the Kokyo Gaien, a large plaza in front of the palace and adjacent to the Nijubashi Bridge, which spans the wide moat surrounding the palace.

As with many cities around the world, Tokyo comes to life at night with its vibrant colours and its mix of cultures, ranging from the old to the modern. Its many restaurants, night clubs, and shops stand out against the backdrop of skyscrapers. However, it is very expensive, more so than other cities I have visited such as New York, Paris, London, or Rome. Eating was another experience. I had eaten sushi on many occasions, but here was an opportunity to eat as the Japanese eat. A conveyor belt or train (Kaiten zushi) of coloured dishes, each colour indicating the cost, steadily passing before you and a gradually increasing pile of empty dishes accumulating in front. Each dish contained a small selection ranging from nigiri (rice balls with fish), norimaki (a dish of dried seaweed), chirashi (seafood, mushroom, vegetables, and rice), and many others, all eaten with the fingers. The final bill being depends on the number and colour of the dishes used.

Kyoto

We reached our next destination, Kyoto, by courtesy of the Bullet Train, or as it's officially known, the Shinkansen. The train, capable of pulling 16 carriages carrying 1,300 passengers, travels at 200 miles an hour with 13 trains an hour leaving Tokyo for Osako. Test runs on a replacement Mag-lev train have already exceeded 360 miles an hour. The mind boggles! Kyoto is located in a valley, part of the Yasmashiro Basin, in the eastern part of the mountainous region known as the Tampa Highlands, and it's surrounded on three sides by mountains. We were based in the New Miyako Hotel, situated in the centre of Kyoto. It proved a most useful location, enabling us to cover much of the city in the days that followed with visits to many beautiful gardens, castles, temples, and shrines. There are 1,600 Buddhist temples in the immediate vicinity of the city and over 400 Shinto shrines. Without doubt the most famous of them all is the magnificent Temple of the Golden Pavilion, richly adorned in gold leaf. Its beauty is reflected in the water of Kyokochi, the mirror pond. Its vista is breathtaking, standing out against a backdrop of rock and pine on a small island overlooking the lake. Its original purpose was to serve as a residence for Shogun Ashikaga Yoshimitsue from AD 1358 to 1409.

At night, we set forth to educate ourselves in the cultural aspects of Kyoto. The Ponto-cho is a small strip of the city with a narrow-cobbled street running from Shijo-dori to Sanjo-doris, west of the Kame River. Since the sixteenth century, the area of Ponto-cho has been the home for geishas, tea houses, restaurants, bars, and brothels. Today the area is home to the Kabererjo Theatre at the Sanjo-dori end of the street. The theatre functions as a practice hall for geishas with traditional dancing, singing, and the playing of traditional instruments, offering a rare chance for ordinary people to see performances by real geishas. For us, it proved to be a colourful and entertaining evening.

Hiroshima

Having a free day on the Wednesday and being templed out, I decided to catch the Bullet Train and spend the day in Hiroshima, 225 miles to the south, which by Shinkansen took just two hours. Another of my wartime memories was when, at 0815 hours on 6 August 1945, the United States dropped the atomic bomb Little Boy, obliterating the city of Hiroshima. I was ten at the time, and the sight of the subsequent pictures in the papers showing the mushroom cloud and one of the only surviving buildings, the Industrial Promotions Hall (now known as the A Dome), left a lasting impression on me. Little was I to know in those wartime years that the bomb, or rather its successors, would become a feature of my service life in the years to come, or that I would visit the city in which the event happened.

On an historical note, the bomb was detonated at 600 metres above the ground, the target being the Aioi T-shaped bridge. The A Dome was situated 150 metres from the hypocentre of the explosion, which created downward shockwave pressure of 35 tonnes per square metre, killing 80,000. A further 70,000 died from radiation sickness in the months that followed. Although Hiroshima has been rebuilt, the A Dome remains as a wreck to serve as a reminder. At 760 metres from the epicentre, two trees remain, one eucalyptus and one willow, alongside which is a covered bunker from where news of the bomb was broadcast. I wonder how long those who sent the fatal news survived their injuries. On the site and close to the epicentre is a monument to a young Japanese girl, Sadako Sasaki, who died of radiation poisoning. She believed that if she built enough paper cranes (birds), she would survive her illness. Unfortunately, this was not to be the case, but her story left a lasting legacy. Thousands of schoolchildren attend the site each year to string paper cranes close to the monument. To me, it was a salutary reminder of the impact that war has on military and civilians alike.

Having returned to Kyoto by Shinkansen train, I spent the following day with the others on a final sightseeing and shopping spree before flying back to London and the realities of life at home.

CHAPTER 19

Slovakia to Africa—A Contrast

At the end of June, I went down to Cromer and met up with younger brother Bobby and his wife, Sue. We spent a week using the caravan as a base and touring Norfolk. By this time, I was almost feeling like a tourist guide, having acquired a fair amount of knowledge of the area over the years. But then, Norfolk (and Forest Park in particular) reflects the peace and tranquillity of our countryside whilst leaving one immersed in history. It's a pleasant way of relaxing and recharging the batteries.

Slovakia—Stredny Silac

Within ten days, I was on my way again, this time flying out to Slovakia and landing at the rather quaint and homely airport of Poprad. There's something nice about collecting your bags from a little kart and walking out to the car, rather than standing around a large and ever-moving series of carousels under the hidden eyes of immigration and customs officials, not knowing if your baggage had actually arrived in the same country. It's also a reminder of the days before air travel became such an essential part of our lives.

Why Slovakia, you might ask. Well, Jonathan and Anna had invested in a holiday home in a little village called Stredny Silac, close to the town of Ruzomberok and on the edge of the Tatras Mountains.

They were heading there as a relief from the intense summer heat in Abu Dhabi, almost reminiscent of India in the Victorian era, when the colonials departed for Simla and the cooler climate of the hills during their summer months. I was invited to join the family for a couple of weeks. Their house, like many in the small villages situated in that area, was of wood and brick construction and set on about one acre of land. It had a variety of outbuildings, including a barn and a basketball court that was turned into a skating rink during the winter, which the locals were free to use.

Although nobody in the village spoke English, I found it was relatively easy to communicate, the Slovaks speaking their own language and we less able Brits using sign language and a sprinkling of German. Situated in a rural setting, with high-rising meadowland beyond the village and the Tatras Mountains providing a stunning backdrop, it gave it an eighteenth-century feel. I could almost sense Dracula's cart trundling through at midnight. Yes, I know it's the wrong country, but the feeling was the same! The village sits within a landscape bowl between the Nizke Tatry mountains to the south and Zapadne Tatry mountains to the north, so it is easy to see why this is a popular ski centre during the winter and sailing and hiking area in the summer.

We spent the days travelling up in the ski lifts to view the scenery from on high, watching the paragliders launching themselves from the top and circling around as they picked up the thermals, thus avoiding a return to earth for as long as possible. What a peaceful existence, and one that reminded me of my early gliding days; how I envied them. At other times, we would drive around to the north of the Liptovska Mar, a very large, man-made lake/reservoir created during the Soviet occupation to supply hydroelectric power to the towns of Ruzumborok and Liptovska Mikulas, situated at either end of the lake. Its secondary use was a sailing centre. On other occasions, we spent our days sightseeing in the many castles or trekking through the forests. The wooded areas, although scenic, were frequented by bears, and there was ample evidence of their presence where they had sharpened their claws on the bark of trees. The fresh marks indicated to me that one should walk a little faster. Not that I'm a coward, you understand. It's just that I look forward to the expectations and excitement of old age, and I can think of better places to get my hugs!

The two weeks sped past, and I was soon on my way by road to Bratislava for the return trip to the UK via Vienna. Jonathan and family returned to finish their holiday before flying back to Abu Dhabi.

Other Commitments

The period from late June to late July was a busy period not only in terms of work but also on the social front. Late June saw me once again spending the weekend with Pat and David up in Northumberland, ostensibly planning our next cycling event. But again, it was the usual recipe: too much good food, too much alcohol, and an abundance of good company. During July, I travelled down to Grantham for the annual reunion at Sheila's old college, Kesteven. The faces are getting fewer and older, but then, I have to remind myself to look in the mirror and refresh my memory of the advancing years. However, it was nice to catch up on the news because I almost feel part of the family these days. On the way back, I made a detour to Grimsby and spent a couple of days with Pat and Bill on their farm in Laceby. In August, Anna and the boys left behind the heat of Abu Dhabi and came to stay with me in Darlington for two weeks, followed by two weeks with Anna's parents down in Bristol. I continued with my work with the local NHS and my gymnastics commitments, in between which I was trying to garner some acclimatisation training for tackling the mountain, the dates of which seemed to get ever closer.

In September 2008, I travelled down to Cromer once more, this time accompanied by David and Pat. Our visit enabled Pat to see more of the Norfolk countryside, plus do peaceful shopping without David, whilst we took to our bikes in an effort to induce some form of fitness regime. Well, that was the intention, but too many hostelries along the way proved somewhat of a diversion. I will just say that we dined well as a threesome and enjoyed the break—not conducive to mountain training!

Apart from work and gymnastics, the remainder of the year centred on arrangement for the Remembrance weekend in London, Christmas with Julie and Nigel once again, and New Year's at Pat and Bill's. As lovely and most welcome as these arrangements are, I'm beginning to feel that they are repetitive and perhaps a burden on those on whom I inflict my company. There was one sad note, and that was the death of Eric just prior to Christmas, after a long illness. Eric and Francis Keithley were a lovely couple and had spent many holidays with us at Purves Hall, which she pronounced *Purvs*, but I hope it wasn't! Although somewhat older than us, they became very good friends over the years, and whenever I was working or visiting Lancashire, I would always call in to see them in Blackburn. His funeral was on 29 December, and it would only be a matter of months before Francis also passed on. I could never envisage her lasting after her soulmate had gone. In fact, I attended her funeral in Blackburn in March the following year.

On the world stage, Obama was inaugurated as the forty-fourth US president. Albania and Croatia were admitted to NATO; strange how the balance of power in Europe has shifted over the past twenty years! In the meanwhile, Russia retaliated against the Ukraine by shutting off all gas supplied to Europe by pipeline through the Ukraine. As Russia supplies over a quarter of natural gas to Europe, this had a knock-on effect, which makes me ask who are the Russians trying to influence? Or is it yet another fit of pique? The Gaza War continued three weeks into the winter of 2008–2009 with the Israeli aim of destroying the military infrastructure of Hamas in Gaza. Swine flu, the H1N1 virus, first identified in 1967–1968 as Hong Kong flu, is deemed a global pandemic as it killed over eight thousand people. Talking of killing, Conrad Muraq, Michael Jackson's doctor, is arrested and charged with his manslaughter. Finally, Barak Obama is awarded the Nobel Peace Prize. *What*? (Must be time for another earthquake or a similar disaster.)

Ascent of Kilimanjaro

Getting to the summit is optional. Getting down is mandatory.

The previous year, I had managed to convince Nigel that we should do something different in the way of a major activity during 2009, and I had it in mind to climb Kilimanjaro in January 2009. Ever since my days in Aden, I had been fascinated by the idea of climbing Africa's highest mountain. This was coloured by my views of the mountain from the air during my many air force visits to Kenya. It straddles the border between Kenya, which had been a British colony, and Tanzania, a former German colony. In fact, at one stage the mountain had been located on the Kenyan side of the border, but Queen Victoria, in her generosity (of which she wasn't renowned), gave it as a present to her German cousin—hence its present location on the Tanzanian side of the border. Having completed the trek across the Atlas Mountains in 2006 with Nigel, which we had enjoyed, it seemed to me a good idea, even if the Atlas were not of the same magnitude. The problem was addressing the altitude and the amount of training necessary, because we were entering an altitude range which, although I had previously experienced in the Himalayas, still presented problems that could not be ignored, namely that of acclimatisation.

Having read into the latest analysis of the difficulties and dangers of altitude sickness, and not wanting to get to the stage where we had to abort the climb, I sought Nigel's medical advice, but I think he was as uncertain as I was as to the likely outcome. It was therefore either working on the assumption that in the land of the blind, the one-eyed man is God and relying on our joint experience (Nigel's medical knowledge, and my experience on Annapurna), or we did something more positive in countering the potential threat. One clearly must be mindful of the dangers of climbing at high altitude, even if you're not tackling Everest. Many people don't realize that Kilimanjaro, at around 20,000 feet, is seriously high—the highest free-standing mountain in the world. Any climb over 18,000 feet is considered extreme altitude, and Kilimanjaro not only exceeds that but can be one of the most dangerous and underrated mountains.

Anyone climbing above 15,000 feet is likely to suffer from mild to medium forms of altitude sickness. Known as acute mountain sickness (AMS), it is caused by dehydration resulting from the higher rate of water vapour lost from the lungs at high altitude. The results can be pulmonary oedema, which is fluid in the lungs, or cerebral oedema, a swelling of the brain. The latter is potentially fatal. The only way to overcome the problem is to acclimatise and to be aware of the inherent dangers caused by the lack of oxygen whilst on the climb. In essence, training beforehand has to be undertaken to condition the body to the changes that will occur. There is a drug called Acetazolamide which can mitigate some of the effects, but if AMS is experienced during climbing, the only solution is to descend to lower altitudes. There is no better advice than to follow the mountaineers' adage: "Climb high, sleep low and acclimatise."

Haunted by the prospect of failure and the possibility of suffering from high altitude sickness, I thought long and hard. How did I overcome this nightmare? Six weeks before we were due to depart, I spoke to experts in the Alpine Club in London, as a result of which I hired a machine called an Hypoxicator. The machine, which acts as a stimulus of the cardiovascular system by breathing reduced oxygen and monitoring the level of arterial oxygen saturation, enables two people to work alternately for about ten minutes at a time. Each day, Nigel and I spent an hour each on the machine and monitored the improvement in the rate of oxygen saturation; added to the training we had undertaken, it no doubt helped in our acclimatisation. It is not cheap, having cost me five hundred pounds for the month prior to the ascent, but at least it gave us some confidence that our trip would not be in vain.

I left Lincolnshire on 3 January 2009, anxious not to unravel all my training and still somewhat concerned over my attempt on Kilimanjaro. I managed three more days on the Hypoxicator before its return to London. I was surprised to find that the Christmas festivities had little impact on the oxygen saturation, much to my relief.

We set off from Durham Tees airport on 7 January and, changing at Schiphol, flew on to Africa arriving at our starting base at Marangu

Lodge in time for an early night's rest. The following day, having collected the additional cold weather kit we had arranged, we travelled for three hours along switchback dirt roads to Rongai, our start point. The following day, we set out for Marangu Gate (1,920 metres), where we met six other climbers and the guides and porters. We set off through the forests at a slow pace as part of our acclimatisation up to Rongai Simba, our first camp at 2,700 metre. All our accommodation during the climb was to be in tents, and in night temperatures of -7 to -10 Celsius, it meant that sleep became very sporadic!

The next day, we set off on an eight-hour climb over high-level moorland and rock. Having climbed to 3,750 metres, we then descended as part of our acclimatisation—climb high, sleep low—to Camp 2 at Kikelelwa Cave at 3,600 metres. Already the nights were very cold, and the first of our party, a Norwegian, was displaying signs of AMS: headaches, loss of vision, and nausea. The sky at night was fantastic, the stars and the galaxy clearly visible against the inky black sky, benefitting from the absence of light pollution.

We set out early the following morning aiming for Mawenzi Tarn at 4,330 metre. The climb was steep and heavy going, the latter part involving climbing up steep rocks to reach 4,500 metre before dropping down to the Tarn (Camp 3), situated in a small basin overlooked by the glowering face of Mt Mawenzi. Once again, the descent formed part of the acclimatisation process. After a two-hour break we had a further stiff climb lasting two hours onto the ridge below Mawenzi before returning to Camp 3, by which time the temperature was down to -10 Celsius.

Another early start on day 5 as we set out on the six-hour climb to Kibo Hut (4,700 metres), the last camp before the summit. We crossed the Saddle, the ridge between Mawenzi and Kibo peaks, on which was perched the wreckage of a light aircraft. Apparently, it had been carrying a group of French tourists from Nairobi when it hit the mountain towards the end of the previous year. All the occupants were killed. We eventually arrived at Kibo Hut somewhat weary, and we collapsed into our tents for two hours' rest, followed by a cup of tea and a briefing before retiring for an early bed. Well, it would be foolish to call it a rest because by 11 p.m., feeling somewhat apprehensive, we set off for the summit, head torches glimmering in the falling snow. As we ascended the snaking rock face and looked back across the range of hills, we could see the lights of others attempting the climb. Farther back were the twinkling lights of the townships. Above us, the stars sparkled as they can only do in the skies in this part of the world—a poetic setting.

Without doubt, this was the hardest part of the ascent. By now most of the party were suffering from some element of AMS. Six hours of hard slog up the famous snake (loose scree, followed by large boulders) traversing towards the top. The route was via Williams Point (5,000 metres), Hans Meyer Cave (5,150 metres), and Jamaica Rock (5,500 metres), during which we were hit by a snow blizzard just below the first summit. We reached Gilman Peak at 6.15 a.m. in time for a hot drink and a bar of instant energy chocolate and to see the sunrise setting the mountain and its shroud of clouds alight with a myriad of colours. The view at the top as dawn broke was fantastic A most exciting and exhilarating moment, but also one of extreme fatigue. I think we were too shattered to take it all in. A shortage of oxygen and a build-up of lactic acid in the muscles were hardly conducive to leaping around in celebration, especially because we still had to circumnavigate the crater rim to the next peak. After a brief rest, we moved on to Stella Point (5756) before finally reaching the main summit, Uhuru Peak (5,895 metres), at 8.30 a.m. Following the obligatory photographs, we retraced our steps to Gilman's Peak and then down to Kibo Hut. The descent, as is often the case, was more exhausting than the climb. The sun, having melted the ice on the surface of the scree, meant it was difficult maintaining one's footing. Even with poles, we still had difficulty keeping our balance, but we eventually made it to Kimbo Hut and, after a brief rest, continued on our way down the mountain to Horombo (3,720 metres) on the far side of the mountain, reaching there at 5 p.m.—an elapsed time of eighteen hours. We didn't need any rocking that night!

Day seven. After another night in tents, we set off at 7 a.m. on the long trek down to Marangu Gate. By this time, I was suffering from constant pain from my old back problem; probably the slippery descent over scree from Kibo plus the constant jarring on the rocky surface had aggravated the injury and created muscular spasms. The eight-hour trek seemed to go on forever. I rode the last mile in the rangers' Land Rover, arriving at the gate before the others—mind you, it cost me a small fortune in beers! There followed a four-hour journey back to the lodge, a most welcome shower, followed by dinner, a quiet celebration, and then the luxury of sleeping in a proper bed. Three of us left the following morning for a day's safari, relaxing in Arusha National Park, before leaving for the airport and the long journey home via Schiphol, arriving at Durham/Teesvalley Airport in the early hours on 19 January.

In summary, it was a fantastic and challenging experience and a unique opportunity to raise money for Cancer Research (UK). Would I do it again? I said no at the time, but the years dull the memory, and less than two years later, I was back in Africa tackling another mountain—but that's another story. You have to reach the age of early senility before these dreams become a reality, and you have to face up to people who suggest you should be more responsible and think of others.

CHAPTER 20

Shangri-La to the Baltic

Shangri-la—a fictional, remote, mysterious place,
synonymous with earthly paradise and situated in the
Kunlun Mountains in the Himalayan range.
Lost Horizon, 1933

The remainder of January 2009 was taken up with NHS board meetings, LTOCA meetings down in London, gymnastics coaching, and presentations to the U3A. By early February, I was on my way again via Amsterdam and Dubai, en route to Kuala Lumpar. I was joined by Jonathan and family, who had flown out from Abu Dhabi, as the boys were playing in a schools' international rugby competition. However, due to the swine flu fears, the competition was cancelled, which we didn't discover until after our arrival in Malaysia. So instead we set off a fantastic holiday in and around Kuala Lumpar before moving on to Kota Kinabalu, in what used to be North Borneo and is now Sabah. Kota means fort or town, and Kinabalu is taken from the nearby mountain and means "revered place of the dead".

Looking back on the holiday, I often regret the fact that I didn't take the opportunity to climb the mountain, but that would have been rather selfish and a missed opportunity of spending time with the family. After all, that was the purpose of the holiday. We had booked into excellent family accommodation in the Shangri-La Rasa Ria Resort. However, because my bookings form had asked for details

273

of where else I had been in the Far East, I had logged my travels around Asia over recent years. I think they assumed it was business travel and would therefore be repeat bookings. How wrong they were. Consequently, because I had been upgraded, Jonathan and family were given the same treatment. We were moved to the Ocean Wing, a most luxurious and opulent facilities; I have yet to see better. The resort had its own nature reserve complete with prang-utans, found only on two islands in the world. I could almost describe it as paradise, a holiday of a lifetime. But all good things come to an end, and we flew back to Kula Lumpar for a few days before Jonathan and family left for Abu Dhabi whilst I made the journey to Rotterdam via Dubai. Then it was on to Tees Valley Airport and home on 20 February.

In April I was invited to deliver a lecture to the Darlington Rotary Club on my tour of China and Japan, which I enjoyed, and from what I understand, so did the audience. This was to start me on a number of such lectures around the north-east, which provided additional help in raising extra money for charities that I was supporting.

History has always been a fascinating subject for me not only for what it portrays but also for the important lessons one could and should learn from the mistakes or successes of others. But it also provides a fascinating insight on people's lives, irrespective of their status or background, and there is nothing more poignant than delving into the lives of one's ancestors. Since the early 1990s, I have been researching and compiling my family history. I've discovered over the years that it is something one must be meticulous about when gathering and assessing the information. Reliability of sources are fundamental, as the further one goes back in time, the less reliable the data. This is especially the case with early census returns and particularly parish records and other less reliable sources. Misspellings and age errors are frequently found, which if not checked can lead to incorrect assumptions.

I took a few days out in June and, as a treat, stayed in the Red Lion Hotel in Long Compton near Chipping Norton. The aim was really to follow up on family history in the Oxfordshire area; my father's relations had lived for some years in Swerford. He had gone to All

Saints College, Bloxham, where I had been briefly educated. My mother's parents and their ancestors came from Oxford and the surrounding area. It was a case of killing two birds with one stone, or should I say many birds. During my earlier research, I had by chance met a couple from Birmingham in the Oxford library, Jane Flynn and Roy Everitt, who by coincidence were looking up one of Roy's ancestors, Baron Everitt—no not a title, but a Christian name—who happened to be the brother of my great, great grandfather. It illustrates the point that names can often become corrupted by a simple error in recording by a clerk, a vicar, or whoever must compile the relevant records. I still correspond on a regular basis with Jane, and between us we have compiled a comprehensive and interesting family history. Jane couldn't get over the fact that Roy and I looked so alike. Frightening, isn't it?

In July, feeling in need of a change of scenery, I sailed from Newcastle on a cruise to the Baltic, spending time in Kalundborg in Denmark, Sweden, and Finland before returning via St Petersburg in Russia and Gdansk in Poland. There was an opportunity to visit Moscow for the day, which I didn't feel inclined to accept. Although things had changed since the ending of the Cold War, I still felt somewhat nervous; perhaps my past history had clouded my judgement, but the days of the KGB activities were still fresh in my mind, and I doubt whether my underlying sensitivities were totally unjustified.

During our time on board, I met Katherine, another singly and a teacher from Edinburgh. Because we enjoyed each other's company, we spent the day in St Petersburg visiting the Hermitage, the Winter Palace, Nevsky Prospect, and the Admiralty Buildings, which had been the headquarters of the Russian Fleet up until the Revolution. I was surprised how many of the old buildings had survived the German onslaught during World War II. In the evening, we attended the Marinsky Theatre (Kirov Ballet) and enjoyed the opera. I'm not normally an opera buff, especially because my experience of the rather dull performances in Germany, but this was the Kirov and therefore an experience not to be missed. The evening was somewhat marred by a torrential downpour as we left the opera house, which left me walking up and down in the rain in an attempt to get a taxi and then trying to locate Katherine amongst the mass of people huddled in the entrance whilst restraining others from usurping my taxi driver with additional bribes, so that we could get back to the ship some distance away.

We soon discovered that despite the changes elsewhere in Europe, little had changed in Mother Russia; bureaucracy still reigned supreme. Having paid off the taxi, we discovered that we had to join a queue of others standing in the rain whilst officials systematically checked our documents before letting us back through the gates. I'm sure it's something to do with the culture rather than the training, the insistence on every little detail being checked and then rechecked. Even so, it was with some feeling of relief that we passed through the gates. However, by the time we were back on board and changed into dry clothes, the euphoria of the evening had somewhat eroded, and we consoled ourselves with stiff brandies before retiring for the night.

The following day, we moved on to Gdynia and Gdansk in Poland and then to Warnemunde on the German North Sea coast. This German port was the former site of the Heinkel aircraft company and was therefore heavily bombed during World War II. Whilst in Warnemunde, where we had docked for the day and had time we to spare, there was something I felt I wanted to do other than wander the streets of the town. I set off by coach to Berlin.

What a difference to the days when we worked in Berlin and the stark contrast that existed at that time between the West, with its affluence and freshness, and the East, living behind the Wall and the barbed wire and existing in a bygone era. I recall those days when I frequently crossed over through Checkpoint Charlie, passing along the bombed-out streets that had changed little since the war and seeing the early morning queues for bread, vegetables, and meat, as well as queues of forlorn-looking people eking out a meagre existence. Very rarely did you see cars, other than those of Communist officials. The contrast in the West couldn't have been more marked, the bustle of traffic set against the brightly lit and well-stocked stores—but that was yesteryear. As I stood at what use to be Checkpoint Charlie, now a tourist attraction, I found it difficult to get my bearings and recall what it had been like less than thirty years before. What had been the Eastern Sector with its bombed-out buildings was now unrecognisable; new high-rise blocks with most of the embassies situated in the residential area of the East, roads filled with cars and brightly dressed people and well-stocked shops. All of which reflected the vast amount of money West Germany had poured into East Berlin during reunification.

Unfortunately, during my perambulations I had a minor accident. I walked into a glass-plated door inside a building close to the US embassy. The result was a split lip, a black eye, and a broken nose, as well as a great deal of embarrassment. Staff at a nearby hotel were most helpful, and I managed to clean myself up and buy a shirt to replace the one covered in blood before returning to the ship, but I couldn't hide my swollen nose, split lip, and black eye, which raised a few questions about what I'd been up to!

Our final port of call was Aalborg in Denmark, an industrial and University City in North Jutland. In 1940 the airfield (being critical for the German invasion of Norway) and the city were captured by the Germans, the first known case of a city being captured by paratroopers. In August of that year, the RAF launched eleven Blenheim bombers of No 82 Squadron to attack the airfield. It resulted in the most disastrous of RAF operations because all eleven aircraft were shot down by enemy fighters or enemy flak within twenty minutes of reaching Denmark.

The passage home across the North Sea was largely uneventful, and we arrived back in the Port of Tyne in the early hours of the morning. Katherine and I agreed to meet for lunch later that month in Newcastle. We settled on Blackfriars, a restaurant situated in a restored thirteenth-century friary close to the city's Chinatown, and spent an enjoyable day in Newcastle before going our separate ways. We still correspond as friends.

In August, we all assembled down at Whissendine to give Jane a surprise fiftieth party. How could someone as young as me have a daughter fifty years of age? The mirror gave me the unwelcome answer: easy! It was a great party, and we managed to sustain the surprise element until she walked through the door. Julie (bless her) and Laura put in an awful lot of work in decking out the hall, as well as making major contributions in organising and providing the food.

Nigel, having rejoined the army while still working at the Memorial Hospital in Darlington, found that he was destined to spend three months over the Christmas at Camp Bastion in Afghanistan. As we were going to have Christmas at Julie's, I decided to take up Jonathan and Anna's invitation to join them before the Christmas break. I flew out to Abu Dhabi on 9 December for a ten-day pre-Christmas returning for Christmas with Julie and Jane and their families. Apart from the usual round of parties with their friends, training in the gym, and swimming, as well as trips out to Dubai, the Oman, and around the coastal area in their boat, it was an opportunity for some unusual Christmas shopping before returning home.

Yes, you are correct: after Christmas with Julie and family, I spent New Year's 2010 in Lincolnshire, once again feeling that I ought really to break the mould! Well, maybe next year.

CHAPTER 21

A Parting of the Ways—Challenging Days

Say what you mean and act how you feel because those who
matter don't mind and those who mind don't matter.
Dr Suess

Back to work with a flourish in January 2010 as the pace of
rationalisation in the NHS increased. Where would the NHS
be, and how would its management system survive unless it had
reorganisation as a regular feature in its strategy? Added to which,
I'm sure that politicians approach it like restacking the deck chairs
on the *Titanic*: it doesn't matter what you do; the result is going to
be pretty much the same. The year 2010 saw yet another change of
direction with Secretary of State Lansley and NHS supremo Peter
Nicholson changing the direction once again, only this time power
was to be vested in the GP-led commissioning boards. Well, that was
the theory. It doesn't take too much nous to sense what is wrong with
the system, and it doesn't rely on hindsight. I used to listen to Nigel
and his colleagues moan on about the growth in managers and over
administration, but I have to admit they were right, and I shared
that opinion: too many mangers earning (or should I say drawing)
six-figure salaries and chasing statistics. My views have always been
"Too many chiefs and not enough Indians" and significant wastage
in chasing dreams instead of reality. Added to which, over the years
there has been too great an emphasis on academic achievements at the
cost of good, old-fashioned nursing. We need to return to it being a

vocation, not a profession, with the patient at the centre of concern. Well, that's my view, and now I will come off my soapbox, but before I do and before you say, "Well, of course, but you were one of those overpaid bureaucrats," let me say that as chairman of the Community Health Services, with 2,500 nurses spread across the north-east, I worked in excess of five days a week for which I was paid £12,000 a year—less than the lowest paid nurse; on this occasion, the NHS certainly achieved value for money!

The months that followed were packed with the ever-increasing demands of the NHS, an organisation that seems to flourish on perpetual rounds of committee meetings, inspections, and statistical returns, which diverted attention away from the clinical staff and most important the patients. One of my areas of responsibilities included the medical staff and facilities in the community, which included community hospitals, clinics, home visits, and prisons. One visit in particular was the day that we arrived at Frankland High Security Prison in Durham. In the process of admission, we had to have our fingerprints and photographs recorded before entering the facility, and there was a similar process on leaving. After our meeting with the governor we were taken on a conducted tour of the facilities during which alarm bells rang and a total lockdown procedure was enforced—an unpleasant experience and the result of prisoners attacking each other. A minor problem occurred on leaving when the system didn't recognise my prints for some reason. It's an uncomfortable feeling being locked in! It was, after all, a prison with which I had a very tenuous connection, as at the time one of the inmates was Ian Huntley, the school caretaker who had murdered two schoolgirls, Holly Wells and Jessica Chapman. His girlfriend and partner, Maxine Carr, came from Grimsby and was the cousin of one of my old school friends, Nancy Suddaby. Well, I said it was tenuous!

The developments that were taking place within the NHS gave place to the merging of Community Health Services with the Regional Hospital Trusts. To my mind, this was counterproductive and would lead to the erosion of services in the community. In addition to which, we had already made our targeted savings through staff reductions and greater efficiency. It was evident that the hospital trusts were

cherry-picking to fund the reductions in staff and costs that they had
to provide. They would therefore seek the savings from nursing staff
in the community: those involved in areas such as midwifery, home
visits, and community clinics to name but a few. I believed this to be
a retrograde step as evidenced by the South Staffordshire Inquiry and
that it was the hospital trusts that needed restructuring. In my mind,
what was needed was a greater emphasis on the clinical provision and
a reduction in the bureaucracy and inefficiencies in management. As
it was most unlikely that I was going to influence events, I decided to
resign. Suddenly I had time on my hands—or did I? A void is quickly
filled, as I was soon to experience.

It seemed to me another of those years when too much happened in
a short period of time. The early months had been taken up with
welcome breaks with Pat and David, my friends in Cumberland.
David and I planned to get in some training prior to tackling the
Trans Pennine cycle route in June and July. It was a new route across
the UK which had just been developed as the Roses Route, although
we were going to do a much longer route which incorporated most
of the Roses Route. The weather wasn't particularly favourable to
our training endeavours, so we cycled a few miles and then relaxed
by sampling the local brew. Some weeks afterwards, I found myself
down in Dorset visiting Sheila and Mike Walker, who'd also invited
Fred and Virginia Mullen, mutual friends. We did the usual thing of
reminiscing over days in the RAF, as one was prone to do once the gin
started flowing. Not that I'm an alcoholic, you understand; it's just the
relaxing atmosphere created by good friends. On the way back, I called
in on the Stainers, friends from way back who also live in Dorset.

The trend in natural disasters continued throughout 2010. The
largest earthquake and the tenth deadliest in recorded history
occurred with the repeated eruptions of Mt Mera, which devastated
the capital of Haiti in January and led to the deaths of 316,000
people. This was followed the same month by an 8.8 earthquake
in Chile, which triggered a tsunami. In April all aircraft in Europe
were grounded following the eruption of volcanic gas from Mount
Eyjafjallajokull (only the Scandinavians could have conjured up such
an unpronounceable name). Not to be left out of it, the southern

hemisphere, in the shape of New Zealand, had a series of quakes in excess of 7.0 between 2010 and 2012. In October repeated eruptions of Mt Merapi and earthquakes in central Java created tsunamis off Indonesia. This was also the year of the *Deepwater Horizon* disaster, when the drilling platform exploded, causing one of the largest oil spills in history as well as the loss of life.

Coast to Coast—By Foot and by Cycle

> Energy is neither created nor destroyed. It just changes shape.
> Sheri Reynolds

Having become a director on the board of English Gymnastics some time earlier, I had commitments down in Leicester, where the English Championships were being held at the beginning of March. Nigel, having got the bit between his teeth, and Julie, who considered that it would be nice to have the house to herself, decided that father and father-in-law would benefit from a walk across the United Kingdom devised by a madman called Wainwright. He (Wainwright, not me!) obviously thrived on masochism. Julie took us across to St Bees and deposited us at the Queen's Hotel, and after dinner she departed with a smile on her face. I wonder why? The following morning after an early breakfast we departed on our trek. The reason for the early start was that Nigel decided that Wainwright had stipulated that one had to secure a pebble from the beach on the west coast in order to deposit it in the North Sea on completion of the walk. As many hundreds of people must have followed these instructions, it's a wonder that coastal erosion hasn't taken place on one side of Britain and a peninsular emerged on the opposite side. Anyway, I can think of many other things I could deposit in those waters, and on a later occasion that would include my bicycle. The rest is but a memory. I do recall asking why we were going north to return south before we had even set foot in the east. But who am I to question such a well-trained action man and man of medicine? He would no doubt respond that it was good for me. Besides which, I recall what Jean Jacques Rousseau said about walking: "I can only meditate when I'm walking. When I stop, I cease to think; my mind works only with my legs."

Our route, for those who might be mildly interested, took us to Emmerdale—no, it was Ennerdale (nothing to do with the TV series)—Rostwaite, Petterdale, over Shap Fell to Keld, and eventually Reith. I stop here only to inform the reader that it was on this section that I lost contact with Nigel, who had his seven league boots on. He also had the maps, the reservation forms, and the name of the overnight accommodation. I had nothing, not even a phone number, just a little money and a raging toothache. I was in a mood that my wife often described as intolerable. I can't think why because I was always under the impression that there was every justification for my actions, especially one of mild disposition. But then, I'm merely a man, and who am I to argue with those who possess female logic? Needless to say, I eventually stumbled on Nigel, the intrepid action man, sitting on the wall and studying his maps on the outskirts of Reith, fully convinced I would find my own way to a destination that I didn't even know existed! With such belief, he should have been a religious cleric.

The section between Reith and Richmond was, to me, easily forgotten. The abscess under one of my molar teeth had by this time felt as though it was lifting my brains (what few I had left) through the top of my head, and this being a weekend, there were no dentists available—what a surprise! Nigel called Julie on the mobile, and she collected me and took me to the medical walk-in centre in Darlington. Even though the staff were part of the organisation for which I was responsible, I have to admit that they didn't recognise me, so quite rightly, I didn't get any special treatment. I wasn't bothered; the way I was feeling, a ship's carpenter could have carried out the necessary treatment. They soon dosed me with antibiotics, which enabled me to rejoin Nigel at Ingleby. By the time we got to Clay Bank Top, followed by the massive hills of Glaisdale, I was beyond caring; besides which, the blisters were beginning to develop out of all proportion to my feet. Eventually, two days later, we found ourselves in Robin Hood's Bay once again, and we were grateful to see Julie with the car to recover our bodies. Two hundred miles in ten days—not bad in retrospect. But then, nothing is bad in retrospect!

And now I come to my other maniacal decision of the year, which some six weeks later would see me cycling across similar countryside in the company of nine like-minded idiots but over a somewhat longer course. This time it was in the absence of the offending tooth, not that I can at my time of life afford to lose many more. As I mentioned earlier, David McKechnie, having no doubt trained exceedingly hard (if not with the bike then at least with the drinking arm), had selected a route that took us from the now familiar watering hole of the Queen's Head in St Bees. The morning ritual started with the half-mile ride to the beach to pick up that mandatory pebble which, during the course of the ride, grew to the size of a boulder. Well, it just felt that heavy. We headed south before crossing the Cumbrian Mountains through Eskdale and then up over the Hard Knot Pass before dropping down to Ambleside at the head of Lake Windermere.

Progressing down across the M6, we made our way to the north of Lancaster, crossing the high ground overlooking Morecambe Bay before descending into the Forest of Bowland, where we picked up the Roses Route and headed for Settle. It sounds short and sweet, but it was anything but. Although interspersed with night stops, of which I can remember little, it was hard going. Farther on, we crossed through Upper Wharfedale and on to Nidderdale and the steep descent into and out of Pateley Bridge. Those hills might be a spectacular sight, but not to a cyclist who has the knowledge that what goes down comes up again. Moving on, we passed south of Ripon, stopping at a watering hole in Bishop Monkton, a village which had once housed my brother-in-law's paint production factory, before we pressed on through Boroughbridge, aiming to reach the YHA Centre in York. Can you image it—Old Age Pensioners (OAPs) and some nearly OAPs accommodated in a youth hostel? I must say it was a place of some excellent comfort, especially for young men like ourselves!

The following morning saw the parting of the ways, with all but three of us having found excuses for having to return to the comforts of modern-day living. Being unable to find a suitably qualified individual to certify our mental health, we said our farewells and set off to great acclaim from those who might in other circles be rated as lacking moral fibre", although some might argue that they had something that we didn't possess—brains! We passed through Stamford Bridge—not, I hasten to add, the home of Chelsea FC but the Battle of Stamford

Bridge in 1066. Well, I suppose there are some similarities between the Vikings of that era and the football supporters of today.

Back to reality. Having absorbed a little more history, we moved on to Driffield, which at one time had been the home of the RAF squadron that I earlier described as almost having curtailed my junior flying career. Here, we managed to cajole a café to remain open to provide us with some sustenance before setting course for Filey and eventually Scarborough, where we then parted company with our third rider, who had decided that it was time to retire with honour and dignity and catch the train home to Leeds. After an overnight sojourn on the outskirts of Scarborough, we said our farewells, and David and I set out on the final leg to Whitby, via Robin Hood's Bay—that's right, yet another pebble! After a brief reunion with Pat, we loaded our vehicles onto the car and set out on the final leg to Darlington.

I bet Harold wished he'd had a bike—he might have avoided that arrow!

CHAPTER 22

The Second Decade

> No man or woman born, coward or brave, can shun his destiny.
> Homer, *The Iliad*

On the international front, 2011 was, on reflection, a rather traumatic year, covering five main areas: the Arab revolutions, the death of key terrorists, continuing economic problems, natural disasters, and several events on the home front. Key domestics issues were to influence the family. The Arab revolutions in January and February, triggered by events in Tunisia and subsequently Egypt, soon had an impact on several other Arab countries including Yemen, Syria, and even the Gulf State of Bahrein. Mass uprisings in the Syrian city of Daraa sent the country sliding into civil war and sent ripples through the rest of the Arab world, especially those countries like Saudi Arabia still ruled by a monarchy. These uprisings became known as the Arab Spring and eventually led to the overthrow of some of the Middle East's well-known dictators and despots, including Hosni Mubarak of Egypt, Muammer Gaddafi of Libya, and Ali Abdullah Saleh of the Yemen. At the same time, the West was still coming to terms with terrorism, particularly the insidious expansion of Islam through al-Qaeda's desire to expand its control. Their most infamous attack was the destruction of the Trade Centre in the United States with the loss of over three thousand innocent people. The Americans, having sworn retribution, finally extracted it. Osama bin Laden, the founder and jihadist leader of al-Qaeda and the instigator of 9/11, was finally located inside a private compound in Abbottabad, Pakistan, and killed by a team of US Navy SEALs; within hours, his body was dumped in the Indian Ocean. Less than five months later, Anwar al-Alaki, the leader of al-Qaeda in North Yemen, who had planned many of the attacks in the Middle East, was killed by a US Predator drone.

The fourth factor during the year was the continuing global economic position which, I have no doubt, arose from the 2008 depression, the cause of which was undoubtedly the collapse of the US subprime mortgage market aggravated by regulatory failure and the subsequent bailout of financial institutions, which merely fuels the problem and in turn leads to an over stimulation of the economy. The problems in 2011 were further acerbated by the unrest in the Middle East and North Africa and the disaster in Japan impacting the economy; oil prices were driven up, which in turn led to cuts impacting on the motor industry. What is it that Newton's third law states? Every action has an equal and opposite reaction. It's back to basic economics: governments and individuals should not live beyond their means. The answer to me is simple, but then, I'm not an economist. However, I am aware that on 31 October the United Nations announced that the world population had that day reached seven billion, so I gather we still have statisticians!

It seems to be almost every year that a number of places around the world are hit by earthquakes delivering substantial damage and loss of life. Earthquakes, tsunamis, floods, asteroids, volcanic eruptions— you name it, it happens, and 2011 was no different. On 11 April, an earthquake of 9.0 magnitude, 80 miles off Sendai and close to the Japanese coast, triggered a tsunami which left 20,000 dead and over 100 million dollars in damage. Worse than that, it destroyed the Fukushima nuclear plant, causing a major nuclear crisis, the second most devastating in human history, leaving residual effects from radiation for decades to come. If one is putting things into pigeonholes, as I appear to be doing, then I suppose mass killings must feature in disasters. One of these that doesn't quite fit is the massacre of the innocents, by which I mean the actions of the Norwegian Anders Behring Breivik, a self-styled anti-Muslim militant, in killing seventy-seven mostly young people attending a political youth camp on the island of Utoya. I frequently reflect on how sad the world can be at times.

Battlefields—Ancient and Modern

For many years, I had entertained the idea that I would like to see some historical battlefields. Well, being a coward of the first order, I've always thought it better to view other people's battlefields rather than have to defend one's own. Having seen the remnants of the two world war locations in Central Europe over the years, which I must say is quite emotional, my focus centred on the older campaigns such as the Crimea, the war that led to fame for Florence Nightingale and others, and of course the infamous charge of the Light Brigade, which resulted in only two hundred out of six hundred surviving. Other names spring readily to mind, such as Sevastopol, Inkerman, and further afield Mafeking, Isandlwana, and Rourkes Drift.

However, I could never seem to fit in a visit at the appropriate time, so I decided that I would expand my interest to embrace ancient and modern history by a visit to Turkey, a place I had only briefly touched down on during my RAF days. In late October 2010, I embarked on a visit to Istanbul, often regarded as the crossroads between East and West, with the aim of seeing the ancient and the modern. The most well-known of sights must be the Blue Mosque, or as the locals call it, the Sultan Ahmet Mosque. Opposite is the intriguing underground reservoir, the Basilica Cistern, which featured in the Bond film *From Russia with Love*. Other locations include the Topkapi Palace, the Byzantine Hippodrome, the Grand Bazaar Hagia Sophia, the Sulaymaniyah Mosque, and of course the Golden Horn.

Having spent a few days in the city soaking up the atmosphere and haggling with the local traders, a habit I picked up in my early days in the East, I moved on by sea through the Dardanelles to Gallipoli. Gallipoli is situated on a peninsular in East Thrace, the western part of Turkey, with the Aegean Sea to the west and the Dardanelle Straits to the east. It is an interesting location, although I remain unconvinced by its strategic position, but who am I to question Winston Churchill?

The Gallipoli campaign, instigated in 1915 by the British in an attempt to divert German troops from the European central fronts, thereby creating a third front on the underbelly of Europe, is considered one of the Allies great disasters of World War I. Not only was the military planning flawed, but the strength and ability of the Turkish Army was underestimated. It is believed that over 200,000 troops on each side were killed; many of the Allied troops, including large numbers of soldiers from Australia and New Zealand (ANZAC), were killed before they even reached the beach, weighed down by their kits and becoming sitting targets on congested beaches overlooked by high cliffs. Many others died from disease during the campaign. It achieved nothing in a military sense, apart from the derision of historians. Mind you, academics are marvellous at analysing events, especially when situated well away from the battlefield and often well after the events, with their marvellous gift of hindsight.

From Gallipoli and the Dardanelles, my journey took me back to Istanbul and then across the bridge to the eastern or Asian coastline of Turkey, to Anatolia. It was a timely reminder that whilst we in the West could get things wrong, the Greek and Trojan strategists of yesteryear could also screw up. Although having no pretence at being a classical scholar, throughout the years I have been fascinated by Greek and Roman mythology and legends. Inevitably, this thirst for knowledge has also embraced the writings of the ancient philosophers such as Plato, Socrates, and Aristotle. Indeed, mythology and legend make up the very cornerstone of ancient Greek history, religion, and philosophy. Their gods and heroes are portrayed as being interlinked and involved in everyday life: Zeus, Athena, Poseidon, and Apollo, amongst the many gods, and Agamemnon, Odysseus, Ajax, and Achilles prominent amongst the mortals. These and other characters are brought alive by writers such as Homer in his Greek epic poems the Iliad, a history of the Trojan War, and the Odyssey, the adventures of Odysseus on his eventual return to Ithaca after the fall of Troy.

Most archaeologists beginning with Heinrich Schliemann, who first excavated the area, believe that the Trojan War may have occurred close to the location of the modern-day city of Hissarlik in Asia Minor. The ancient citadel is situated at the edge of a cape projecting into the Aegean, between the Dardanelles and the Gulf of Edremit. The Trojan War, which arose through the elopement of Helen, wife of Menelaus King of Sparta, with Paris, the son of King Priam of Troy, lasted some ten years until the fall of Troy; its capture was enabled by the concept put forward by Odysseus of building the Trojan horse. Helen eventually returned to Menelaus after the death of Paris and the conclusion of the war. Oh, dear, the fickleness of women!

Down the coast, sixteen miles from the sea on a promontory and some two miles north of the river Caicus, sits the city of Pergamon, overlooked by its Acropolis, an ancient centre of healing. It was the home of the famous Pergamon Library, the contents of which were lost when Mark Anthony gave the library to Cleopatra and it was transferred to Alexandra. You just can't trust the Egyptians to look after anything, including their own country. During the time of the writing of St John, Pergamon was one of the world's most important cities. Whilst an enjoyable and interesting visit, it left me with more questions than answers as I headed south to Ephesus and Izmir.

Ephesus was one of the twelve cities of the Ionian League during the classical Greek era when its population of 250,000 made it the largest city in that part of the world. It's famed for its Temple of Artimis, one of the seven wonders of the ancient world, and the library of Celsius which once held 12,000 scrolls. Once the home of Disciple John, it is purported to be the place where John brought the Virgin Mary to live, having promised Jesus that he would look after her. What is claimed to be the house of Mary is situated some four miles from the town. I suppose there must be some credence to the claim because four popes and most of the Roman Catholic Church have at one time or another made the pilgrimage here. Who am I to dispute it? I went along for the experience. After brief visits to Pamukkale, Antalya, and Izmire, the journey across this part of Turkey was at its end, and I headed for the airport and the return to the UK. There is much more that I could add about my visit to Turkey, but I'm sure that would simply dull your attention span, and the last thing I want to do is to make this into a travel log.

In my absence, my brother-in-law Martin had died, and unfortunately I missed his funeral. The remainder of the year was spent playing catch-up before Jonathon, Anna, and the boys arrived for Christmas. The year 2010 soon gave way to 2011. No, strangely enough, I didn't spend New Year's in Lincolnshire; as I promised myself, I stayed at home. It wasn't all altruistic because within two weeks I would be heading out to Africa once more, and I had to have some semblance of fitness. Added to which, I think it was right to not impose myself too much on others no matter what they might say and however much I enjoy my fish and chips at Steels in Cleethorpes.

Ascent of Mt Kenya

> Only those who will risk going too far can
> possibly find out how far they can go.
> T. S. Eliot

Having tried unsuccessfully to persuade Nigel to join me, I set off on my own in early January 2011 to attempt the ascent of Mount Kenya, Africa's second highest mountain. Yes, I know I said never again, but you have to understand that I'm somewhat of an inveterate liar! Although slightly lower than Kilimanjaro, Mt Kenya is a harder climb, being more of a technical ascent. On a more serious note, having said I would never repeat the experience of struggling up mountains, I was intrigued by reading Felice Benuzzi's book, *No Picnic on Mount Kenya*. It is the story of three Italian prisoners of war who escaped their British captivity from POW Camp 336, Gilgil (Kenya), merely to climb the mountain—a daring escape and a perilous climb. After successfully scaling the mountain, they returned to captivity for the rest of the war. And you think I'm mad! Having read the book, I felt compelled to give it a try. There was one quote in Benuzzi's book that fascinated me and in some ways inspired me to do what he had done, to climb the mountain.

> I emerged at last, stumbled a few steps and then I saw it;
> an ethereal mountain emerging from a tossing sea of clouds
> framed between two dark barracks a massive, blue-black

tooth of sheer rock inlaid with azure glaciers, austere yet
floating fairy-like on the near horizon. It was the first
17,000-foot peak I had ever seen. I stood gazing until
the vision disappeared among the shifting cloud banks. I
remained spell-bound. I had definitely fallen in love.

The attempt didn't get off to a very auspicious start when the airline
KLM delayed its scheduled departure from Durham Tees Valley
because of adverse weather conditions in Amsterdam. We had boarded
the aircraft, and the pilot kept us on the runway for sixty minutes,
which was exactly the time before the departure of my connecting
flight to Nairobi. The captain drifted between optimism and
pessimism as he reviewed the situation, and then the staff informed
me that though the connecting flight couldn't be delayed, I would be
able to see, on my arrival, if it had left—some comfort, some logic.
Arriving at Amsterdam at the appointed time of departure and not
knowing which dock it was leaving from was like competing in one of
those mindless TV games. Schiphol airport staff assisted the chaos by
removing the flight from the indicator board, thus suggesting that it
might have already departed. I'm sure my test was to establish a new
world record for the cross-terminal Heart Attack Stakes. Luckily the
aircraft had technical problems, so I was able, with a few well-directed
arguments, to board just as the doors closed. Little did I know that my
bags had not enjoyed the same degree of success. I have long held the
view that I have an innate ability to move in different directions to my
accoutrements when travelling by air. It is called Everett's Second Law
of Predictability.

The flight was full of people travelling to the African continent. The
food was of dubious quality, the service was somewhat chaotic, and the
noise precluded sleep, all of which made for an uncomfortable journey
of a little over eight hours through the night. I did have the temerity to
point out on several occasions that neither my overhead light nor my
screen were working, and I could not therefore read or watch films, but
to no avail. The joys of travelling in economy class. A young baby then
ensured that the only other option available, sleep, had subsequently
been removed from the menu. I arrived in Nairobi, tired and somewhat
irritable, to find that my bags containing all my essential clothing and

energy foods, together with my climbing equipment, had not made the connection. I was informed that it might arrive the following day, by which time I was scheduled to have started my climb some ninety-five miles away from the arrival airport. What I wasn't told at the time was that I would have to pay seventy dollars for its delivery. The motto of this airline partnership should be "We delay, you pay".

To this day, I suffer from recurring nightmares associated with missing connecting flights, trains, buses, and ships and the loss of bags and other important possessions, which to no small measure is connected to this experience. Yes, I know, I'm a psychiatrist's dream!

The bags did arrive at Mountain Rock Bantu Centre late in the evening of the next day, delivered by the very company through whom I had arranged the climb. How ironic! I guess very little has changed since I was last in Kenya in the 1960s. That meant that my acclimatisation was reduced by a further twenty-four hours, and this was to have an impact later in the climb. When climbing Kilimanjaro two years earlier, we had concentrated on acclimatisation to avoid high altitude sickness. Unfortunately, the Kenyan guides did not seem to share the same concerns. To climb over 17,000 feet in three days is hard enough, but to lose twenty-four hours and have little time to sort out essential equipment is tempting providence.

After a good night's sleep and a reduction in my blood pressure, as I adapted to a more laid-back approach to life in Africa, we set out by Land Rover on the start of our trip along the early morning crowded roads. Very soon we departed from the metalled roads and headed up over heavily rutted lanes for about three hours towards the entrance to the National Park, eventually arriving at Sirimon Park Gate somewhat bruised and battered by the continual jolting despite the relative slow journey. Having retrieved the kit from the vehicle, Sirus, my guide, introduced me to our cook and three porters, who were busy sorting and repacking all our climbing kit and rations. They were to stay with us for most of the route, except for the climb to the summit/

The next day we set off on our initial five-hour hike through Montana Forest, covered in bamboo and rosewood, up to Old Moses

Hut at 11,000 feet. Here we had an overnight stop in freezing and uncomfortable conditions. I've had better nights on the mountains in tents. At by least travelling alone, apart from my support team, it was a way of meeting others who were attempting the ascent—people with whom I could converse and share my concerns.

We left camp at 6 a.m. and for the next eight hours traversed expansive moorland carpeted with tussock grass, exotic rosewood, heather, and unique giant Lobelia and Senacio plants. The forest and bamboo areas that surround the lower levels of the mountain are not without some danger created by the presence of buffalo, elephants that wander to the levels of glaciers, and even lions. The lions have been known to attack people on the ascent of the mountain. However, the area has its softer side, for it was here that I witnessed the lack of fear in the birds and animals that surrounded us; so tame were the birds that they would eat from my hand when we stopped for an occasional snack during the day.

The journey seemed a never-ending, criss-crossing of valleys and streams; the moorland rising from the Nanyuki River involved many steep climbs and descents before we finally entered the Mackinder Valley, which we reached in the late afternoon. Here I had my first close view of the mountain in all its glory, set in a juxtaposition against the moorland with its own peculiar flora and fauna. The jagged peaks of the mountain looked truly awe-inspiring as I looked across the west face of Batian to the subpeak of Lenana looming high above us. I began to understand why this mountain range had a reputation for its stark but entrancing beauty. Not for the first time, I wondered just what I was doing taking on such a daunting challenge. We eventually reached Shipton's Hut at almost 14,000 feet for our second overnight stop, the conditions being much the same as at Old Moses, but at least it was an opportunity to meet other climbers and get to bed early, ready for the final leg the following day. There was no choice—no lights!

I said everything was compressed in time. Here we were on day three, up at 2.30 a.m. in freezing conditions, ready for the attempt on the summit. For the first time, I suffered from nausea; whether this arose from the food or the first signs of altitude sickness, I was unsure. But it left me searching for further signs such as severe headache, which had it occurred would have necessitated me abandoning the climb. Faced with a further climb of almost 3,000 feet, the going became harder; a mixture of scree and rocks of varying sizes giving way to high-level rock, and towards the top was an almost vertical wall to scale with the only light from our headlights. The rocks were difficult to negotiate because most were coated in layers of ice. I began to question my sanity, attempting such a climb at the age of over seventy-five.

This is a mountain that has no easy way to the top, and unlike Kilimanjaro it is more of a technical climb; the last few hundred feet, like many mountains, is a test of resolve. However, I eventually made the summit just in time to witness the sunrise. Having experienced it on Kilimanjaro, this was no less impressive as I looked down on the clouds and saw the horizon burst into a myriad of colours ranging from deep red through orange, yellow, green, and deep blue.

After twenty minutes at the top taking photographs, I set off with my guide, who had climbed the mountain many times before. On the descent, about 500 feet from the top, I lost my footing on a very narrow ledge and fell about 15 feet on to rock and scree before rolling another 15 to 20 feet. I heard a loud crack and felt intense pain in my right knee, which made me think that I had either broken the leg or snapped the tendon. However, because I could move my leg after a few minutes, I realised that the sound came from my headlamp and glasses, which were smashed as my head hit a rock. More to the point, I had stopped just short of a significant drop. Perhaps someone was telling me that it was time for me to retire! My immediate relief gave way to anger as I reflected on my lack of concentration and then to embarrassment at the thought of screwing up in front of the guide. We eventually made very slow progress down to Camp 2. After a welcome cup of tea brewed on one of those portable stoves that are the dream of every mountaineer, we moved on the long grind down to Camp 1, a distance of over eleven miles. All told, it had been an eighteen-hour day that I thought would never end.

The next day at 6 a.m., and following a light breakfast, we set off for our return to Sirimon Gate. Perhaps it's just me, but I always find the downhill elements of mountains the most demanding, sapping energy and playing hell with the muscles and back! It is a fact that most accidents in climbing occur on the descent rather than the ascent. I must admit on this occasion, despite the adrenalin kick of having summited, I wasn't feeling particularly happy with life. As the day progressed, I seemed to get progressively slower. It didn't help that in favouring my right knee, I managed to trip several times on the deeply rutted track. After slow progress, almost a crawl, and with the help of the guide, I eventually arrived at Sirimon Gate, much of the trail having been but a blur. Having finished our trek and packed the kit into the Landrover, I said farewell to our porters, but not before handing over the usual tips and excess clothing, which seems to be a feature of climbs and treks. We travelled back to Mountain Rock Lodge via Nanuky, which was a bumpy and painful ride of over two hours.

Whilst my initial impression of the Mountain Rock Lodge was somewhat clouded by its rather decadent state, my return after a few days on the mountain gave me a different perspective, and I began to view it as the Safari Hilton. Perhaps it was the long-awaited cold beer that influenced my view, or the fact that I was only there for a short while before returning to the UK. After all, the hotel did have showers with some hot water, and of course with the accompanying cockroaches who seemed to enjoy sharing the facilities with me. Having showered off the mountain dust, I returned to my bedroom in the nude to find an uninvited guest working his way through my bags, throwing clothes and accoutrements in all directions. His threatening stance and menacing glare convinced me that this was not the time to have an altercation which I would clearly lose. After all, male baboons are not the friendliest of creatures. I'm not sure what he intended to do with the articles he took with him; probably he thought that dressed in my underpants, socks, and T-shirt, he would appeal to his female counterparts. Have I got news for him. It never worked for me, and I'm sure it wouldn't for him!

The evening meal was a further problem in communication. I declined the offer of mutton or goat, having survived it on the mountain, and instead opted for chicken. One would have thought I had more sense.

The meal that arrived had three chicken heads mounted on a bed of cold rice, the poor creatures' eyes having glazed over long before mine. I knew how they felt. Needless to say, I did try to explain to the waiter that not even in the UK did we eat such sophisticated delicacies.

My return to Nairobi coincided with rush hour, if you can describe it as such, a time of the day when everyone has the right of way on either side of the road. I'm not talking just about motorists—pedestrians, cattle, dogs, cyclists, chickens, and young schoolchildren walking the few miles home, and big mamas were having their afternoon chats. Massive clouds of dust swirled over the roads, coating everything in a fine red dust. Did I say roads? What I really meant was a series of potholes joined at intervals by strips of hard core and on some rare occasions tarmac. The journey of less than one hundred miles took a back-breaking six hours. After several delays in Nairobi and at the Schiphol airport, which was par for the course, I arrived home in the early hours of the following day. On reflection, climbing the mountain was perhaps the easiest part of my experience!

In summary, "Vini, Vidi, Vici"—I came, I saw, I conquered. But there's more to my visit than that, and there's more to Africa than clambering up a few mountains. To me, it's not only about the indifference and corruption; neither is it just about the poverty that permeates the continent and is brushed aside by the many despotic politicians. It's not about the romantic notions of Africa with its unique natural resource or its idyllic settings of mountains, rivers, deserts, and wild animals. Africa's uniqueness is about all of these things: a wild and largely untamed but fascinating continent.

CHAPTER 23

Back to the Realities of Life

Every man has a sane spot somewhere.
Robert L. Stephenson

It was back to work with a vengeance for yet another period of change and transition in the National Health Service. Who said this was a part-time occupation? Over the next few weeks, there was the never-ending cycle of visits, meetings, and discussions across the north-east from Richardson Hospital, Barnard Castle and Darlington in the south to Fern Court, Ramside and Easington in the east, and Stanley and the Dales in the West, with Durham sandwiched in between. Plus, there was the eternal procession of meetings at the NHS Headquarters, north of Tyne.

As I said earlier, by March 2011 I had already decided that I'd had enough of the politics of the National Health Service, both internal and external, and I resigned my position as chair of the Community Health Services, a position that paid a pittance and was beginning to interfere with the rest of my life—a life that I suffered under the delusion of having under my control. At the end of March, I had a meeting with Sir Peter Carr in which I outlined why I was leaving, expressing my disillusionment with the continual change of direction and what I considered to be a lack of leadership. His description of the progress being achieved, in his view from the top, didn't exactly accord with mine or, I believe, any other sane knight of the realm. We politely differed in our opinions and parted accordingly.

My sister-in-law Sheila succumbed to cancer during April, so Julie and I travelled down to Grantham to join the family for the funeral on Friday, 15 April, travelling back the same day because I had already agreed to spend that weekend up in Northumberland with Pat and David. A week later, I informed Brandy that she was about to have another wonderful holiday at Ketton Hall, her kennels, whilst I packed my warm weather clothing and headed for Abu Dhabi to stay with Jonathan and family; my final opportunity to visit as they were planning to return to the UK, exchanging the oil rich for the oil poor. Two weeks flew by, culminating with a trip to the top of the newly built Burg Khalifa, the world's tallest building, which had been completed the previous year. I recalled the 1950s when, as a mere youth, I had exceeded my expectations and travelled to the top of the Empire State Building, which at that time was the tallest in the world. Somehow this didn't feel the same, with a much faster and more comfortable transition to the top. Shortly after the lift started, I did ask Jonathan how long it would take to get to the top. The look I got with the response, "Dad, we've arrived," was one of pitiful sympathy in the certain knowledge that his father had entered that era of elderly decline. Originally called the Burg Dubai, this new skyscraper was renamed after Sheikh Khalifa bin Zayed Al Nahayan, the ruler of Abu Dhabi who generously bailed out the now indebted Dubai with £6 billion—I suppose a mere drop in the oil ocean. I'm only envious because I don't have a wallet big enough to house that sort of loose change! Of course, my visit was somewhat overshadowed by the royal wedding of William and Kate, and the infamous bum wiggle of her bridesmaid and sister Pippa.

The Everett contribution to the National Health Service continued in my absence when Julie submitted her body for its MOT, having had her right rotator cuff recreated—Darlington's answer to the Bionic Woman.

London Transport Old Comrades Association

Upon returning to the UK on 5 May, I had a quick turnaround and then went down to London for the London Transport Old Comrades Association (LTOCA) AGM and lunch. The following day, I had dinner in the RAF club before returning to Darlington to get a quick change of clothes, collect the dog, and then travel down to Forest Park, Cromer, for a few days of maintenance work on the caravan and some training rides on my bike.

As a director of London Transport and an ex-officer in the armed services, I had been invited to become the president of the LTOCA in 1994, a position I'm very proud to continue to this day. The primary objective of the LTOCA is to perpetuate the memory of those who made the supreme sacrifice in the service of their country and to preserve the spirit of comradeship among all ex-service personnel. The main event is participating in the Remembrance Day Parade in Whitehall each November, preceded by the annual dinner, but LTOCA also aims to provide assistance to colleagues and their families during the rest of the year.

In 1920 King George V granted a unique honour to what was then the London General Omnibus Company (LGOC), the forerunner to London Transport which was eventually to become Transport for London. This honour established London Transport as the only civilian organisation to march alongside the armed forces in the Remembrance Day Parade. The honour was in recognition of the service rendered by the men of the LGOC who served as soldiers and drove their buses to and from the front line in France during World War I. Although changes have taken place over the years, London Transport maintains the privileged position of last in line on Remembrance Day and first in line at the Cenotaph.

London Transport also played a significant role on the home front during World War II, supporting the fire services as part of the Home Guard and the ARP and providing essential service. Throughout the Blitz on London, tube stations provided shelter and facilities in 86 medical posts for 63 million users. More than 7 tonnes of food and

12,000 gallons of tea and cocoa were carried on specially converted refreshment trains every day to support those being sheltered. A little-known aspect is that throughout World War II, the LT Works at Chiswick constructed a significant number of Halifax bombers that were ultimately to play an important role in the destruction of German wartime industry. Between 1942 and April 1945, over 700 bombers were constructed using 500 different subcontractors. The nucleus of the organisation was established at Chiswick and subsequently developed out to Aldenham before taking over a new factory at Leavesdon Airfield, near Watford. The organisation assumed responsibility for the final erection, test-flying, and delivery of complete aircraft. The 710th aircraft off the production line was called *London Pride*. Also, a closely guarded secret was the provision of a 5-mile tunnel 4 yards in diameter and situated under 3 stations at Wanstead, Redbridge, and Gants Hill. It comprised of 300,000 square feet of factory space for the production of aircraft parts, together with a subterranean canteen for 600 people and 4 mess rooms seating 1,600 people. With additional entries at Cambridge Park and Daneshurst Gardens, no employee in the factory had more than 400 yards to walk to the place of work—a very important aspect during the Blitz. London Transport staff also contributed to a LT fund dedicated to paying for the production of Spitfire fighter aircraft, two of which carried the London Transport logo on the side of the aircraft and flew with the No 308 and No 350 Squadrons.

Being conscious of the lack of training and my even greater lack of fitness, and with a little over two months before my next act of madness, I decided to escape to Cromer in the hope that I could at least mount the cycle and pedal a few miles. I say two months, but that's overlooking the fact that I had other commitments during that time. Alas, I spent some time down at Forest Park sorting out the garden, relaxing, and yes, I did do a little training. Nevertheless, it was nowhere near the mileage that was necessary in preparation for my next challenge. However, I comforted myself with the old adage "Where there's a will, there's a way".

The Holy Land

> Is he not sacred, even to the gods, the wandering
> man who comes in weariness
> Homer, *The Iliad*

Earlier in 2011, I had been invited to join His Honour Judge Ian Alexander, Great Chancellor of the Order of Knights Templar, and other Knights to make a pilgrimage to the Holy Land. One of the objectives of the visit was to make a donation, on behalf of the Knights of the Great Priory of England and Wales, of £500,000 to the Ophthalmic Hospital of St John in Jerusalem; the second objective was to enjoy ourselves. For the remainder of the visit, we toured the country, although our crusade was slightly different to the journeys pursued by Richard the Lionheart and less of a threat all round. It was a most interesting visit combining the historical aspects of a country central to the Christian and other faiths in so many ways, with the everyday events of modern Israel.

Jerusalem

We set out on Thursday, 16 June, the day before my birthday, arriving in Jerusalem that evening. In all, the pilgrimage (tour) was to take twelve days. The Holy Land is a term that refers in general to the whole area in between the Jordan River and the Mediterranean Sea. To both Christians and Muslims alike, the perceived holiness of the land was one of the unique factors that motivated the Crusades; if you're a cynic, the others were money and power. The first day of our visit being a Friday, and the start of the weekend (Friday and Saturday were the Jewish holy days), the roads were fairly crowded, so we were taken to the Mount of Olives, one of three mountain peaks in a range which runs along the Kidron Valley just a few hundred yards to the east of the old city of Jerusalem. It is a location where Jesus came frequently to teach and prophesise to his disciples. At the foot of the mountain lays the Garden of Gethsemane, the name being derived from the Aramaic "Gat Smane", or oil press. It is here that Jesus was betrayed by Judas and where he is said later to have ascended to heaven (Acts 1:9–12).

The olive trees that grow in the garden are reputed to be over 900 years old, carbon-dated as far back as 1092 and planted from the same parent tree.

The Kidron Valley (Qidron in Arabic and Cedron in Hebrew) runs along the eastern wall of Jerusalem, separates the Temple Mount from the Mount of Olives, and continues east through the Judean desert towards the Dead Sea, descending 4,000 feet along its 20-mile course. The area of the Mount of Olives is sacred ground, covered by a massive cemetery. There is an end-day prophesy that it will be the epicentre of God's fight with the enemies of Jerusalem. The Bible describes that on the Day of Judgement, "a great earthquake will strike Israel, such as has never occurred before causing a rift that will run from Jerusalem to the Dead Sea and the Mount of Olives will be split in half" (Zechariah 14:3–5). I was thankful that the Day of Judgement didn't coincide with my visit to Jerusalem!

Bethlehem

Moving on from doom and gloom, our next port of call was Bethlehem, located five miles south of Jerusalem. It perches on a hill at the edge of the Judean desert, and it was here that Mary gave birth to Jesus in a cave where there was a manger used by the animals. Here too, one thousand years before Christ, it was to become the birthplace of David, second king of Israel. The name Bethlehem means "House of Bread" in Aramaic and Hebrew and "House of Meat" in Arabic, which gives one food for thought! Our journey to Bethlehem was a strange experience because as we approached the town, we were confronted by the "separation wall" constructed by the Israelis to restrict the flow of terrorists. It was almost like crossing into East Berlin during the Cold War era with the high concrete walls and the barbed-wire checkpoints. The barrier that runs along the northern side of the town, within close proximity of houses, has severely affected the economy and movement of the town's residents. Out in the countryside, it was a different environment: Bethesda, the Jordan Valley, Jericho, Beit She'an, Capernium, the River Jordan, and the Sea of Galilee. All of it so steeped in biblical history.

Bethseda

The next day, Saturday (their equivalent of our Sunday), we set out for Bethseda. One thing that you notice very quickly is how small the country is with distances soon covered. Mind you, it would have posed more of a problem in Jesus's time. Bethseda is a small fishing village on the shore of the Sea of Galilee. It is here that Jesus walked on water, fed a crowd of five thousand (the loaves and fishes), and gave sight to the blind man. It was also the home to Peter, Andrew, and Philip, who gave up fishing to follow Christ. In the afternoon, we visited the Church of the Holy Sepulchre, built by Constantine's mother, Helen, in AD 326, torn down several times and rebuilt.

One of the most controversial sites in Christianity, said to be the original burial place of Christ and venerated as such, is Golgotha, the Hill of Calvary. It is now a site shared by many religions: Greek Orthodox, Roman Catholic, Eastern Orthodox, Anglican, and others. It poses the inevitable question: which has got it right? I was more impressed by the alternative we went to see, Golgotha and the Garden Tomb. In 1883, near the Damascus Gate, General Gordon (he of Khartoum fame, who was murdered by the Mahdi in 1885) found a rocky escarpment shaped in the form of a skull with caves as eyes, which more aptly fits the description in the Bible. The site would certainly make executions very visible and ominous. Nearby is the Garden Tomb, reputed to have been occupied by Jesus and having the grooves in which the rolling stone would have fitted at its entrance. Situated at the base of the Golgotha escarpment is a modern-day bus station. Well, some people must move with the times!

The Old City

We returned to the Temple Mount, the site that was first consecrated by the Israelites of Exodus, and watched the devout religious sects at the Wailing Wall, lodging their prayers in the crevices between the limestone blocks of the wall. The wall, also referred to as the Katel and believed by devout Jews to be the Western Wall of the Second Temple, is in the Old Quarter of East Jerusalem. It is 187 feet high, built of thick corroded limestone, and about 1600 feet long, although most of it is engulfed by other structures. It is an enigma because it supports the foundations of the Al Aqsa Mosque, Islam's third holiest site after Mecca and Medina. The Dome of the Rock that surmounts Temple Mount was built in 691 by al-Malik to rival the Holy Sepulchre, and his son al-Walid went on to build the al-Aqsa Mosque in 705 for Mohammad's night journey to Jerusalem and back to Mecca (Koran 17:1). From the top of the rock, Mohammed began his ascent to heaven.

Moving on through the Old City, we entered Zedekiah's Cave, also known as Solomon's Quarries, a five-acre underground limestone quarry that runs for a considerable distance under the Muslim Quarter of the Old City and under the Holy Mount Moriah. The quarry was carved by the masons, labourers, and many slaves over several thousands of years. Herod the Great (73–4 BC) certainly used the quarry for building blocks used in the renovation of the Temple, as did Suleiman the Magnificent many years later in rebuilding the city walls.

Day three saw us once again heading out towards Galilee. Mind you, it can hardly be avoided. This time we were aiming for Tiberius on the western shore of the Sea of Galilee. Since the sixteenth century, Tiberius has been considered one of Judaism's four holy cities, along with Jerusalem, Hebron, and Safed. The city has, for thousands of years, also been known for its hot springs, which are believed to cure skin and other ailments. Its name derives from the fact that when established, it was named in honour of the Roman Emperor Tiberius.

Jordan Valley

Passing on down the Jordan Valley, we eventually arrived in Jericho, believed to be one of the oldest inhabited cities in the world. Described in the Old Testament as the City of Palm Trees, it has copious springs which have attracted inhabitants over thousands of years. It is the traditional place to which the Israelites returned from their bondage in Egypt, led by Joshua, the successor to Moses. The name Jericho recalls the Israelites marching, trumpets sounding, and walls falling down. It's a wonderful story of faith and victory, but did it really happen, and if so, was it in the way it is described? For seven days, they marched around the city until the walls fell. There are many ideas of how this happened, and there is clear evidence that an earthquake occurred at this time. However, if God did use an earthquake, it's still a miracle that it coincided with the seventh day of the march of the Israelites, and as claimed in the Bible, it was "by faith that the walls of Jericho fell down" (Hebrews 11:30).

Our next destination was Beit She'an, about twenty miles south of the Sea of Galilee. One of the most ancient settlements in Israel, throughout history it has played an important role due to its strategic position at the junction of the Jordan River and the Jezreel Valley. Even today its position is vital, sitting as it does at the crossing point into Jordan. In the Crusader period, the settlement was part of the Belvoir fiefdom, and the ruins of its castle remains until this day, as do the remains that are evidence of Roman occupation, such as the Amphitheatre and the Roman Baths.

The following day, Monday, we found ourselves back at the Sea of Galilee, this time on the northern shore close to Capernaum at Tabgha at the foot of the Mount of Beatitudes. Tabgha (Greek for "seven springs") is where Jesus came after receiving the news that Herod Antipus had beheaded his cousin John the Baptist, and it's where he fed the crowd of five thousand who had come to hear him with five loaves and three fishes. It is also the location where he appeared to the disciples and told them to cast their nets on the opposite side of their boat, and the place where he challenged Peter three times. Mount Beatitude is the site where he preached the Sermon on the Mount.

Golan Heights

On the way to the Golan Heights, we stopped off in Banias, at the base of Mount Hermon and close to the ancient Roman city of Caesarea Philippi. It is adjacent to a spring, a grotto, and related shrines dedicated to the god Pan. The Golan Heights, also called the Syrian Golan, forms a rocky plateau 3,300 feet high in the Anti-Lebanon Mountains that overlooks southern Syria. Seized by the Israelis in the closing stages of the six-day war (1967), it is located only forty miles from Damascus, which is clearly visible from the Heights. It also borders Lebanon to the north and Jordan to the south, and it is therefore of major military strategic importance. Moreover, it provides one-third of Israel's water supplies. The Israelis have important military intelligence-gathering facilities spread across the plateau, and though we could visit some of the now disused bunkers, it was impossible to gain access to those currently in use. However, looking out over Syria, one can understand why the Israelis wish to hold on to this advantage.

The evening was spent in accommodation in the Kibbutz of Ein Gev. Three of us caught the bus, loaded with armed male and female soldiers obviously on changeover of shift, which took us into the local town, where we spent the evening viewing the sights. The following morning, we packed our bags and left by coach for Cana of Galilee, where Jesus attended the wedding at which he turned the water into wine. What a pity we now can only reverse the process! Cana is close to Nazareth, the birthplace of Christ and the town in which he grew up.

Situated close to Nazareth, at the eastern end of the Jezreel Valley and 11 miles west of the Sea of Galilee, is Mount Tabor, a hill of about 500 feet rising in splendid isolation from the surrounding plains. It has often been surmounted by a fortress due to its strategic importance; but by the end of the fourth century it had become a church and later a monastery, and it was considered by the Crusaders as a most sacred site. Why? Well, the answer lies in the fact that the church houses a rock that was believed to be the very site of the Transfiguration, when Jesus is transfigured or metamorphosed, becoming radiant when conversing with God and the prophets.

In the afternoon, we moved down to the River Jordan to Yardinet, the place where John baptised Jesus. We also were given the opportunity of a second baptism whilst being fully immersed in the River Jordan. Not exactly what I expected, with the waters being exceptionally muddy with large rocks underfoot. However, it was an experience that not many have the opportunity to undergo. We returned for a second night at our Kibbutz, and the following morning after breakfast, we set sail on the Sea of Galilee. In the afternoon, we left for our journey to Acre via Montfort Castle, a Crusader fortress dating back to the times of the kingdom of Jerusalem. The fortress is built on a narrow and steep cliff projecting from a larger hill above the southern bank of Nahal Kziv in the upper Galilee region, about eight miles northeast of the city of Nahariya and close to the border with Lebanon. It's a most impressive location and a very defensible position from which Saladin was denied during the Crusades.

Acre

Crossing to the coast, our next visit was to Caesarea Maritima, situated some thirty miles south of Acre. Originally a Phoenician city, it was rebuilt with a man-made breakwater to allow ships to land. It was created as the new Roman capital by Herod the Great, who built his palace here and dedicated the new city to Augustus in the tenth century BC. It was captured by King Baldwin the First in 1101 during the First Crusade. A legend grew up that in this city was discovered the Holy Grail, around which so much lore accrued over the next two centuries. The old city of Acre (Akka) is a large walled city on the shores of the Bay of Haifa, ten miles north of Haifa. An ancient Hebrew legend tells that the sea flooded the world, and when it reached the shores of Acre, it stopped short, as is written in the Book of Job (38:11). "Hitherto shalt thou come, but no further." As the largest natural port in Israel, it has a long history of conquests and ruling empires. Its name appears on the tribute lists of Pharaoh Thutmose III (sixteenth century BC). During the twelfth century AD, it was one of the Crusaders' main fortifications and ports, as well as their last foothold in the Holy Land. One of the most impressive sites is the massive underground tunnel built by the Templars in the twelfth century to connect their fortress on the south-west of the city with their harbour facilities on the south-east.

Two days later found us in Tel Megiddo, some twenty miles south-east of Haifa. As implied, the city is a Tel, twenty-five different cities built on each other. Strategically placed at the head of a pass through the Carmel ridge overlooking the Jezreel Valley from the West, it was a site of great importance in the ancient world because it guarded the trade route connecting Egypt and Assyria. It was therefore the scene of many historical battles. One of Egypt's mighty pharaohs, Thutmose III, waged war upon the city in 1478 BC. To the Roman Empire, it became an important military artery known as the Via Maris, The Way of the Seas. According to the Bible, it is Armageddon the site of the final battle before the second coming (Revelation 16:16).

The Dead Sea, Masada, and the Dead Sea Scrolls

Saturday, 25 June, saw us heading south once more towards the Dead Sea and Masada, an awe-inspiring sight. Masada, meaning fortress in Hebrew, is an ancient fortress located on the top of an isolated rock plateau on the eastern edge of the Judean Desert, overlooking the Dead Sea. Herod the Great built his winter palace on the top between 37 and 31 BC. The cliffs on the eastern edge of Masada are some 1,300 feet high, and the plateau (1,800 feet high) is reached by three very narrow, winding, and hair-raising paths that lead to fortified gates at the top. Although I was used to some steep and precarious climbs, I found this one of the most nerve-racking and exhausting climbs. Imagine doing this in full armour! A fact for the historians amongst you: the siege of Masada by the Roman army ended with the mass suicide of the 960 Jewish occupants (men, women, and children) at that time. That really must have been an awesome sight to confront any attacker.

The Dead Sea is the lowest point on earth, situated at 1,300 feet below sea level, and is part of the 4,000-mile Great African Rift Valley. Although fed by water from the surrounding mountains, no water flows out of the Dead Sea; instead, it evaporates in the high temperatures. Ten times saltier than water found in the oceans, it has such a high specific weight that you can literally float on the surface. Indeed, once floating on your back, it is difficult to turn over— something I didn't particularly enjoy, with visions of staring into the sun until the end of time. They do claim that the waters and the environment contain therapeutic qualities, being high in magnesium (good for bronchial conditions), bromine (relaxes the nervous system), salt (draws the toxins from the pores of the body), and medicinal mud containing sulphur (for the treatment of psoriasis, eczema, arthritis, dermatitis, etc.).

Located on a plateau about one mile from the Dead Sea, near the Israeli Kibbutz of Kalia, lies Qumran, the site of one of the world's most significant historical finds, the Dead Sea Scrolls. The scrolls were accidentally discovered in 1946 when a young Bedouin shepherd, Mohammed Edh-Dhib, fell through the roof of a cave. When pulled out by his two cousins, they retrieved seven scrolls. Subsequently, a series of twelve caves around the site of Wadi Qumran were opened between 1946 and 1956, and hundreds of scrolls, stored in pottery jars, were discovered. It is believed that these form part of an ancient library. A collection of 972 texts in Hebrew, Aramaic, Greek, and Nabatacan, written on both parchment and papyrus scrolls, and bronze carvings has been recovered. The originals are now held in a Jerusalem museum.

The Eye Hospital

We arrived back in Jerusalem on 26 June and during the day walked through Old Jerusalem and along the Via Dolorosa, along which the fourteen Stations of the Cross are commemorated, ending in the Church of the Holy Sepulchre. As Knights Templars, we were particularly interested in the area set aside for the first king of Jerusalem, King Baldwin I. Later, three of us visited the King David Hotel, the scene of many recent historical events. The evening had been set aside for our visit to the St John Eye Hospital Group, a charitable foundation which operates an ophthalmic hospital in Jerusalem and satellite eye care clinics in the West Bank, the Gaza Strip, and East Jerusalem, where the rates of blindness are ten times higher than in the west because of the interbreeding between families; especially in the Arab areas, eye disease is widespread with far-reaching consequences. In recognition of the work carried out by the hospital, Queen Victoria granted it a royal charter, and it has continued its work with the voluntary and financial support of our order. Patients receive care regardless of ethnicity, religion, or ability to pay. Our cheque for £500,000 was gratefully received, and I'm sure it will help them achieve some of their objectives.

The last day of our visit took us to the port of Jaffa and then on to Tel Aviv for our flight to London. There is much more we garnered from this visit and more that I could relate, but suffice to say that from every respect, this was a most interesting and rewarding experience. It gave one a different perspective on a part of the world that, whilst it continues in conflict, shares common history.

International and Domestic Developments

There was hardly time to recover before a double problem. My brother Graham had another fall and had been moved across to Queen's Hospital in Nottingham on 14 July, and Dave (brother-in-law) had been admitted to Harrogate with heart problems on 16 July! I visited both before returning home, after putting Brandy back into kennels. The following week, I was off once more, this time travelling to Manchester to attend grandson Jack's graduation. I know what you think: I'm too young to be a grandparent. I put it down to G and T, which keeps me going. Jack had worked extremely hard during his final year, gaining a first-class honours in economics and business management. His girlfriend, Jess, had also received her nursing diploma the previous year. We were all delighted, especially Jane and Kevin, who by this time had been admitted back into the fold, but only on temporary membership. I am of course talking about Kevin; I wouldn't wish you to think that I treat my daughters that way! We celebrated in some style with dinner in a restaurant near Sheila Mackie's home in Cheshire. I regretted that my Sheila couldn't have been there. She would, like me, have been immensely proud that the first of her grandchildren had done so well.

The remainder of the summer was equally hectic with both the English and British Gymnastics, the World Gymnastics Championships in Tokyo, the World Trampoline Championships in Birmingham, the Pre-Olympics Qualifications in London, board meetings, and of course the regional competitions to consider. There was even time to fit in journeys down to Forest Park to sort out a few maintenance problems, mainly replacing much of the wooden decking, during July, August, and September. And that's not forgetting the annual Kesteven College reunion in between.

Turning to the lighter side, it was a year in which we at home could join in the celebration of another royal wedding, that between William and Kate, on 29 April. We weren't invited, of course, although I noticed that some lesser celebrities were present! You would have thought that a young RAF officer and would-be king would be aware of the protocol! My sister celebrated her eightieth birthday that year and invited us all to attend her celebrations. Gordons supplied the gin whilst M&S took care of the food! Never mind, I might still be around when the next royal gets hitched. I was also invited to Pat and Bill Gladding's golden wedding anniversary thrash—was it really that long ago? The marriage, I mean, not the party.

Jonathan and Anna decided during 2011 that it was time to return home. The boys needed to move on to secondary education, added to which there was a need to consider the future for the family. Jonathan was offered the position of managing director of PMES, part of the same Ultra Electronics Group in the UK. As this was to be a final excursion for me, I went out to Abu Dhabi, for what is likely to be the final time, in May prior to their return home. Nigel went off to war again in November (what some people will do to avoid having Christmas with their family). This time it was chasing pirates off the coast of Somalia and the Yemen as part of NATO's Operation Ocean Shield on board the Royal Fleet Auxiliary *Fort Victoria*. I suspect it was an opportunity for these noble reinforcements to sun themselves on the deck, supping their drinks, whilst the marines went off in their inflatables to invite a few Somalis back to the party—invitation by gunpoint only. They did manage to return with thirteen of them after sinking their boat. Well, it was either come back and join the party, or provide lunch for the sharks! In the meanwhile, as compensation, I had Christmas with Julie and the children; I shouldn't address them as children because now they are mature young adults. Jonathan and family headed off to Bristol for Christmas with Sue. New Year's I spent at home once again, and so ended another year. Where do they all go to?

CHAPTER 24

New Challenges

Challenges are what make life interesting, overcoming
them is what makes life meaningful.

Joshua Marine

Let me return to the more mundane events which occurred during
2012—mundane to some but important to me. During April I
received news that my static caravan down at Forest Park had suffered
because of burst pipes during the heavy and prolonged frost, and this
had caused substantial damage. The entire carpeting had to be ripped
out, jet heaters were put in place to dry the frame out, and a new
boiler and piping were fitted. This news I could have done without
immediately before I was about to embark on our project for the year,
or rather one of two: a thousand-mile cycle ride down the Danube
averaging sixty-five miles a day (note I still work in miles). It was
intended that our route would take us from the source of the Danube
at Donauschingen in southern Germany to Budapest in Hungary,
having transited Germany, Austria, Slovakia, and Hungary.

Challenging the Danube

David McKechnie decided that we would drive out to Germany,
collecting Graham Hardingham from Newark on the way down
because we were setting off from Ramsgate to cross by Euro Tunnel.

Why Ramsgate, that conurbation being on the north-east coast of Kent, whereas the Tunnel is situated on the south coast? Well, if you're going to have a Yorkshireman as navigator, you don't argue these minor points. Needless to say, the anomaly did eventually dawn on David as we crossed the Thames and headed north to Ramsgate, but it was too late to change the bookings. Ramsgate is not the most inspirational of locations from which to set out to conquer the world. It's a good job the Germans didn't select it as their chosen location for their invasion, otherwise they would have lost the war a few years earlier, starved into submission and driven back by the damp and cold. Apart from travelling salesmen and contractors—the modern-day terminology for handymen/labourers, of whom there were quite a few—and local residents who didn't seem to appear at night, there was little sign of life or activity. Well, each to his own, but one thing I know: this is not an area in which I would plan to pass my sunset days.

The Source of the Danube

The following morning, we set off early for Folkestone, twenty-six miles to the south, arriving to join the train an hour later. The journey through the tunnel was quick and uneventful, so we were soon on our way down through France. After a number of comfort breaks because it was a significant distance, we arrived at Donauschingen in time for dinner at the Airport Hotel, where we were to leave the van and start out on the Sunday morning to Fridingen. But first we had to visit what is claimed to be the source of the Danube in Donauschingen, a pond in the Royal Garden into which one pitches money, just like the Trevi Fountain in Rome. However, I soon established why David was so keen to set off from here. It is not only the source of the Danube, it is also the source of the Royal Furstenberg Brewery. What a pity it was a Sunday! Having arrived just outside a small village in the middle of nowhere, David's front wheel rim exploded. What a start, miles from any large habitation and any hope of finding a cycle shop. I eventually found some German canoeists down on the river and, in my very poor German, managed to establish that there was nowhere open on Sundays in this part of Germany. However, their leader did offer to take David and bike into Fridingen, where he could probably get it replaced the following day whilst Graham and I cycled on. Punctures, tyre replacements, and spokes we had anticipated, but not exploding wheel rims.

The Swabean Alps

Our aim was to complete the ride in twenty days, with rest days in Vienna, Regensburg, and Budapest, which meant that we would have to average about sixty miles a day; a schedule we had to stick to as we had prebooked accommodation and travel arrangements. We didn't hang around to admire the countryside, although at the pace we were going, there was plenty of time to do that. We cycled on through Eningen, situated at the foot of the Swabean Alps to Leipheim, and then went on to Marxheim. Day six saw us passing through Ingoldstadt in the centre of Bavaria renowned as a setting for *Frankenstein* by Mary Shelly. It is also the HQ for the Audi car company. We were comforted by the thought that we had a day in hand when we reached Regensburg. Located at the confluence of the Danube and the Regen Rivers, Regensburg dates to pre-Roman times. The town is dominated by the Gothic Dom (Cathedral) with its twin towers looking down onto the medieval stone bridge that spans the Danube. During 1943, it was the target for the RAF, being the home of the Messerschmitt Bf109, rival to the Spitfire, and housing a major oil refinery. In more modern times, it was also the home of Pope Benedict XVI, who lived here from 1969 to 1977 whilst he was professor of theology at Regensburg University.

Pressing on the next day, we stopped for a beer and some lunch in a pub near Deggendorf, where we were engaged in conversation by the local fire chief, the bar owner, and the fire crew; they were immaculately dressed, and none of them spoke English. It was therefore up to me to bridge the gap, which I did with some difficulty. Nevertheless, it was a very entertaining and relaxing break, which left us with the view that getting back on the bikes was the last thing in our minds. By now we were averaging sixty-four miles a day, which we maintained until reaching Vienna. On the way we passed through

Linz, the third largest city in Austria and the home of Joseph Kepler, who discovered the law of planetary motion. It also had an unsavoury past, having been the place in which Hitler spent his childhood and where during World War II, the Mauthausen concentration camp was located, not that it's mentioned in the local history. I find on these visits that the Germans and Austrians suffer from a national form of amnesia when it comes to events that occurred in the 1930s and 1940s. On through Melk, whose skyline is dominated by the Benedictine Abbey standing high on a hill above the town. We reached Vienna in the early evening, tired and ready for a good meal, a drink, and a rest.

Austria and Vienna

Vienna, the capital and the largest city in Austria, lies close to the borders with the Czech Republic, Slovakia, and Hungary. Apart from its reputation as the city of music, it is also said to be the City of Dreams because it was the home of the world's first psychoanalyst, Sigmund Freud. Surrounded by the Russians following the end of World War II, it became a hotbed of international espionage, as illustrated in Graham Greene's novel *The Third Man*. The Russians eventually pulled out in 1955, probably anticipating the retreat of communism that was to occur some years later. I had been to Vienna a few times in the past and so spent the day resting rather than sightseeing. I'm glad I did because from here on in, the temperature increased significantly as we rode through the countryside.

Slovakia—Bratislava

Bratislava, the capital of Slovakia, straddles the Danube, which is spanned by the Novy Most Bridge. It has had a multiplicity of influences on its history, having moved through times when it was controlled by Romans, Hungarians, the Ottoman Empire, Austria, and Czechoslovakia. It was annexed by the Germans, taken by the Red Army, and then went back to Slovakia in 1993. After staying the night, we moved on the following day to Komorno, a distance of seventy-one miles. The town sits at the confluence of the Danube and Vah rivers and straddles both banks, being linked by the Elizabeth Bridge. The part of the town on the other side is known as Kormarom. Following the Danube, which was becoming ever wider as it swept on its course down to the Black Sea and some 46 kilometres from Budapest, we reached the town of Esztergom on the right bank of the Danube; as well as being the oldest town in Hungary, it forms the border between Hungary and Slovakia.

Hungary—Budapest

We were now well on our final stretch to Budapest, and by this time we had crossed the Danube so many times I had lost count and almost lost interest as bridge followed bridge, but I must say the scenery was stunning. The Danube enters the city from the north, encircling Obuda and Margaret Islands as it flows towards the flat plain of Pest on the northern bank and the hills of Buda to the south. Buda and Pest were overrun by Genghis Khan and his Mongol armies as he stretched his armies into Europe. The two parts of the city were united in 1874. Now the capital of Hungary and the "Queen of the Danube", the city is the seventh largest in Europe, and its Parliament building is the third largest in the world. We stopped for a drink on one of the many river restaurants before heading for our final overnight stop in the Baross City Hotel, close to the Keleti train station from which we were due to depart two days later, heading north once again. This left us the whole of Tuesday to explore the city.

We took the opportunity to make the most of our time in Budapest, and although I had been here on a couple of previous occasions, there was still so much to see and so little time in which to make the most of our visit. Following a comprehensive tour of the city and having celebrated our achievement with Hungarian food, wine, and music, we packed our bags and departed by train the following day, heading for Donaushingen once again. It was an opportunity to see different aspects of the countryside previously given scant regard from the saddle and our journey home via Ramsgate and Newark—a journey that had more appeal to the sense than two wheels. Notwithstanding my bias, it had been a challenge and a journey that proved to be yet another exceptional experience, but I doubt—no, I know—that I will not do such a long ride again.

By June the hardships of the ride had firmly retreated to the rear of my brain, if indeed I had one, for here I was in July, back in the saddle and setting out on yet another coast-to-coast challenge.

> Only by suffering can we find ourselves.
> Fyodor Dostoyevsky

The Slow Wheelers of Nottingham

On 6 July, I set off with the "Merry Men of Nottingham"—well, actually the "Slow Wheelers of Sutton-on-Trent", and not all men. We had a girl to show us the way well, or at least that's my story! This time is was a slightly different route, some two hundred miles in four days, and yet another pebble to carry across the country. Heading off from St Bees to Thelkeld, it wasn't long before we encountered the first of many punctures, break failures, chain breaks, and sundry other problems (such as torrential rain) that confront cyclists. By the time we reached the ascent to the Whinlatter Pass, the group had become fragmented and out of contact with each other as visibility all but disappeared. I missed the vital turning to Whinlatter and parted company with the rest of the group, which resulted in me heading four miles north to Cockermouth, a deviation of eight miles. By the time I got back to the Whinlatter turning, the roads were flooded. I had no option but to wade on, by which time I was freezing cold, wet, and suffering from the first effects of hypothermia. I was still five miles from Keswick, added to which the light was failing fast and my front light had smashed during one of my falls. I had no signal on my mobile, and once again I questioned my sanity. By the time I reached the outskirts of Keswick, I was walking and muttering about fatherless sons who had abandoned me to the elements, but here I had a stroke of luck. I actually got a mobile signal and discovered that the others were relaxing in a pub in the centre of the town. And there I was, thinking they might be worried about their missing colleague! Ben, one of the other cyclists, was also missing, and his father set off in the recovery vehicle to find him—a dream gone wrong? A mere forty-one miles up and down rolling hills and through some of the prettiest countryside that England has to offer; in the company of friends, great banter, and glee; and washed away in one of the wettest days in Cumbrian history, with a month's rain in less than 24 hours and 124 local flood alerts.

We set off the following morning from our overnight stop at Troutbeck with the rain still falling, once again heading into a headwind with Monty's words ringing in our ears: "Today is much easier—just 45 miles if we don't get lost, and relatively flat terrain apart from the 3,500-foot ascent. We could easily burn off 4,000 calories." Never, ever believe anything you're told by a Guardian reader and a rabid socialist. We stopped for refreshments at Appleby in Westmorland before pressing on to Ravensdale, eventually arriving at the campsite surrounded by sheep, where the recovery crew had parked their own caravan, complete with bar, in a farm situated some two miles west of our hotel. Rob, Jeremy, and others proceeded to distribute large jugs of pink gin and tonic, which we despatched with gusto. By the time we attempted to leave, getting back on our bikes presented a major problem. The cycle ride of some two miles in the dusk in a somewhat drunken stupor is best forgotten for the anoraks amongst you. The barn in the farmyard housed a number of old buses, including a London red Routemaster. I always thought there was something odd about folk in Westmorland.

The following morning, as we left the Black Swan, hurtling down hill at thirty-five miles per hour, the front brakes on Graham Hardingham's bike became unhinged, probably in sympathy with the rider. This was not an immediate problem because he wouldn't need them for the next few miles up the Hill of Death. We eventually reached the summit to see the recovery team's Dell Boy caravan perched aloft and playing the theme tune from *Rocky 2*. Nevertheless, the thought of hot-spiced drinks inspired us up the last few hundred extremely steep feet. After a short recovery, we set off once more with the certain knowledge that what goes up must come down. The sun came out as we crossed the border into Yorkshire, Rob's explanation being that it only shines that way in "God's own county", whatever that means. The next ten miles were pure joy with spectacular scenery.

Hardingham, showing nerves of steel, threw caution to the wind, pressing on downhill with only his back brakes to restrain him. We eventually made Reeth and stopped for a late lunch, the full Sunday roast with Yorkshire hospitality. (Words such as "Lunch is only served between 12.30 and 1.30 p.m." springs readily to mind, as did "Well, it's the best we can do at this time of day".)

The following day to Osmotherly was a more relaxing ride. The Yorkshire Dales beckoned with numerous fast descents, crossing of rivers and streams and then climbing back. After sixty-eight miles we arrived ready for a meal and a few beers, but we were in time to see the England football team lose (yet again) on penalties. Upon departing from Osmotherly the following morning, Hardingham wasn't in the best of moods because the landlord had refused to give shelter to his bike. Graham responded by inferring that he had received better treatment during the war at the hands of the enemy. I'm not too sure which tablets Graham was on or which war he meant. Needless to say, our departure was once again uphill, steep enough to want you to walk, if only pride would let you. Monty has that unfailing ability to find a hill anywhere, even in the Fens. What spectacular scenery, looking down over the Tees Valley to the North Sea. By now the route was undulating (that's Yorkshire for hilly) as we hugged the ridge of the Cleveland Hills, passing through a cluster of small villages. We stopped at Danby for lunch only to find everywhere closed, as did every other facility in the town. Well, this was still Yorkshire, and customers are a nuisance. As we reached Glaisdale the roads became even hillier if that's possible, winding up and down through the moors via Egton to Grosmont.

We rested our weary limbs at the Railway Tavern adjacent to the station, much to the delight of the anoraks amongst us who eulogised over the age of steam. The steep hill out of the town was yet a further challenge, and even Graham had to drop down to a gear that I didn't know existed—it's one above stop! For those who don't know, the Moors are not flat, undulating stretches of heather. They consist of many stretches which are more closely associated with the Himalayas—places where cyclists and walkers should be roped together. One such location is Glaisdale in the Esk Valley, where the road drops vertically into the village and out in a similar manner—but uphill, on the far side. This is the Beggar's Bridge, built by Thomas Ferris in 1619. Ferris was a poor man who hoped to wed the daughter of a wealthy local squire. To win her hand, he planned to set sail from Whitby to make his fortune. On the night he left, the Esk was swollen by rain, and he was unable to make a last visit to his intended. All I could think was that he was lucky nobody else stepped in! After several years, he eventually returned from his travels a rich man, and after marrying the squire's daughter, he built Beggar's Bridge so that no other lovers would be separated as they were. That should touch the heartstrings of our female readers. especially those who wait that long to catch their men!

We toiled over the rest of the route, especially the hill up into Sleights, before eventually reaching Robin Hoods Bay, where we celebrated in style—yes more G & T at the local caravan site, where our trusty supporters were gathered, before descending into the bay and shedding our pebbles once more. I could have got a job building Hadrian's Wall with the number of pebbles I had collected and delivered over the years.

CHAPTER 25

Sixty Years on from the Coronation

In 2012, it was to be another year with those ever-recurring themes: achievements in the developing world, set against the muscle flexing in those countries pedalling their own ideologies. January was marked by Iran's continuing drive to enrich uranium. The United Nations was concerned over the proliferation of nuclear developments for nonpeaceful means and was of the opinion that Iran was not striving to use the building of nuclear plants for domestic purposes, so it imposed economic sanctions. By late February, Iran had retaliated by banning all oil exports to the West, specifically aimed at Britain and France. Subsequently, there has been much postulating on what might happen, the increased rhetoric from Iran suggesting support of Hezbollah attacks on Israel, the possibility of Israel attacks on Iran's nuclear plants, and the ever-present problem of the conflict in Syria. Whilst it remained a concern on the worldwide stage, national thoughts were more focused towards the two major events at home: The Queen's Diamond Jubilee, of which there had only been one other monarch who had reached that remarkable milestone (Queen Victoria), and of course the "Home" Olympics.

The year also marked sixty years since Queen Elizabeth II ascended the throne on 6 February 1952 following the earlier death of her father. As head of the Commonwealth of 54 nations which, at 2.2 billion comprises almost one-third of the world's population, her jubilee was celebrated around the world. The Diamond Jubilee was marked by a spectacular central weekend, which included a massive pageant on the River Thames, street parties throughout the country, and a series of regional tours throughout the UK and Commonwealth visits by other members of the royal family. At the age of eighty-six and with a husband in his ninetieth year, it would have been impossible for her to have visited all the Commonwealth countries. Whilst she and Prince Philip concentrated on celebrations at home, the younger royals took on the visits to the other Commonwealth countries.

Whilst from a national perspective attention was being focused on two major events, the second being the Olympic Games, there were other important events, including the inevitable disasters. First, the positives. On 4 July, the firing of the Large Hadron Collider at CERN in Switzerland led to the possible discovery of a new particle that is consistent with the Higgs boson theory. Peter Higgs is a British theoretical physicist who predicted the discovery of a new kind of elementary subatomic particle which acts on others to give them mass. If the Higgs field does exist, it would be a monumental discovery for science and human knowledge opening doors to many fields. It is interesting to note that it was the editor of the journal at CERN who'd originally rejected Higg's theory as preposterous!

Curiosity, the Mars rover, reached the red planet in August and started its major exploration in search of the composition of the surface, the climate, and possible signs of previous life on Mars. This was seen as a precursor to human exploration of the planet at some future date. In October, the Austrian Felix Baumgartner made that incredible free fall from 39 kilometres at the edge of space, reaching a speed of 1,342.8 kilometres per hour—the first human to break the sound barrier in free fall and survive. Again, from a national perspective, there was also the news in December that William and Kate were expecting their first child. Finally, and to many of us the most gratifying news of all, was that the world did not end in December as some had predicted based on interpretation of the Mayan theory!

As one would expect, there are always the downsides, the cream-stealers in life, and 2012 was no exception. The major occurrence was the devastation created by the super storm as Hurricane Sandy struck the east coast of the United States. It caused $50 billion in damage, was the second largest storm in history, and resulted in 125 deaths across 17 states. The second event, although hardly in the same league, was the *Costa Concordia* disaster, when the Italian Captain Francesco Schettino managed to hit the rocks and submerge the luxury liner off the Italian Island of Giglio on the coast of Tuscany, resulting in the deaths of 32 passengers and crew. Although the liner, one of the largest ever built, didn't sink, she was scrapped as the resultant damage cost over $500 million—Italy's equivalent of the *Titanic*.

On a personal note, I had a call from Graham Hardingham telling me that the consultants had advised him that he had terminal pancreatic cancer—devastating news not only for Graham but for the rest of us. Only a few months previously, we had been enjoying the highlights cycling alongside the Danube with David McKechnie, during which Graham was only just coming to terms with the loss of his wife, Barbara, from an autoimmune disease the previous year. Life can be a bitch!

The Home Olympics

> The Olympics shows the Community what gymnastics is all about.
> Bella Karolyi

Because the Olympics were being held in the UK for the first time since 1948, it was for me, and all those involved in our sport, one of the dominant features of 2012, and as such I feel it warrants a separate mention. Let me start by returning to the beginning of the year.

By the end of the first week in January, I was fully immersed in the activities of British Gymnastics. Following a winter of hard preparation (I hasten to add for the gymnasts, not me), they had the chance of competing in London for the Olympic Test event for men's gymnastics. The British men's team failed to qualify at the Tokyo World Championships, which was a prerequisite for the Olympics; during the previous year, they'd finished only eighth in the team event instead of third. It was therefore of vital importance that GB finished at least third in this qualifying event (what in some circles would be described as a repêchage), otherwise we were out of the Olympics both as a team and as individuals. The team spent the whole Christmas away from their families, training and training. Not only did they qualify, but they also finished first. It's amazing what you can achieve when you keep away from the turkey, the festive spirit, and other distractions! The rest of January, February, and March was a flurry of gymnastics activities including training, awards presentations, and English and British board meetings, added to which we were hosting the World Acrobatics Championships and the National Championships in Birmingham. Finally, the most important event was the Olympic Games in London during July and August.

During the weeks, down at the National Sports Centre in Lilleshall Shropshire, I took time out to visit the nearby small and picturesque town of Much Wenlock. What was the attraction when everyone else was fully focused on the Olympic Games? I've said it elsewhere in this epistle: one must always be guided by the lessons of history, and where else in this Olympic year then at the home of the modern Olympiad? Contrary to popular myth, Baron Pierre de Coubertin did not conceive the idea of the modern Olympics in Athens in 1896. He had befriended Dr William Penny Brooks, who some years earlier in 1850 had established the first such games in Much Wenlock. Having taken over his father's practice and with wide-ranging interests, particularly in health and well-being, Brooks became a local magistrate in 1841 and developed a strong desire, based on his experiences, to promote moral, physical, and intellectual improvement. His work focused on the structured physical exercise and education for the working classes as well as the introduction of physical education in British schools. This ethos was firmly established in the first of the Much Wenlock Games of 1850, open to all comers or in his words, "Every grade of man".

In 1865, he wanted to expand the games nationally and established the National Olympic Association, a sports association for athletes, with the first Festival at Crystal Palace in London attracting over ten thousand spectators. With such success, Brooks wanted to expand it internationally and establish it in Greece, but the Greek politicians declined. To the Greeks, it was reverse psychology: "Beware of the Englishman bearing gifts!" At this stage, the young de Courbitin entered the scene, having received an invitation from Brooks to visit Wenlock in October 1890 to see the "Olympian Games" firsthand. It was this visit that inspired de Courbetin's quest for the modern Olympics. Moving forward, Brooks, who by this time was a member of the Olympic Congress was unable to attend the Congress in 1894 due to ill health and died months before seeing his ideas formalised in the first games in Athens in 1896. The Wenlock Games have been held every year since that time.

As directors of British Gymnastics, our focus had to be on the sport of gymnastics, for which we had been set a target of at least two medals. Consequently, the rest of our year centred on the Olympic Games and the associated activities. It was of course the year of the highly successful Home Olympics. The gymnasts exceeded our expectations by gaining four medals, an achievement that had a significant impact on our future funding. The accumulation of a small number of medals might seem insignificant in the round of things, but one can't ignore the impact it has on the sport and people's perception of the athletes. Louis Smith and Beth Tweddle went on to enhance their newly acquired status with appearance on TV and winning events outside the sport, all of which did a great deal to focus public attention on the achievements of the sport, which was further recognised by their award as MBEs.

I love those who yearn for the impossible.
Goethe

Grimsby

After a somewhat hectic family Christmas in Darlington with Jonathan, Julie, and families, it was time to hit the road again. I spent New Year's at Laceby with Pat and Bill and a nostalgic return to Blundell Park watching Grimsby Town FC playing Lincoln in a 1-1 draw, following which I had my photograph taken with the match ball. Blundell Park seemed so much smaller than when I was last there. Perhaps I've become used to the modern-day Premier League and the more sophisticated facilities. What a pity that the standards of behaviour, both on and off the pitch, hasn't met the same standard. The following day, it was lunch with Pat and John Platt at the Angel in Louth, and then on to Forest Park to negotiate the sale of the caravan. It was a somewhat nostalgic journey to Norfolk, and whilst parting with the caravan was parting with happy memories, the increasing costs and the lack of opportunity to use the facilities left me with little choice. I could use the additional money to more effect in holidays abroad, added to which I was beginning to feel that my gymnastics commitments were akin to being in full-time employment but without the benefit of pay!

British Gymnastics

The start of 2013 was not the most auspicious, having to travel through heavy snow to gymnastics competitions, seminars, and board meetings in Sheffield, Liverpool, and Birmingham. By the beginning of March, in a reshuffle and two years into my appointment to the board, I found myself elected by the board as president of British Gymnastics. It was what politicians would describe as the baby-kissing role, but in terms of gymnastics it was more of a "handshake and passing out awards" type of responsibility. Nevertheless, I felt it an honour that I could be of some use to the sport in general and BG in particular. Whilst on the subject of gymnastics, the men's team, now comprised of some of the younger members and some of the established gymnasts who were working towards the next Olympics in Rio, had an outstanding success at the European Championships in Moscow, securing five medals. We were beginning to recognise that Britain has really secured its rightful place at the top table of the sport. However, it was not a time to be complacent. Having said that, who would have thought back in the 1960s that we would have been outcompeting the East Europeans who for decades had been the dominant force in world gymnastics?

Later in May, we entered another prestigious period for British Gymnastics in that we played host to the FIG, the International

Federation of Gymnastics. This organisation is the governing body of international gymnastics and is dedicated to developing gymnasts and coaches, as well as setting the standards for the sport from the Olympics down. It comprises 128 nations as well as representation from four continental bodies: the European, Pan American, African, and Asian and Oceania groups. The Congress meets every two years in different countries, but its members and committees work throughout the year. Many of the individuals representing the nations have been involved at high level in the sport over the years, either as active gymnasts, coaches, and judges or as administrators, and often a mix of all categories. The week of meetings in the newly developed Albert Dock area of Liverpool culminated in a dinner held in the Hard Day's Night Hotel, a Beatles-inspired hotel that was part of a Grade II listed building dating back to 1884, situated in North John Street, just a stone's throw from the Cavern, with its strong associations with the early rise of the Beatles. The dinner was held in the Blake Restaurant, so called after the artist Sir Peter Blake, who designed the cover for the celebrated *Sergeant Pepper's* album. Clearly with so many middle-aged and elderly delegates, the Beatles theme was appropriate, as was the location.

For those who may not be as geriatric as me, I should point out that the Cavern, at 10 Matthew Street, was opened as in 1957 as a jazz club, and contrary to his different style, it is often seen as the birthplaces of the Beatles and many groups that followed thereafter, but this is not necessarily so because they had developed as a group in Hannover, Germany, before returning to the UK. Nevertheless, the Beatles made over 292 appearances in the Cavern between 1961 and 1963, a period during which they were discovered by Brian Epstein. In the decade that followed, many other well-known artists cut their teeth in the Cavern; these included groups such as the Hollies, the Rolling Stones, the Yardbirds, the Kinks, Queen, and the Who, as well as many individuals including Cilla Black, Sandy Shaw, and Elton John to name but a few. Many speculate on why Beatlemania swept the world at that time. Perhaps it was that their musical genre reflected the social and cultural changes that were occurring during that era. There was certainly no doubt that the group developed their distinctive music over that decade and those that followed. Rooted in Skiffle and 1950s rock and roll, which in turn embraced American blues, it developed a unique and original input through innovation based on many genres of music, from pop ballads through classical to psychedelic rock and Indian meditation. There is little doubt that they touched the pulse of an emerging generation to the extent that they have become the best-selling band in musical history. But back to the main theme, the last night of the international gathering.

As a relative latecomer to the gymnastics world, I found it fascinating meeting with and talking to the great and the good. Many spoke several languages, and one lady in particular spoke fluently in eight different languages. Me, I struggle with one, maybe two! It is on occasions such as these that you discover how small a cog you are in the grinding wheel of life. One fascinating woman I chatted with at dinner was Nellie Vladimirovna Kim from Kazakhstan, who represented Russia and was one of the truly great gymnasts of the 1970s. We all recall her teammates, the diminutive Russians Olga Korbut and Ludmilla Tourischeva and the Rumanian Nadia Elena Comaneci, but few recollect the great Nellie Kim, who outshone them over the decade. She is a colossus (I hasten to add in reputation, not stature) who straddled the decade as an awesome competitor, amassing six Olympic medals, ten world titles, and ten European medals amongst her many achievements. She was also the first female gymnast to achieve the perfect score of ten in both the vault and floor competitions at an Olympic Games.

Following on from the Olympics, it was also a busy and successful year for British Gymnastics. Earlier in the year, I had been appointed deputy president and then in May was elevated to president. It was another brilliant year with many of the British gymnasts disciplines attaining world championship and European titles—without a doubt the best year we have ever had in the sport.

National and International Events

In terms of international events and our national economic position, 2013 was hardly setting out a dynamic form. Indeed, it was the usual mixed blessings with the possibility of a "green shoot" recovery in the economy. Like many countries, we had for too long been living in a fool's paradise, borrowing massively to support a welfare lifestyle we clearly could not afford. Perhaps the job criteria for the chancellor of the exchequer should be based on the ideal housewife: living within one's budget, "if you can't afford it, don't buy it". It reminds me very much of my early married life when we scrimped and saved to buy our first washing machine rather than buy it on credit. I suppose the downside of this was that one didn't get a credit rating, but at least we didn't borrow beyond our means.

A fall in oil revenue, a fall in demand for products, a manufacturing downturn, and retail skimming along the surface of a 0.3 per cent increase in GDP—hardly a story of success. Missing a triple-dip recession did little to warm the blood; neither did the prolonged cold spell in the weather, with March being the second coldest since records began.

The early months of 2013 saw the French mount operations in Northern Mali to counter the activities of the African wing of al-Qaeda following their murder of hostages in Algeria. In Russia a meteor, on entering the Earth's atmosphere, exploded over the city of Chelyabinsk, injuring 1,500 people and showing once again how vulnerable we are to such events. Woe betide the day when a more substantial piece of rock penetrates our atmosphere. In the Middle East, Syria became entrenched in the throes of a civil war, and Iran continued to thwart UN resolutions and reject proposed visits by UN inspectors. Further afield, North Korea stepped up its rhetoric and the beating of war drums by moving its missiles to the east coast, reopening its nuclear plant, and declaring that it was still at war with the South.

The year was to see the passing of two world leaders. In February, the pope made the unique decision that he was going to retire—something that had not happened in many hundreds of years. The new pope was subsequently elected in March and was the first to come from South America. This was followed in April by the announcement of the death of Baroness Thatcher. In the words of Boris Johnson, London's mayor, "She was the greatest Prime Minister since Winston Churchill." That comparison is most apt because she was as brave in peace as Churchill was in war. She knew the consequences of failure in confronting aggression in the South Atlantic, communism, the megalithic European community, the unions, and the IRA; all of which posed substantial threats to these islands. Indeed, you could say that she was ever ready to pick a fight on a matter of principle. True, her policies created division, but they also restored the "Great" in Britain, thus ensuring that Britain's voice was once again listened to on the world stage, whilst at home her policies brought an end to years of economic decline. She was accorded full honours at her funeral in London later that month. It was an occasion marred only by the hatred and nostalgia of the extreme left, who have never been able to come to terms that the world has moved on and left them behind.

The year 2013 marked the United Nations' adoption of the Arms Trade Treaty, regulating conventional weapons. However, there seemed to be little agreement in other directions, especially over Syria and elsewhere in the Middle East. Nature once more intervened to remind us how fragile life can become on our planet. Major earthquakes were experienced in Asia, Central and South America, and Japan, and there were flash floods in India, America, and Mexico. Later in the year was the most destructive typhoon in the Philippines killing over ten thousand people and making millions homeless. It was also the year that saw the arrival of the next generation of the royal family, with the birth of Prince George of Cambridge.

CHAPTER 26

A Return to the Mountains

> Insanity is doing the same thing over and over
> again, but expecting different results.
> Albert Einstein

If that quote by Einstein is so, then it is much more comfortable to be mad and know it than to be sane and have one's doubts. Whatever the reasons, in July 2013 I once again took time out for the first of my personal challenges of the year, flying out to Peru and climbing the Inca Trail through the Amazon rainforest and down to the ruins of Machu Picchu. This was to be followed by a second journey in October when I set out for the Himalayas and Everest as part of my fundraising commitments. In retrospect, two such challenges in the space of a few months might be considered too ambitious, but who knows?

Peru—The Andes and the Amazon

The Andes form the longest mountain range in the world, rising only 100 miles from the Pacific coast with many peaks exceeding 6,000 metres (20,000 feet), part of which is the Vilcambamba range to the north-east of Cuzco, sitting between the two great rivers the Urubamba and the Apurimac, which in turn feed the mighty Amazon.

Perhaps the most arduous part of my visit to South America, however, was the travel to and from the continent. Regarding the pearl of wisdom "If you've time to spare, travel by air", nothing could be closer to the truth. The elapsed time from leaving Darlington in the north of the UK, via Madrid and Lima, to arriving in Cuzco in Peru was twenty-eight hours, and it certainly couldn't be classified as a relaxing start to the journeys I was to face over the next few days. The ancient city of Cuzco, the historical capital of the Inca Empire, is surrounded by minor peaks of the Andes and sits at an altitude of 3,500 metres, or a little over 11,000 feet, almost three times the height of Ben Nevis. The streets of the city are narrow and stepped, rising out to the nearby hills, and are often impassable to all but pedestrians.

The hotel to which I had been allocated was situated at almost the highest point in the city and a good half a mile from the centre as the crow (or should I say the condor) flies. This meant carrying luggage and backpacks weighing about 25 kilos up about 640 steps. A not too difficult task for a healthy person at sea level, but at this height the air is thinner, and each lungful is half that taken at sea level; therefore, strenuous exercise becomes difficult, the heart pounds, and breathing is more onerous. When climbing in Africa, we were always told "slowly, slowly" because it takes time for the body to acclimatise—a timely reminder that I needed to bear in mind for the days to come, especially after so little time to adjust to the change in altitude. Going from sea level to over 11,000 feet overnight was hardly conducive to an aging body. Not for the first time, I began to wonder if I had pushed my luck in selecting a firm with a name like Exodus to arrange for my well-being in South America!

With this in mind, the next two days were put to good effect in helping the body to adapt to the higher altitude, albeit over a truncated period of time. Walking as far as possible both within the city and in exploring the various Inca sites in the locality helped, but sleep at nights was spasmodic, reflecting the changes occurring in breathing patterns. Time also had to be set aside for repacking essential items because the maximum weight allowed on the trail had been recently revised down to ten kilos, which included sleeping bag and wet weather gear. The rest of the clothes had to remain in the hotel. I find this the most difficult aspect of decision making in climbing or trekking: what is essential and what is desirable. The problem is that you never know the difference until the desirable becomes the essential!

In the early hours of the following day, I awoke to blue cloudless sky with the warmth of the sun, even at this altitude, beginning to make itself felt. Leaving by coach from Cuzco's city centre, our party of twelve consisting of Australians, Canadians, Irish, Welsh, and of course other Brits were, accompanied by our Peruvian guides and set out to conquer the Andes Well, that's what it felt like! The rules for climbing mean that you must do it in groups with at least two trained guides. What never fails to surprise me when travelling in such groups is the competitive elements who must lead from the front. Not quite so in this case, I hasten to add. Entering in at high altitude does tend to calm people down, and wise heads prevail.

Our route followed the Classic Inca Trail, starting at Piscacucho and running alongside the Vilcanota River, which nestles beneath the snow-capped Nevado Veronica Mountains. At midday, we found ourselves passing the Inca ruins of Llactapata before reaching a side valley near the hamlet of Huayllabamba, by late afternoon, where we were to camp for the night.

The following day proved to be yet another early start. Awake at 5 a.m., we set off an hour later for what was to be the longest and most strenuous day, over eight hours of continuous clambering over rocks; some would call them paths. Initially, we climbed up the mountain to where the path runs through an area of rain forest and a section of polylepis woodland in which wildlife abounds: hundreds of different rare birds, including the hyperactive hummingbirds beating their wings at over eighty times a second; butterflies (Peru has over 3,700 species, more than any other country in the world); and peculiar animals and rodents such as the viscacha, a cross between a squirrel and a rabbit.

Our route continued up and around terraces of cultivated fields surrounding the ruins of Llulluchapampa and then ever upwards, towards the Warmihuanusca (Dead Woman's) Pass at a height of 4,234 metres (almost 14,000 feet). After a brief respite in the hope of rebalancing our oxygen intake and putting on our waterproofs, for by now a fine persistent drizzle and low cloud enveloped us, we started a long, steep descent to our camp for that evening at 3,600 metres (12,000 feet) in a scenic valley overlooking the Pacamayo River for a most welcome rest. Already three of the group were showing the classic symptoms of acute mountain sickness, and one was taken down by stretcher.

By now we had established the pattern of rising at an early hour. After breakfast, we set off on yet another climb to reach the Runquracay Pass at 3,930 metres (just under 13,000 feet), passing the ruins of Sayajmarca and re-entering the rain forest through an old Inca tunnel, before camping on the ridge overlooking the ancient Inca settlement of Phuyupatamarca, still at a height more than 12,000 feet.

The following morning, I was up very early to see the sunrise as the first rays crossed over the snow-capped peaks. From the high ridge, we started down the infamous Inca steps, a two-kilometre descent with sheer drops to the river thousands of metres below, eventually arriving at the Inti Punka, the Inca Gate of the Sun, where we had our first view of Machu Picchu, with the familiar sight of its awesome mountain, Huayna Picchu, looking like a predatory condor with its outstretched wings sheltering the settlement below. After passing the edge of the ruins, we descended to the Urubamba River and camped near Puente Ruinas. What a delight to be able to wash again and to know that the hardest part of the challenge was now behind us.

However, those dreaded early morning starts were not yet at an end. Up at 3.30 for an even earlier start to the day at 4. Why? Well, the aim was to be in Machu Picchu in time to catch the first rays of the sun illuminating the mountains and then bringing light and life to these ancient ruins. The remainder of the day was spent exploring the ruins of this now famous archaeological site dating back to about 1450, its location rediscovered by the American Hiram Bingham in 1911. By late afternoon, having absorbed as much as we could and to sidestep the tourists who travel up in their busloads, we set off for

Aguas Calientes, where we caught the train for our return to Cuzco and a celebratory dinner with the group and our guides.

The following day, our last in Cuzco, was to be a recovery day—a day relaxing in our hotel or climbing nearby hills to loosen up sore muscles. We decided that was not to be and set out to fulfil our roles as tourists, packing everything into the last few hours. From nearby Inca sites at Sacsayhuaman, situated 3 kilometres from Cuzco, with its enormous stone blocks up to 9 metres in height and weighing over 125 tonnes and carved to be fitted with precision to avoid the impact of earthquakes, to Quenco, an Inca medicine man site. By the afternoon, we found ourselves in the town of Puca Purcara and then moved further out to the Sacred Valley—too much details to expand on in this brief outline.

In summary, it was a hard challenge that exceeded expectations in a setting that was not only breathtaking but also awesome in its historical content. My only regret is that whilst in Peru, I didn't think about adding another week to my sojourn and extending the tour by sailing out to the Galapagos Islands. Now, that really would have been the icing on the cake. Well, maybe that's an idea for a future date. Would I do Peru again? I think not; once is enough to protect its mystique. Besides which, there are even more challenges ahead and so little time to achieve them all: Everest in October following on from Peru, which in a way provided some degree of acclimatisation. But let me hasten to add, nothing prepares you for the mightiest mountain of them all: Sagamantha, mother goddess of the world.

> Learn from yesterday, live for today, hope for tomorrow.
> Albert Einstein

Everest and the Himalayas

Chomolungma or Sagamantha (Goddess Mother of the World), or Everest as it is better known, straddles the Nepalese and Tibet border and rises to a height of 8,848 metres or 29,035 feet. Named after Sir George Everest, the surveyor general of India, who was the first to produced detailed maps of the Indian subcontinent including the Himalayas, Everest is without doubt the greatest mountain of them all.

Since early childhood, it has always been my dream to climb to the summit of Everest. However, I'm realistic enough to know that this is a dream I will never attain. Had I started out much earlier in life, this might have been possible (somehow, I doubt it), but then, this is what dreams are made of. My fascination with the mountain goes back to my youth, reading about those early expeditions carried out during the 1920s. It was those three attempts in 1921, 1923, and 1924 that laid the foundation on which future attempts were based by identifying routes, changing weather patterns, and climbing conditions, making the final conquest achievable. From a personal perspective, it remains the unsolved and compelling mystery of what happened to Mallory and Irvine during their ascent of the mountain in 1924. Did they reach the top, or were they killed by a fall in their attempt to reach the summit? Much of the evidence suggests that they suffered a fall on their way down, but the paradox is that it doesn't confirm that they had reached the summit before so doing.

Despite many attempts in the 1920s and 1930s, it was not until Hilary and Tenzing made their historical attempt on 29 May 1953 that the summit was eventually conquered. They reached the top at 11.30 after a gruelling climb up the southern face, and after fifteen minutes at the top, restricted by the lack of sufficient oxygen and during which time they searched for but failed to find any positive evidence that Mallory and Irvine might have reached the summit, they started their descent.

This in no way attempts to belittle the astonishing achievement of Hillary and Tensing; it simply poses the question as to what might have been. Nevertheless, it is a topic which has been openly debated not only by many of the leading climbers of their day but also by those who knew the determination of Leigh and Mallory to overcome all obstacles to achieve his goals. However, we shall never have conclusive proof. Suffice to say, Everest remains an enigma even though it has been conquered many times. To me, it was to be the second challenge of the year, and one, I'm delighted to say, that would see me in the company of Jonathan for the first time. Although I had been in the

Himalayas before, on Annapurna, this was to be my first visit to Everest; I had flown over it in the 1990s, but it's never the same as feet on the ground.

Jonathan flew back from working in the Oman, and we set out from London Heathrow on Friday, 11 October, on what was anticipated to be an eighteen-day visit to Nepal. What we hadn't planned for was the typhoon (cyclone) in the Bay of Bengal coinciding with our arrival in Kathmandu. I hasten to add, it was nothing like the ferocity of the one that struck the Philippines the following month, but it was still of some significance. However, it delivered a major impact on its outer fringes, bringing torrential rain, high winds, and heavy cloud to Nepal and in the process dumping some three metres (nine feet) of snow on Everest Base Camp, which due to avalanches and resultant deaths closed the area for some days. Consequently, no flights to Lukla, the starting point to our journey across the Himalayas, were possible during the first three days. It was a period during which we travelled each day to the airport in Kathmandu to be processed and reprocessed, along with hundreds of others, only to be disappointed yet again. These were days when we should have been acclimatising on our way to Everest.

An added pressure was learning that our baggage allowance to Lukla could not exceed ten kilogrammes. Considering the equipment we were carrying, this left us with a major problem of what to leave behind, knowing that the climate on Everest could drop to -27 Celsius—hardly conducive to lightweight clothing! This was a problem I alluded to in regard to our time in Peru. On the evening of the third day, we had a meeting with our agent, who had arrived from the UK and decided to cut our losses. Should a window of opportunity appear on day four, we would hire helicopters, because it was clear that fixed-wing aircraft could not operate through the mountains to reach Lukla. The airfield at Lukla is a narrow, 400-metre strip set at a steep incline. At one end sits the terminal building abutting the solid wall of the mountain, and at the other end is a sheer drop into the valley some 500 metres below. Little wonder that it has the deserved reputation of being the most dangerous airfield in the world! Just before midday on day four, for a brief period the weather improved sufficiently for us to leave Kathmandu on our forty-five-minute helicopter flight to Lukla. Even for me, this was a breathtaking landing, in low cloud with poor visibility and buffeted by heavy winds. After scampering out of the helicopter, we quickly retrieved our bags and set off into the village to grab a cup of tea and await the arrival of the others because each helicopter could only carry three people.

Two hours later, with our baggage secured to a line of yaks, we set off on the two-day trek north leading to the Sherpa capital of Namchi Bazaar, contemplating what it would be like on our return journey, when we would have to take off from Lukla, downhill in a heavily laden light aircraft. It's at times like this that you wish you could afford the luxury of a helicopter; however, that was a dream for later. The immediate need was to concentrate on quickly acclimatising whilst absorbing the incredible scenery on the way up through the villages of Chepling and Monju, to our first overnight stop at Phakding at 2,800 metres (8,400 feet). Although we only covered seven miles in distance, the ever-changing gradients took us almost seven hours to overcome—something to which we would have to adapt as we progressed towards the high mountains.

The following day, we passed through the guarded entrance to the Sagamantha National Park, crossing over high suspension bridges and frequently meeting yaks, pack horses, and individual Nepalese, who were themselves carrying loads of more than fifty kilos, descending in the opposite direction. We soon started the steep and continuous ascent towards Namchi Bazaar. Namchi lies in a natural amphitheatre on a ridge at over 11,000 feet, surrounded by mountains, and it's the advanced gathering point for many of the expeditions setting out to Everest and the higher Himalayan range. However, being three days behind schedule, we pressed on with yet another steep climb, passing through the villages of Kenjuma and Kunde. Here we visited the Edmund Hillary Hospital and the monastery in Khumjung, where for a small donation we were shown the only yeti skull in the world, on which scientists have cast doubts. On our way to Tengboche, we stopped for a lunch break at the Everest View Hotel, built by the Japanese as a tourist attraction but regarded by many as a white elephant. Here we had our first dramatic views of the snow-capped mountains dominated by Abu Dablam, whilst in the distance Everest soared above but behind the wall of Nuptse and Lhotse. This was to be a familiar aspect of Everest: always hiding itself but from time to time revealing its majestic form. As one of our group described it, "It's like a Victorian lady lifting her skirts to reveal just a little of what might lay beyond."

By now we were acutely aware of the thinning air at altitude. After leaving Abu Dablam behind us, we descended to the trail that meets the Dudh Koshi River (the Milk River), so called because of its foaming white glacial waters cascading down from the Himalayan range. We crossed many bridges spanning the fast-flowing river before ascending steeply to the little hamlet of Phunki Thangkha and then on to Thyangboche. The following day saw us descending as we crossed the rapidly flowing Imja Khola before climbing through the valley to Pangboche and a steep climb to Dingboche at almost 14,000 feet. By this time, I was feeling the effects of my knee, having twisted it as I slipped on the ice, which no doubt aggravated an old injury to the anterior cruciate ligament (and the consequential damage to the cartilage) during my misspent youth playing football. It was a problem that I had suffered with on Kilimanjaro, Mt Kenya, and in the Andes. I should have anticipated this happening, but I didn't. Whatever the reason, it was certainly painful and had an adverse effect on my progress over the icy boulders.

Progress was slow, and from time to time we witnessed many avalanches and (far more worrying) rockfalls that cascaded to the front and rear of us. It was frightening because some of these rocks were of significant size, and more to the point we had no hiding place. I can now envisage what it must have been like for those killed in the avalanches that occurred in the same region in the months that followed. These mountains, like many others, can be most challenging and unforgiving.

Nevertheless, we pressed on, anxious to reach our destination. The trail at this point climbs steeply out of the village to Dugla at the end of the of the terminal moraine of the Khumbu glacier, and following a further steep climb, that brought us to Chukpo Lari, a beautiful, isolated, and poignant place where scattered large cairns are located as memorials to the many climbers who have died on Everest. Carrying on past the hamlet of Lobuje, we headed northwards, following the Khumbu glacier towards Gorak Shep at an altitude of almost 16,000 feet, where we were to night stop and then move on to reach Everest Base Camp. After celebrations and many photographs, Jonathan and I moved on to the Khumbu glacier and built a small cairn in which we placed a photograph of Sheila and said a few private words. She had made it to Annapurna, and had she been alive, she would have wanted to be with us. We returned to our overnight stop in Gorak Shep, preparing for an early morning ascent of Kala Pathar, following which we would start our descent towards Namchi Bazaar.

As with all mountain descents, an element of euphoria creeps in, and this can be dangerous. You relax your guard and attempt too much, too quickly. I was hardly doing that, but we were descending rapidly, and I felt under increasing pressure with my knee problem. Despite having a knee brace, the pounding of the bone was painful and slowed my progress. Our guide decided that we should hire a yak, horse, or mule to get me down to Lukla, but then the cardinal sin of pride came into play: I was damned if I was going to be a wimp taking the easy option. Nevertheless, as we reached Phakding lower down, common sense prevailed, and I traversed the remaining ravines and bridges on the back of a very tolerant horse that I hired. Sitting high on a horse without a saddle or reins and looking down the steep precipices left me in no doubt as to my lack of sanity, especially as we crossed the high, narrow suspension bridges, sitting high above the side netting, feeling the bridge oscillating under the weight of yaks, horses, and heavily laden porters, and looking down into the gorge 1,500 feet below. I can recall little of the journey down, except for the journey would end as I clutched on to my trusty steed. What's the saying? You only live once, unless of course you're a Buddhist!

I eventually arrived in Lukla ahead of the others, but I was soon joined by Jonathan, who was adamant in wanting to prove that his commando training was not in vain by running (or rather, leaping) from rock to rock down the mountain. I think he spent too long in the Falklands watching the rock hopper penguins, but then, I always thought that Sandhurst was a training school for maniacs. Perhaps I'm simply displaying my jealousy of youth, or should I say relative youth. We were soon joined by the rest of the party, and after a few outlandish celebrations and a good night's sleep, we eventually boarded our aircraft and, with eyes closed, took off from Lukla bound for Kathmandu. There followed further celebrations with our signed footprint being attached to the ceiling of the Everest Ascents Club, amongst those of many who had preceded us, including most of the well-known climbers. Amongst the hilarities of the evening was witnessing Lal, one of our Sherpas, fall asleep into his soup. It was nothing to do with the consumption of too much alcohol, you understand, but simply fatigue, or so he would have us believe. Mrs Lal did not believe it and was not amused!

The Aftermath of Everest

I'm not afraid of death, I just don't want to be there when it happens.
Woody Allen

After the sad partings at Heathrow and the promises (however vague) of meeting again soon, Jonathan and I departed for Stafford well and truly shattered. The following morning, I awoke to niggling chest pains, which I attributed to indigestion. Sadly, this was not the case, and I spent the next frustrating seven days in Stafford and Stoke Hospitals recovering from a heart attack caused by multiple small pulmonary embolisms. Whether it was the results of the fall, the flight, or old age, who can tell. The result was two months of recuperative training and a multiplicity of tablets, many of which were to counteract the effects of the others. Added to which, I had other things occupying my mind and time.

I spent New Year's 2014 again in Laceby courtesy of the Gladdings, during which time I was invited to watch my old club Grimsby Town, now out of the Football League and nestling in the Conference League, attempting to show some semblance of cohesive football without a great deal of conviction. This was hardly what I needed in the process of recovering from a heart attack, but nevertheless it was an interesting and nostalgic event and a welcome break. As usual, I visited the site where we scattered Shelia's ashes, laid a few flowers, and chatted to the tree in the vain hope that she might be listening. It was hard to come to terms with the passage of time; this was almost ten years since she passed away. Thank goodness it was an isolated spot because I'm sure anyone passing would have regarded me as a nutcase. It's at times like this that you sometimes question what is to come, and if there is life after death, then why can't there be some form of communication? Now I'm getting too philosophical!

By the beginning of February 2014, frustration was beginning to overtake common sense (or so my daughters told me), and I was gearing myself up to getting back on the mountains: a minnow in the guise of Ben Nevis, this time in the company of son and grandson and what few of the "Yak Attackers" had come for the weekend. Jonathan had already taken both boys up Snowdon and Scafell, so at least for James, it was one in each country. Needless to say, boys never grow up, and they spent their time at the top involved in a snowball fight whilst I sat and viewed the scene from the summit, which on every mountain leaves you with a lasting impression of both grandeur and achievement. However, I was becoming aware that climbing, and dare I say excessive physical activity, was beginning to have an impact on my body. It was something that I had to address later in the year because I was now suffering from two prolapsed discs in the base of the spine.

Setting aside my minor problems, it was shattering to hear of the tragedy on Everest barely four months since our return, with the death of eighteen Sherpas. A massive ice formation, known as a Serac, broke off an overhanging glacier just above Base Camp. It was immense, a piece the size of 657 buses and weighing the equivalent of 31.5 million tonnes. It triggered an avalanche of snow and ice which thundered down onto the Khumbu icefall, burying everything in its path. During our time on Everest, we had witnessed avalanches and rockfalls too close for comfort, which are terrifying because you're never quite sure which one has your name on it.

This was the year in which the UK was battered by a series of storms and the remnants of US hurricanes, exacerbated by a change in the

Gulf Stream, raising speculation of a change in the weather patterns brought about by global warming. Inevitably, this gives rise to the doomsday prediction of the UK and Europe returning to another ice age. However, I take comfort in that no two scientists ever come to the same conclusion!

On the domestic front, I continued with my rehabilitation, increasing my walks to ten miles every day, much to the angst of Brandy, my dog, who accompanied me. But as I said to her, she's got four legs as against my two, so she's really only doing half the distance! It was during the year that Julie fractured all her metatarsals whilst on holiday, followed shortly by Nigel being admitted into hospital for an operation on his spine which put paid to his army career, although he continued as an NHS surgeon. There was one benefit, although he didn't see it that way: he could no longer return to Afghanistan.

In June, I took a break from gymnastics, Masonic, and other commitments—I think some people call it retirement—and spent a couple of weeks in the Cape Verdi Islands. I'm not quite sure where the *verdi* comes from because these are volcanic rock groups in the middle of the Atlantic, albeit surrounded by marvellous sandy beaches. Although in the company of many hundreds of holiday makers, it was nevertheless a holiday of solitude; next time I'll take a group holiday. Yet again, the airlines had heard about my desire to enjoy myself rather than commit to reckless holidays, and so that I didn't feel deprived, they relieved me of the worry of how much baggage I should take. You've guessed it: I was delivered to Cape Verdi Islands and my bags to Frankfurt. Now, that shouldn't have been too difficult to resolve, except that there were no flights from Frankfurt to Cape Verdi. To make matters a little bit more demanding, there were no clothing shops in the hotel complex or indeed on the island. We were once again subjected to Everett's Law.

It could be a sign of old age (I prefer years of maturity), but the months appeared to be flashing past, full of activity and growing concern for events over which we have no control. It has been described as the sport that takes your breath away. Certainly, the Commonwealth Games held in Glasgow during July and August lived up to our expectations as far as British Gymnastics was concerned. The home nations amassed twenty-six medals, with England being the predominant body with nineteen. This was our best result in many years, if not ever. Sir John Major, our newly appointed patron, joined with his wife, Norma, in supporting our gymnasts. It was evident that the time, effort, and money we had put into the sport was now showing dividends with a crop of new, young faces entering the higher echelons of the sport.

Following my sojourn in Glasgow, I left for Cheshire to join the Northwood Cricket Club's tour of Cheshire, but not before I spent a day viewing where we used to live in Buxton many years ago. I played in two matches and umpired in the third, but I think I realised that at the ripe old age of seventy-nine, it was perhaps time to give up the pretence of playing, as the ball seems to travel faster as you face it, either with the bat or in the field. The bat also appears that much heavier and narrower.

The rest of my year was taken up with a strange collection of events: gymnastics, British Championships, and board meetings; my niece Danielle's wedding; two funerals, which seem to get more frequent, one being my aunt, who at the age of ninety-five was the last surviving member of my mother's family; and visits to Maidstone and Nottingham to attend the disbandment of the Lancers, and to celebrate the 160th anniversary of the Charge of the Light Brigade.

Order of the Fleur-de-Lys

Finally, I made a visit to Queens' Chapel in Cambridge in October, where I was made a Knight Chevalier of the Order of the Fleur-de-Lys, a French Military Order of Chivalry. Nothing to do with the Everetts' tenuous connection with Normandy. It's just that they offered, and I accepted!

"OK, but why Cambridge?" you might ask. There are two strands to the answer. The first deals with the chapel itself, and the second related to the origins of the order. The chapel was founded in 1448 by Margaret of Anjou, wife of Henry VI, and Elizabeth Woodville,

Queen Consort of England. Margaret was the daughter of Rene d'Anjou, who founded the Order of the Fleur-de-Lys. The order was originally called the Ordre et Compagnie du Lys and consisted of knights and gentlemen-at-arms of the Scottish Army in France, who also formed part of the French king's bodyguard. In 1420 the Earls of Douglas, Buchan, and Murray had joined together and led some six thousand knights and soldiers to help the king of France fight the English—not so much out of loyalty but as mercenaries. Five years later, Charles VII created two elite bodyguards from these men, the Garde du Roi and the Garde de Corps du Roi. The Fleur-de-Lys was established in 1439 during the Hundred Years War by Rene d'Anjou, regnant king of the two Sicilies, titular king of Jerusalem and Hungary, and Duke of Anjou, Bar, and Lorraine, in recognition of the assistance they had provided Rene in regaining the kingdom of Naples.

They fought with Joan of Arc and Rene at Orleans. By 1780 they had been absorbed into the British and Swedish armies, the Scots becoming the Scots Guard. If you don't want them as effective enemies, then make sure you have them under your control. We're back to the old adage "Keep your friends close and your enemies closer". The order then became a charitable organisation, and it was transformed into an Order of Chivalry in 1840. Its grand patron is HRH Princess Elizabeth of Serbia and Yugoslavia, who is cousin to the Duke of Kent and second cousin to Charles, Prince of Wales, and its sovereign grand commander is the Most Noble Chevalier Comte Hugh de Montgomery, a descendent of Rene d'Anjou.

Returning to Elizabeth Woodville, she was the spouse of Edward IV from 1464 to 1483. The Woodville children included the princes in the Tower and Elizabeth of York. Through Elizabeth she was the maternal grandmother of Henry VIII and the great grandmother of King Edward VI, Queen Mary I, and Elizabeth I, as well as being the great grandmother of Mary Queen of Scots. Through her daughter, Elizabeth of York, she is the ancestor of every monarch since Henry VIII and the Scottish monarchs since James V. How complex life can become. You might add that there's nothing like keeping it in the family!

International Events

This was a turbulent year in which several external disturbing developments occurred: the annexation of the Crimea and Russian intervention in the Ukraine, the rise of Islamic terrorism, and increased tension between Israel and Hammas, threatening Middle East peace and the impact of a worldwide glut of oil. The Ukraine has been caught between the East and the West for much of its history. In February 2014, the pro-Russian president resigned over his decision not to sign a trade deal with the EU, and following riots, he fled to Russia. Pro-Russian rebels in the Crimea, clearly acting under instructions from Putin, called an immediate but questionable referendum to rejoin Russia. Encouraged by this success, pro-Russian separatists, supported by Russian military, seized regions in the east of the country. The United States and the EU retaliated by imposing sanctions on Russia, whilst the G8 expelled them from their gatherings. It was also in July 2014 that MH17, a civilian Malaysian airliner, was shot down by missiles, and all passengers and crew were killed. An independent investigation group subsequently announced in May 2018 that it had conclusive proof that the aircraft was shot down by a Russian BUK missile system of the 53rd Antiaircraft Brigade of the Russian army, which had crossed the border into the Ukraine. All of this has raised the spectre of a return to the Cold War.

Malaysian Airways also suffered the loss of another aircraft, MH370, en route from Malaysia to Beijing in March 2014. Subsequent investigations showed that despite heading for Beijing, its disappearance occurred in the southern hemisphere to the north of Australia. Despite pieces of debris being washed up in Madagascar, Mauritius, Mozambique, and South Africa, as well as one of the biggest maritime searches in history, no other traces have been found, and the search was finally called off in 2018.

However, from my viewpoint the most disturbing factor was the rapid rise of the Islamic terrorist group ISIL, which declared a "caliphate" under its own strict version of Islamic law. Its rapid advance to take over large sections of Iraq and Syria earlier in the year went largely unopposed. However, it wasn't long before the United States and some Arab countries formed a coalition, although the Americans were reluctant to put boots on the ground, and so it became an aerial war of attrition. There is little doubt that this brutal and barbaric ideology based on medieval culture needs eradicating, but this needs greater involvement and commitment by the wider Muslim community. Will this happen? I doubt it.

Ever since Hammas was elected to power in Gaza, the daily conflict with Israel has continued. In June, the kidnapping and killing of three teenage Israelis and the continued firing of missiles into Israel brought the inevitable response, with the bombardment and occupation of Gaza. There seems little hope of this problem ever being resolved.

After five years of stability, between June and December, the price of oil fell by almost 40 per cent from $115 a barrel to below $70. A variety of reasons are postulated by the economist: the failure of OPEC to agree to a cut in the level of production, turmoil in the Middle East (notably Libya and Iraq), sanctions imposed on Russia because of its actions in the Ukraine, the expansion of shale gas production in the United States, and last but by no means least the significant impact of the weak economies throughout the world. But for how long the market will stay depressed, no one knows.

CHAPTER 27

Europe—Is This Disintegration?

> Democracy is when the indigent, and not
> the men of property, are the rulers.
> Aristotle

Perhaps the first rumblings of potential changes in Europe were evident from the Scottish push for independence, which many of us thought had been put to bed once and for all with the positive vote to remain part of the United Kingdom in the referendum of the previous year, 2014. Clearly the almost clean sweep of the SNP—with the return of fifty-six MPs to Parliament following the election in 2015, which saw the Conservatives returned with a majority—raised the issue yet again. The backlash was a clamour for self-government for the English and a strengthened determination to renegotiate membership of the European Union—issues that will, like the ghost in *Hamlet*, linger on. But of greater threat to the integrity of the EU was the near collapse of the Greek economy. How apt that the quote above should come from a Greek philosopher and from the cradle of democracy, because as we moved into 2015 we could be seen to be acting out yet another Greek tragedy with the players, in this instance Prime Minister Tsipras and Finance Minister Varoufakis, arguing that Greece, as the birthplace of democracy, should not have to bow before its creditors to resolve its debts. How naïve, and dare I say predictable, a left-wing statement. Sitting with combined debts of 360 billion euros, it beggers belief that they should prevaricate over implementing the reforms demanded by the EC as a means of providing debt relief.

"Greece cooked the books to get into the Euro. The country was riddled with corruption, inefficiency and tax evasion; living beyond its means, racking up giant fiscal and trade deficits." Not my words, but those of the Reuters News Agency on 22 June 2015. It is hard to imagine any commercial organisation being allowed to operate in a more reckless and irresponsible manner and refusing to pay its debts; it would not survive. Neither, I fear, will Greece unless it accepts the demands to reform its fiscal policies. It is hoped that having reached the precipice, they will not suffer from vertigo when looking down at the abyss below. Such a move impact will impact on not only Greece but also on the future stability of the Euro and the EU, as well as those to whom the debts are owed – Germany (57.23 billion euros), France (42.98 billion), Italy (37.76 billion), Spain (25.10 billion), and all the other nations (including ourselves) who contribute through the IMF and raise questions over the UK's future in Europe. Hence, one of the reasons for the UK decision, by referendum, to leave the EU.

Another more worrying factor was the free movement of labour, which in the early days enabled workers within the EU to take up work in other member states. Open borders within Europe was a concept that became highly questionable through mass migration, over which the UK had no control. Firstly, there were the economic factors arising from new members of the EU seeking higher living standards in other member states. Secondly, there was mass migration from the Middle East and Africa, which was largely uncontrolled on the southern flank of the EU. All of which was exacerbated by the increasing threat of terrorism by conflicts inflamed by ISIL and other extremists under the cloak of migration.

The tectonic plates of politics were on the move, the first eruption of which was the shock result (to some) of the UK referendum, which declared in favour of the UK leaving the EU, subsequently referred to as Brexit. This in turn resulted in a change of leadership and the realignment of many within politics on all sides. In a sense, politicians now had to listen to the will of the people. Never since Cromwell and the earlier imposition of the Magna Carta had democracy been so evident.

Isn't it strange that the nearer history gets to oneself, the more uncertain it becomes? The decision to leave or stay in Europe was never going to be clear-cut. Turning the clock back to the years when we were part of EFTA, a free-trading element of nations seeking closer ties with Europe and struggling against the intransigence of the French under De Gaulle, Europe had an appeal as the European Economic Community. And that was what was intended, not a massive, unaccountable, bureaucratic superstate manipulated by nonelected officials. There is little wonder that those, like me, lost the appetite for an ever-larger freeloading, undemocratic system with uncontrollable movement in and across its borders. Yes, you might have guessed: I'm a Brexiter, so blame me!

Before reading gloom and doom into a parting of the ways, we should look at an example of survival within Europe with a country that is not part of the EU, and here I talk about the small but not insignificant country of Switzerland. It is not part of the European Union yet sits in the middle of Europe; it has its own deal with the EU yet trades with many countries including China and Japan without being constrained by any of the EU rules; it has the highest wages in Europe yet exports 5 per cent more to the EU than the UK does; and per capita it is the second richest country in the world.

Whilst this might have been the first sizable earthquake, there was more to come following the US presidential elections when, against all the odds, Donald Trump was elected and the Republicans had complete control of the Senate and Congress. Like it or not, the people had spoken, and democracy was once more on the march. In the two years since his election, he has astonished many by his use of the social media to express his views, his naïve comments, and his involvement in wider diplomatic activities. Indeed, one could hardly describe them as diplomatic. During his visit to Europe in July 2018, he undermined the British approach to Brexit, attacked Germany for its use of Russian gas, and attacked NATO for its lack of investment—hardly an encouraging approach to its major allies. Whilst on the subject of NATO, another worrying factor is Trump's heavy-handed approach to Turkey, a key ally in the protection of southern Europe, which could have an adverse effect especially because Turkey is in severe economic straits and could turn to Russia for assistance.

His subsequent meeting with Putin, from which he excluded even his own advisors, mirrored Chamberlain's pre-war meeting with Hitler, reflecting an attitude of appeasement. The worrying aspect of Trump's "America first" is the possible return of the United States to an isolationist world similar to that which existed in the 1930s. In his speech, Trump set aside the Russian annexation of Crimea, its military involvement in the Ukraine, the Novichok chemical attack in southern England, and the US indictment of twelve military officers for conducting cyber warfare against the United States during the 2016 elections. Within the United States, there were major concerns over his humiliating performance in contrast with Putin's control, with the press declaring this an historic low in US diplomacy.

Domestic and International Issues

Let me return to more mundane and domestic issues during 2015. You will probably have guessed that the new year started in Laceby once again. What did I say about breaking the habit? However, it is always nice to return to your roots and refresh your views and attitudes towards life. Added to which, it's nice to party! January, February, and March were months filled with gymnastics activities—regional, national, and international events. In March, my number four grandchild celebrated her twenty-first. It can't be that long ago that I was celebrating mine—I wish! In April two further significant events occurred. Alexander, granddaughter number three, left for China via Canada to start a career teaching English to Chinese students. A week later, my younger sister Gill went into Leeds Hospital for a fusion of discs in her back, only to discover that she had widespread cancer of the bowel, liver, and lungs, to which she succumbed within months. It was shattering news to all concerned and brought home to me the realisation that it was over ten years ago that Sheila had also died of this dreadful infliction. Such news is a battering ram, especially to the family, and I can understand the difficulties Dave, her husband, faced. It was a forceful reminder of what I had lost.

April witnessed the largest burglary in English legal history when four elderly men managed to relieve the Hatton Garden Depository of £200 million. I say the largest in legal history on the assumption that King John and the robber barons of the Middle Ages achieved greater success. Strange to say that in all these cases, little of the proceeds are ever recovered, merely recycled.

The following month saw the arrival of Princess Charlotte, swelling the ranks of the younger royals.

Talking of getting a battering, it was in May 2015 that all the pollsters were predicting a hung Parliament following the general election, but they were taken by surprise when the Conservatives were returned with a clear majority. Labour didn't fare so well, especially in Scotland, where they lost out heavily to the SNP, raising the spectre of yet another round of devolution debate—too soon and too provocative. Miliband resigned, leaving Labour in turmoil, followed by the resignation of Nick Clegg as leader of the Lib Dems and the emergence of the veteran left winger Jeremy Corbyn.

These weren't the only batterings. In April, an earthquake measuring 7.8 hit Nepal and caused extensive damage across the country, resulting in the deaths of over 9,000 people. Two weeks later a second earthquake with a magnitude of 7.3 struck west of Namche Bazaar and close to Mt Everest, causing an avalanche which struck Base Camp at ferocious speed, killing 17 climbers, injuring over 60 others, and trapping many other climbers farther up the mountain. The Base Camp on Everest is particularly vulnerable because it is situated on a shoulder of rocky glacial moraine, below the Khumbu icefall, a maze of moving crevasses and glacial ice cliffs. It is estimated that a further 1,000 people in Nepal were killed because of this second earthquake. It is devastating to see the impact that those has had on a small and impoverished country. Life can be so cruel.

On the subject of cruelty, terrorist activities increased during the year as ISIL extended its reach. In January Boko Haram massacred 2,000 in Nigeria, and ISIL in Libya beheaded 12 Christians whose only sin was to believe in a different religion. In Kenya, terrorists of Al-Shabaab killed 148 university students, and in June a lone terrorist murdered 30 British tourists on the beach Sousse in Tunisia. In the meanwhile, ISIL had joined forces with Boko Haram and set about destroying ancient cities and monuments in Iraq, Syria, and the Levant—mindless morons who think they can eradicate history and change the world with their distorted ideology. In Europe, we had a bloody wave of bombings and shootings, with 130 people killed in 6 attacks across Paris, sponsored by ISIL terrorist groups.

It is an aspect of history that always disturbs me in that although wars are the result, in one way or another, of fanaticism and greed, the underlying factors can often be created in the name or cause of religion. The Middle East conflict of today has its roots in the division between Sunni and Shia Muslims arising from the struggle as to who should lead the Muslim community following the death of the Prophet Mohammed. Sunnis form over 85 per cent of the faith and are the orthodox branch. The name is Ahl-al-Sunna, meaning "the people of tradition", whereas Shia is the more hard-line element, which in turn has spawned al-Qaeda and ISIS or ISIL with its inbuilt desire to remove anything which is in opposition to its beliefs.

Our insurance against war is military strength in support of political will, something of which we should always bear in mind if we are to live in peace. Early in May 2015, I was invited to Richmond Castle to witness the queen presenting the colours to the newly formed Royal Hussars, an amalgamation of the 9th and 12th Royal Lancers and the Queen's Royal Lancers (formally the 17th and 21st Lancers). Like many others, I become confused over time in trying to recall many of the old, established elements of the British Army as cut after cut over the years has completely reshaped military history. But then I am, or was, a simple RAF officer. Whenever we restructured, we simply shelved the squadron concerned until such time as it could be resurrected in another form! As holders of the Elizabeth Cross, in recognition of the loss of their son in the Bosnian conflict, my friends John and Sylvia Nicholas were presented to the queen. Barry had been a twenty-year-old member of the Royal Engineers Bomb Disposal Group when he was killed whilst clearing mines following the conflict.

On the suggestion of John and Sylvia, I joined them and other friends of theirs on the *Queen Mary 2* for ten days in May, a very special occasion because Cunard were celebrating the 175th year of its formation. We sailed around the UK visiting several ports associates with Cunard's history, from Cork to Oban and from Belfast to Glasgow, before meeting up with the *Queen Elizabeth* and the *Queen Victoria* in the Mersey. The highlight of the celebration was seeing these three massive liners doing a simulated dance, turning through 360 degrees, during which the Red Arrows flew over streaming their red, white, and blue smoke. Almost a million people watched from the shores whilst the beams of laser light lit up the "Three Graces' displaying the history of Cunard and Liverpool. It took me back to 1957 and my return from national service in Malaya, when I saw Liverpool in a very different light!

A word about the Three Graces. For nearly a century, the three magnificent architectural structures in Liverpool, the Royal Liver, the Cunard, and the Port of Liverpool buildings, affectionately known as the Three Graces, have dominated the skyline as a testament to the city's worldwide commercial reputation when, at the turn of the century, it established its trading dominance, primarily with the new world and the colonies. As the Echo Arena has become a focal point for British and International gymnastics, I have become a regular visitor to Liverpool, but there is still something special and vibrant about the city both in its commercial activities and its night life, which over the years became a favourite haunt for groups such as the Beatles, Gerry and the Pacemakers, Freddie Mercury, and individuals including Cilla Black, Acker Bilk and more.

The Year of the Octogenarian

> Age doesn't arrive slowly, it comes in a rush. One day nothing has changed, a week later, everything has.
>
> James Salter, 2013

In 2015 I became an octogenarian. It's difficult to cope with when you brain tells you that you are approaching thirty, although things aren't quite as they use to be. Setting aside the philosophical debate on yesteryears, I had to face the inevitability of how other people viewed advancing years; from the very young who regarded it as an age beyond the grave (but then, didn't we all at one stage?) to the very sympathetic who realised that they were fast approaching that stage of life themselves, and even others who had moved a step beyond. Unbeknown to me (well, almost), Julie, Jonathan, and Jane, together with their relative partners, had decided in the timely Everett tradition that this event was not going to pass unnoticed by the general public. I had an inkling that something was afoot when Julie advised me in no uncertain terms that what I had planned for the weekend of the 13–14 June had to be changed. As daughters are prone to do, she had been monitoring my calendar activities on an almost daily basis. Other parts of the jigsaw started to fall in place with comments from friends like, "Take care, and we look forward to June." Maybe they thought I was so gaga that I wouldn't notice. I also saw one of the cards sent to my sister after her operation, which ended, "See you at Brian's Surprise Party!"

Nevertheless, the outcome was a fabulous party at the Bridge Hotel in Wetherby, Yorkshire, with friends and family from all over the country, which went on into the early hours of the following Sunday morning. Julie had trawled through my address book and computer to great effect and contacted over 150 friends. I have been endowed with three very remarkable, loving, and generous children to whom family is everything, and my eight grandchildren are following their example. I have never felt so proud and humble as I did on that day, surrounded by family and friends.

It was also another phenomenal year for the scientific world and indeed for humankind. The space probe New Horizons, launched from Earth over nine years previously in January 2006, as part of the NASA Deep Space Network, advanced towards the Kuiper Belt, passing Pluto at a range of 3.11 billion miles and travelling at a velocity of 50,000 kph (31,000 mph). Pluto, a dwarf planet measuring only 2,370 kilometres (1,473 miles), could fit into an area the size of Africa with plenty to spare. The pictures transmitted took over 18 hours to reach Earth but were of outstanding clarity. It marks the completion of visits to all 8 solar system planets from Mercury and finishing with the dwarf planet Pluto. The second major achievement came in July when scientists at the European Large Hadron Collider discovered a new particle, a new form of matter called a Pentaquark. This was only a year after the same device had confirmed the existence of the Higgs boson particle. It's a truly remarkable period of discovery and exploration, but I'm sure that future developments will push the boundaries further back in time.

On a more personal note, in August 2015 I took this frail frame of mine on a cricket tour of Cheshire with the more able members of the Northwood Cricket Club. I know, I did say that last year was the last, but I blame the decision on this eighteen-year old trying to break out of a body that has entered its eighth decade. The retribution was fast and furious, unlike my attempt to chase after a catch on the boundary, as I crashed on my shoulder, which resulted in a torn rotator cuff and a subsequent frozen shoulder. I spent the rest of the tour as a drinking spectator! There followed twelve weeks of rehabilitation treatment at the Darlington Stadium. Whilst not really the most relaxing of treatments, it had its benefits, because I looked out over the pitch and was able to watch the "All Blacks" training prior to their winning the world rugby cup.

As the president of British Gymnastics, I was heavily involved in events leading up to the Rio Olympics. We hosted the World Championships in Glasgow, which proved a great success and illustrated once again that when our nation sets its mind to organising major events, it is second to none. From a personal perspective, it confirmed what we had set out to achieve some ten years before: to produce gymnasts of outstanding quality and to move the sport to the forefront of world competition. It is therefore with some gratification that we can look back on all the recent successes and look forward with confidence to the next decade.

It would not be inappropriate to finish off with a word about the weather, which we Brits frequently put at the front of our concerns— as though we don't have enough to worry about! Every two to seven years, the warm waters of the Pacific Ocean expand eastwards, and it appears that they are now the warmest since 1998. Even without global warming, temperatures have reached new records. At last, international agreement has been reached over the need to curb emissions, but this does not mean that action will follow, added to which we now see the United States turning its back on the agreement. Severe droughts in Africa and heavy winters and floods in Europe appear to be the likely outcome in the years ahead, but who knows?

CHAPTER 28

Freemasonry and Chivalric Orders

No, We're not a Funny Bunch of People.
Johnny Lancaster

Freemasonry

This is totally out of context, and certainly out of the time thread that I hope is passing through this epistle, but nevertheless I thought I should refer to what my offspring refer to as the "funny handshake club", especially because I've been involved in Freemasonry for over forty years, a period that has taken an inordinate amount of my free time, albeit willingly committed. Freemasonry is probably one of the world's most misunderstood organisations. A well-known actor friend of mine, Johnny Lancaster, wrote a book some years ago entitled *No, We're Not a Funny Bunch of People*, a book on Freemasonry written by a Freemason, which probably explains it far better than I can.

Whilst working in the Ministry of Defence in 1975, I was invited to lunch with friends working in GCHQ, some of whom I had worked with in Malta. It was at this time that I was invited to join Freemasonry. Although I knew nothing about the organisation or its origins, I was aware that my paternal grandfather had been a Freemason, but my father had not. They had never raised the subject with me, and neither had anyone else. Whilst weary of any such links and largely ignorant of what was involved, I was somewhat hesitant, especially because I was, at that time, security cleared at the highest level in my MOD employment—but then, so were they! Perhaps it's something to do with the fact that people who deal in secrets are more likely to keep secrets. Hence, my career in Freemasonry took off.

For many years, Freemasonry was its own worst enemy, hiding behind a cloak of secrecy and therefore allowing the myth of it being a secret society to develop unchallenged. It is not, nor has it ever been, a secret society but rather a society with secrets, generated from its medieval traditional links with the local fraternities of stonemasons, who from the fourteenth century regulated their craftsmen by qualifications and experience, the recognition of which demanded secret signs and passwords restricted to the various levels of entry determined by the guilds. Masons could only gain employment and entry to their relative lodges through such a code of recognition, which included passwords and pass signs. It's not so different from the distinction made between officers, NCOs, and other ranks in the armed services, who don't have signs and passwords, but they do have ranks to determine their status, and to a certain extent they reside and dine in different quarters.

Freemasonry as we know it today formally came into existence in the UK during the early eighteenth century, although it probably had its informal links with the craft going back into the Middle Ages. Today, it is a fraternal organisation of like-minded people from every walk of life, race, and religion, sharing common values. It is one of the world's oldest and largest nonreligious, non-political, fraternal, and charitable organisations. Indeed, over the generations its members have and do include royalty, heads of states, religious leaders, and those of high standing in every profession. Freemasons are taught to practice charity and to care not only for their own but also for the community as a whole, both by charitable giving and by voluntary efforts and works as individuals.

It is the second largest donor of charity within the UK, having donated over £100 million in recent years, all from within its own membership; that is unlike the largest, the Lottery Fund, which draws its money by commercial means. Since 2015, Freemasonry in London has given over

£2 million to enable a second air ambulance; this provides a rapid-response, advanced trauma team to operate within the M25. It was this aircraft that was quickly on the scene following the tragic death of five people on Westminster and PC Keith Palmer in the ground of Parliament Bridge during a murderous attack by the killer Khalid Masood in the name of ISIL. It has also funded similar services in other parts of the country. Following the tragic fire in the Grenfell Tower block in London, the London Masons provided funds for the fire brigade to purchase two extended height aerial vehicles at a cost of £3 million, as well as five rapid responder cars for the London Ambulance Service. It provided St Bartholomew's Hospital in London with a £2 million CyberKnife, a frameless robotic radiosurgery system used for treating benign and malignant tumours, only the second such system in the UK.

In addition to which, the 230,000 members of its 8,000 lodges in the UK make individual or group donations amounting to several million pounds each year to many national and international charities. Moreover, it is a worldwide fraternity, and in America alone in 1992 (I don't have more recent figures), $400 million was donated to charity. What I have omitted to say is that one's career in Freemasonry is not restricted to the mainstream of the organisation but in time branches out to embrace the many side orders, of which there are some sixteen, ranging from the Royal Arch to Knights Templar and the Knights of Malta to Mark Masonry and Allied Degrees.

Like any large organisation, it has its critics, some of whom propound conspiracy theories and antireligious concepts, and some who would liken it to the Mafia. Well, they would—it helps them to sell books! Nothing could be further from the truth. It is a society of men concerned with moral and spiritual values based on kindness, integrity, fairness, care for the less fortunate, and a belief in a supreme being whose presence overarches all religions. Others have argued that it is a preserve of men, a male hegemony, but this overlooks the fact that there are now female freemasons with their own lodges. Over the years, I have given many lectures within the community to explain our aims and objectives and to debunk the myths that have surrounded the order. I have to say much of it is generated by the media because nothing sells better than mystery, drama, or bad news! I recently watched a programme called *Granchester* in which the local masons were portrayed as racist, bigoted thugs in a secret society. If that truly is the case, then why do we attract so many Asian, African, and other ethnic people of all religions? We ask only that Masons believe in a supreme being. One has to wonder where the bigots really reside. Is any research ever carried out, or is it just in the mindset of a few who have their own misguided political agendas?

My Masonic career, if you want to address it as such, culminated in 2017 when I was promoted to one of the highest offices within Freemasonry, that of grand officer, and invested as such by His Highness the Duke of Kent. I was also invested the following year as a grand officer in the Royal Arch. However; life doesn't end here; there is still much to be done and not a great deal of time in which to complete everything that I would wish. But then, there never is.

Chivalric Orders

In the course of my Masonic career, I've established contact with many people of like minds, and as such it is inevitable that in the course of time, one is invited to attend various functions and, in the process, become involved in similar organisations. There are three orders of chivalry that fall into this broad category, although they are not necessarily related. The first more closely associated with Freemasonry is the Scottish Masters of St Andrew, or as it is better known on the Continent, the Directoire Ecossais de Belgique, which has as its offshoot the more esoterical Order of Elus Kohen. The second is the Order of the Fleur-de-Lys, incorporating the military Order of the Crescent and the Order of St James of Altopascio. And the third is the Healing, Teaching, and Chivalric Order of St Raphael.

Scottish Masters

It is probably apposite to point out that, as with so many other things French, there are differences between our two countries, especially within the maze of French Masonry. British masons, mainly of Irish and Scottish origin, introduced Freemasonry into France in 1726. Despite it being a Christian chivalric organisation rather than Catholic, it expanded very quickly because whatever was English in the eighteenth century was considered to be highly fashionable, especially by Parisians. During those early years, much of masonry was adapted to meet Gallic taste, and the workings therefore became known as the Scottish Degrees, or as it is known today, the Scottish Rectified Rites, and was considered to be an aristocratic order restricted to the local nobility whose aim was the material revival of the Order of the Temple—the former Knights Templar who had been disbanded on the orders of King Philip V and the French Pope Clement in 1310. Now it's perceived to be an extension of Freemasonry and the knights, on the continent of Europe they are known as Chevaliers or Knights Beneficent of the Holy City (CBHC). The order has spread across northern Europe over the years, and that part with which I am now associated is within the Grand Legation of Belgium, headed by the Directoire Ecossais de Belgique. It is known as the Loge St Georg in the Province of Ypres, a town well-known for other reasons.

The Order of the Fleur-de-Lys

As mentioned earlier in the book, the Order of the Fleur-de-Lys is an independent sovereign order of chivalry under the royal patronage of HRH Princess Elizabeth of Serbia and Yugoslavia. It has within it two further orders: The Order of St James of Altopascio and the Military Order of the Crescent. I am a knight of the order with my current position within the order being grand herald. My role is the examination, approval, and granting of "arms" to those so entitled and in maintaining the history of the order and its members. It's a rather privileged position, especially with my involvement in heraldry and history in general, and it has generated a steep learning curve in my knowledge of the intricacies and methodology of heraldry adopted over the years.

The Order of St James of Altopascio was formed in the middle of the eleventh century between 1057 and 1086, when its headquarters and hospital were set up in Altopascio to provide spiritual and medical assistance to pilgrims travelling from France to Rome, as well as protection as they traversed the forest of Cerbia. It was granted the right to pass freely anywhere within the empire without paying taxes, and in 1190 it was granted imperial recognition by Henry IV. On 5 April 1239, Pope Gregory 1X granted the order "rule", elevating the knights to the same level as the Knights Hospitaller (St John of Jerusalem).

There is at this point a need to reflect on what I wrote earlier regarding the disbandment of the Knights Templar on the orders of the French King Philippe IV and the French pope in Avignon, Pope Clement V, in 1307 leading to the death by burning at the stake in 1310 of the grand master of the Templars and the flight of others. Some of those in France quickly joined the Order of St James for their own protection. In 1520, Charles V elevated the Knights in Altopascio to the same category of other knights. Today there exist Knights of the Tau Cross in Altopascio, which is within the Order of the Fleur-de-Lys.

The military Order of the Crescent was founded by Rene d'Anjou in 1448, and it is comprised mainly of French aristocrats but did not survive long, as in 1460 it disappeared and became absorbed by the Order of the Fleur-de-Lys, of which Rene d'Anjou was the first head, and in which it now resides.

The Order of St Raphael

The Healing, Teaching, and Chivalric Order of St Raphael is an international order of Christian chivalry which exists to perpetuate the ideals and traditions of chivalry in a modern world. The order is named in honour of St Raphael, who was said to hear the prayers of holy men and bring them before God. The main purpose of the order has always been to aid the cure of those who are sick in mind and body. The second purpose is to preserve and pass on knowledge to others; it is especially concerned with the wisdom of philosophers and men and women of learning. There is, within the order, a military chivalric Order of St Mark. Membership is only by invitation, but the order is open to all religions. Within the order, I have been appointed as the grand treasurer with responsibility for its financial standing.

CHAPTER 29

One last Mountaineering Challenge

*I don't regret the things I've done, only the
things I didn't when I had the chance.*
Anon

After Everest, I said that was the last of the mountains I would climb,
but then I am delusional because there was one last challenge that
always seems to feature in my dreams: I'm stuck on a narrow ridge
looking down thousands of feet into a crater, fearful of falling into
the fire below—could that be Hades?—and then I wake up. After
giving it some thought, I started to plan an ascent of four active
volcanoes during one week in October 2016. I know—sheer madness,
but a challenge, nevertheless. And as has been the case with all my
other challenges, I committed myself to raising funds for charity. That
way I couldn't chicken out at the last minute. To make sure this was
achievable, the volcanoes had to be close together, so I selected four
in Sicily and the Aeolian Islands in the Mediterranean: Vulcano, Mt
Pillatus on Limpari, Stromboli, and Etna on Sicily.

Volcanoes are usually associated with those areas where the earth's
crust is broken into seventeen tectonic plates, which move into or away
from each other, although not always the case. As you will no doubt
gather, I'm not a volcanologist, and I don't intend the delve into or
explain the science. Suffice to say that having climbed the dormant

Vesuvius in Italy and witnessed Fuji in Japan, I was keen to see at close hand other strata-volcanoes, especially those that sit across the Aeolian Islands

Sicily and the Aeolian Islands

For over 2,500 years, Sicily, located at the cross roads of the important trade routes between North Africa and Europe, has been of significant importance as an island. Even today it provides a vital sea route for refugees escaping despotic regimes and seeking new lives in Europe, but they're exploited by people smugglers in the process. The island of Sicily derives its name from the three Bronze Age tribes who settled there in 15 BC—namely, the Secani in the west, the Sucel tribe in the east, and the Elymians in the north. Later cultures ranged from those of the great ancient nations, including the Phonecians, the Greeks, and the Romans, through to the Arabs and Normans in the Middle Ages, and then the French and Spanish in sixteenth and seventeenth century. Finally, it was annexed as Italian territory by Garibaldi in 1860. It is of course the renowned home of the Cosa Nostra, or the Mafia (Arab word mu'afah, meaning protection—a very appropriate title!). These days the Mafia is not as dominant as it was, presumably because much of its activities have become a worldwide operation.

Situated in the Tyrrhenian Sea, the Aeolian Islands form a volcanic archipelago stretching eighty-seven miles north-east of Sicily in an arc towards Italy. They were created by the movement of the African continental plate against the European plate. It is at these boundaries that most active volcanoes occur. Volcanic activity on these islands has provided very fertile soil conducive to organic growth, and many areas around the volcanoes have active fumaroles giving off sulphur fumes, and in some parts are thermal waters which are considered beneficial to health by the locals.

The Aeolian archipelago is named after the demigod of winds, Aeolus, who according to legend was the son of a mortal man and an immortal nymph. Zeus appointed him controller of the four winds, the Anemoi Theumai, which the gods had locked within the island of Aeolia. In Homer's Odyssey, we learn of the mythological story of Odysseus returning home from the Trojan Wars, having lost his way, and ending up on the island where he was befriended by King Aeolus. After staying for four weeks and wanting to get back to his homeland, he was given an ox-skin bag by the king containing the four winds with which to assist him in his return to Ithaca. I will not go into the problems Odysseus faced on his return journey, for as the title suggests that was his odyssey, but because of his crew releasing the winds when he was asleep, their ship was driven back to Aeolia, where Aeolus refused further assistance. Consequently, many years passed before they got back to their native land.

The flight from Heathrow was via Milan to Catania and then by boat to Lipari, the largest of the Aeolian Islands in the Tyrrhenian Sea and part of the volcanic archipelago which stretches from Etna on Sicily to Vesuvius on mainland Italy. After a good night's sleep, we departed early the following morning with the guide by boat for the first ascent of the sulphur ridge surrounding Vulcano. The Greeks called it Thermassa, the workshop of the Olympian god Hephaestus. The Romans believed that it was the chimney of the god Vulcan's workshop and that the earthquakes that ensued were due to Vulcan making weapons for Mars and his army to wage war. Following the trek down from the top, we wallowed in the hot springs and mud baths surrounding Vulcano, noted for its steaming fumaroles and hydrothermal activity amidst the ever-present smell of sulphur (a most unusual experience), before returning to Lipari.

I recall years earlier, during our stay in Naples after climbing Vesuvius, we visited Solfatara Crater, one of forty smaller volcanic outlets of the Phlegnean Fields, some six miles outside Naples. Its largest fumarole, or volcanic vent, is Bocca Grande, which ejects steam in excess of 320 degrees Fahrenheit. The bubbling mud at its centre contains seven gases together with water which is rich in more than nine minerals. The emissions of hydrogen sulphide, which can be extremely hazardous, smell strongly of rotten eggs. I remember the astonishment of one of friends, who was a volcanologist from one of our universities, when the guide invited us to poke sticks through the surface, which resembled the floppy surface of a baked rice pudding. Some people don't appreciate the forces of nature with which they are dealing. I've had a healthy respect for volcanoes ever since!

The day following our arrival in Lipari saw us trekking to and climbing Mt Pilatus (6,384 feet), which had last erupted less than three3 months previously on 12 August, mainly ejecting pumice. Lipari has the largest deposit of pumice in the world. It is also renowned for obsidian, a hard, black volcanic glass. On the way down from the volcano, we trekked across the south side of the island before getting an early night in readiness for the trip to Stromboli.

Day four was the boat to Stromboli and an early evening boat ride around the northern flank of the mountain to see the Sciara del Funco, the stream of fire, a lava flow that runs down the mountain side. Stromboli is a vast underwater volcano some 8,900 feet above the seabed. It has been in continuous minor eruption for the last two thousand years and can be seen from far afield, hence its nickname, the Lighthouse of the Mediterranean. After an early night followed by a morning at leisure, we set off the following afternoon with the aim of reaching the summit by sunset thus, enabling us to have the best close-up sighting of the volcanic activity.

The next day, we departed by boat for Milazzo and a transfer to Taomina before a hike to the mountain lodge on the southern edge of Etna, where we were to spend the night. Etna, standing at 11,000 feet, is one of the most active volcanoes in the world with near continuous activity. It has seventeen craters, but only three are currently active. It had erupted early in May and again in August, and we were told that although volcanic activity was relatively calm at the surface, seismic activity was high. The emissions of S02 had increased to 7,000 tonnes per day, which could indicate fresh magma and signs of deep-seated explosive activity. Added to which, there were high winds that made it difficult standing, let alone moving. That leaves one with a question: "Why am I doing this?" It was such a relief to get down and spend a relaxing evening in Catania before returning home the following day. Job done! I was intrigued to read sometime later that because of the geological and atmospheric conditions on Etna being similar to those on Mars, scientists have tested robots on the mountain. They certainly tested me!

It was an extremely fascinating but daunting experience. Too often we in the northern hemisphere tend to regard these exhibitions of nature, in its extreme, as something which is remote and therefore of little concern. But close up, the force with which they can erupt, and the resultant damage generated, reminds you that all is not gentle when facing nature.

CHAPTER 30

Out of Africa

I dream of Africa which is in peace with itself.
Nelson Mandela

I do wonder if this dream to which Mandela refers can ever become a reality. Africa may have been regarded by historians as the birthplace of humanity, but it has also been a continent rent asunder by colonialism, tribalism, corruption, conflict, famine, and disease. Yet it remains a wondrous place full of natural beauty, exciting, daunting, and challenging. If Mandela's dream is in regard to his native South Africa, then perhaps one day his dream will be fulfilled. I do not see such a proposition for other parts of the continent.

Over several years, I have visited many parts of Africa from Tunisia, Morocco, and Libya in the north; Egypt and Sudan in the east; Somalia, Kenya, and Tanzania in the south-east; Botswana and Zimbabwe in the south; and Senegal, Nigeria, and Sierra Leone on the west coast. All are so very different in terms of culture and history, and some in terms of the environment, but they all have that magical element of being part of Africa.

Having had a brief sojourn in southern Africa in my national service days, and in a quest to slake my thirst for history, especially in regard to those early colonial days of an expanding British empire, I decided that in July 2017 I would once again set foot in southern Africa, but this time to walk the ground and see for myself those areas of historical setting. Besides which, isn't it the place from which our ancestors branched out across the globe? I'd always been intrigued by the writings of others describing the developments in South Africa, especially in the 1800s; the Zulu Wars, the Boer War, and more recently the fight for independence. And perhaps I would also have the opportunity to tackle just one more mountain, albeit much lower than some of my previous challenges in Africa: Table Mountain.

After two days in Johannesburg and the surrounding area, we travelled down the Panorama Route to the Kruger National Park, one of the world's largest game reserves covering almost 20,000 square kilometres. Created in 1898, it has a high density of wild animals and birds. It is renowned for its big five: lions, leopards, elephants, buffaloes, and giraffes. Why those five in particular, I know not, for there are some 137 animals there, many of which in my view are equally exciting, such as the cheetahs, hippos, gazelles, and crocodiles. The wide and diverse range of birds is quite incredible: over 500 species, from the larger vultures and eagles down to the tiny hummingbirds. Added to which, there is the impressive variety of flora and fauna—flowers such as the leopard orchid, wild hibiscus, and the impala lily—and trees ranging from the tall jackaberry or African ebony to the mopane tree with its kaleidoscope of colours. The mopane is also host to the mopane moth, the caterpillar of which is harvested, dried, and used as a food source.

We were soon on our way to Mbabane, the capital of Swaziland, or should I say eSwatini as recently renamed by its king on the occasion of its fiftieth year of independence. He considered the name Swaziland too British. Here we go again, recreating history to delete colonialism. Perhaps we Brits should celebrate our independence by renaming our country to delete our history of Roman colonialism! Why Swaziland, you might ask? Well, it was the shortest route to get to the Zulu battlefields of Isandlwana and Rorkes Drift.

Whilst on the subject of colonialism, the Zulu wars resulted from just that. In 1878, the British governor of Natal wanted to turn all of South Africa into a British dependency, and one of the obstacles to that aim was the Zulu leader King Cetshwayo. In January 1879, the British, under Lt Gen the Lord Chelmsford, moved into Zululand. For whatever reason, the British made some very poor tactical decisions. First, they underestimated the size and fighting ability of the Zulu army, who were formidable and courageous warriors, adept at hand-to-hand fighting with their short assegai spears and shields. Second, the British force was split over a considerable distance and thereby weakened on all fronts. The commanders also made tactical errors in their positioning and support beneath the sphinx like hill of Isandlwana and suffered a decisive defeat with 1,700 killed. The white stone cairns that mark the mass graves of the British on the slopes of Isandlwana are poignant reminders of the losses that occurred. A short distance away, across the Buffalo River, was the small mission station of Rorke's Drift, manned by about one hundred troops and civilians under the command of Lt John Chard and Lt Gonville Bromhead. For the next twelve hours a force of more than four thousand Zulus led a sustained attack on the station before departing, having killed seventeen troops at a cost of some four hundred of their own. A total of eleven Victoria Crosses were awarded in recognition of this courageous defence, the greatest number in history for one day's action; some historians suggest it was also to assuage the loss at Isandlwana. But then historians, like politicians, are often cynics. Nevertheless, despite the loss of British prestige, King Cetshwayo was deposed a few years later, and his territory was absorbed under British rule.

The remainder of my time in South Africa involved visits to the Boer War battlefield of Talana. We took a journey to Hermanus to watch the whales entering the bay, only they failed to appear on the two days we were there! We made visits to the winelands of Stellenbosch and Franschoek, Cape Point and Boulder Bay, and of course the grand finale, Cape Town and the Table Mountain. I must be careful—this is beginning to read like a travel brochure!

The Boer War was between the British and the Boars, who inhabited a combination of the Orange Free State, under Marthinus Steyn, and the South African Republic (SAR), under Paul Kruger. The underlying causes for the war were the control of the Witwatersrand gold mining area, discovered in 1886. But the primary reason was the desire of the British government, under Lord Salisbury, to secure British dominance in Southern Africa. The Boers, on the other hand, were fighting for what they regarded as their independence. The war started in 1899 and lasted for two and a half years. Initially the Boers gained the upper hand with their guerrilla tactics of hit and run and their blockades of towns such as Ladysmith, Mafeking, and Kimberley. The British, under Kitchener, struck back with a scorched earth policy, burning farms and settlements. At its height, the British deployed over 500,000 troops against the 80,000 of the Boers at a cost of £200 million. Many of the tactics were to colour British military strategic thinking (rightly or wrongly) during the First World War. Besides which, it was not a good thing because the ground and the environment involved were so different.

During the Boer War, the British made what might be regarded in hindsight as strategic errors. I've found hindsight a wonderful attribute because you can rarely be wrong. Much of the blame for the failings of the British Army in Africa were attributed by the press to its commander, General Sir Redvers Buller. Historian Richard Holmes quotes from what was said at the time: "He was an admirable Captain, an adequate Major, a barely satisfactory Colonel and a disastrous General." But this is overlooking his strengths, as historians, critics, and especially those in power are prone to do. He was an innovator in countering the Boer tactics of guerrilla warfare and introducing tactics which changed modern warfare, such as covering artillery fire. Alas, he did not survive his critics and was dismissed from the service despite having his request for a court martial refused and his appeal turned down by the king.

Three leading statesmen played a role in the war, especially at the Battle of Spion Kop, a battle that was to shape their future: Botha, who led the Boers; Ghandi, who had left India as a barrister to work in South Africa and became a stretcher-bearer working for the British army; and Churchill, who was a correspondent acting as a courier. But as history tells us, nothing in life is that simple. Louis Botha was to go on and become the leader of the Union of South Africa, having first served as prime minister of the Transvaal. Mahatma Gandhi was a complex character who fully supported the empire and was of the view that whites and Indians were bonded by a common Arian bloodline that was not shared by Africans—somewhat of a racist view. He was later to lead the struggle for independence in India. Winston Churchill, having created popularity back home by his exploits, was to become a politician and eventual wartime leader of Britain.

During the course of his activities during the Boer War, Churchill was taken prisoner after his armoured train was ambushed by a Boer force, allegedly led by Botha. Churchill escaped to be somewhat of a national hero at home. Before escaping prison, he left a letter of apology on his bed which read, "I have the honour to inform you that as I do not consider that your Government have any right to detain me as a military prisoner, I have decided therefore to escape from your custody." He made his way to Mozambique, forging rivers and hiding in various mine shafts to avoid capture.

As a matter of interest, I've often wondered what the link was between Liverpool Football Club with its Kop stand and Spion Kop. It arose from an article by the sports editor of the Liverpool Echo in 1906, who likened the spectators on the mound at one end of the ground to resembling soldiers standing on Spion Kop, a reference to the heavy losses suffered by the local regiment during that war in South Africa.

Cecil Rhodes

Whilst on the subject of colonies and colonial rule in Africa, I was intrigued to read in the *Telegraph* in January 2017 reference to activists who were campaigning to remove the statue of Cecil Rhodes from Oriel College in Oxford on the grounds that it symbolised racism and colonialism. In particular, it mentioned that a twenty-three-year-old South African student, Joshua Nott, who had been a leading activist against Rhodes and his statues in South Africa, had just been offered and accepted a Rhodes scholarship at Oriel College, Oxford. I can fully understand his change of mind: if you can't change history, take advantage of it!

Rhodes was born in 1853, the fifth son of a vicar. He was a sickly child and sent out to stay with his brother in South Africa to recover. He returned to the UK in 1873 to attend Oriel College, Oxford, but only stayed for one term. In 1871 he bought a claim to diamond mining, which led to the formation of the De Beers Company. In seventeen years, he had acquired nearly all the small diamond mines around Kimberley. By this time, he also headed the British South Africa Company, which on behalf of the British government annexed the territory of Mashonaland, later to become Southern Rhodesia, and so named in his honour. Cecil Rhodes went on to become prime minister of Cape Colony from 1890 to 1896. His greatest legacy has been the Rhodes Scholarships. Since its foundation in the 1820s, Rhodes Scholars have included people like President Bill Clinton, physicist Leonard Huxley, astronomer Edwin Hubble, leading scientists, philosophers, physicians, prime ministers, governors general, historians, and many leading figures from other walks of life—too many to list here.

It is true that Rhodes was a racist, a believer in white supremacy, and a staunch colonialist, but in the late nineteenth century he was a dominant figure in South Africa. Like it or not, you cannot and should not attempt to change history. What you should do is learn from it.

Return to Cape Town

I had viewed Table Mountain initially from our ship all those years ago, when it was shrouded in low cloud; it looked dark and threatening as it towered over the city like a great defensive wall. Its very presence seemed challenging. It was also a time of apartheid, when segregation was determined not by social status but by the colour of your skin. Now, on my return the city and the surrounding area, the mountain, looked somewhat benign, almost inviting. Who am I to refuse such a challenge? So, on a blue, cloudless day I took up the challenge. The view from the top was fantastic, looking out across the city whilst in the background, looming grey against the horizon, lay the infamous Robbin Island, noted for its famous prisoner

Nelson Mandela, the first black president of South Africa who spent eighteen of his twenty-seven years as a prisoner on the island. Much as I wanted to get across to the island and get a feel for what life would have been like, incarcerated for what would have been a lifetime, it was not to be. You have to admire Mandela because despite the hardships and the depravation, he never gave in and never showed any signs of resentment and bitterness. Unfortunately, I didn't get across to the island because the sea was far too turbulent for any movement by ship, and the high winds precluded movement by air. Maybe there will be another time.

A word about Mandela. He was a controversial but charismatic figure who spent most of his life as a South African revolutionary political leader. With fears of a civil war looming, F. W. de Klerk, the then president, released him from prison in 1990. Once established as president, Mandela was instrumental in the drive for national reconciliation but retired after one term in office. His fight to overcome apartheid became a beacon for democracy for many around the world.

Conflict in Africa

It is not only South Africa that has experienced unrest during recent years. There are many areas of the continent that have undergone significant change since the pre-independent days of the 1960s. Conflicts have become a distinct characteristic of the continent both north and south, but more especially the area of sub-Saharan Africa, which stretches from Mauritania in the west to the Sudan and Somalia in the east.

When you consider what has happened since decolonisation developed in the 1950s and 1960s, there have been a series of civil wars: Sudan, Chad, Angola, Liberia, Nigeria, Somalia, Burundi, Rwanda, the Republic of the Congo, South Sudan, and Dufur, to name but a few. Inevitably this has led to a breeding ground for terrorists such as Al-Qaeda and its many Islamic variants such as Boko Haram, Al Shabab, and Islamic Maghreb, leading to instability throughout the area.

The causes are many and varied, but inevitably there were corrupt and inept political elites supported or controlled by military powers, heavily predicated on using the country's rich resources rather than improving low living standards, which only encourages support of terrorist organisations and leads to armed conflict and coups and counter coups. Even as I write, what was considered a democratic improvement in the voting process in Zimbabwe is now appearing to unravel into anarchy following the coup in 2017.

During 2017, General Constantino Chiwenga, the head of the army, visited China. Days later he instigated the army-led coup that removed Mugabe from power. Emmerson Mnangagwa, a one-time supporter of Mugabe, and known as Ngwena (crocodile), assumed power as president of the Second Republic. Incidentally, Zimbabwe is the name given to the former British colony of Southern Rhodesia. The latest indications are that Mnangagwa, as the current president, has been elected with 50.8 per cent of the vote, which has sparked off rioting. It now remains to be seen if democracy will survive in Zimbabwe.

Involvement of External Powers in Africa

Inevitably, it is in such times of change that others seek out opportunities, whether it is through trade, military opportunity, or political influence. Such events are developing throughout these areas of Africa. Both Russia and China are stepping up their involvement as the United States withdraws from some of its commitments.

The Chinese government has established what it has said are commercial and military agreements with Djibouti. In addition to funding a £3 billion rail project between Djibouti and Ethiopia and a £230 million freshwater pipeline, China has established its first overseas base in Djibouti. Located close to the port of Doraleh and also to the only US base in Africa at Camp Lemonnier, barely a few miles away, it is supposedly a support facility for the Chinese navy as well as being a commercial port outlet. It is interesting to note that it occupies a strategic location on the Bab-el-Mandeb and overlooks the Gulf of Aden. Aden has always been of significant importance, which raises the question why British defence policy (withdrawal from east of Suez) caused us to vacate this important location situated on such a vital route for both trade and oil supplies.

In contrast to both Russia and China, US influence in sub-Saharan Africa has diminished in recent years. Russia has increased its involvement and is looking to expand its influence across the continent, Approximately, twenty-eight of fifty-five African nations now have trade agreements with Russia. Why the interest in Africa? The answer lies in both commercial and military opportunities, not least of which are the vast rich natural resources, gold, diamonds, oil, and minerals which are being exploited across the continent, which give rise to the opportunity for investment and trade, seen by the Russians as an essential offset against trade sanctions imposed by the West. For example, Russia has started plans to build a £2.3 billion platinum mine in Zimbabwe, and it committed £3 billion to build and operate a crude oil refinery in Uganda, developing the world's largest diamond deposits in Angola and bilateral trade agreements to explore vast oil deposits in Sudan. Russia military involvement is significant, with peace-keeping activities that now outstrip the combined totals of the United States, UK, and France. It also has other military activities such as the training of Nigerian special forces, the opening of a Russian language school in Kinshasa, and of course the ever-increasing arms sales to a number of African countries.

CHAPTER 31

The Final Challenge

Life would be infinitely happier if we could only be
born at the age of 80 and gradually approach 18.
Mark Twain

Uncertainty still prevails in the world, but nowhere more than in
Europe, where greater strains are being placed on the European
Union, such as changes in leadership in both Spain, arising from a
vote of no confidence, and in Italy, where elections have led to a hung
parliament. There are five countries within the EU who have debts
larger than their economies: Greece, Portugal, Eire, Italy, and Spain.
Greece in particular has been struggling for two years and, at the time
of this writing, goes for elections on 17 June 2018 or the second time
in six weeks because of its debt crisis. Elsewhere, the ongoing Turkish
currency and debt crisis has reached $453.2 billion of external debt,
giving rise to financial contagion across the Western world. At the same
time, the United States appears to be drifting back into isolationism
with Trump's policy of "America First", which could lead to a tariff war
by which no nation benefits, causing consternation amongst its allies
and possible implications for the whole Western alliance.

Meanwhile at home, the uncertainties arising out of Brexit, the
inflexibility of Brussels, and the difficulties of the government holding
together a fractious group within Parliament does not auger well for
our own future. Representing the people, but not representing their

views! I'm of the opinion that politicians of whatever shade are not good poker players, and if they are, they have the tendency to play with the wrong cards—or conversely, they are playing the wrong game. That's why when the electorate becomes frustrated, they shuffle the pack.

There isn't a year that goes by without some form of natural tragedy taking us by surprise, and one has to say in this day and age, these things are so unpredictable. Here we are in July 2018, possessing all manner of highly technical instrumentation by which to make certain predictions, and yet once again we get caught out: the Fuego volcano. Perhaps there is more to this long, hot summer than we can imagine.

Across America and Back

On a more conventional theme, or should I say unconventional theme, I started my long walk for charity at the end of February 2017 and aim to finish before the end of the summer of 2018. This time it is for Alzheimer's' (Dementia) and entails a walk across North America, the East Coast to the West Coast, up to Canada and then back to the East Coast. Clearly, I couldn't afford the time or the costs to physically complete the task on the North American continent, so it meant simulating it wherever I happened to be by walking the same distance, approximately five thousand miles. However, the mileage has to be on the roads, not on the treadmills or other artificial aids. The route I selected started in South Carolina and crossed through Atlanta, Dallas, Phoenix, and on to San Diego before moving up the West Coast. The second leg traversed the West Coast through to San Francisco and then across the Canadian Border at Vancouver. The final leg was from Vancouver via South Dakota and the Great Lakes to Pittsburgh and New York. I did think of flying out so that I could make the grand finale in real time, but the costs would have far outweighed the income from gifts, so I thought that I would make my own donation to the charity.

As I approach the autumn of my youth, or so it seems, I like to think that to some extent I fall into Mark Twain's category of declining humanity. It's a view that I've long shared with Mark Twain over many years. I would simply add to have all that knowledge, wisdom, wealth, and experience, plus a youthful body to go with it, would indeed be a challenge worth having. So, what remains to be done before I reach my "teens"? Well, I think that it's time to draw a line in the sand as regards the extremes in fundraising and to recognise that I'm no longer eighteen. Therefore, as I reach the closing chapter of this epistle, I shall settle back into what others call retirement. It remains for me to finish my walk across North America and back, scheduled to be completed before the end of 2018, having walked six thousand miles in less than twenty months. Not bad for an eighteen-year-old in an eighty-three-year-old's frame! After all, walking is no more than one step away from your past and one step closer to your future.

In June 2019 I will have finished my second four-year term as a nonexecutive director on the board of British Gymnastics and as president. I shall hand over to my successor prior to the Olympic Games in Tokyo. On the one hand, I will enjoy the additional time this will give me without withdrawing altogether from a sport which I feel passionate about. On the other hand, I shall miss the challenges, the companionship, and the opportunity to be involved in developing a sport which has made significant advancements and achievements in the last ten years—a period during which we have moved from being an also ran on the world stage to one where we are one of the main contenders.

Russian Increased Involvement

As the decade moves towards its final years, and as many of us also head in the same direction, it is perhaps appropriate that we reflect on the direction in which the world is heading. Oh, for Merlin and that crystal ball. On the political front, we see a darker side in the re-emergence of a more sinister and ruthless Russian state—first in its overt actions over the Crimea and the Ukraine in general and the cynical support of oppressive regimes such as Assad's Syria, and second in its more covert approach in dealing with those who oppose or even question the manner in which the regime under Vladimir Putin is developing. There is blatant disregard for the democratic rights of states or individuals, as well as the assassination of those who have opposed the Motherland. From a personal perspective, there are three aspects that cause me concern: the cynical support of rouge states and terrorism, the covert introduction of biological and chemical elements against international conventions, and the selective assassination of those who might question the state.

The most cynical action taken by the Russians in recent years was the poisoning of Sergei and Yulia Skripal in Salisbury during March 2018 through the use of a chemical nerve agent Novichock developed by the Russians in the 1970s and 1980s. It is said to be the most fatal of nerve agents ever developed, five times more potent than Sarin gas (developed by the Nazis) or VX. It was designed by the Russians to be undetectable. It prevents the normal breakdown of a neurotransmitter acelylcholine, which causes muscles to contract involuntarily, leading to respiratory failure through the result of copious fluid secretions filling the lungs and resulting in cardiac arrest. There is no known cure, although there are a number of antidotes, including atropine and diazepam, which could help if introduced in sufficient time. Its use, as with all nerve agents, is banned under UN law.

Sergai Skripal was a former colonel in Russian Intelligence who became a double agent for British Intelligence and was subsequently arrested by the Russians. Following negotiations between the UK government and the Russians, he was eventually exchanged for a Russian counterpart. It is believed that the assassination attempt was carried out by members of the GRU military intelligence service acting under direct orders from Putin. One must never forget that Putin himself was a member of the KGB, of which the GRU is a less acceptable adjunct, so such an assumption would not be outside the bounds of probability. Added to which, it is a message they would want to send to potential spies in the future: betray us and pay the price.

The assumption from evidence gathered is that the Novichock was transported in a perfume bottle and smeared on the door handle of the Skripals' house. The police have retrieved the bottle following the death of Dawn Sturgess, who, it is believed, found the perfume bottle in a nearby park toilet. It is suspected that several Russians were involved in this covert operation and that police have identified two from facial recognition, both of whom left the country under false identities shortly afterwards. They were originally identified as Alexander Petrov and Rusian Bellingent, and both have alleged connections to the Defence Ministry. However, this could have been a botched effort arising from conflicting interests between Russian intelligence agencies.

Subsequent revelations by Bellingcat, an award-winning online investigative team, has established conclusively that the individual named as Rusian Boshirov is in fact Colonel Anatoliy Chepiga, of the elite Fourth Spetznaz Brigade under the command of the GRU. A BBC team, following up on this investigation, visited the village of Beryokovkoy close to Russia's border with China and some five thousand miles from Moscow. It's a village in which Anatoliy spent his childhood. A woman in the village identified Anatoliy in the photograph, and she said he had recently visited his home in the village, accompanied by his son.

It is not unusual for such agents to be trained as military attachés in embassies. But it is most unusual for a highly ranked military individual with twenty military decorations, including Hero of the Soviet Union, to be given such a task. It would normally be carried out by a field operative of a lower rank. That implies the order for the attempted assassination came from a very high level, if not from the very top. Whatever the truth behind the attack, it led to a serious diplomatic breach, with the UK expelling twenty-three Russians and accusing the Russians of an attack on British sovereignty. The United States then expelled a further sixty Russians, and many other countries did the same. As a result, there has been heightened tension, with increased military activity on the borders and in the air being monitored by NATO.

Conversely, we see what the likely transitions are towards more agreeable positions with the United States in the attitudes of Korea and China, so perhaps all is not doom and gloom, although the waters are being continually muddied by Trump. I like to believe that I'm an optimist and look for the good in everyone and retain my hope for the future despite all the obstacles and my doubts. Whilst on the subject of China, it has overtaken the United States as the world's largest trading nation, and by the end of 2018 it is estimated to have the world's largest economy.

Domestic Issues

On the domestic front, the uncertainty surrounding Brexit continues to create concern. There are those who consider things have changed significantly since the referendum and want there to be a further referendum. Then there are those who say the UK government and the EU should deliver what the electorate called for. The country is divided, as is parliament, and I'm sure there is equal concern across Europe; nothing is ever what it seems. It appears to me that both sides are playing a dangerous game of brinkmanship.

On a more personal note, there will be other parallel ways that bring this decade and these memoirs to a conclusion. I well remember a film entitled *Four Weddings and a Funeral*, a romantic comedy starring Hugh Grant and Andie MacDowell made in 1994. Perhaps it's a time we live through, but at my time of life, the sadness for me is that funerals become more frequent than weddings. In the early days, it was predominantly about parties, engagements, weddings, and christenings. In later years it's the more depressing loss of family, in my case involving both of my sisters and my older brother, as well as several friends. Alas, from my perspective, it's been the opposite of the film—it's been four funerals and a wedding. The one ray of sunshine has been the wedding of Jack and Jess, the first of my grandchildren to launch into marriage. Like many youngsters these days, they chose the unusual route, having bought a house together and planned their wedding well in advance, and selecting a venue which challenged everyone's travel plans. How about a farmhouse, miles from anywhere, on the edge of Dartmoor? It was a great occasion with many friends and relatives, some camping out. But novel as it was, I'd rather the comforts of the hotel I had. That's the sadness of advancing years: comfort before adventure. Now here I am, a year later, awaiting the arrival of my first great grandchild. How Sheila would have loved being the grand matriarch, and the child is due on Sheila's birthday. Alas, that will never happen in our family—it'll be late as usual!

The downside has been the loss of another sibling when Shirley departed from us in mid-2018 after suffering for some time with dementia. It is so sad to witness people suffering the loss of mental faculties, especially when they have difficulties recognising their own kith and kin. As with family tradition—well, our family in particular—funerals become more a celebration of life and, despite the loss, a time of celebration. Well, any excuse for a family party. Years ago, it was us listening to stories about the great aunts and great uncles. Suddenly, I discover we are them, and here we are telling sons and daughters, nieces and nephews, about the good (bad) old days. A fantastic opportunity for a get-together, no expense spared, which Shirley would have been furious to have missed. But like all of these losses, though it provides many happy memories, it does leave a gap.

Jane and Richard had to get back for work, but Jonathan, Julie, and I stayed on for a day because they wished to visit old haunts, one of which was the RAF Staff College at Bracknell, where we had lived in 1974 whilst I attended the college. Suddenly I realised that well over forty years had passed, and things are not what they might have been. The college buildings, a lovely eighteenth-century country house set in many acres of lawns and with gardens and sculptured woodland, have disappeared, giving way to what can only be described as modern chicken coops. These modern flats of multiple shapes, sizes, and colours were obviously the dream child of some up-and-coming architect and lack any relationship to the setting in which they've been placed. However, at prices in excess of £500,000, somebody must like them. Part of the parkland has been left intact, and Julie and Jonathan were able to identify some areas where they had played as children. The only association with the Royal Air Force that remains is the local council's naming of roads, such as Hurricane Gate, Tornado Close, Halifax Road, and Buccaneer Road—so imaginative!

Upon returning home, it's interesting to find that little changes year on year. We are still struck by many of the natural disasters, and we seem reluctant to learn the lessons of the past. I refer in particular to the deadly eruption of the Fuego volcano in Guatemala, which caused villages such as El Rodeo, San Miguel, and Los Lotes to be buried beneath pyroclastic flows of molten lava and ash, affecting more than 1.7 million people, with 3,000 evacuated and over 800 dead or missing. This was the volcano's most violent eruption for over 100 years, and it sent ash to levels in excess of 33,000 feet. Pyroclastic flows are fast-moving mixtures of gas and volcanic materials such as pumice, rock, and ash. The flows can travel at speeds in excess of 700 kilometres per hour, close to the speed of a modern jet airliner, at temperatures between 200–700 degrees Celsius, burning and burying everything in their paths. This is similar to the destruction of Pompeii and Herculaneum in AD 79 when the flows took minutes to travel many miles.

The National Institute for Seismology and Volcanology said it gave the relevant warning in plenty of time, but this was not heeded by the civilian authorities, and timely evacuation did not take place. Heavy rain, causing fresh landslides of volcanic mud and warnings of new pyroclastic flows, added to the problems. As I said, we never seem to learn.

CHAPTER 32

Days to Remember

When you go home tell them of us and say, "For
your tomorrow we gave our today."
John Maxwell Edmunds

When I joined London Transport in 1992, I was asked by the board
of directors, as one of the more recent officers to have served in the
armed forces, to lead the LTOCA contingent on the march to the
Cenotaph in Whitehall each Remembrance Day. I was subsequently
invited by the London Transport Old Comrades (LTOCA) committee
and members to become the president of the LTOCA, a position I've
held by election each year ever since. There has only been one occasion
that I haven't been able to march to the Cenotaph or lay the wreath.

The objectives of the LTOCA are to perpetuate the memory of those
who made the supreme sacrifice in the service of their country and
to preserve the spirit of comradeship amongst all ex-service personnel,
past and present. These objectives are achieved through participation
in the march to and from the Cenotaph in Whitehall on Armistice
Sunday each November; attendance at the Field of Remembrance
at Westminster Abbey, at LT's own memorial in Broadway, and
at County Hall; and the holding of a reunion dinner on the Friday
preceding Remembrance Sunday in London, where the guest of
honour is usually one of the heads of the armed services. Many of
our members also make the pilgrimage to the battlefields of both

World Wars in Europe and to the special services at the Menin Gate in Belgium and the Dunkirk beaches in France. However, the association also is involved in several other activities throughout the year, ranging from assistance to old comrades and their families, visits to many battlefield sites, and developing and maintaining links with other services or ex-service associations. It has also been TfL practice, over the past twenty-five years, to hold a reunion luncheon for the LTOCA marchers.

But let me return to the reasons why an organisation such as London Transport has such a special place in what originated as a military parade organised by the Royal British Legion following the 1914–1918 Great War. In 1920, kind George V granted a unique honour to the London General Omnibus Company: to become part of London Buses and the forerunner of today's Transport for London. This honour established London Transport as the only civilian organisation at that time to march alongside the armed forces in the Remembrance Day Parade. The honour was in recognition of the service rendered by the men of the London General Omnibus Company, who served as soldiers and drove their buses, carrying troops and equipment to and from the front line in France during World War I. Although changes have taken place over the years, London Transport, in its various guises, maintains the position of last in line on Remembrance Day in Whitehall each year.

In 1919, George Gwynn, a driver at Merton Garage, wrote,

> I left on 22 October 1914 with the very same bus (B1219) as had been in service between Raynes Park and Liverpool Street. She had done good work, taking part in the First and Second Battles of Ypres, the Battle of Le Bassee, the Battle of Neuve-Chapelle and the Battle of Loos. Did her bit in our Somme offensive, and again at the Battle of Arras, at Cambrai, and also at Messines Ridge. Then again she did some good work in rushing reinforcements up to Bailleui … and then loaded with some of our brave troops to Mons.

Also, a closely guarded secret was the provision of a 5-mile tunnel, 36 feet in diameter and situated under 3 stations (at Wanstead, Redbridge, and Gants Hill), providing 300,000 square feet of factory space for the production of aircraft parts, together with a subterranean canteen for 600 people and 4 mess rooms seating 1,600 people. It had additional entries at Cambridge Park and Daneshurst Gardens. No employee in the factory had more than 400 yards to walk to their place of work—an important aspect during the Blitz.

In addition to those from London Transport who made the ultimate sacrifice in both World Wars, there were many who served in both conflicts or have seen active service in the various emergency theatres of war that have arisen subsequently, including the more recent events in Europe, the Middle East, and Asia. As the years progress, it becomes more difficult to retain links through our older members. Nevertheless, there are a growing number of new veterans arising from the many peacekeeping operations involving British servicemen and women around the globe. Indeed, there are a few within our organisation still actively involved as reserve forces in support of operations overseas.

Knowing of my involvement with the LTOCA and my interest in military and family history, my children and grandchildren have organised a family tour of the European battlefields to mark my eighty-third birthday. Like me, some of them have heard of the personal recollections about life in the trenches during World War I, especially the horrific stories of the Somme where 19,000 British and Commonwealth soldiers were killed in just one day—a very sobering thought. "Theirs not to reason why, theirs just to do and die." Our visit is going to be a comprehensive tour exploring the World War I sites of Flanders and the Somme, Vimy Ridge, Essex Farm, Tyne Cot, Thiepval, and the Menin Gate in Ypres.

During the 1980s when I was in Germany, we made many journeys back to the UK by road and often into or through France, to the south or on visits to Paris. We frequently passed many of the individual cemeteries and monuments, some small with perhaps no more than twenty soldiers graves and others such as Thiepval, the largest British war memorial in the world commemorating over 72,000 soldiers. However, during our time in Germany, there was never sufficient time to stop, much to my regret. More recently, I've been making several trips a year to Brussels, Ostend, and Ypres for meetings, but there is never sufficient time or the opportunity to visit any of the sites. It is always something I've wanted to rectify.

Sheila's father served as a young soldier initially in the Manchester Regiment during World War I and was injured on the Somme. After some weeks recovering in the UK, he was returned to take part in the Third Battle of Ypres, one of the bloodiest battles of the war, in 1917; it is frequently referred to as the Battle of Passchendaele. Heavy rains had turned the Flanders fields into a quagmire during the battle that raged for three months over a five-mile stretch of countryside and claimed the lives of some 325,000 Allied soldiers and 260,000 Germans. The irony is that by early 1918, the Germans had recovered the lost territory, albeit at great cost. Almost 600,000 fought and died over barely 5 miles of territory! It was the war to end wars, in which more than 7.6 million individuals took part in a global conflict that shapes the world in which we live today, and where women for the first time took over the traditional roles which had previously been carried out by men who could then join the war. It was a war that didn't end wars, because within twenty-one years World War II started.

Like many of those who survived the war, Jack Holland was very reluctant to talk about his experience, although over the years I was able to coax a little from him. To me, it seemed he suffered (as many did) from the survivor guilt complex. On occasions when I did get him to say something, his eyes would glaze over as though seeing it all happening again and reliving the conditions: the smell, the noise, the atrocious weather, and the fear. He described how on one such occasion, he regained consciousness to find himself in a massive shell crater partially filled with water, and with no idea where the rest of his platoon were.

On the opposite side of the crater was an exhausted German soldier. Neither spoke the other's language, but Jack offered him his drinking water bottle, in which he had some rum. I didn't ask him where he got it from! Jack was the only one who still had his rifle, and he took the German back to his own lines. From all accounts, the German was none too reluctant. This saved Jack from being charged as a deserter and receiving a death sentence. In those days, there was no such thing as shell shock, or as we would call it these days, post-traumatic stress disorder. As to other stories, they were few and far between, and I found this to be the case with others of that vintage who had been through similar experiences.

CHAPTER 33

Back to Where It Almost Began

Things happen once only and are never repeated,
never return. Except in memory.
Damon Galgut

Although I'd travelled back to Malaya, or Malaysia as it is now called,
I had never gone back to Singapore and Changi to rekindle my early
days in the RAF. That was a time of many memories. It had always
intrigued me as to what might have changed over sixty years, and
when the chance arose in 2018 to visit, I leapt at the opportunity to
combine a cruise in the Far East with a return to a place of happy
memories. Alas, it is the case of something only happening once, and
it can never be repeated. Memories should be left as such; one should
not seek to live them again.

Hong Kong

In August 2018, I departed the UK to fly to Hong Kong. A former
British colony situated at the mouth of the Pearl River, Hong Kong
comprises three main areas, Hong Kong Island as well as Kowloon and
the New Territories, both on the mainland. Hong Kong was handed
back to the Republic of China at the end of its ninety-nine-year lease
in 1997, and it now has special status as an autonomous territory
within China. As well as being a major port, a global financial centre,

and the world's seventh largest trading entity, it is also the fourth most densely populated region in the world. Since the Chinese assumed control, there has been considerable new building, especially of high-rise flats, on reclaimed land.

Two things I had set out in my bucket list of things to do was to take the traditional Star Ferry from Kowloon to Hong Kong Island—a must for anyone visiting the island. The second was a tram ride on the historical rail to Victoria Peak, also known as Mt Austin; it's the highest point on the island and provides a spectacular view of the surrounding area. On the third day I boarded the *Voyager of the Seas* and set sail for Vietnam. In retrospect, I was grateful for the fact that I'd missed typhoon Mangkhaut by a matter of days. Although it didn't wreak the same degree of havoc as it did in the Philippines, it still left substantial damage.

Vietnam

To many, Vietnam is synonymous with the war in the 1960s and the support of the Americans in opposing the spread of communism, but it had its roots in the 1950s. Prior to World War II, the French had ruled over the region as a colonial power since 1887, hence the name for the region being French Indochina. The Viet Minh, under Ho Chi Minh, fought a terrorist campaign against the Japanese invaders and, following the war, against the French who attempted to reinforce colonial rule. Between March and May 1954, the French troops faced a humiliating defeat at the battle of Dien Bien Phu, marking the end of French rule in Indochina. The North came under communist control, and the Viet Minh was dissolved in 1960. In the meanwhile, North Vietnam, with Chinese and Russian military and economic aid, infiltrated South Vietnam in support of the Vietcong, who had been waging a terrorist campaign in the South since the Japanese invasion. In the process, the Vietcong had built an elaborate complex of tunnels stretching for seventy-five miles in which they stockpiled weapons and supplies, concentrated troops, and even established basic hospital facilities and shelter for families. The tunnels had ventilation systems concealed in trees or rocks adjacent to the routes to the tunnels. Added to which, access points were often booby-trapped' with mines or other more basic traps, and the whole system was well concealed by natural vegetation.

It was one part of this complex that I wanted to visit, close to what had been an American base very near Ho Chi Minh City (formerly Saigon) and now referred to as the Chu Chi Tunnels. As I was to discover, the tunnels were narrow and claustrophobic and often infested with scorpions, snakes, and venomous centipedes, so I didn't spend too much time admiring the scenery. Whilst some of the access points had been widened, they didn't take account of the modern Western body shape; I'm far from corpulent and still had a struggle to drop down into the tunnels.

Few people realise that at the height of the Tet Offensive in 1968, the United States had almost 500,000 troops in the field supported by 850,000 South Vietnamese and allied troops, but they were opposed by a much larger North Vietnamese force that was supported by 170,000 Chinese, 81,000 Russians, and 600,000 North Koreans. The casualties were equally dramatic, with 1.1 million North Vietnamese killed as against 250,000 South Vietnamese troops and over 58,000 US troops. The war came to an end in 1975 with the fall of Saigon following American withdrawal in 1973, and it culminated in the reunification of the North and South. Whilst it is still a communist country in political terms, since 1986 it has adopted a market-orientated economy which has led to substantial economic growth.

Thailand

Once again, a country that reverts to a name we never knew in our school days when it was always Siam; in later years, it was linked to the book by Margaret Landon entitled *Anna and the King of Siam*, later adapted as a film and play called *The King and I*. It's a story about Anna Leonowens, a widow with two children who was invited to Siam by King Rama IV (better known as King Mongkut, who reigned from 1851 to 1868) to teach his children English language and culture. During his reign, he opened up his country to Western influence.

In touring Bangkok, the capital of the country and the most populous centre of over 8 million people, one experiences the blend of cultures where East meets West. The roads are awash with scooters carrying anything from one to a family of four. Alongside the busy roads are both modern and traditional shops with residential housing situated immediately behind them. Situated alongside the Chao Phraya River delta the city is surrounded by an area occupied by 14 million inhabitants. On the side of the river sits the Royal Palace surrounded by an artificial canal, thus forming an island known as Rattanakosin Island. The Grand Palace has been in existence since 1782, when the Chakri Dynasty was founded by King Rama I. As a Buddhist country, its royal citadel has many wats (Buddhist royal temples or sacred precincts). The most famous, the Wat Prachetupon, houses the golden reclining Buddha. There was one thing I shall always remember: riding in a tut-tut, a motorised version of a rickshaw, and wondering if I would survive the traffic that didn't seem to differentiate between left and right.

To avoid this seeming like a travelogue, I haven't covered all are ports of call or all the aspects of the visits we made; suffice to say they were many and varied. I was of course concentrating on memory lane and the return to Singapore and Malaya, or should I say Malaysia.

Singapore

In due course we arrived in Singapore, but there was little of the harbour front that I recognised. It was sixty years ago since I'd seen it, and the world has moved on. As I implied earlier, never go back searching for memories; leave them as dusty reminiscences, intriguing to those who follow but meaningful only to oneself.

Much of the seafront is farther out to sea, clearly a sign of land reclamation and the construction of massive buildings that screen off those areas I used to know, such as the Padang and Collier Quay. Even China town seemed to have retreated in land, and had it not been for the cathedral dwarfed by super towers and Raffles, I would have been lost. Not wanting to lose face or indeed direction in front of Steve and

Jackie, I suggested we take a taxi into Chinatown, where we had lunch before going on to Fort Canning Hotel and then a visit to the Bunker on Fort Canning Hill, a location from which the British retreat from Singapore and eventual surrender in 1942 was coordinated. In the words of Winston Churchill, it was "the worst disaster and largest capitulation in British history".

I know that hindsight is always a gift the further one retreats from the actual event, but even I have to question the inadequate defence of Singapore all those many years ago. As a simple airman, two things stay uppermost in my mind. First, why did the military planners—and I use military in its general term—commit and eventually cause the loss of two powerful warships, the *Prince of Wales* and the *Repulse*, to the northern coast of Malaya to attack the Japanese invasion force without adequate defence either by land or air, especially when it was known that the Japanese had control of the air at that time? Both vessels were sunk by Japanese torpedo bombers after the fleet commander, Admiral Sir Tom Phillips, failed to call for air support, favouring radio silence. Second, given they had a superior military force and knew that the Japanese were running out of ammunition with overstretched lines of communication, why wasn't more damage done to the causeway to delay the enemy longer? I know that there were other considerations, such as lack of food and water. Nevertheless, it still appears an easy capitulation. But as I said earlier, hindsight is a wonderful thing.

Above all, what I wanted to see where the changes to Changi since my time as an airman in the 1950s. The establishment of Changi as an airfield was initiated by the Japanese, who used Allied prisoners of war to build the runway during 1943–1944. Following their surrender after the dropping of the atomic bombs on Hiroshima and Nagasaki, ironically the runway was completed by Japanese prisoners of war in 1946 when the RAF took over Changi. The other infamous association with Changi, apart from the many atrocities during the Japanese occupation of the island, was the Changi Prison, which I had visited during the 1950s—a place of many dark memories.

Changi is now one of the biggest air hubs in the Far East. The massive changes to the airfield and associated complex, the modern road systems and high-rise buildings, have changed the whole perspective. I remember the main street of the village lined on both sides with corrugated roofed, timber shops. There were names such as the Lucky Silk Store, selling everything from silks to watches, from tape machines to binoculars. There was also a tailor's shop—I think it was called Singh's—where you could have a shirt or a suit made overnight. The cinema was replaced by a bus terminus and eating stalls scattered throughout the village, which resembled one of those settings for an old western film. However, many of the roads still retain the old RAF-associated names such as Hendon Road, Farnborough Road, Cranwell Road, Biggin Hill Road, and many others. Ah, such memories!

We were to return to Singapore on two further occasions during the cruise, which gave us ample opportunity to see as much as we could, including a Singapore gin sling in Raffles and, on our final visit, a visit to the top of the Marina Bay Sands hotel overlooking the F1 Grand Prix circuit, which gave us the opportunity to see the final day's practice. The top of the hotel is shaped like an open-topped boat with both ends overlapping the triple towers and containing a glass-bottomed swimming pool as well as an observation point. If you don't suffer from vertigo, you certainly will after going there. I was less affected by a visit to the world's tallest building, the Burj Khalifa, in Dubai.

Penang Island

This was my first visit to Penang since competing in the Malaysian Athletics Championships in 1956, and though George Town remains very much as it was, the surrounding areas have changed significantly over the years. There are now two bridges connecting the island to the mainland. The Penang Bridge, built in the 1980s and 8.5 miles long, is built to withstand earthquakes of 7.5. The second bridge, the Sultan Abdul Halim Muadzam Shah to the south, is 14.9 miles long and was opened in 2014. It was constructed to resist seismic activity near the

Sunda tectonic plate. Previously, visits to Penang had to be made by ferry from Butterworth on the mainland.

Kuala Lumpur

I've lost count of the number of times I've been to Kuala Lumpur and the Batu Caves, a location that always provides the wow factor to all the visitors; Jackie and Steve were no exception. We had two problems. We arrived on a major Buddhist holiday and left in a monsoon of some deluge. However, it took away nothing from the experience. An hour later, we were in the centre of KL viewing the Pretonas Towers, at 1,483 feet the tallest twin towers in the world. Unfortunately, it was a public holiday, and the tower was closed. However, the KL Communications Tower at 1,381 feet was open. The downside was the crowds generated by the holiday! Nevertheless, it was a breath-taking view despite the overcast weather.

Our visit to Phuket, and thereby a return to Thailand, marked the beginning of the end of our saga. Phuket's major attraction has to be the beaches, particularly on the north-west of the island. However, it was this very area that was struck by a tsunami on Boxing Day 2004 following an earthquake in the Indian Ocean, which caused devastation and the death of 250 people on the island. On the north-east side of Phuket is the Phi Phi Island, better known to many as the James Bond Island.

CHAPTER 34

End of an Era

A story has no beginning or end: arbitrarily one chooses that moment
of experience from which to look back or from which to look ahead.
Graham Greene

And so we move towards the end of the second decade of this
millennium, a period of social, economic, and political crisis. The
European debt crisis impacting on Greece, Ireland, and Portugal,
with perhaps a few other nations such as Turkey heading in a similar
direction. The crisis arising from the Arab Spring impacting on
Egypt, Tunisia, Libya, Bahrein. The Yemen and Syria, to name but
a few, where many thought democratic improvements would occur,
but instead disorder reigned supreme and extremism stepped in to
fill the void. The Syrian Civil War bringing the superpowers head-
to-head and resulting in a European refugee crisis, further fuelled by
the conflicts in central Africa and as far afield as Afghanistan and
Pakistan. The movement of people being further exploited by so-called
people traffickers in North Africa and elsewhere. The major impacts
being experienced in Turkey and the central Mediterranean countries
such as Italy and Greece, all of which is now beginning to influence
political direction stemming from the reactions of voters across
Europe.

Relationships with and within the European Union

I can't conclude without further reference to our membership of the European Union and the referendum which started us on the road to Brexit or, as is hoped for, a different form of relationship with the other member nations. Don't hold your breath because there are too many vested interests at play to have a simple and acceptable solution to the problem, not only within Europe but elsewhere.

Maybe it's this influx of migrants that influenced the way the referendum on our leaving the European Union transpired, created by the desire to control our own borders and the fear of losing jobs. However, I think it was more complex than that. From my perspective, this was only one of the problems. There were other factors such as the bureaucracy of unelected officials in control of events in Brussels, the gravy train of highly paid and ineffective politicians, and the ridiculous costs of moving the complete organisation from Brussels in Belgium to Strasburg in France each month. Added to this were the vested interests of individual member nations.

Although it may have some points in its favour for holding together a disparate conglomeration of nations it is not a United States of Europe, and neither was it ever intended to be so. In the days when the UK was seeking membership of the EEC and being frustrated by that demigod of France, Charles de Gaulle, I was solidly behind the concept. But what started as an economic community has long since developed into a European Union, heavily influenced and controlled by an unelected commission which determines policies, procedures, and the legal aspects of all its citizens. Certainly, there are some controls imposed by elected officials, namely the MEPs, but they are mainly concerned with local interests, and as Nigel Farage said when addressing the Parliament two years ago, most of them lack experience of the real world. Setting that aside, the European Parliament has become a large, expensive circus—and a travelling one at that.

The European Parliament consists of 751 MEPs from 28 members states, the number being based on each country's population. Germany has the largest number with 96, France has 75, and the UK has 75.

The total cost of the European Parliament is approximately £1,568 billion per year. The main five contributors, who between them pay 50 per cent of the total, are Germany, UK, France, Italy, and Spain. In 2017 the UK made an estimated gross contribution of £13 billion after rebates.

Each month the European Parliament moves the three hundred miles between its headquarters in Brussels in Belgium to Strasbourg in France and back again. Why? Because the status of the circus was set in stone by the European Treaty in 1992, which states that this can only be revoked if all member states agree, and clearly France is never going to do so. Again, I ask why? The answer is obvious: it is hugely beneficial to France in the financial support of Strasbourg and the local area. I call it the travelling circus because of the large number of clowns it employs, and it has a vested interest in continuing the moves, which I will touch on later. The monthly Strasbourg meetings, which last for only four days (and therefore forty-eight days a year), add an extra £93 million to the annual budget. The move involves 1,000 politicians, officials, and employees being moved on two chartered trains whilst about 2,500 cases of documents are transferred on five lorries. It's a ridiculous cost to taxpayers, all to solve the nationalistic egos of politicians. Although MEPs have voted with a majority of three to one to end the farce, it is not going to happen for the reasons I've already outlined.

Why do I call it a gravy train? On top of their salaries, which amount to the equivalent of £7,105 per month, they have £3,838 office allowance, travel allowances of £3,788 (first class rail and business class by air), and daily attendance allowances of £272 per day (for hotels and meals). There's no wonder some people clamber to get on the train!

Whilst leaving this last decade of my epistle, and whilst on the subject of Europe, I can't help making some reference to my transport issues and the inherent problems of car ownership and security issues. In March 2018 I discovered what many already are aware of: the use (or rather misuse) of technology and its indirect links to Europe, which is now becoming my favourite subject. Having been the proud owner of a German Mercedes car for the best part of eighteen months, I discovered that the manufacturers of this so-called prestigious car have not given much thought to its security. The vehicle, having reposed securely on my drive overnight, went absent without leave one morning in May, which I only discovered as I was about to leave home at 10 in the morning for a journey south. I had a moment of senior citizenship, trying to recall if I had left it somewhere and promising myself to take less alcohol the previous night, before remembering that I had both security lights and cameras fitted to the house. When I checked the CCTV, it revealed two youths calmly walking down the drive at 2 a.m., getting into the car, and driving it away—all within the space of twenty seconds. How? Well, apparently electronic keys used on some modern cars can be cloned anywhere and at any time from a distance of three metres—for example, in a car park and without you knowing about it. Then all they have to do is to follow you home or find out where you live. Some security! As the police said, my car is probably stolen to order and on its way to Europe in a container ship.

Trump: The Enigma

> I'm afraid you're entirely bonkers, but I'll tell
> you a secret—all the best people are.
> Lewis Carroll, *Alice in Wonderland*

And then of course we come to our loose cannon, Donald Trump—a friend to everyone and an enemy to all. He has angered his allies in Europe and has (or would appear to have) moved close to Putin. Is it that he's heard the adage "keep your friends close, but your enemies closer"? I can appreciate his desire to meet his promise to put America first, and his demands for the Europeans to meet in full their commitments with regards to paying the costs of NATO are fully justified. However, his actions in generating a trade war, especially with China, can only bring harm to the world economy. This is looking more like a return to the isolationist policies of the 1930s. How much of this is manoeuvring, I can't say, but his actions are both unpredictable and destabilising. He met with Putin in Helsinki shortly after his own legal system indicted twelve Russian military officers for conducting cyber warfare against the United States during its elections. He made no reference to Russia's annexation of the Crimea, and neither did he raise the topic of the Novichock chemical attack in southern England. All this took place without his close advisers in attendance. Add to this his criticism of the German chancellor and the undermining of Virginia May's Brexit position, and there is little wonder that even back in the United States, his actions have been heavily criticised, including by his own Republican Party, who termed his attitude of appeasement a humiliating performance in contrast to that of Putin. John Kerry, the former Democratic secretary of state, described his comments regarding Germany as disgraceful, destructive, and counter to US interests. It was also described in the US media as an historic low point in US diplomacy.

Equally worrying is his rhetoric and his use of social media to send his messages to the world. His exchange with President Rouhani, threatening to reimpose sanctions, is similar to the rhetoric exchanged with Kim Jong-Un of North Korea. But one has to ask whether it will work a second time; I'm not sure that it even worked on the first occasion. Looking at recent US intelligence, it suggests the North Koreans have already started redeveloping their missiles. However, Iran is not North Korea. Moreover, one has to consider what the likely impact will be on his relationship with America's important allies in Europe, who together with the United States signed the treaty with Iran. Especially because Trump now states that anyone trading with Iran, in any way, will have sanctions imposed on them.

Don't get me wrong. There are many aspects of his policies that are in the interests of the United States, and quite rightly these will be uppermost in his mind. Nevertheless, some of them will have far-reaching consequences on many others and an adverse impact on international trade.

CHAPTER 35

Final Reflections

I knew who I was this morning, but I've
changed a few times since then.
Lewis Carroll

Having lived through what I consider to be one of the most dramatic ages in the history of humankind, I muse on what we can look forward to in the years to come. Apart from man's inherent ability to be in a continuous state of conflict, be it domestic or universal, there have to be some significant events or achievements. I read recently of some interesting predictions made by others. I will try to put these in some semblance of order, time-wise, although I'm unlikely to be around to see the prophecies confirmed.

- 2029: The arrival of the first artificial intelligence machine that can function on intellectual tasks.
- 2030: World population to reach 8.5 billion
- 2036: 50/50 chance of curing the aging process
- 2038: 32-bit computers will overflow (where have I heard that before!)
- 2050: The world's population will have increased to 9.3 billion, an increase of 0.8 billion in 12 years. (We are running out of space.)
- Hypersonic travel will have arrived before 2050. Boeing has already revealed a concept of a hypersonic airliner flying at

speeds of Mach 5 (3,800 mph) and cruising at a height of 95,000 feet, which would enable flight times from New York to London of less than two hours. (Mind you, it will still take you as long to go through arrivals procedures at Heathrow!) Work on hypersonic missiles travelling at these speeds is already underway, with the aim of being into service by 2021.

- In the same decade, it is anticipated that a space elevator (planet-to-planet transport system) will be envisaged. (Beam me up, Scottie!)
- By the year 2050, the UK could have Europe's largest population and the largest number of migrants (UN prediction). Whatever happened to Brexit?
- Before the year 2050, China, India, the United States, Brazil, and Mexico will be the largest economies in the world (Goldman Sachs prediction).
- A century later, in 2160, Scientists predict that some people will have reached the age of 150. I was obviously born too early!

Environmental Implications

Predicting what is likely to happen in the near future is one thing. Trying to forecast what may happen in the long term is quite another and certainly beyond my capabilities. Nevertheless, the biggest concern has to be the environmental implications for our planet arising from changes that are taking place now and not in the distant future. There is no doubt that weather patterns are changing; scorching temperatures in unusual areas, massive forest wildfires, excessive droughts over large areas, melting ice fields causing a rise in sea levels, and extensive flooding and violent storms are but a few of the indicators.

Some of these factors are cyclic, created by powerful weather systems such as El Nino, a phenomenon that occurs every three to five years—and one that has a large-scale ocean atmospheric climate interaction linked to periodic warming of parts of the Pacific Ocean. This can have a large-scale impact on global weather patterns, such as creating droughts in Africa and Australia and typhoons in Japan and China. Others causes can be attributed to man's use of resources, or should

I say excessive use of resources, the overall effect of which has a detrimental impact on the environment.

These changes are undoubtedly having an increasing and accumulative adverse effect. One doesn't have to be a scientist to see the signs that are emerging through global warming: increases in air mass temperature, changes in the arctic sea, flood occurrences as atmospheric moisture increases, added storm intensity, and an increase in forest fires (which in turn add to carbon dioxide emissions).

Scientific evidence gathered in 2016 revealed temperatures that continue long-term warming trends. Average surface temperatures have risen by two degrees Fahrenheit since the late nineteenth century, driven in the main by man-made emissions, most of which have occurred in the last thirty-five years. As we have seen in recent years, the climate is getting drier, and rainfall is becoming more volatile. However, there are some things we can change, and must change, if our planet is not to become a Mars of the future. Changes have been agreed at the international level in the past, so it is not beyond the capabilities of nations to address these issues without delay, as has happened with the problems associated with depletion in the ozone layer.

The Hole in the Ozone Layer

What is the ozone layer, why is it important to life on our planet, and what has happened to it in recent years? It is a layer, or more important a shield, in the earth's atmosphere that absorbs about 95 per cent of the sun's most damaging ultraviolet radiation. Without it, life on earth would end; the radiation would damage the DNA of plants, animals, and humans, and the food chain would collapse, causing widespread extinction.

Although scientists had previously predicted problems, it was not until May 1985 that a paper was published by British Antarctic Survey scientists Farman, Gardiner, and Shanklin revealing one of the most disturbing discoveries: a rapid decline in the ozone layer. Their findings, based on observations leading up to 1984, showed that the level was estimated to be some 35 per cent lower than in the 1960s. The hole measured over the Antarctic was the size of that continent and bigger than Europe or the North American continent.

Why was the effect centred at the earth's poles, what was the cause, and how could it be contained? The very low winter temperatures, especially at the south pole, cause stratospheric clouds and ice particles to form, which in turn (through chemical reaction) enhances ozone depletion. A large percentage of these chemical changes can be attributed to us.

Since the discovery of chlorofluorocarbons (CFCs) in 1928 and their production by DuPont in 1930, they have been used in a multiplicity of manufactured goods ranging from aerosol sprays to spacecraft, from refrigerators to solvents. It was in 1974 that scientists Sherwood Rowland and Mark Molina, in examining the effects of CFC on the environment, demonstrated beyond reasonable doubt that CFCs had the ability to prevent the chemical interaction between chlorine and nitrogen, thus adding to 80 per cent of the damage to the ozone layer. For their work in this area, they were in 1995, awarded the Nobel Prize for their pioneering work in atmospheric chemistry alongside the Dutchman Paul Crutzon, who coined the phrase *Anthropocene* to describe man's drastic impact on the earth.

The fact that there had been a rapid decline of some 35 per cent in the ozone layer, increasing at a rate of 3 per cent per year, led to a ban on CFCs and their replacement by hydrofluorocarbons (HFCs), which don't contain chlorine and so have zero effect on the ozone layer. This was agreed by thirty nations at a meeting in Montreal, which brought about the Montreal Protocol in 1987, the details of which were extended to other nations in the 1990s following intervention by President Reagan and Prime Minister Thatcher. Although there are now signs of recovery, and there has been a 4 per cent improvement year on year in the depletion of ozone over the last decade, and the use of CFCs has been largely eradicated, there is still a residual effect from existing CFCs which will exist in the earth's atmosphere for up to one hundred years. We are not out of the woods yet, but at least Armageddon has been avoided.

Other Impacts on the Environment

There are other elements that are having a major impact on our environment and which could and should be better controlled: the pollution of our oceans, carbon emissions, and global warming. Over 300 million tonnes of plastic are manufactured every year, and it is estimated that some 8 million tonnes ends up in our oceans. Whilst it is extremely versatile and very useful in everyday life, plastic is also virtually indestructible. Most of it finishes up in the environment, either in landfill sites where it will take forever to decay, in lakes or rivers, and eventually in the oceans—with disastrous consequences for marine life. The residual impact is that although it eventually breaks down in the ocean into smaller elements, these in turn attract toxins, which are hydrophobic and are absorbed by plastic. Inevitably these are ingested into marine life and in turn enter the human food chain. There are other factors impacting on our oceans and the marine life therein, such as carbon emissions that are acidifying the waters, increasing global temperatures that are destroying coral reefs, and overfishing, which is depleting the food chain.

Let me not be too downbeat about these problems. My only worry is that the world was taken by surprise when the depletion of the ozone layer was identified. I dread to think that a similar complacency might exist when it comes to the other problems associated with the environment. My particular concern is that President Trump, as leader of the greatest industrial nation, was the only one to show disdain for action on climate change when the G7 met in 2018. I fear that this is more to do with trade than with the environment. As Newton postulated, "every action has an equal and opposite reaction," and if we are not careful, we will bequeath a planet to others that will no longer be habitable.

Reflections

As I sit here in my study on a glorious summer morning in 2018, one of the hottest on record, I reflect on the life I've led and the opportunities I've had. I feel not only grateful but highly honoured to have shared my life with so many marvellous people from all walks of life. But as I leave this one small footprint in my transit through life, my greatest pride and achievement is, without doubt, my family: my children and grandchildren and their loved ones. Nobody can have a greater degree of satisfaction in seeing the love, consideration for others, commitment, determination, and achievement that they have displayed throughout their lives, which leaves me immensely proud and humble and aware that this is a great and lasting tribute to their mother, who will always be remembered as an angel amongst angels. I'm also aware of the great debt of gratitude I owe to the many friends we as a family, in its widest sense, have made in this transitory period of life, as well as the love, support, and help they have provided.

While reflecting on these many memories, I can't help but think about the issues they raise and the lessons that I hope I've learned over the years from the observation of others, which in some small way may have influenced me. There are some values that spring readily to mind, such as humility. You can't help but feel humble when in the company of those who have risked their lives for others—for example, the VC and GC holders and other highly decorated people or those who have devoted their lives to helping others who, without exception, remain modest in regard to their exploits and expectations.

I suppose the other thoughts reflect my transition from the days of youth and immaturity to old age and a greater awareness of others (notice I didn't say maturity)—such aspects as patience, understanding, tolerance (yes, even in old age), and sympathy, and dare I add tact, determination, and diplomacy. I believe these traits have helped in forming my footprint in life, one small footprint in time, which pales in significance when compared to so many others who occupy this galaxy of ours.

I end with just one last request to my family and friends:

> Remember me not for what I might have been but for what
> I was—and for the times we shared together.

Lightning Source UK Ltd.
Milton Keynes UK
UKHW040921180119
335737UK00002B/13/P